Avid Xpress Pro Editing Workshop

Steve Hullfish

Jaime Fowler

San Francisco, CA

Published by CMP Books, an imprint of CMP Media LLC
600 Harrison Street, San Francisco, CA 94107 USA
Tel: 415-947-6615; Fax: 415-947-6015
www.cmpbooks.com   email: books@cmp.com

Senior Editor:	Dorothy Cox
Managing Editor:	Gail Saari
Cover Layout Design:	Damien Castaneda

Distributed in the U.S. by:
Publishers Group West
1700 Fourth Street
Berkeley, CA 94710
1-800-788-3123

Distributed in Canada by:
Jaguar Book Group
100 Armstrong Avenue
Georgetown, Ontario M6K 3E7 Canada
905-877-4483

Library of Congress Cataloging-in-Publication Data

Hullfish, Steve.
 Avid XPress Pro editing workshop / Steve Hullfish, Jaime Fowler.
    p. cm. -- (DV expert series)
 ISBN 1-57820-238-8 (alk. paper)
1. Video tapes--Editing--Data processing. 2. Motion pictures--Editing--Data processing. 3. Digital video--Editing--Data processing. 4. Avid Xpress. I. Fowler, Jaime. II. Title. III. Series.

 TR899.H848 2005
 778.5'235'0285536--dc22

                          2004024553

For individual orders and information on special discounts for quantity orders, please contact:
CMP Books Distribution Center, 6600 Silacci Way, Gilroy, CA 95020
Tel: 1-800-500-6875 or 408-848-3854; Fax: 408-848-5784
bookorders@cmp.com; www.cmpbooks.com

ISBN: 1-57820-238-8

Dedication

To my mom and dad who instilled in me the importance of writing and creativity, and my wife, Jody, and the children, Haley and Quinn, who lost a lot of quality time so that I could get this finished. Without their patience and understanding, this book never could have been completed.

—*Steve Hullfish*

To my children, Lauren, Brendan, and Joshua

—*Jaime Fowler*

Acknowledgements

We would like to thank everyone at CMP for their patience and skill at shepherding this project to its successful completion, especially Gail Saari, Dorothy Cox, and Paul Temme. I would also like to thank Jim Feeley for introducing me to the talented and dedicated publishing team at CMP and for giving me my first writing gig.

There is also an important "second family" that has always provided knowledge and wisdom, and that is the great team of folks up in Tewksbury (Avid Technology) who are always happy to lend a hand and provide the right tidbit of information at the crucial moment. A special thanks to Steve Chazin for his help in providing the finishing touches to the final draft.

Thanks to the good folks at Artbeats for providing images.

Equally important in providing a constant barrage of crucial information are all my many friends on the avid-L listserve. Talk about getting schooled! We'd especially like to thank (in no particular order) Wilson Chao, Terry Curren, Bob Zelin, Frank Capria, Greg Glazier, Steve Bayes, Andre Brunger, Charles Vanderpool, Dave Spraker, Jeff Kreines, Jeff Sengpiehl, Job ter Burg, Pete Bradstock, and Pete Opotowski.

Contents

vi Contents

xii Contents

Index **455**

Chapter 1

Introduction

ABOUT THIS BOOK

Chances are you've picked up this book and thought to yourself "Another Avid book, how interesting!" Yes, there are a lot of books out there about Avid products. They cover the entire gamut of functions, buttons, menus, and interfaces. Hasn't everything been covered? Not exactly.

Xpress Pro Workshop is just that: a workshop. This is a look into how two editors approach a specific editing application. Because there are two of us, there is some balance. Avid products are designed so that different editors with different styles and workflows and needs can all utilize the same interface. Our experience and styles are different, and so are the unique approaches to the Avid Xpress Pro. Together we cover a wide range of video and film postproduction topics. What sets this book apart from reading the manual or from reading other Avid books is that we strive to not just tell what the buttons and commands do, but how this applies to your unique postproduction problems. We call this the drill and the hole approach. Nobody really needs a drill. What they really need is a hole. So in addition to explaining how the drill works, we explain all the aspects of the "hole." In other words, how do the features of Xpress Pro solve the problems that you need to solve? What we are attempting to do with this book is concern ourselves as much with the application—or use—of the editing features as with the features themselves.

1

We show you tips or pointers on how to work more efficiently, how to avoid painful mistakes (all of which we have personally made at one time or another), and how to attain fluency on Avid systems. As you become more comfortable with the system, you will find ways to make it your own. That is, you will examine the tools available, determine which are best for you, and make those tools more accessible on a custom interface.

The ultimate goal of any editing machine is to create a person-machine interface that can communicate near-instantaneous information. You make a decision; the machine shows you the edit. You change the edit; the machine shows the changes immediately. It is this symbiosis that will allow you to seamlessly go from thought to screen with rapid speed and efficiency. It is also this approach to editing that gives you the opportunity to think creatively. And if you can think creatively, you would be, as the late Edward Dmytryk put it, "a miracle worker." It is one thing to push buttons, but quite another to find creative solutions to problems that we frequently face in postproduction.

Beyond the range of normal editing comes the zen-like feeling of proficiency. The editing system becomes an extension of yourself, because you know how to control it, how to make it do the things that you need done. When you've reached this zone, nonlinear editing can be done almost as fast as you can previsualize the cut in your head.

This book was created with those thoughts in mind.

ABOUT XPRESS PRO

Avid Xpress Pro is the result of generations of software development by Avid Technology in Tewksbury, Massachusetts. Although Avid didn't invent nonlinear video editing, it certainly made it popular. Now, with dozens of different systems in practically every corner of the world—including the North Pole—nonlinear has become the accepted standard.

One of the reasons Avid has been such an industry leader is the development of the GUI (graphical user interface). The GUI on Avid systems is the gold standard that other developers seek to attain. There is nothing as comprehensive nor as ergonomic as an Avid interface, because it was developed by two very different types of people: programmers, who were specialists in creating innovative interfaces, and editors, who knew what the interface needed and how it must work. Unlike many other software manufacturers, Avid listened very carefully.

Those of us who were fortunate enough to be there in the early days saw how quickly the interface was developed and improved through direct feedback. Avid was smart enough to listen and, at the same time, to follow the rules of interface and software development. As a result, the current interface used on Xpress Pro and other Avid systems was born. The interface that you see on Xpress Pro varies somewhat from other Avid models, but in essence, they all work exactly the same. You will find that any Avid system has similar functions and capabilities. The process of adding new functions and technologies has changed the basic systems very little.

When asked if we can edit on an Avid, we answer "yes." When asked *which* Avid systems, we also answer "yes." The reason being that they all work the same, though some have more functionality than others. If you understand all of the functionality available on Avid systems, you can operate any Avid system.

Xpress Pro software is compatible with both PC and Macs. As a result, we use a certain nomenclature for keystrokes in this book. For example "Ctrl/Cmd" means that on a PC, use the Control key, and on a Mac, use the Command key (also called the "Apple" key, or our personal favorite, "Splat") When a keystroke of Alt/Option is mentioned, it refers to using the Alt key on PC, the Option key on the Mac. If you have a two- or three-button mouse on a Mac, you can right-click to get the same contextual menus that are on the PC version. If not, Ctrl+click usually does the trick. And which computer works best? We use both platforms and they both work great.

SCALABLE ARCHITECTURE: THE NEW INDUSTRY STANDARD

You could compare editing systems to a human brain. The right side, which would be the more creative tendencies, has the GUI, the operator interface. The left side contains the nuts and bolts, or the hardware. Xpress Pro is a type of software whose time has come. It is completely reliant on the hardware inside of your computer. With an optional Mojo, it can do more. But the bottom line is that there is no need for coprocessors these days. Previously, nonlinear editing systems were almost completely dependent on coprocessing. The first Avid Media Composers used five separate cards to enable it to store and play back video pictures and sound. The pictures, we might add, were pretty awful by today's standards. AVR 1, Avid's first low-resolution images, was referred to half-jokingly as "shower curtain resolution" because of its blurry images. But now, the home PC works fast enough and can process enough information so that there are no required extra coprocessors to run the equipment, and the imaging is well above most broadcast standards.

This is a milestone in technology. What it signifies is that we can take a software CD and a hardware key (a dongle) and plug it into any recent model PC or Mac and make it into an editing system. The democratization of video editing gives more people the opportunity to learn how to edit using the tools that are standard in the industry. There is still an art and a craft to editing, and there is always the need to be able to communicate with a client. These things truly differentiate the professional from an amateur. But the systems are plentiful and far less expensive than in their infancy. As a result, anyone who is willing to put in the time can learn the craft.

Scalable architecture is a term used collectively by various manufacturers of editing and compositing systems that refers to the software's ability to adapt or continue as technology increases. In the case of Xpress Pro, it means that while you may only be able to play out a few streams of real-time video today, next year may offer a faster CPU, which, in theory, could allow you to play back more real-time effects than previously. Of course, the software will have to change somewhat to accommodate new operating systems and new chipsets. Nonetheless, it does appear that we are on the road to completely CPU-dependent editing systems.

Will coprocessors go away? Not for the foreseeable future. For some of the high-end compositing engines, CPU speed isn't enough. For complex effects, coprocessors will continue to be necessary for real-time viewing. Of course, one never knows what technology tomorrow may bring.

COMPONENTS OF AN XPRESS PRO SYSTEM

An off-the-shelf computer, an optional small external processor, Xpress Pro software, and a consumer DV camera can form the base of a professional nonlinear editing system with an advanced feature set, zero additional compression, and the ability to capture and output broadcast quality video.

Avid's Specifications

Avid Technology has tested many of the latest computers, RAM, drives, video cards, FireWire devices, decks, and software for compatibility with Xpress Pro. Before buying each of these components, it is recommended that you visit the Avid website, www.avid.com to see if your components have been prequalified.

Prequalification of the components assures that Avid software and hardware will work correctly with your system. However, there are many forums, newsgroups, and list-servs on the web where alternatives are discussed. For the most part, Apple Macintosh computers are a preconfigured setup.

If you're something of a PC tech, you might want to build your own system. The key to doing this is to follow the general guidelines from Avid's specifications, then do some research on what might work better, or, in some cases, cheaper. If you are not comfortable with this type of thing, do not attempt it. The results could prove less than successful, and experimentation can prove expensive.

Computer

The type of computer required for Xpress should correlate directly with the type of media produced. In order to work efficiently with uncompressed 1:1 video with the optional Mojo and to be able to take advantage of real-time effects, a very fast CPU would be necessary. If you're using only Xpress Pro software, the speed of the CPU, while better for processing effects and rendering them, is less important.

The first Xpress Pro configuration shown at the National Association of Broadcasters Annual Convention in April 2003 was a Compaq XW8000 workstation configured with Dual Xeon 2.4GHz processors. This configuration proved to be successful in its showing, with faster render times and a responsive interface. The point to be made is that the faster the CPU, the more processing power. The more processing power, the better your operational results will be. Moving through a multitrack Timeline with real-time effects and audio scrub will task any CPU.

If you're using a Mac, be sure to make sure that your system is approved for Xpress Pro. Most of the latest Macs are, but changes in chip configuration and other hardware might affect how well Xpress Pro will run. Sometimes these changes will cause Avid to issue a new minor release of the software, allowing it to play well with the latest Macs. The Xpress Pro software can run fine with most Macs. But Mojo has very specific requirements. If you're using Mojo, be sure it is compatible with your system.

PCs are generally a little easier to configure. For Xpress Pro software-only configurations, think big, fast, dual processor and generally an Intel Pentium chipset. There are plenty of people running AMDs as well with Xpress Pro, but Avid does not "support" these chipsets. So, if you prefer AMD, how do you know if it works? The forums on Avid's website have comments and suggestions from users all over the world. Chances are that someone somewhere has used Xpress Pro on a similar configuration. The forums also discuss the latest drivers, video and sound cards, and other peripherals that can be used.

A Word about the Internet and CPU Tweaking

If you intend to use your Xpress Pro with the Internet, it is highly recommended that you use solid antivirus protection that can expand to include information on current viruses. The Internet is full of all kinds of nasty viruses and things that just shouldn't be on your system. These viruses can damage data as well as hardware. Arm yourself before venturing out onto the World Wide Web.

Some computer experts, particularly of the PC variety, enjoy the hobby of overclocking and computer tweaking to get the most out of their systems. The tweaks that may help some applications run faster do not generally work on Avid systems. A word of warning here: Avid systems tend to run your computer through the paces pretty thoroughly. Software tweaks and hardware overclocking can be highly dangerous. While beta testing for Avid, we ran some system tests and found that CPUs, RAM, video cards, and drives were running at a very high sustained pace. Increasing voltages to RAM, the CPU, AGP, and PCI peripherals is extremely dangerous and could quickly fill the room with the smell of burning silicon. A few extra megahertz of speed isn't worth the risk. If you want to overclock and tweak, do it on another CPU.

Memory

Faster RAM means faster rendering and a more responsive editing interface. Quantity is important, but don't cheat yourself on quality. Every Xpress Pro can use at least 1 GB memory. There are two very popular types of ram for PCs: RAMBUS, which is very quick and responsive, and DDR, which, when put in a dual channel mode, can be just as fast.

DDR RAM is dependent on two things: first is a dual channel capability. Not every computer motherboard is made for dual channel DDR. Be sure to check before purchasing your computer to make sure that it is dual channel capable. If there are not two rows or buses for RAM installation on the motherboard, you can be sure that it is not dual channel capable. Second are the RAM chips themselves. Some can be used for dual channel, while others will not guarantee successful use in dual channel configurations. Dual channel RAM literally doubles your processing, rendering, and interface response. It is better to have less RAM in dual channel mode than more RAM in single channel mode, so spend your money wisely. You can roll the dice if the RAM is not guaranteed for dual channel, but it probably isn't worth the expense. Put your money into quality hardware.

For Macs, you should use the RAM specified by Apple for your system. The more RAM you use, the better. 1 GB of RAM is ideal for any Xpress Pro system. You can get away with having less, but it will limit the number of things that you can do while editing.

Video Card

Xpress Pro supports a number of display cards, some of which are expensive. The reason is that the system relies upon Open GL technology, which is relatively new and thus more expensive than older display cards and technologies. OpenGL allows for faster processing and rendering. But Open GL is required for any 3D effects. Without an Open GL card, 3D effects will not properly work and some real-time effects will not play back. While you may not be able to afford the card that is the best, look for one with a high amount of RAM and quicker processing. Bigger and faster cards can make the difference between long renders and a relatively comfortable session.

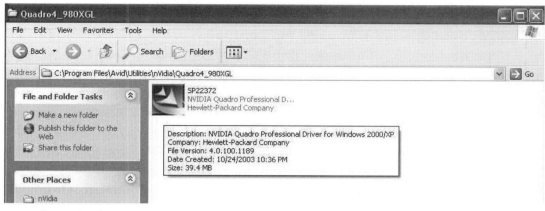

1.1   The Nvidia drivers

Xpress Pro software was written primarily for the Nvidia chip set (though this dependence could change in the future). There are a number of manufacturers who use this chipset, including PNY and Best Data. The recommended video card is Nvidia's 980 Quadro 4 XGL. However other Nvidea and non-Nvidia chipsets can work quite well, so long as they are Open GL compliant for 3D effect processing.

Xpress Pro software may come with a special set of drivers for the Nvidia card. Once you've installed the Xpress Pro software, you can find these on your Windows system at [drivename]:\ Program Files\Avid\Utilities\nVidia. On the Mac, they should be at MAC HD\Applications\Avid\ Utilities\nVidia. The drivers adjust video so that both moving and still pictures will match color, luminance, saturation, and hue in Xpress Pro. If you purchased a different video card, you will have to adjust the settings so that the two match.

Without Open GL hardware on the Video Card, the system relies upon Open GL software to process pictures. Software-only Open GL is not adequate for many of the effects in Xpress Pro's effect palette.

Again, be sure to check Avid's website for approved video cards at www.avid.com.

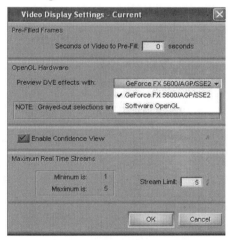

1.2   Software versus hardware Open GL selection

Sound Cards

Most CPUs come equipped with sound cards and they work just fine. Check the CPU specs to see what kind of sound is capable for output from your system. If you purchase the optional Mojo, your sound will run through the FireWire connection. If you are using Xpress Pro software only, you might consider using a third-party sound card. These are not generally supported by Avid, but you can check the Xpress Pro forums to see which cards will work. In general, it would be wise to just load the basic sound drivers. Sound cards come with all kinds of nutty extra-special configurations and software. Start with the basic driver and try it out with Xpress Pro first before bringing in the fancy options. On both PC and Mac, we've used the internal sound configurations and they work just fine. If you're just beginning to build your system, you might consider adding a third-party sound card later. Better to "trick out" your system as you go.

1394/FireWire Card

An IEEE 1394 or FireWire input has become somewhat common these days on computers. Xpress Pro will support the early generation FireWire 400 cards as well as built-in IEEE 1394 buses already installed in computers. Most Apple G4 and all Apple G5 systems have FireWire built in. This is also true for most PCs. FireWire cards are a fairly inexpensive buy for those computers who don't have built in connectors.

A common misconception among DV users is that IEEE 1394 or FireWire is the same as MiniDV or Digital Video. This simply is not so. OHCI compliant IEEE 1394 is a protocol that allows for a data stream running at 400Mbps. This stream can contain anything, including digital or analog video. To clarify, an uncompressed stream of 601 video can go into a 1394 card and can be ingested by an Xpress Pro system. So FireWire/1394 is not DV, it's a method of carrying information much like SCSI. As a result, there is no compression of any 1:1 video flowing through Mojo to your FireWire card on your computer.

FireWire devices for your Xpress Pro system may vary, but can include:

1. DV and DVCAM Decks
2. Drives
3. Transcoders
4. Mojo

If you decide to use more than one FireWire device, it would be wise to consider adding more FireWire cards to your computer. One of the disadvantages of a single bus card is that the signal path can become congested when sending a FireWire signal to the computer from a video source and then sending it back out, to, say, a drive or a transcoder. It is easier and more efficient to use multiple buses, i.e., multiple cards, to prevent such congestion. If you have the optional Mojo, it is mandatory that it be on a separate FireWire bus. Putting other devices on the same bus will cause equipment failure. Basically, Mojo is a bus-hog and it won't allow other peripherals to function, at least not well.

Transcoders

If you use Xpress Pro without Mojo, you might find that a transcoder is very handy. Transcoders allow you to put analog video and sound through a FireWire connection to your computer and they also allow you to play it back through FireWire to an analog deck. If you're using VHS, Beta, U-Matic, or any non-FireWire capable deck, a transcoder will be useful. There are several makes and models of these transcoders, and it's important to choose the right one for your needs.

For example, if you just need composite video and audio going into FireWire, you can find a good transcoder for under $300 (U.S.). If you need to input and output component video, the price is quite a bit higher.

Avid Mojo

If you purchased the optional Mojo, you don't need a transcoder. Mojo takes in any form of analog video and encodes it through a FireWire connection. If your source deck uses component analog video, you can connect it to Mojo with the optional component cable. Mojo will input and output S-Video, composite, and component video. It also allows you to create and play back uncompressed media on Xpress Pro. Mojo will also allow real-time playback of effects in uncompressed mode. We'll talk about all of that later.

Display(s)

A good quality monitor is absolutely necessary for Xpress Pro. Be sure to choose one that can display 1024 × 768 pixels in 32-bit color or better. Because of the amount of information that you need to display in order to edit, some prefer to use a dual monitor configuration. This can be easily achieved, provided that the right video card is used. While dual monitor display is a welcome comfort, remember that Open GL is a must for your system.

LCD displays are of great value to video editors. Their biggest advantage is space. If you have a system with relatively little space between the keyboard and monitor, LCD displays can increase the distance of focus, making it much more comfortable for you to view the interface. Be sure to pick an LCD panel that has the characteristics mentioned previously, as well as one with a wide viewing radius and a good contrast ratio.

Video Monitors

A video monitor is a must for viewing the edited images full screen. In order to view the images on the monitor, you must have a video card that is capable of video output, a transcoder, or the optional Mojo to be able to see the video display of your cut.

Many different types of monitors are available. Some are made for basic viewing, others for presentation, and more expensive video monitors for broadcast. Should you be using your Xpress Pro system for broadcast projects, it is recommended that you seriously consider using a broadcast monitor, which normally provides the highest fidelity of picture reproduction, as well as information about both horizontal and vertical sync.

Speakers

There are many self-powered speakers available at computer stores and professional audio supply houses. The range of these speakers can vary considerably as can the price. Some may sell for under $20. But you get what you pay for. If budget allows, try to find a better quality speaker in order to monitor the fullest range of sound. Shielded speakers can reduce magnetic interference. When placed in close proximity to your monitors, the speaker magnets can cause distortion of images and in some cases, do permanent damage to your monitors. Be sure to find shielded or lower power speakers to prevent this from occurring, or if you want a cheaper solution, keep the speakers at least two feet away from the monitors.

Waveform and Vectorscope

In some cases, you may be producing a final broadcast output with your Xpress Pro. In these cases, you will need a waveform and vectorscope to monitor the output of video signals from your system. Prices on these scopes can be very high, but there are some inexpensive alternatives that display on either computer CRT monitors or even using broadcast video monitors instead of the more precise hardware scopes.

Drives

Your media needs to be stored on a drive or set of drives that do not contain your operating system. It is advisable to use drives that have higher speeds, bigger cache sizes and more reliability. Almost all drives have been tested by any number of IT specialists and the information is published on the internet. Keep in mind that, for playback of media in a continuous stream, the sustained throughput is important, as well as a low data error rate.

If you intend to play back uncompressed media, Avid recommends a dual channel SCSI Ultra 320 card with at least four SCSI external drives that can be striped in an array. Drive striping allows the drives to read in tandem to allow faster throughput. ATA 100 and SATA (serial ATA drives) are not recommended by Avid, but you might find limited success with these, especially if they are striped together. While it may seem more attractive to buy a single bigger drive, the more drives that you have in a striped configuration, the less wear and tear they will get. The biggest drawback to any striped drive array is failure. The failure of a single drive will cause loss of data of all the drives that are striped in the array. For example, if you happen to buy four 1 TB drives and stripe them together, the failure of one of the drives would cause a data loss of—you guessed it—4 terabytes. Yikes!

If you're not using Mojo and the uncompressed option, you can probably get away with using single drives. Just remember that faster is more important than bigger. The drive should spin at a minimum of 7200 rpm.

When using a laptop with Xpress Pro, you can either use external SCSI or FireWire drives. The internal drive, which contains your operating system, spins at a slower speed than most nonlaptop drives. As a result, you will possibly experience some serious playback problems if you use the internal drive. However, in a pinch, it can work for offline resolution and shorter pieces. If you are using Mojo and use FireWire drives, they have to be completely different buses. For example, if you are using Mojo and have a built-in FireWire port on your laptop, you'll need a separate cardbus FireWire card for any external drives.

Keyboards

Most experienced editors rely much more on their keyboards than the mouse. There are a number of different keyboards out there that will work with Xpress Pro. Any USB keyboard will do the trick.

But some editors appreciate the fine art of the colored keycap, where specific reference is made not only to the alphanumeric characters on the keyboard, but also to the Avid-specific functions on that key. Well, there's good news. There are a lot of manufacturers out there who are willing to sell you an Xpress Pro compatible keyboard with fancy Avid keycaps on it. These keyboards definitely separate your computer from the rest of the hoi polloi, and all of the Avid functions are etched right along with the characters on the keys. But there's bad news, too. Once you start customizing your keyboard settings, you might not like the original configuration on that fancy multicolored Avid Xpress Pro keyboard. And if that happens, the keyboard is just for show. What should you do?

Some editors will print the symbols on sticky clear plastic sheets and attach them to the keys. Others buy the fancy keyboards and leave it alone. And some will find the most comfortable standard keyboard and leave it as it is. Choose whatever method helps you to use the keyboard more, and you will find yourself increasing rapidly in proficiency. Most important is comfort. If you edit a lot of hours consecutively, you will need a keyboard that doesn't strain your wrists. Find the one that is most comfortable on the wrists.

Pointing Devices

Most editors use a mouse, but it isn't always the best solution. If you feel discomfort after a long edit, you need to find a more ergonomic pointing device. There are graphics tablets, track balls, and some space-age-type peripherals out there that will make it easier on your wrists. Recently we tried a new device called Fingerworks, which tracks finger movement on a special pad that is similar to a mouse pad. Do a thorough search, especially if you already have some carpel tunnel issues. You're going to be pointing and clicking a lot.

RS-422 Adapters

In order to allow Xpress Pro to remotely control RS-422-controllable non-FireWire tape decks, you'll need an adapter. If you're using FireWire decks or non-remote-controllable decks, these adapters aren't necessary.

For Mac users, you can obtain either a special adapter card or a USB to ADB adapter from Keyspan. Either of these works great. You will want to speak to your Avid sales representative for more information on these adapters and whether or not you will need one.

For PC users, some non-FireWire decks can be controlled using Addenda's Rosetta Stone. Rosetta Stone translates from an RS-232C interface on your PC's Com port to the RS-422 interface on some decks.

For the latest information on compatible decks and cameras that can be remote controlled with Xpress Pro, visit the Avid website.

Software

Xpress Pro software works in conjunction with your operating system, QuickTime, and other software to create a solid postproduction package. Installing, managing, and updating the software is up to you. Here are a few caveats:

1. Never change horses midstream. It's a good rule of thumb not to update your Xpress Pro or operating software in the middle of an ongoing project. Why? Some think this is superstitious, but if you've worked around software enough, you know better. New software introduces new operational challenges, new features, and, yes, new bugs. It's

better to wait until your current projects are finished before installing any new software. If you have a project that will last several months, find a good stopping point and archive everything. You can always revert if the new software causes problems.

2. Make sure that both the operating system and your current version of Xpress Pro are compatible. We'll mention it again a few times—go to the Avid website and be sure to check before installing anything new.

3. When you're in the middle of a project, avoid installing any new software of any kind. If it conflicts with Xpress Pro, it will cause a serious headache. Better to wait.

The Operating System

Most people think of the operating system on their computer as transparent. It exists in order to drive the computer. But it also exists in order to drive your software. Xpress Pro is compatible with both Mac and Windows, but only under certain conditions. Whenever a new release of either Mac OS or Windows XP is put in the marketplace, everyone wants to jump on the bandwagon and try out the latest features. But it's not a good idea to go running to your local computer store to install the latest OS for your system until Xpress Pro is approved on the new OS. If you do, you're taking a chance that the OS isn't supported by Avid. And if it's not supported, that means that Xpress Pro might not even work.

On a Mac, the Software Updater in the Control Panels can be used to automatically connect your system to the Internet and update the latest release of OS. On the PC, you can update your system with the latest software by going to the link in the Start menu.

Your Xpress Pro Software

Your Xpress Pro software comes with a number of different applications. It's best to load the software CD and follow the instructions carefully. But before you do, there is the inevitable "Read Me First" document that comes with every piece of software. Our advice: read it. With some releases, there are specific warnings that might relate to your computer, your workflow, or the software itself.

To clarify, there might be a need to upgrade your operating system, your computer, your graphics card, or other peripherals. There may be warnings that the software is not compatible with other software that you might frequently use.

Here's a good example: on a recent version of Avid software, it recommended on the Read Me First document that Windows users increase their page file size to the maximum. Some didn't bother to read this, and as a result, they complained, only to realize that they did not RTFM (Read The Fantastic Manual). No one wants to look goofy, just read the danged thing!

Avid's software changes frequently, too. With new releases come new features, bug fixes, and options. Be sure to check Avid's website for the latest downloads for Xpress Pro.

Okay, ready to load the software? Not so fast! First we have to discuss the dongle. The dongle is your hardware key. This authorizes your use of Xpress Pro. It's a little handy purple USB device with a big white card attached. On one side is the PC serial number. On the other side is the Mac serial number. It doesn't matter which computer you use, the dongle can work in both. Most importantly, don't plug in the dongle until you have installed the software and the Sentinel drivers. The Sentinel drivers tell your computer how to look at the dongle to verify it. If the drivers aren't loaded and the computer restarted, you could actually damage the dongle.

Put in your CD and the Main Menu comes up. Load Xpress Pro. From there, you can load all of the software components, the utilities, FilmScribe, EDL Manager, Avid Log Exchange, the whole thing. It's better to just follow the instructions and install everything at once.

When you're finished installing everything, shut down the computer and plug in the dongle. Then start it up. Xpress Pro will be in the Avid folder inside your Applications folder on your Mac. If you're using a PC, it's in the Avid folder inside of the Programs folder.

C'mon, everybody, let's launch Xpress Pro! Woo-hoo!

Now that you're up and running, let's customize everything. Xpress Pro can be configured to meet your specific needs. To learn how, just turn the page.

Chapter 2

Settings

When most people begin to learn a new application, the first priority is to just *do* something with it as quickly as possible. And once that first stage of discovery is complete, many people never turn back to see what they may have missed in the learning process. One of the biggest areas overlooked when this "learn by intuition" method is used is how to customize the application.

WHY CUSTOMIZE YOUR SETTINGS?

Customizing your settings is crucial to getting the most out of any application, and Xpress Pro is no exception. As a matter of fact, most Avid products are designed to provide as many highly customized settings as possible because so many people edit in so many different ways on a vast spectrum of projects. Customizing the way Xpress Pro works leverages your time and effort because you only have to customize things once for most settings. Some settings you'll want to tweak on a per-project basis. Once that customization is complete, your settings work quietly—behind the scenes, under the hood—to maximize your effort with every keystroke and decision. That means that you really can't afford *not* to set these items properly right from the start.

Virtually the entire Avid experience is affected by the various customized settings and views. Most of these settings deal with specific areas from other chapters in this book, but we chose to devote a chapter just to settings and other customizations. This stuff is basically "set it and forget it." One of the few exceptions to this rule involves the various Bin settings and views. Bin-related settings are covered in the Organizing the Edit chapter because Bin settings are often changed or revised and because these settings are crucial to media management and organizing bins,

Beyond understanding where and how to customize the various settings and views of your Xpress Pro, we'll be explaining the reasons *why* you'll want to set them in various ways. The reasons are very dependent on *how* you edit and *what* you edit. We'll approach these reasons from our own experience and from our discussions with many editors over the years, but you may need to take the basic knowledge and examples given in this chapter and figure out for yourself how they apply to your specific work.

WHAT CAN YOU CUSTOMIZE?

The nerve center for customizing the interface and toolset is the Project window's Settings tab, which I often call the Settings list. But there are plenty of additional ways to customize beyond the Settings list. The Timeline is configured from its own Fast menu. Also, the Composer window can be customized apart from the setting that is specifically devoted to the Composer window. Bin views are customizable and Toolsets can also be customized without going into the Settings list.

The Settings tab in the Project window not only acts as the main location for adjusting settings but also allows you to copy, paste, save, and transfer settings. It also lets you turn certain settings into site-wide defaults. In Avid-speak, any individual Avid editing product, such as Xpress Pro or Media Composer, is considered a "site." You can apply certain settings so that they act as the default settings for all users and all projects on a specific "site." If you are managing a large number of sites at your facility or on a project, these "site settings" can be transferred to all sites. This is useful so that everyone is doing everything the same way and that projects can easily be moved through the postproduction pipeline.

VIEWING THE SETTINGS TAB

We'll start our exploration of settings in the Settings tab of the Project window. Even the list in the Settings tab can be customized! Clicking on the Fast menu in the upper left corner of the Settings tab calls up a list of groups of settings and views. The first three choices are Active Settings, Base Settings, and All Settings.

The Active Setting is very useful to keep down the signal-to-noise ratio of information. It displays all the settings that are active. This basically gives you your current operational settings with no other distractions. This means that the list is easy to navigate and you can quickly find what you want if something is not acting the way you want it to. The other advantage to this view is that you can instantly look at the list and determine if there is a setting that you did not expect was active or if you are missing a setting that you believed was active. So this acts as a quick troubleshooting view.

Base Settings is similar to Active Settings in that it is a restricted view. It will show more settings than Active Settings because if you have multiple base settings, the Base Setting view will provide all of them, regardless of whether or not they are active (see Figure 2.1). The main settings that are excluded in Base Settings are all of the Timeline and Bin views, Title Styles, Workspaces, and the import and export settings. Since most people activate and alter all of these excess items from their respective menus, the only reason to really see these in the Settings list is to copy and swap them with other projects and users. You may find other reasons for viewing these items in the Settings list.

All Settings lets you see every Timeline and Bin view and all of the import and export settings, as well as Title Styles and Workspaces. Generally, this is way more information than you need for day-to-day editing procedures. The main use of this view is to copy, swap, and save these settings.

The other choices in the Settings tab's Fast menu are Bin Views, Export Settings, Import Settings, Timeline Views, Title Styles, Workspaces, and Workspace Linked. All of these views are very specialized and obviously isolate specific settings when you are look-

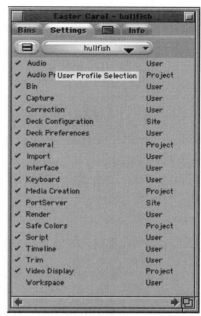

2.1   This is the Settings tab of the Project window, showing only the Base Settings.

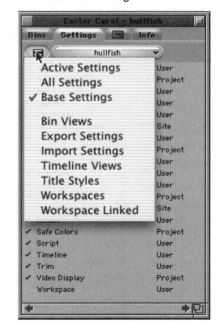

2.2   The Fast Menu icon allows you to customize the settings list.

ing for them for a reason. There may be uses for these specialized settings that you can devise in your specific workflow, but during most of the editing process the first three settings—Active, All, and Base—are the most useful. I prefer to have a restricted amount of information so I can quickly find things in the list, so I rarely use the All Settings.

TRADING SETTINGS

There are lots of reasons to copy, trade, or save settings. One of the main reasons is to enforce standard operating procedures across all of your editors (meaning the people who edit, not the equipment), and editing, logging, or digitizing stations. Exporting settings is the way to get all of your projects to have the same audio sample rate, to use a specific type of timecode, or to have certain exports done identically.

The logical approach would probably be to show you how to copy and swap settings at the end of the chapter, when you can better understand the value and reasons for swapping these settings, but we'll show you how to do it now, so you can import all of the settings from the DVD into your own user settings as examples.

We'll run through five exercises to show you how to do this. The first thing we want to do is bring all of the settings in from the DVD. Some of these are specific settings we devised for various purposes and some just reflect our personal preferences for various settings.

1. Put the DVD from the back of the book into your DVD drive.
2. Launch Xpress Pro and open a new project called Settings Test.
3. Click on the Settings tab in the Project window.
4. Go to File>Open Settings File (or Ctrl+O/Cmd+O).
5. Navigate to the DVD drive>Customization Chapter>Settings Files.
6. Choose the file XpressPro_Settings_Collection. This opens a new window in your project.
7. Drag the keyboard setting titled Blank from the new window into your Settings tab in the Project window.
8. Close the XpressPro_Settings_Collection window.
9. In your Settings tab, you may not see the new setting. This will depend on what is checked in the Settings Fast menu. To see the new setting, you will need to have All Settings or Base Settings chosen in the Fast menu.

10. Click to the left of the words Keyboard Blank to *activate* that setting. Or to open the setting, *to see it*, double-click on the word Keyboard. You know that the setting is active when there is a checkmark to the left of the setting name.

11. With the Keyboard Blank setting activated, you'll discover that your keyboard no longer works for editing.

Many people find the blank keyboard setting is handy to use when they take bathroom breaks so that their clients can't meddle with their sequence while they're gone. Or, if you have a mean streak, load this up into a coworker's settings, activate it, and see how long it takes them to figure out what's wrong! This setting is also very handy as you determine which buttons to map to your keyboard. Print the Blank keyboard out enlarged to a landscape-oriented 8 1/2 × 11 in. piece of paper and pencil in the various buttons you want to map.

Sharing Settings En Masse

The second exercise involves the creation of a settings file—similar to XpressPro_Settings_Compilation—that can be shared with other editors.

To share all of your settings—or to save settings to a CD, to save them for placement on a network server, or to save them to email to a friend—there are two basic methods that can be used.

The simplest method is to simply copy the file at the desktop level, without the use of the Xpress Pro application at all. Navigate to the Avid Users folder. This is in various places depending on your platform and version, so if you don't know where it is, do a search for "Avid Users." On my Mac, the search results in: Macintosh HD>Users> Shared>Xpress Pro>Avid Users. And on the PC, it's C:\Program Files\Avid\Xpress Pro\Avid Users. Your results may be different. Inside the Avid Users folder will be a folder with your user name on it. Inside that folder are several files. The one that contains the settings in your Settings tab also has your name on it and has the suffix .avs (Avid Setting). You can copy this file and save it anywhere you want.

Saving copies of your settings outside your Avid User folder is a very good idea. Settings often become corrupted and if you haven't saved them, they will need to be re-created from scratch. Saving them to a CD or a USB thumb drive is an excellent way to be able to move your settings from one machine to another if you are freelancing on multiple systems. In a large editing facility, it is good to have your settings saved to a central server so that they can be accessed from all of the editing systems.

SAVING MULTIPLE SETTINGS FILES

The desktop method may be a little too general for you if you want to share multiple settings with other editors. With the previous method you are sharing *all* of your files. If you want to be a little more selective in what you share, you'll need to do it from within Xpress Pro. Here's how:

1. Launch Xpress Pro and open the Settings tab in the Project window.

2. Go to File>New Settings File (or Ctrl+N/Cmd+N).

3. This opens a small window called "Untitled."

4. Drag the specific files you want to share from your Settings tab to the "Untitled" window. You can use Ctrl+A/Cmd+A to select all of the settings in either the "Untitled" window or the Settings tab. Also, most methods of selecting groups of files—such as Shift-selecting—will work in either location.

5. Select the "Untitled" window and choose File>Save Copy of File as…

6. Give your file a name and save it where you want it.

SHARING SPECIFIC FILES BETWEEN USERS

The third exercise involves swapping a specific individual setting with another editor. We'll loan one setting to another editor and borrow a different setting from the same editor. To do this we need to do a little setting up first, assuming that you don't have another editor working on your system. To set this up, go to the desktop and drag the "Joe Editor" file from the DVD drive>Customization Chapter>Settings Files to your Avid User folder on your hard drive.

Warning

On some systems there are two levels of users. The first is a level simply determined by the computer's logon name. The second level of user is created from within Xpress Pro. This creates a folder with your computer logon name nested within the Avid User folder. Inside that folder is another folder with your Avid user name. These are often identical names, which can be confusing. You need to drop the "Joe Editor" file into the folder labeled with your computer user logon name.

1. Launch Xpress Pro and open the Settings tab in the Project window.

2. Go to File>Open Settings File (or Ctrl+O/Cmd+O).

3. Navigate to the Avid User folder and find the Joe Editor folder. Inside that will be the Joe Editor Settings.avs file. Click on it.

4. This brings up a window called "Joe Editor Settings.avs."

5. Drag a single file from your Settings tab (for example, the "Blank keyboard" file) to the "Joe Editor" window. Drag a file (for example, "E-mailable QT Export") from the "Joe Editor" window to your Settings folder.

IMPORT A USER PROFILE

The fourth exercise demonstrates how to import a new user profile into your system. The setup of exercise three basically explained how to do this from the desktop, but this procedure can also be done from within the application. This is the basic procedure you would use if you copied your settings to a CD and wanted to import them to someone else's Xpress Pro or other Avid product.

Warning

Copying settings between Avid products is possible, but not necessarily recommended. Due to differences in capabilities and versions of certain products, imported user settings may not deliver dependable, predictable results. It is recommended that you re-create your user settings from scratch whenever moving to another product or version. To assist you in re-creating your user settings by hand, Avid recommends that you print out your settings, especially your keyboard settings.

1. Launch Xpress Pro and open the Settings tab in the Project window.

2. Click and hold down on the User Profile Selection button at the center of the Settings tab above the list of settings. This button probably has your name on it. This will reveal a pulldown menu.

3. From the pulldown menu, select Import User or User Profile.

4. Navigate to the DVD drive>Customization Chapter>Settings Files>Alan Smithee folder and hit the Choose button.

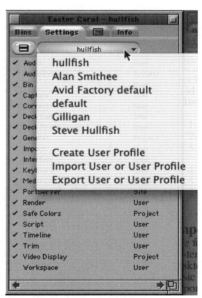

2.3   Settings pulldown menu

CREATING SITE SETTINGS

The fifth exercise explains how to create a site settings file that will dictate the settings of all new users and projects on your Xpress Pro system. This is ideal for establishing your post house's ground rules or standard operating procedures and is an effective way to impose structure on projects that will be touched by multiple people. These site settings can be copied and pasted at the desktop level once they have been created on a single system.

Whenever Xpress Pro launches a new project, it looks to a few files for specific settings that will be applied to that project. First it looks to the Site Settings folder for general information about how to configure new projects on your specific computer. When new users are created, the Avid also looks to this Site Settings folder to see what default settings should be applied to new users. With established projects and users, Xpress Pro looks to the folders with specific settings for those projects and users.

Warning

Site settings *do not* apply to established users or projects.

To create a site setting:

1. Launch Xpress Pro and open the Settings tab in the Project window.

2. Go to File>Open Settings and navigate to either the Programs folder (PCs) or the Applications folder (Macs). Inside that, follow this path: Xpress Pro>Settings>Site Settings. If you are an experienced Avid editor on another product, you are probably used to being able to find the Site Settings in the Special menu of the application. This is not true of Xpress Pro.

3. Once you have opened the Site Settings file, a window titled "Site Settings.avs" appears. This window is probably empty at this point.

4. Drag any settings from your Settings tab into the Site Settings window. Any file dragged to Site Settings will be the default setting for any new users or projects created from then on. Common site settings specify audio sample rates, default Media Creation settings, and timecode specifics, especially for the NTSC crowd.

5. Close the Site Settings window to save the new settings.

CUSTOMIZING THE SETTINGS IN THE LIST

Let's start figuring out how to make these settings work for us. The next section will tell you how and why to set all of the settings available in the Settings tab. There are additional settings that will help you edit and organize, but we'll get to them next. Don't necessarily read this chapter linearly. If you start to read this chapter and don't feel you're getting enough out of it, skip to the next heading. If you want a good setting to start with to show you how valuable this stuff can be, check out the Keyboard setting.

Audio Setting

The Audio Setting can save you time and effort every day because it lets you choose the default pan. This is an important option because nearly all field tapes (camera originals) are not really stereo. They are simply two mono channels that you don't really want panned left and right. In this instance, "centered" is the best choice. Without this setting centered you'll need to center all of the audio you digitize from a typical field tape manually. You do want to be careful

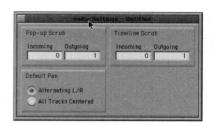

2.4   Audio Settings

that if you set and forget this option at centered any stereo music files or other true stereo audio will need to be manually panned left and right. You could also create two versions of this setting: one for stereo and the other for mono signals.

Audio Setting also lets you choose scrub parameters. (Scrubbing is when you jog back and forth over a section of audio to determine the IN or OUT point.) If you sample incoming frames (the default), the position indicator is at the beginning of the last sampled audio point. So if you have just heard a sound, that means you are parked at the head of that sound. If you sample outgoing frames, the position indicator is at the tail of the last sampled audio point. Which option seems right to you? Which way will help you find the right edit point? I use the default, but now that you understand what this feature does, maybe you'll change it. Also, scrub parameters can be set to play more than one frame to improve legibility, but this may make it hard to accurately determine exact frames for editing. You can set different scrub settings for pop-up windows and the Timeline. I think this would just get confusing to try to remember which was set how, and constantly adapt to it.

Audio Project

Despite the many parameters that can be set in Audio Project settings, for me, its main purpose is that users can specify a sample rate of 32, 44.1, or 48kHz. Which of them you choose is really a personal or house preference. The higher the sample rate, the better the audio quality, but if you are going to use mostly sources that start out as 44.1kHz (like CD audio), it may be better to choose to edit at that sample rate because the difference in audio quality between 44.1 and 48kHz is going to be difficult for anyone to distinguish, especially on a video project. If you are delivering your project as computer files of some type instead of video on a videotape, you may want to consider the final file requirements as you determine your sample rate. If you are being asked to deliver a QT file of

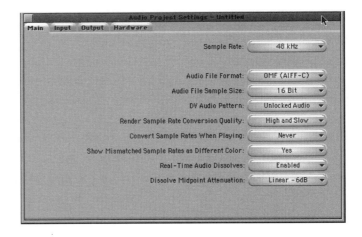

2.5 Audio Project Settings, Main tab

320×240 at 22.050kHz audio sample rate, you should choose 44.1kHz since it is evenly divisible by your target sample rate.

My general preference is 48kHz since most of my digitizing and all of my layoffs go to DigiBeta. (It is possible to lay a 44.1 project off to DigiBeta too, but the native rate of a DigiBeta through its AES/EBU audio inputs is 48kHz. A 44.1 project would need to be laid to DigiBeta using the analog spigots.)

32kHz is the DV tape audio sample rate and should really only be used for those projects shot with a 32kHz audio sample rate.

In the most recent software releases of all Avid projects, including Xpress Pro, a lot has been added to the Audio Project setting that historically has resided elsewhere. The other choices in Audio Project's main tab are:

- *Audio File Format:* OMF .wav, OMF (AIFF-C), or SDII. OMF .wav is the choice for creating files that are compatible with most Windows applications. OMF (AIFF-C) is mostly for compatibility with ProTools, but there are other third-party applications that can also read or write AIFF-C, so if you are considering collaborating with an outside audio specialist or sweetening your audio in a different program, this is an excellent choice. SDII is a choice if you are working on a Macintosh-based Xpress Pro; it allows for compatibility with some other Mac applications and many early Avids.

- *Audio File Sample Size:* 16 bit or 24 bit. Generally 16 bit will be the best choice here if you are going to collaborate with another Avid video editing product. Meridien products can only read 16-bit audio files. If you will be going to ProTools for audio finishing and audio quality is a priority in your project, use the higher definition 24-bit audio file sample size. ProTools can read either sample size, but most

ProTools sessions are conducted in the 24-bit space because of the increased sample resolution.

- *DV Audio Pattern:* Locked or Unlocked. This choice is provided because some devices check the DV Audio Pattern and you will need to comply with the requirements of those devices. Locked Audio Precisely locks the audio clock to the video clock, maintaining the same number of audio samples in each phase cycle. Unlocked Audio allows some tolerance in this relationship, but never allows the margin to exceed ±25 audio samples per frame.

- *Render Sample Rate Conversion Quality:* High and Slow, Balanced, or Low and Fast. This allows you to basically choose slow, medium, and fast conversions of sample rates. If your project is 48kHz and you import a 44.1kHz file or attempt to use a 44.1kHz file from another project, it will need to be converted to the sample rate of your project in order for it to be laid off to tape. Depending on the quality needs of your project and how much time you have for this conversion, you can pick one of the three choices. High and Slow means the quality will be high, but it will take longer. Low and Fast means a low quality conversion, quickly. And Balanced is the choice for all you fence-sitters out there who just can't decide.

- *Convert Sample Rates When Playing:* Always or Never. It is possible for the system to play back audio from two different sample rates in the same sequence, but not to lay them to tape. If you want to always be able to hear your mismatched sample rate audio while you're editing, choose Always. If you'd rather know up front that the media needs to be converted to a different sample rate, then choose Never. Never is a good choice because when you are ready to do a digital cut— these mismatched sample rate segments will not play.

- *Show Mismatched Sample Rates as Different Color:* Yes or No. Yes allows this parameter to show you any mismatched sample rate audio in the Timeline sequence. No will not show you where the mismatched samples are.

- *Real Time Audio Dissolves:* Enabled or Disabled. Generally, anything with real-time performance is a good thing. You should have this enabled. You should disable this feature, however, if you are experiencing any audio performance delays on your system.

- *Dissolve Midpoint Attenuation:* Linear −6dB or Constant Power −3dB. Don't worry about theory here or what the difference is between linear and constant. What matters is how you like your audio cross fades to sound. Try a nice long dissolve between two music sources with the settings one way then the other. If you disable real-time audio dissolves, set the midpoint attenuation to Linear and render the dissolve; then set the midpoint attenuation to constant and render the dissolve. You will be able to play back the two different types back to back. (A rendered file will not be altered.) By the way, attenuate just means to lower the volume. As in "Please attenuate the bass response, it seems a little bottom-heavy." Which dissolve do you like better? In some advanced audio programs like Pro-Tools, you can actually draw a graph of the response of the dissolve. This allows you to have some of that control.

The Input tab of the Audio Project Setting allows you to alter the gain of an input source and to alter your input source. If you do not have Mojo, your only choice here is OHCI. With Mojo, you can also choose RCA (the RCA audio inputs on Mojo) or DV (the DV input on the back of Mojo).

With Mojo you are presented with the chance to use a Passthrough Mix tool for lowering or raising the monitoring levels of your input signal. (See Chapter 8 "Audio" on page 217 for more on the Passthrough Mix tool.)

You are also allowed to add +6db of gain to the incoming signal.

The Output tab gives you an output gain and a Master Volume gain. It also allows you to bypass Clip Gain, Real Time EQ and/or Auto Gain settings during output. You can also choose to output in stereo or mono. Output Gain lets you calibrate the volume of the overall output, so that your tape deck or recording device can be set to a unity setting (a centered or détente setting). Master Volume allows you to deviate from the calibrated setting if you have mistakenly mixed an entire sequence a little too hot or too low. This Master Volume will also lower speaker volume. The Bypass buttons allow you to output audio so that the Xpress Pro ignores any of the Audio Mix tools adjustments to individual clips and real-time EQs that were set by the Audio EQ tool or by any of the Auto Gain features, such as rubber-banding. With Mojo, you are also presented with the option to output in stereo or mono.

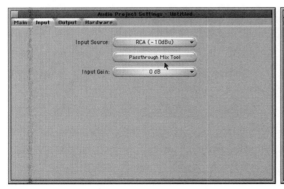

2.6   Input tab

2.7   Output tab

The Hardware tab basically lets you see your audio hardware specs. There is nothing here that you can set or customize. This is for informational purposes only. Your Hardware tab may look different depending on whether you have Mojo or not.

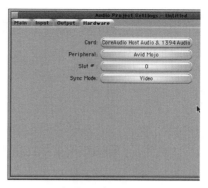

2.8   Hardware tab

 In order to increase the convenience of switching between sample rates, input types, or scrubbing parameters, you should make multiple audio settings and click between them as necessary. To create multiple settings, click on a setting and Ctrl+D/Cmd+D. Rename the duplicated setting with a descriptive name and alter the settings. I have two Audio Project settings: one for 44.1kHz audio and one for 48kHz.

Bin Settings

We're going to include a discussion of the Bin settings and Bin views in "Bin Management" on page 106 in Chapter 4. To see how these settings can help you, check there.

Capture Settings

General Tab

The Capture Setting has five feature-packed tabs. The first one is the General setting. The top two radio buttons dictate how the deck reacts after a capture is complete. These are two seemingly innocuous, but fairly important buttons. In general, if you are digitizing fairly quickly, on-the-fly or capturing numerous clips in a row, you will move through your tasks quicker if the radio button for Pause deck after capture is selected. If you select Stop deck after cap-

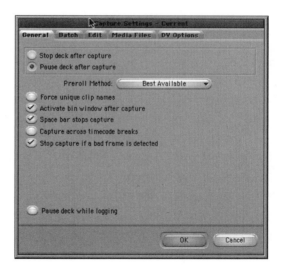

ture, the deck will stop completely, and the playback heads spin down, causing a momentary delay if you want to continue searching for another clip. Where the Stop deck after capture setting comes in handy is if you are going to do an unattended capture. Some-

Faux Composer for Xpress

While there is no Composer setting in Xpress Pro, as there is in many other Avid products, I want to point out that, for those of you who are used to Avid Xpress or XpressDV, the Composer window in Xpress Pro can be configured to display standard Media Composer–like side-by-side source and record monitors. This is a huge advance. I have spent all my time on XpressDV and Xpress Pro using fairly small computer monitors, and even with the limited screen real estate, I still like having this option on Xpress Pro. If you drag the window into an aspect that is similar to a single monitor (e.g., fairly square), it will turn into a single monitor. If you drag into an aspect that is similar to two side-by-side monitors (e.g., fairly wide compared to its height), it becomes dual monitors. Dragging the monitors so that there is almost no height to them at all will allow you to use the dual Timelines of source and record, plus the dual tracking information and buttons, without the loss of screen real estate. You can drag these windows so that the video displays are quite small, but still usable. That's the way I use them, since I am usually monitoring the actual video on the "client monitor."

Also, for those used to higher-end Avid products, the Composer Setting is where you normally switch to 16:9 aspect source and record monitors. In Xpress Pro this is done by right-clicking/Shift+Ctrl-clicking on one of the monitors. This calls up a pulldown menu that allows you to select or deselect this option. Setting 16:9 here does not affect the client monitor. If you want to view 16:9 in the client monitor, you need a monitor capable of displaying 16:9 natively.

One of my other favorite settings in Composer is the ability to create a center duration window that sits between the source and record monitor and tells you how far it is between the Mark in and the Mark out. This choice does not exist on Xpress Pro. To make up for the loss of this important button, I typically call up the Timecode window in the Tools menu and set it to IO and size it pretty small. This works quite well as a replacement.

times as I walk out the door for the night, I'll start to capture a fairly long clip that I intend to work from the following day. I don't want to have the deck's playback heads spinning against the tape all night after the clip has been captured because it could ruin the tape and it puts a lot of wear on the heads. So when I digitize something overnight or even over lunch, I will set the deck to Stop deck after capture.

Preroll method is chosen from a pulldown menu on the General tab. The choices are Best Available, Standard Timecode, Best Available Control Track, and Standard Control Track. The fastest method of preroll is generally Standard timecode because the deck is transported directly to the preroll point first. With the other methods, the tape must shuttle to the IN point, then preroll back slowly, using the control track before prerolling. Best Available uses adaptive preroll, which means that it first tries to do a full preroll using timecode, then, if that fails, it tries it again using the full preroll amount using control track, and if that fails, it tries again, using the available amount of preroll instead of the specified amount of preroll. Standard Control Track rolls to your IN point using timecode, then prerolls using the amount of preroll specified. Best Available Control Track is an adaptive preroll that first attempts to do the preroll as Standard Control Track, and if that fails, then it attempts to determine the maximum usable control track and uses that. The idiot-proof version to use is probably Best Available, because it will try to use the timecode first, so this speeds capturing while still allowing Xpress Pro to attempt the other options if timecode does not work.

The next choice is Force Unique Clip Names. This depends on how you name clips. This is a pretty good thing to have turned on, since it forces some sense of organization on you. On some projects with huge amounts of clips, you might not realize if you accidentally name two clips the same thing by accident, like WS Sunset. If you turn this on, it would warn you that there was already another clip with the same name. (This does not prevent you from renaming clips so that they have the same name or from importing clips with the same name. This just affects captures.)

Activate Bin Window After Capture is the standard method that most Avid products use when capturing. It assumes that you have not named the clip while it was capturing. If you like to name clips during capture or prefer to name clips after you get a bunch of them into the system, then you can turn this off. It will keep the cursor and active window from moving to the bin. Set this according to what keeps you working the fastest. Your standard operating procedure for when you name clips will dictate this.

Space bar stops capture is a setting that a lot of older, linear editors will relate to. It's kind of like the All Stop button (that was usually renamed to what the French would call the Oh merde! button.) I rarely have an emergency where I want to stop a digitize as fast as possible, so I would not turn this on. It could also mean that a careless brush of the keyboard in the middle of a long capture would end the capture unexpectedly, which would be a greater reason to say "Oh merde!"

Capture across timecode breaks is a little bit misleading. It doesn't actually allow you to capture across timecode breaks. It allows you to start a capture, and when the system encounters a break in timecode, it ends the capture at the timecode break and saves the clip. Then it continues capturing after the timecode break, creating another clip.

Warning

There is a threshold to acknowledging timecode breaks. If the break is under a few frames, the Avid is unable to detect it. This means that frames after the invisible timecode break will actually be mis-timecoded by however many frames were missing in the timecode break. Breaks of this size are fairly rare, but if you digitized an entire tape from beginning to end and that tape had 20 or 30 four-frame breaks in it, by the end of the tape, the frames would be off by up to 4 seconds. I believe this small timecode error only occurs with certain DigiBeta cameras. Stop capture if a bad frame is detected allows you to end the capture if the system detects a bad frame. This is another one of those personal preferences. I would not turn this on, because I'd rather the entire digitize take place, regardless of the bad frame, because the clip, or the part of the clip with the bad frame, may never end up in the edit anyhow. And if it did, then you could always redigitize later. However, if you were capturing something—perhaps without timecode—that you did not want to redigitize and you needed the entire feed completely clean, then this would be a good thing to turn on.

Pause deck while logging is basically a feature that people choose to turn off if they are logging from a deck during a live shoot. If you log during a live shoot with the typical Avid behavior, the deck would either pause or stop the tape when you select an OUT point. On a live shoot this could obviously be disastrous. However, if you are logging from a tape that has already been shot, you would normally want the tape to pause when you enter an OUT point so that you could record a name for the clip so you wouldn't miss anything while you were naming the clip. You could also choose to not pause during logging if you just wanted to keep the deck rolling at all times.

Batch Tab

The top two radio buttons are mutually exclusive. If you select Optimize for disk space, Xpress Pro only captures the source material plus any handles that have been assigned. No matter how close the clips are—and when you consider handles, it's actually possible for clips to overlap—the tape stops at the end of one clip and rolls to the preroll point for that clip before starting another clip. If Optimize for batch speed is selected then any clips with the same video resolution and audio sample

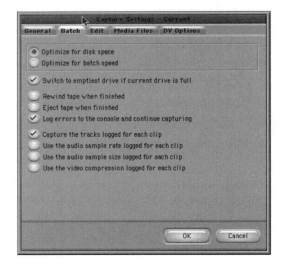

rate that are within 5 seconds of each other will be captured as a single clip. This makes the batch capture go faster—minimally—but it can also waste disk space—minimally—since it captures small amounts of material that will not be used in your sequence. This is really fine tuning here, but lots of Avid editors have been asking for the ability to optimize for batch speed for a long time, so, if you're one of them, do a little happiness jig.

Switch to the emptiest drive if current drive is full automatically switches to another media drive when the current target drive is full. This switch occurs between captures. Xpress Pro cannot capture part of a clip to one drive and the other part to another drive. This is a very important selection to make for capture sessions that are largely unsupervised. If you are diligently watching your batch capture, then not selecting this simply calls up a dialog when the disk is full and you manually select another drive. Wonder why anyone would NOT want this turned on? It's to prevent capturing material to a disk that could be reserved for another project. Often times, drives need to be portable and get sneakernetted to a different machine. But if your project were to randomly select that drive as it batches, the drive could "walk" with your valuable material still onboard. The reverse can also happen. If you want all your media on a certain drive so that it can "walk" then you'd be in trouble if random clips were digitized to a different drive when your drive became full.

Rewind tape when finished is an option that basically does what it says. If that's what you want, then this is the setting for you. This can slow down batch sessions, however, because you have to wait for the tape to rewind before starting the next batch. However if you only have one deck and a policy of leaving all tapes stored rewound, then this will work for you.

Eject tape when finished is a similar setting to the above setting. It's a very handy setting if you have are batch-digitizing using an assistant editor with a tape deck in a far away control room, because it is a visual and aural clue that you need the next tape fed into the machine. This instance will be fairly rare with Xpress Pro compared to the higher-end Avids (I work like this all the time with a Symphony), but it can serve as a visual and aural clue to you, even without an assistant, if you get distracted at the end of batch. The ejecting of the tape will alert you that the batch is complete. Another great benefit for all of us trying to save our pennies is that ejecting the tape saves wear and tear on your tape heads.

Log errors to the console and continue capturing is selected even if I'm paying close attention to a batch capture. I don't want some little thing to stop the capture. If it's bad, I can always kill it later. This setting is especially important to turn on if you are batching largely unsupervised.

The next four settings are very similar in nature: "Capture the tracks logged for each clip," "Use the audio sample rate logged for each clip," "Use the audio sample size logged for each clip", and "Use the video compression logged for each clip." These should basically be set on a case-by-case basis. Generally I turn all of these off. When I batch-capture I usually want things to be very uniform, so I'd prefer to override any of those setting with what I select in the Capture tool. For example, if you are rebatching an offline edit, those clips were probably captured or logged at a low resolution. Since you want to uprez the clips, you do not want to follow what the old clips say. Similarly, if you are batching a bunch of tapes that a production assistant or assistant editor or even a producer had logged, they generally don't know exactly how you are planning to capture, so you'd want to override their logging decisions. Often, when logging, people—including editors—aren't paying much attention to sample rate, sample size, video resolution, or even logged tracks. And if you logged it yourself, thinking that you'd digitize everything at 1:1, then discovered you needed to digitize at 15:1s because of a lack of disk space or another unexpected project, you'd want to be able to override that log.

Edit Tab

This tab enables you to display the Splice-in and Overwrite Edit buttons in the Capture tool and to indicate the amount of handles you want before and after the IN and OUT points. This choice is here because many editors wanted the ability to instantly cut something into the Timeline from the Capture tool. While I have never used this option, it would come in handy for news editing situations and for cutting in new footage on very tight deadlines. If you're strictly a post house type of editor, I'd keep these off to minimize that signal-to-noise ratio of stuff that you have to look at. But if you work at a place like in "Broadcast News" where you're diving across the newsroom and sliding under filing cabinet drawers on your knees to deliver a tape at the last minute, then you will probably have this on and be happy for it.

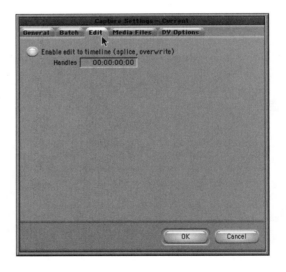

Media Files Tab

This largely has to do with the way media is stored to the drives. This is under-the-hood stuff, but you may have a reason for setting certain things a certain way. Generally, this is set-it-and-forget-it stuff.

Capture to a single file, 2GB limit limits any media file to 2GB upon capture. That's not a lot of time when you're dealing with uncompressed. I prefer to leave this option off. Turning it on may help speed up the response of the Capture tool in getting ready for a new clip, but it'll quickly be offset by the amount of time you spend recapturing stuff that got cut off in midstream by this setting. This setting is the opposite of the Capture to multiple files selection. This allows any length recording as long as you have the drive space.

The companion setting for Capture to multiple files is Maximum (default) capture time (30) minutes. This allows you to select a length of time that is pre-allocated on the drive when Capture multiple files is selected. The default is 30 minutes. You will want to pay close attention to this setting if you digitize longer items. You don't want to underestimate, certainly, but setting this for a very long time causes the Xpress Pro to spend time pre-allocating that space. If you find your Xpress Pro taking too long between each clip, reduce this number.

Switch to emptiest drive when *n* minutes left switches target drives during capturing when a drive gets full. With the cost of drive time dropping constantly, I'd set this number fairly high. Maybe 5 minutes—more if you can afford it—2 minutes at least. Remember, the media database files on those drives need to be rewritten and updated all the time. If there's not enough space on the drives, these files can't be written properly and you'll see weird lock-ups and possible crashes and other problems. Also, remember that anytime you render, the primary target drive for those renders is the same drive that contains the source material for the render, so space needs to be saved for that.

DV Options Tab

All of these selections relate to what happens when the Xpress Pro encounters scene breaks (based on the time-of-day information stored and transmitted on DV video). If you select DV Scene Extraction the system can do one of three things when it encounters a new scene:

1. It can add a locator (if you choose the Add Locators option)

2. It can create a subclip (if you choose the Create Subclips option)

3. Or it can do both (if you choose the Both option).

This depends on how you like to work. Some people would prefer to have lots of broken-up subclips in their bins for easy identification, while others find tabbing through locators to find their shot is less choppy. Fence-sitters, you know which option is for you.

Correction Mode Settings

The Correction Mode Settings aren't going to speed up everyday editing, but they'll obviously have more and more effect on your day-to-day work as you start to incorporate color correction on a regular basis. The Correction Mode Settings have two tabs. One affects the manual correction features and the other customizes the AutoCorrect features.

In the Features tab, the first item is a pulldown menu that defines the way color labels are saved. The choices are None, RGB, Name, and Name and RGB. In Color Correction (CC) mode, you can save the color swatches in the Color Match area that you create by using the Eyedropper tool to sample pixels in your images. The choices in Saved Color labels define the default naming scheme for these colors. The name it refers to is some kind of standard semidescriptive name; for example, I sampled a red pepper and a glass of beer from a product shot and got the respective color names of Firebrick and SaddleBrown. (I was not on the committee that created these names, and some name choices are a little odd, like an orangey yellow color (R = 207, G = 121, B = 26) named Chocolate. However, you can't blame Avid for the naming scheme; it is derived from the standard HTML color naming scheme.) RGB is simply the numerical red, green, and blue values separated by commas. For the pepper and the beer, these numbers were 171, 36, 24 and 148, 71, 7 respectively. These numbers and names have little to do with your purpose for saving them, so it could be argued that the only description that should be given is a name that describes its purpose, like Ideal Joe Flesh Tone, or Client Logo Color or Client Approved Beer Color. The use of the default descriptive name and RGB value is especially redundant since a swatch of the actual color actually sits in your bin when you save it and seeing the color with your own eyes is better than any description.

Real Time Image Updating enables the active monitor to update on-the-fly while you manipulate the color controls in CC mode. The speed of the updates will be largely dependent on the speed of your specific system. As Avid pointed out when it released the DNA line (which includes Xpress Pro), these are products designed to take advantage of the native processor speed of the systems on which they're run; so the faster your computer is, the better Xpress Pro is going to run.

Obviously to do good color correction, Real Time Image Updating is pretty important, so you may wonder why you'd turn it off. Well, if you are having performance issues (only while in CC mode), you may want to turn this off. If you do, you can still make corrections, it'll just take a while for the monitor to indicate the correction you made. You can also toggle this mode on and off by pressing Alt/Option to temporarily get the opposite state. On my system this setting actually does not make a lot of difference.

Eyedropper 3×3 Averaging is an important setting that affects the way that colors are sampled using the Eyedropper in Color Match. Because adjacent pixels in an area that may seem to have a homogeneous color can actually vary quite widely due to noise and other factors, you can set the Eyedropper to average the color values of a 3x3 block of pixels surrounding the center pixel at which the Eyedropper tip is actually aimed. I use this option because the average is usually a better indicator of the actual color of the area. You just want to be aware that you have this on, especially if you are pointing at a pixel that is very near an area of another color, because the average of the pixels could include the values of the colors in the adjacent area.

Show Eyedropper Info. If you read our book, *Color Correction for Digital Video,* or any of Chapter 12 "Color Correction" on page 341, you know how important the numerical values of the RGB channels are in evaluating your images. I can't imagine turning this off, but if you find that these numbers are more noise to you than signal then turn off the numbers with this setting.

Eyedropper Picks from Anywhere in Application allows you to do just that. If you want the option to pick a color from the interface itself or somewhere other than the video portion of the image in one of the three CC monitors, check the box next to this setting.

The AutoCorrect tab does not affect the AutoCorrect functions in Color Correction mode, because these corrections are done in the order that you use them. Where this tab works is in the Effects mode. When you drop a Color Correction effect onto a clip from the Effects mode's Image group, it autocorrects that clip according to the parameters set in this tab.

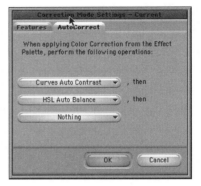

The AutoCorrect tab has a note that states: "When applying Color Correction from the Effect Palette, perform the following operation:" Then there is a pulldown menu with the following choices: Nothing, HSL Auto Balance, HSL Auto Black, HSL Auto Contrast, HSL Auto White, Curves Auto Balance, and Curves Auto Contrast. When you click on the one pulldown, another pulldown appears below it and the word "then" appears next to the first pulldown. The same is true for the next pulldown, so you can have it perform three separate operations consecutively. This is necessary because the order in which the corrections occur and the type of auto correction applied *does* make a difference. To understand the choices offered here, see Chapter 12 "Color Correction" on page 341.

The choice of Nothing exists if you only want to use one of the two or two of the three corrections. In this case, in the final pulldown, select Nothing.

Deck Configuration Settings

Deck Configuration lets you configure specific decks that you use all the time. This is a faster alternative than Auto-configure, especially if you only have a couple of decks.

To configure a deck, double-click Deck Configuration in the Settings scroll list of the Project window. Select a Channel Type and Port depending on how you are controlling your deck. (Direct Com Port, FireWire, V-LAN). Frame accuracy is important in batch capture situations, so you should not use FireWire for deck control. It's fine for a one-time capture, but not for projects that will need to be batched. (This is not an Avid problem. This is inherent in the deck control of FireWire.) Click on the Add Deck button to open Deck Settings and either Auto-configure or manually choose a deck. (For FireWire decks, it will probably be more successful to manually configure the deck from the Deck Type

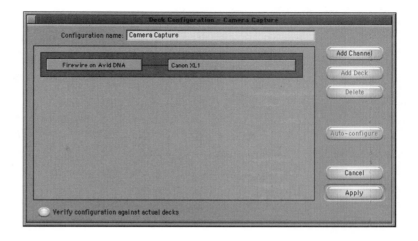

2.9   Deck Settings

pop-up menu.) Now use Deck Settings to really customize the way your deck responds. (See the next paragraph for more info on this). Once all this is set, you can choose to Apply the configuration. Hook up any of your other decks to the computer and configure them the same way. Each of these decks can be named and called up specifically. You don't have to use the technical name for the deck, like DVW-A500. You can call it whatever your facility has labeled the deck in the tape room, such as "VTR13" or "Big Bertha." There is also an option to Verify configuration against actual decks that checks to make sure that the deck you've chosen is actually the one attached to the computer.

To customize the Fast Cue parameters, analyze how your deck responds as it fast-forwards to a specific timecode destination. Does it overshoot timecodes in FFWD? Setting Fast Cue properly can speed tape searches and batch digitizing. Avid custom-tailors these parameters according to the factory settings of each specific deck, but you may find that the ballistics of your deck are not quite in tune with the factory settings. You can also use Deck Configuration to have one deck get deck control from one port and another deck from a different port. Many people either switch control cables back behind their decks or buy control patch panels or switches when all you really need to do (if you only have a couple of decks) is to attach them both to separate ports and assign them in the software.

If you just want to use Auto-configure, instead of configuring your decks and saving them, there is something that will speed up the Auto-configure process. What the computer is doing as the Auto-configure render thermometer is filling up is searching through a list of deck templates to match them with the deck that it finds on the other end of the com port or FireWire cable. There are hundreds of deck templates to match (e.g., my folder has 345 deck templates.). However, you probably do not own hundreds of different models of decks. Personally, I'd only need five at the most (three VCRs and two audio decks). Locate the deck templates in your Avid folder and delete any deck you don't think you'll own or rent anytime soon. The only exception is that you should save the Generic decks, because that's what the Avid uses if it isn't sure what deck it's found. On a Mac, these templates are in the Applications/Avid Xpress Pro/SupportingFiles/Machine Templates. On a PC, check Programs/Avid Xpress Pro/SupportingFiles/Machine Templates. If you're the cautious type, you don't have to delete them, you can move them to a separate folder called "Decks I wished I owned, or am glad I don't." The next time you Auto-configure it will be instantaneous.

Deck Preferences

Deck Preferences provides global settings for basic deck control for any deck connected to Xpress Pro.

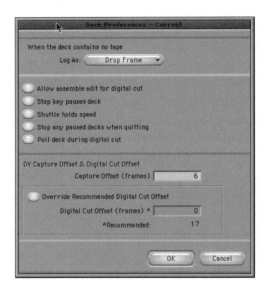

The first choice, When the deck contains no tape Log As: pertains to logging only without a tape in the deck obviously. If there is a tape in the deck, this setting doesn't matter. This allows you to set a default for the type of timecode used in logging. Set this for the type of timecode you most regularly receive for logging purposes.

The next choice is to Allow Assemble Edit For Digital Cut. This records frame-accurate digital cuts without striping entire tapes. (Remember, frame accuracy is not possible with FireWire control.)

Stop key pauses deck is fairly useful when you're digitizing quickly. If you do not select this option, then every time you hit the space bar, the deck will stop as opposed to pause. The difference is that stopping a deck means that the heads spin down and it takes more time to get the deck back up and rolling for the next clip. Having the deck stop does help keep head and tape wear to a minimum, however. This only pertains to the space bar and not to the stop button in the Capture tool.

Shuttle Holds Speed is an option that doesn't work for me. I prefer shuttling along and letting go of the shuttle when I want to pause the deck. This is the behavior I'm used to from when I started editing with linear edit controllers. However, if you just want to set the deck at a specific shuttle speed without having to hold the shuttle exactly in place, then this is the option for you.

Stop Any Paused Deck When Quitting is a useful option for saving wear and tear on tapes and decks. This automatically stops a paused deck (that you might have forgotten about) when quitting the application. I'd personally like to see this setting changed to Stop any paused decks when quitting the Capture tool. Sometimes I don't quit Xpress Pro for days.

Poll Deck During Digital Cut is the default option, and I have always opted to leave it on. It is possible that the performance hit that can result from displaying the polled data (timecode info and record status) can result in degraded video quality, like visible noise. If you turn it off, it only means that the timecode of the deck is not displayed in the Digital Cut window during the digital cut and the Record button doesn't flash. If your deck is within eyesight, then you really don't need this turned on, since you can see the timecode on the deck and you can see that it is recording. If you don't experience noisy digital cuts, you can probably leave this option on.

DV Capture Offset & Digital Cut Offset Capture Offset (Frames) is a setting for those capturing DV footage using FireWire, but controlling the deck and receiving timecode data from the DV deck via V-LAN or a Direct Port (RS-422). The default setting for this is 0, or no offset. To determine the correct offset, digitize a few clips and compare the timecodes of the captured footage to the timecodes of those clips as you watch them straight off the tape. If, for example, frame 1:00:00:12 from a captured clip in the Xpress Pro is actually frame 1:00:00:08 on the tape, then set the offset to –4. You are restricted to an offset range of –6 to +24.

Similarly, if you are experiencing an offset when you do digital cuts to DV decks, you can choose Override Recommended Digital Cut Offset and then determine the amount of the offset needed and type that amount into the Digital Cut Offset (frames) entry area. You should try several short digital cuts to make sure that the offset is consistent. If the offset is not consistent, then the deck you are using is probably not capable of timecode accuracy.

Desktop Play Delay allows you to synchronize the playback of the video and audio signal as it is viewed on the computer monitor and the client monitor. Adjust the slider until the two views are synced.

Export Settings

Export Settings are provided in the Settings tab basically for the purpose of copying and sharing these settings, though you can also activate them from the Settings tab. This is particularly good for drag-and-drop exports, since the Export dialog doesn't come up when you use the drag-and-drop method. Chapter 14 is devoted entirely to exporting, and the settings will be covered in depth in that chapter.

General

Temporary File Directory assigns a location to the temporary file that is created when a drag-and-drop export is executed. The temporary file is located in the same folder as the Avid application by default. But since these temporary files can be quite large, you may want them to be sent to another location with plenty of space.

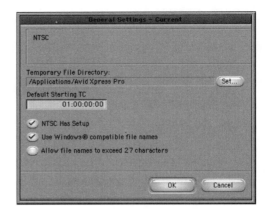

Default Starting TC specifies the default starting timecode for each new sequence. Most stations and post houses have a standard operating procedure for the starting timecode of their programs. This is a common question of many beginning Avid users. Typing a colon (:) between any of the numbers will indicate NDF timecode. A semicolon (;) indicates drop frame, which is the standard timecode type for broadcast. My default is set at 58:30:00, so that I can put 60 seconds of bars and tone and 30 seconds of slates and black, then start my program at 1:00:00:00. Some networks prefer to start shows at 10;00;00;00 or 11;00;00;00. Check with your broadcaster before laying off a tape, or you'll probably be doing it again.

NTSC Has Setup is basically for all NTSC editors except in Japan. This means that your legal black levels will start at 7.5 IRE on a waveform monitor. If you set it to NTSC Does Not Have Setup, then your legal black level will be set at 0 IRE. If you are unsure of how this should be set, ask an engineer at the broadcast outlet or duplication that generally receives your finished edits to help you.

Use Windows® compatible file names prevents you from using the characters /\:*?<>| in bin, project, or user names. These characters are not allowed in Windows file names. This option is helpful for moving bins and projects from Macintosh to Windows platforms. If you have an IT department and you aren't at a completely Mac-centric place, you should definitely have this on. It can also help in archiving project data and locating and sharing data across WANs and LANs.

Similarly, the Allow file names to exceed 27 characters is generally unchecked to provide better Windows compatibility. You should try to develop a naming scheme that stays under 27 characters for all your files, but if you don't want to be constrained by that, then check this setting.

Import Settings

Import Settings are provided in the Settings tab basically for the purpose of copying and sharing these settings, though you can also activate them from the Settings tab. This is particularly good to do for drag-and-drop imports, since the Import dialog doesn't come up when you use the drag-and-drop method. Chapter 11 is devoted entirely to importing and the settings will be covered in depth in that chapter.

Interface

The Interface Setting has two tabs: General and Appearance.

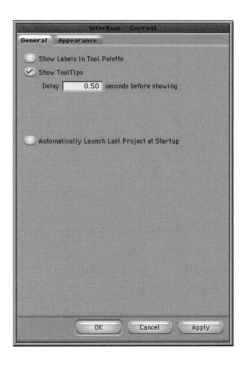

The General tab starts with Show Labels in Tool Palette and Show ToolTips. Both of these settings are very good for beginning editors. They enable little labels that explain what the buttons mean in the Tool Palette (accessible from the Fast menu between the Source and Record Monitors), and all of the other places where buttons are available, respectively. If you already know what all the buttons' names are, then you should turn off these two settings. At the very least, set the Show ToolTips Delay to at least a second. Otherwise, the system will constantly display the labels for the buttons as you mouse around the screen. The General tab also has a very noninterface setting included on it: Automatically Launch Last Project at Startup. If you generally like to always go back to the last project you were working on when you start up Xpress Pro, then this is the perfect time-saving setting for you. If you're like me, you work on so many different projects at a time that you'd probably waste more time quitting out of projects that you didn't want to go into. I keep this unchecked.

The Appearance tab of the Interface setting is where all the heavy lifting takes place. Although if you aren't really a cosmetic person, these settings could easily go untouched. Basically all this does is change the color scheme of the various backgrounds, buttons, bins, and tracks. I never minded the original color scheme of the Avid interface, so I stick with Spartan myself. Although, I have to admit that I think the Swoosh button style with a nice shading looks very cool and doesn't interfere with my editing. Experiment at your leisure, but remember that the purpose of the interface appearance should support your primary goal of easily grasping what you are trying to edit. If the color scheme you choose makes it difficult to tell which track or button is active or causes you to hunt for things that are sitting in plain sight, then something is wrong. Your color scheme should be easy on the eyes and easy to understand at a glance. Also, if you do a lot of color correcting, it should be as neutral as possible. (Note that the interface colors we chose for display in this book were chosen so that they would *print* clearly in black and white. This is not our preferred interface design.) If you do a lot of color correction, be careful of really funky appearance settings.

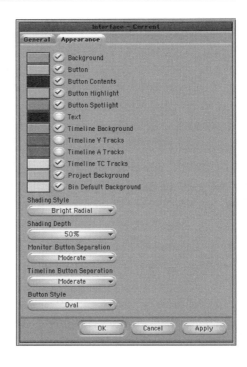

Keyboard

The keyboard is where customization is really, really important. My personal keyboard is radically customized, but many would argue that keeping your keyboard settings as close

to the default as possible is very smart since this layout is the most widely used, so that you can sit down at almost any system without having your personal settings with you.

To best customize your keyboard you should really pay attention to the commands you use every day as you edit. Anything you do with the mouse should be added to your keyboard if possible. To do this, call up the Command Palette (Ctrl+3/Cmd+3) and open the Keyboard Setting from the Settings list. Select the Button to Button Reassignment button at the bottom left corner of the Command Palette. Now simply drag the buttons from the Command Palette to the key on the keyboard that you want to assign. It is also important to map often-used File menu pulldowns. I have various pulldowns mapped including Audio Mix, Audio Tool, Render In/Out, Effects Editor, Batch Digitize, New Title, Color Correction toolset, and even Xpress Pro Help. To map these pulldowns, simply select the Menu to Button Reassignment button in the lower right corner of the Command Palette. Then click on the keyboard button you want to assign (i.e., you have to mouse-click it in the keyboard setting, not press the button on your actual keyboard) and click up into the pulldown menus like you normally would to select a pulldown.

Sometimes, in order to map certain file menu pulldowns to keyboard keys, you need to set up the circumstance that enables that pulldown first. For example, you can't map Render In/Out unless you have an effect in the Timeline with an IN and an OUT marked on either side of it. I have Render at Position, Render In/Out, and Expert Render all mapped to my keyboard.

You can have multiple keyboards for multiple tasks. To make multiple keyboard settings (for example, a trim keyboard, an effects keyboard, an audio keyboard, a color correction keyboard, and an editing keyboard), simply duplicate the keyboard setting in the Settings list (Ctrl+D/Cmd+D) and name each of them by clicking in the space between the word "Keyboard" and "User" and typing a name. You can switch between them from the Settings menu by clicking just to the left of the word "Keyboard" or by linking them to workspaces and then switching workspaces with the workspace buttons.

I've considered using multiple keyboard settings, but never thought I'd be able to keep them straight. There are also several MUI-devices (manual user interface) like Contour AV's ShuttlePro, onto which you can map keystrokes. There are also several controllers by JLCooper that can control the Avid.

My customized keyboard was developed by mapping the blank key to all of the buttons and then doing a screen capture of the blank keyboard. (There's a copy of this blank keyboard on the DVD.) I blew up the screen capture to a full sheet of paper and penciled in various important commands and file menu pulldowns, then located the ones I used most directly under my fingers so they didn't have to move. This is similar to the theory behind the QWERTY keyboard for typists. The most commonly used letters of the alphabet are positioned so you can type without moving your fingers at all. (Although, as a historical note, the typewriter was also designed to keep the little metal strikers from jamming up on the letters that are often used together.)

To decide what you might want to map, call up the Command Palette (Ctrl+3/ Cmd+3) and look at every button on each tab. If you don't know what every button does, find out. Keep a list of all the buttons you use all the time and the ones that you think might be useful. Then go through each of the pulldown menus and add any of those selections that you use frequently to the list. Create groups of these buttons that you think you'll use the most and keep them together where they're easiest to reach. Keep in mind that the groupings that Avid developed for their default keyboard layout were very well considered and the product of quite a bit of research. Even though my keyboard is drastically different from the default, my keys still fall into groups that maintain the same color groupings of Avid's default keycaps.

While I don't recommend that you edit using my keyboard settings, I'll explain mine to help you as you make decisions about why to map buttons to certain keys. I re-mapped the JKL default keys to the comma (,), period (.), and slash (/) keys, so that I don't have to reach too far up into the keyboard. I can also easily get my fingers positioned over them without looking down at the keyboard by tracing my middle finger along the space bar until it ends, then sliding up a row. Just like the default, I mapped the Mark In and Mark Out keys centered directly above my JKL keys. Then I developed a highly efficient mapping so that allows my hand to stay nicely in place with limited movement: I mapped the Remove Mark In and Remove Mark Out to the shifted keys directly under Mark In and Mark Out. And to access Go To In and Go To Out, I use a simple modifier key (Alt on PC and Option on Mac) in combination with the Mark In and Mark Out keys. Thus I have six buttons under two fingers. Just above my Mark In and Mark Out keys (K and L respectively) I have my editing buttons on I, O, P and {. This allows me to play through material, reach up a row and mark an IN and OUT, then reach directly up another row to Lift, Overwrite, Splice, or Extract. I also have the Mark Clip button nearby (with Remove Mark Clip on the Shifted key), Extend Edit, Remove Effect, and three different kinds of renders. I have other things mapped as well, but they aren't as important to my day-to-day editing.

Another way to use the keyboard more is to memorize any of the keyboard shortcuts that are built into the pulldown menus. I have Audio tool mapped my F12 key, but I could also get to it with Ctrl+1/Cmd+1. Pick a different keyboard shortcut every day or every week and practice using it instead of mousing.

Tools	Toolset	Windows
Audio Mix		
Audio EQ		
Automation Gain		
AudioSuite		
Audio Tool		⌘1
Audio Punch-In		
MetaSync Manager		
Calculator		⌘2
Clipboard Monitor		
Command Palette		⌘3
Composer		⌘4
Console		⌘6
Capture		⌘7
EDL		
Effect Editor		
Effect Palette		⌘8
Hardware		
Locators		
Media Creation		⌘5
Media Tool		
Project		⌘9
Timecode Window		
Timeline		⌘0
Title Tool		
Video Input Tool		⌘-
Video Output Tool		

I've seen a lot of people's keyboard settings. The most common keyboard settings use the default settings as a starting point, then people tend to strip it of the keys that they never use. Then, the primary place for personal commands is the function key row and/or mnemonic Shifted keyboard positions, such as putting the Title tool button on the Shift+T key or the Render key on Shift+R. There are also editors who come from other editing systems, including linear systems like GVGs, who map their keyboards to be similar to their old system. As long as you're using the keyboard instead of the mouse, you're in much better shape. Most linear editors started with GVG-like settings, then converted. Same for film editors, who first demanded an external shuttle knob, then tossed it and used the JKLs.

Avid likes to point out the fact that you can transfer user settings between products and versions, but in reality, user settings really should be created from scratch in every new version. This is actually a pretty good idea anyway, because each version brings new tools and it's pretty easy to get into a rut of using the same tools that you've always used. Exploring new tools helps get you out of your comfort zone, which is a good thing creatively. So each time you go to build a new user setting, check out all the new features in the Command Palette, the pulldown menus, and the settings. When you're done, print out a hard copy of your settings so you can quickly reset them when you switch products or versions.

 Don't forget the rest of the GUI when mapping buttons. The visible keys on the screen are an excellent place for two different kinds of buttons: those that you rarely use, so you need to see them, and those that are used in conjunction with mouse movement anyway, such as Collapse. It's almost impossible to set up a Collapse without using the mouse, so while you're mousing anyway, you might as well just click up above the Timeline to execute that command instead of keyboarding it. Which buttons make the most sense above the Timeline? Which are important to have under either monitor?

Media Creation

The Media Creation Setting has seven tabs. Don't get too intimidated though—the Capture, Titles, Import, and Mixdown & Transcode tabs are all identical and it's usually best to just kind of gang all of those decisions together.

The first tab is the Drive Filtering tab. This determines where your media can go. You can elect to Filter Based On Resolution, which limits your media to drives that Avid believes are capable of handling the throughput needed to stream out that resolution without skipping or dropping frames. If you really want to be able to digitize or transcode

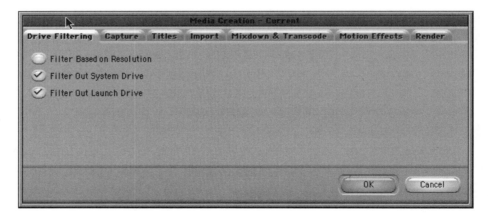

or consolidate to a drive that you can't see from the interface, turn off Drive Filtering. Especially when consolidating, you will want to do this so that you can archive media to drives that you don't intend to use for playback. For example, even though a CD or DVD wouldn't be up to the demands of real-time 1:1 playback, you can certainly use them for archiving.

Filter Out System Drive and Filter Out Launch drive are both excellent preferences to make if you are on a system that has huge external media drives, but many portable Xpress Pro systems count on using the internal drives to save media.

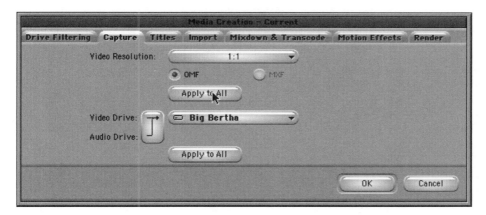

The Capture tab (plus the next three tabs, Titles, Import, and Mixdown & Transcode) all allow you to select a default resolution. This is very helpful and it's an excellent setting to save to your site settings to create a site-wide default resolution. You can easily override this in the Capture tool, but it gives you a standard starting place that is right for your needs most of the time. The Apply to All button below it allows you to assign that same resolution for Titles, Imports, and Mixdowns & Transcodes.

The button under Apply to All lets you select a default drive. By clicking the vertical button to the left of the drive button, you can opt to split your audio and video media onto two separate drives. This can often improve throughput. Apply to All puts all of the Titles, Imports, and Mixdowns & Transcodes onto the same drive.

 Splitting audio and video onto two separate logical drives does not do any good unless the drives are physically different and not just two different partitions of the same drive.

Warning

The Motion Effects tab in the Media Creation setting only allows you to set a drive, which you could Apply to All, but you probably already did that in another tab.

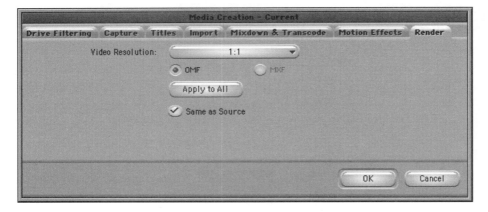

Renders can be done in an assigned resolution or can be done Same as Source by checking the box next to that choice. There is no drive to assign because renders are written to the same drive that their source media is written to.

PortServer

PortServer allows you to connect and disconnect from LANShare and to Auto-connect or not at launch. If you don't have PortServer, don't worry about this, and if you do have PortServer then you know more about it than we do.

Render

There aren't many options in here that are going to save a lot of time. You can set a sound that plays at the completion of a render, in case you like to nap or take a few bites of kung pao squid while rendering.

The next choice in this window is the ability to set a default for motion effects. This basically depends on the kind of work you do. For cutting offlines, you can probably set this to Duplicated Fields. The motion will look a little choppier, but your renders will be faster. For online work, I'd go with Both Fields, although the best result depends on the motion within the clip itself. If you're looking for a final quality render the first time around, you'll need to chart which styles give you the best results and set it for that. You won't be able to set a default motion effect style that will give the best results *every* time, but the goal is to have the default give you the best shot at getting it right most of the time on the first pass. Similarly, you can also set the default for Timewarp motion effects. Finally you can set the quality of the renders for regular segment and transition effects. This largely depends on whether you're using the machine to do offline or online work.

Safe Colors

For a detailed explanation of how and why to set Safe Colors, see "Color Correction Tool" on page 349 in Chapter 12.

Script

The Script Settings allow you to customize the font, size, margins, and color of scripts that are imported as bins if you like to use the script workflow for your editing. This was developed for a feature film work-flow, but any project can take advantage of it. You can import a script from any word processor or script writing software and link clips to the lines in the script. The takes are laid out in a graphical form against the script itself allowing the editor to see which lines of the script have coverage by certain takes. Select the options that allow you the greatest

signal-to-noise ratio of information. The Script functions allow you to see your work laid out in a format similar to script supervisor marks, which are used on scripts for most feature and entertainment work. The advantage is that you can electronically draw the lines, use multiple takes from a single line, show on- and off-camera characters, and cut using the script rather than a bin. While the script function is great for most formatted and scripted programs, it also can be used, to a limited extent, to cut documentaries. For example, if the doc is already done by "paper cut" and scripted, you can add selected B-roll footage to the script without having to do a search-and-destroy mission.

Using the advanced script functions, you can tell Xpress Pro where a line exists within the script on any given take. Usually when editing dramatic material, you use best line over continuity. If you have several takes of a line in the script and it is recorded into the script function, you can click on the line and play back every take, effectively determining which take is the best one. It saves a lot of time when you approach the cut in this way.

Or as one director put it, "It's not the time it takes to take the take that takes the time; it's the time between the takes that takes the time to take the take."

Think about it.

Timeline

The Timeline Settings are very important because this is where so much of your day-to-day editing takes place. You should really take some time to understand all of these settings and customize them according to your workflow. Timeline Settings are fairly basic, but we'll also discuss Timeline views, which really need to be customized for each editing task throughout the day or for particular projects or types of projects.

There are two tabs for this setting: Display and Edit. The Display tab has five check boxes affecting the look and behavior of the Timeline.

Show Toolbar is fairly new to the Avid veterans, who may be coming from other products. This option allows you to have a row of buttons along the top of the Timeline. I like this new addition to the Timeline. It does take up some screen real estate, so you have to determine if it's worth the space to have the buttons there, especially on a single-screen computer setup. This toolbar also gives you permanent access to a nice-sized audio meter.

Show Marked Region highlights the region from the Mark In to the Mark Out in purple. I like this on, but it annoys some people. The region will not turn purple if you don't have any tracks selected. Sometimes it's helpful to have this on, since it's easier to notice than looking for the Mark Ins and Outs. One of the main reasons to turn it off is that it makes it difficult to see clip colors. Try editing with it both ways to determine what's best for you.

Show Marked Waveforms only displays audio waveforms between a marked IN or OUT point instead of over the whole sequence. Sometimes drawing the audio waveforms for an entire sequence can grind an editing session to a halt. If you like to see the waveforms, but don't have time for them to constantly redraw, try this option. To see the waveforms in the Timeline, you still need to activate them in the Timeline Fast menu, but the Show Marked Waveforms limits the display to the marked area. The name of this setting is actually a little misleading, because it doesn't *show* marked waveforms, it actually *limits* waveforms to marks.

On most newer Avid systems, you can use Ctrl+./Cmd+. (period) to halt a long waveform redraw. Once the redraw has been stopped, you can go to the Timeline Fast menu and deselect audio waveforms. Or switch to Show Marked Waveforms. This method is known as bagging the redraw.

Highlight Suggested Render Areas After Playback is a new setting made necessary by the ability of the DNA products (including Xpress Pro) to attempt to play back any effects. The suggested render areas are marked in the Timeline with various colored lines that indicate the confidence that Xpress Pro has in being able to play back parts of the sequence without needing to render. A thin red line in the Timecode track indicates areas that definitely need to be rendered. Yellow lines indicate areas that were difficult to play back. And blue lines indicate that playback may be hampered due to disk speed limitations. Rendering isn't really going to help the appearance of blue lines. Your only option there is moving that media to faster drives. See Chapter 9, "Effects", for more detailed information on this.

Show Four-Frame Display shows the head and tail of incoming or outgoing frames of video in the Composer window when you drag a segment in the Timeline. This is handy to see where you're dragging something, but sometimes it is slow. Enabling this depends on whether you want to be a speed demon and get every bit of system performance you can get (turn this off if that describes you) or if you like the visual cue that this setting provides. This really depends on your video card memory and RAM speed.

Remember, things that hurt system performance but add to your ability to recognize the correct editing location better may end up being faster in the long run than the purely faster setting approach for the computer. You and the computer are like a team in a three-legged race: if you allow the computer to go faster, but hamper your own abilities, you're really slowing the entire process in the end.

The Edit tab allows you to set the Start Filler Duration. In the Clip menu there is a selection for Add Filler to Start. The default for this is 1 second. If you regularly use this feature and commonly add a larger number of seconds than 1, then this setting could save you some time by allowing you to add, for example, 10 seconds or 60 seconds of filler at the top of your sequence with a single pulldown or button click (if you have the pulldown menu mapped to a button). A good example of a smart setting here would be if you set your default starting timecode for new sequences to 58:30:00, then you could set Add Filler to Start to be 1:30:00 and you'd be starting your edit at 1:00:00:00 with a single keystroke.

Recent releases of Avid software allows you to look for flash frames so that you do not accidentally lay-off a show with errant frames. One of my editing jobs was cutting promos, and as I cut the promos for major sitcoms, I saw plenty of flashframes; for example, you could tell that in one version of the cut they had tried a wideshot, but later decided to use a close-up, but when they cut the close-up in, they'd mistakenly left one frame of the wideshot. And these are primetime network sitcoms and dramas. So to prevent this, you get a choice with this setting to determine just how many frames are considered a flash frame. This is a good thing. If you're cutting an MTV music video or a trailer for the X-Games or something, you may use shots that are only two or three frames long. So you can set a threshold for the length of a bad flash frame. If you are cutting news or documentary, you can probably set this threshold much higher, since you'd rarely want a shot under a half a second. I don't really use this feature, but if I did, I'd probably set it to warn me about anything under 10 frames.

Auto-Patching automatically patches the enabled source tracks to the tracks enabled in the Timeline. I find this to be handy, so I have this enabled. Try it to see if you like it and if it saves you time. There's really no downside to turning this one on.

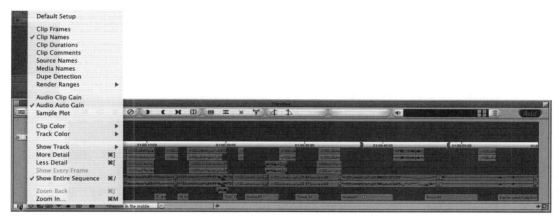

Auto-Monitoring is generally a handy tool to reduce clicking. It simply makes the video monitor icon in the Timeline (the thing that determines which is the highest video track you're monitoring) follow along with your most recent video patch. So if you're monitoring v1 and you patch a new title onto v2, you will be monitoring v2 automatically if this setting is selected.

Default Snap-To Edit allows you to have every Timeline segment edit snap to the transition at an edit. In XpressDV, this was the only way the Timeline worked. In Symphony and other higher-end products, Snap-To Edit is optional. For Xpress Pro, this setting allows you to choose which behavior you prefer. I find that it is a little limiting for the way I cut, but if you want to quickly and easily be able to drop stuff right at the end of a clip, then turn this on.

Dupe Detection Handles allows you to choose the size of the handles, in frames, to use for dupe checking. Basically this is a film thing, because certain ways of cutting film negative require the destruction of different numbers of frames of the negative. But this can also be used to look for duplicated shots in video.

Timeline View

In the Settings list, this just lists all of the Timeline views you've created using the Timeline Fast menu and other Timeline manipulations (enlarging tracks for example) so you can select or copy them. It's very smart to create several Timeline views for different purposes. Some of mine include a Timeline view with 8 audio tracks and 12 video tracks squeezed as small as possible with the timecode track in between the audio and video tracks and no clip text. (Moving the Timecode track in between the audio and video tracks is not possible with Xpress Pro unless you know our secret.)

I also have one with the audio tracks pretty big and the Auto Gain (rubber-banding) turned on. I have another version of that same Timeline view, but with waveforms turned

Moving Timecode Track

Although the timecode track can't be moved in Xpress Pro, we have created a hack that probably makes this book pay for itself: you can create a Timeline view with the timecode track in the middle on another machine and import it into Xpress Pro. That setting has been created and saved for you on the DVD. Import it and you too can have the timecode between audio and video. This serves at least two great purposes. It lets you easily differentiate visually between the audio and video tracks and it allows you access to the timecode track no matter how many tracks you have and how little screen real estate you have. Often, when I am editing with dozens of tracks, if I want to turn sync locks on all my tracks, or if I want to see the timecode track, or click on it as a shortcut to escape the Trim or Effects mode, I have to scroll all the way down to the bottom of the Timeline. With the timecode track in the middle, it is almost always accessible. Putting this on the disk makes me believe there really is a Santa Claus.

on. If you do lots of multi-layered video effects, you could have a version where each video track is a slightly different color or maybe even turn on Clip Frames to help you get a better idea of what part of the effect is on each track. I wouldn't want to leave Clip Frames on for all my editing, but if you're zoomed into a small, complex portion of a sequence, it could actually save you time by allowing you to visualize things faster. You could also have views to show color corrections or to show offline media or create a view that scrolls the Timeline. Explore the things that are helpful to you and set up Timeline views with descriptive names.

Clip Frames is crazy to me. I don't know why you'd want these on, except for my suggestion to use them for small areas of dense effects. Most sequences are so long that you don't even get a single frame on a segment, and if your edit is so short that you *do* display a frame on each segment, then you really don't need the feature. But many people requested this feature for many years, so there must be some point. Having this on is a *huge* redraw load, though.

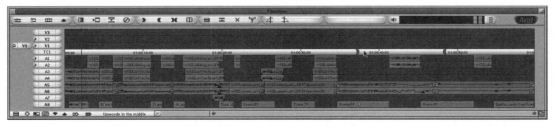

2.10 Eyes will probably gaze in wild wonder in at this screenshot of an Xpress Pro Timeline with the timecode in the middle!

2.11 Timeline view with Clip Frames enabled.

Clip Names, Clip Durations, Clip Comments, Source Names, and Media Names are options to get good textual information as you are editing. What each one does is fairly self-explanatory. Figure out how any of this information will help you in the Timeline. If it just creates a lot of noise instead of signal in the information that you need to help you edit, then don't use it. But that information can help you as you edit. Less text info from these options can help Timeline redraws. The way to get the best of both worlds is to have multiple Timeline views and only turn on the ones that you need, when you need them. I always keep a super-clean version of a Timeline view (with all options turned off) so if redraws are taking too long I can call that up.

Default Setup	
✓ Clip Frames	
✓ Clip Names	
Clip Durations	
Clip Comments	
Source Names	
Media Names	
Dupe Detection	
Render Ranges	▶
Audio Clip Gain	
✓ Audio Auto Gain	
Sample Plot	
Clip Color	▶
Track Color	▶
Show Track	▶
More Detail	⌘]
Less Detail	⌘[
Show Every Frame	
Show Entire Sequence	⌘/
Zoom Back	⌘J
Zoom In...	⌘M

To help me find where I am in the Timeline compared to the pages of a script, I use Clip Comments turned on in the Timeline. Then I segment-select all of the clips (usually in the audio track, like a narrator) that pertain to a single page of the script and pulldown the Sequence pulldown menu (hidden above the Sequence Monitor image, under the name of the current sequence) to select Add Comments. This brings up a dialog that allows you to type a comment for the clip or clips. I keep this to single numbers—instead of something like "page 01"—since that makes it easier to see when the sequence is lengthy and zoomed all the way out. If you really want to speed up this process, map the Add Comments menu selection to your keyboard, then all you have to do is lasso all the clips from page 1 of the script, hit the Add Comments button, type "1," and you're done.

Dupe detection shows you if you have parts of the same shot twice in your sequence. See the previous Timeline section in this chapter.

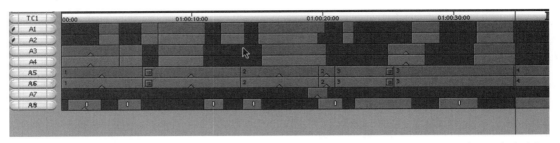

2.12 A Timeline view with Clip Comments turned on. Each audio segment had a comment that included the page of the script it was from. Now you can easily find your place in the script in the Timeline.

Render Ranges indicates unrendered portions of your sequence with a thin red line at the top of the tracks in the Timeline that need to be rendered. You can either choose to see All the areas in a sequence that need to be rendered or Partial only to indicate only the segments where the renders were interrupted and still need to be completed. Choosing None disables the Render Range feature.

Audio Clip Gain provides you with a visual reference in the Timeline for the audio levels set from with the Audio Mix Tool. This is indicated by a black line providing the Clip Gain level with gray lines to indicate various audio db levels.

Audio Auto Gain is similar to Audio Clip Gain, but it allows you to place keyframes on the black line that indicates the Auto Clip Gain level for the purpose of rubber-banding. Audio Clip Gain and Auto Clip Gain are not mutually exclusive. They can be displayed at the same time, but this may cause confusion when trying to apply keyframes.

Sample Plot allows you to see the audio waveforms for your audio tracks in the Timeline (see Figure 2.15). This function can really slow a system down, so we recommend that you only use this feature when you really need it. My rule of thumb for enabling waveforms is to turn them on only when I am not monitoring video. This will really open up some system resources. So, without video playback, most Avids are very, very responsive, even with waveforms selected on the Timeline. You can use this feature in conjunc-

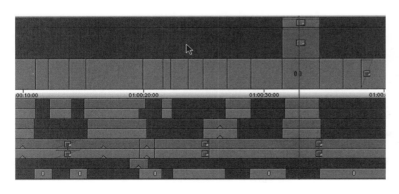

2.13 Timeline view with Render Ranges set to All. The thin red lines indicate effects that have not been rendered.

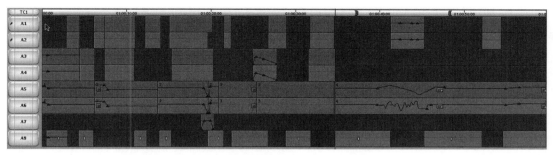

2.14 Timeline with Auto Gain on and rubber-banded keyframes set.

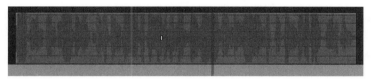

2.15 Audio waveform produced by Sample Plot

tion with the Timeline setting to only draw the waveforms between Mark In and Mark Out. See the section on "Timeline" on page 50 in this chapter.

 When you monitor waveforms try to get the audio tracks as "fat" as possible. By using Alt+Ctrl+L/Option+Cmd +L you can expand the waveform *inside* of the track. The same modifiers with "K" shrink the waveform inside the selected track. Of course Ctrl+K/Cmd+K shrink the selected tracks.

Clip Color lets you see different clip colors in the sequence. The three basic options for clip color are Local, Source, and Offline. Local clip colors are those assigned from within the Timeline. Use local clip color to designate specific portions of the show. For example, segment-select all the clips in a show open and color them green, then color all of the bumpers blue. Or color each show segment a different color to make it easier to jump around in the show. I also sometimes use local color to organize interview footage. I'll cut huge chunks of unscreened interviews into a long Timeline, then, as I listen to them, I'll color-code each answer. When I get done screening all the footage, I can easily drag all the colors into groups. Now I can watch the groups to see which comments intercut with others in the group, or which comments are the strongest or are redundant.

 Warning If you are trying to get Local Clip Color to work and the Set Color choice is grayed out in the Edit menu, you need to turn on Clip Color>Local in the Timeline first. That will enable you to select Set Color from the Edit menu.

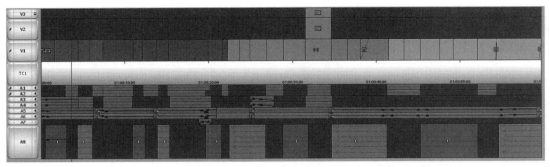

2.16 Timeline View with Local clip color. Varying shades of gray correspond to colors. See Figure 2.16 on DVD for a color version of this image.

Source color is used when you want to see the clip colors that were chosen in the bin. If you color-code all the interview footage from a single person in the bin, then turn on source clip color, you will be able to locate all of those clips in your sequence. Sometimes I do this if I have to add lower third titles to someone in each show segment. By color-coding the interviewees, I can easily tell if they show up in certain show segments. Or use this option to show all the offline media in a segment.

Warning

When using clip color to show offline media, you can't really rely on this as your only means of detecting offline media for long sequences because you could easily miss shorter clips, even when you're fairly well zoomed in.

Track Color is a setting where I tend to stick with the default. Some editors use absolutely blinding combinations of Day-Glo track colors, but that can really fatigue your eyes. It is definitely useful to have each track a slightly different color. With a big effects stack it could help determine which tracks to enable.

Show Track allows you to hide or display any tracks. I don't usually mess with this, but for a sequence with a large number of video tracks, you could choose to hide them when working exclusively with audio, or vice versa. Generally, I find that there's no reason to hide these tracks because if I have a lot of tracks in a

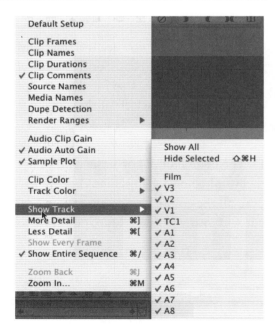

sequence, many simply don't get displayed in the limited real estate of the Timeline.

Showing More Detail or Less Detail isn't really a function of the Timeline view as much as it is being able to zoom into the Timeline. I have never used these from the Timeline Fast menu because the keyboard commands for these functions became second nature early on. To zoom in or out of the Timeline in increments, use Ctrl+[/Cmd+[(to go in) or] (to go back out) and then Ctrl+/ or Cmd+/ to see the entire Timeline.

Show Every Frame seems to me to be a huge waste of system resources. I suppose you could try to edit this way. It shows you every frame of video in the Timeline across the top of each video track. This really doesn't tell you very much and it really takes a lot of computing power to do screen redraws with this setting enabled.

Title Styles are listed in the Settings list so you can select or copy them. These styles are a great way to speed up creating titles. And since Title Styles are user settings, it's important that you can see them in the list, because if someone else has to edit on your project, or if multiple editors are working on the same show or campaign, then you can copy these Title Styles into another user's settings. Creating Title Styles is done while you're in the Title tool. (For more on this subject see Chapter 10 "The Title Tool" on page 299.) Once you've got a style you like, you can save it as a Title Style. One of the great time savers with Title Styles, especially if you work on a show that relies heavily on a few basic looks for fonts, is to assign a function key to a style. Then to create a title in that style, you simply hit that function key and start typing.

Trim

The Trim Settings window has two tabs: Play Loop and Features.

The Play Loop tab allows you to set the preroll and postroll for Play Loop while in trim. The defaults are a good place to start. Most linear edit suites gave a preroll time of 5 seconds, but this was more about how long it took to get a tape to lock up properly than how much time you need to determine the proper timing of a trimmed edit. I don't know anyone who includes an Intermission time. The object here would be to develop a customized time for pre- and postroll that allowed you to see enough material surrounding the trim to let you make a good choice without wasting any extra time prerolling or postrolling around the edit point.

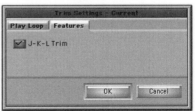

The Features tab is a little misleading since there's only a single feature that defaults to the on position. J-K-L trim allows you to control the direction and timing of your trims. This is a great feature that many people asked Avid to add to the Xpress Pro interface. I'd leave this on even if you don't use it.

Video Display

Video Display allows you to determine various ways to improve the performance of video playback from within the system.

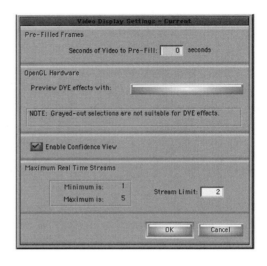

The Seconds of Video to Pre-Fill text box delays playback the number of seconds you specify. During this Pre-Fill time, Xpress Pro prepares to playback the sequence from the Timeline locator to the end of the sequence. For especially long or complicated sequences setting this number fairly high increases the chances that Xpress Pro will be able to playback the sequence successfully. The maximum Pre-Fill time is 10 seconds.

The OpenGL mode allows you to assign an OpenGL video board to use for playback of video. Any OpenGL cards installed in your computer will be selectable from the pulldown. If you don't have an OpenGL card, there will be no selections in the pulldown and a software OpenGL "card" will be used for playback.

Enable Confidence View allows you to view incoming or outgoing media in the Record monitor while you capture media or lay off a digital cut.

Assign a Stream Limit number in the text box for the number of video streams you want the Record monitor to attempt to display.

Workspaces

Workspaces are very powerful. They allow you to call up multiple tools and arrange windows in a set arrangement using a single keystroke. Common Workspaces to set would be:

- Audio Workspace with Audio tool, Audio Mixer, and maybe EQ, AudioSuite, and Auto Gain

- Digitize Workspace with Digitize tool, Audio Tool, Console, and scopes

- Effects Workspace with the Effects Palette and a customized effects keyboard setting

The three choices you're confronted with in Workspace Mode are Activate Settings Linked By Name, Continually Update this Workspace, and Manually Update this Workspace.

Activate Setting Linked by Name is an incredibly powerful feature. If you had an Audio Workspace and an Audio Bin View and an Audio Timeline View and an Audio keyboard setting, you could link them using this feature so that whenever you called up the Audio Workspace, your bins would display certain audio information prominently, your Timeline would have expanded audio tracks with audio waveforms and audio levels enabled and your keyboard would be reset to give you certain audio tools at your fingertips.

Warning Be aware that audio settings are placed in alphabetical order, so if you make a Digitize Workspace and assign it to the W1 key, then make an Audio Workspace and attempt to assign it to the W2 key, the Audio Workspace will get placed where you had mapped Digitize because it is now first alphabetically. You can choose to simply number your workspaces, but I like names better because it makes linking settings easier to understand. Otherwise, you'd need Timeline views, bin views, and keyboard settings that were just numbers.

The other two options in this are mutually exclusive. If you choose to update automatically, then every time you change something while a specific workspace is open, that's the way it will be next time. With manual updating, you need to make a conscious decision to change the workspace. To me, it's almost pointless to have workspaces if they're updated automatically, because they would be constantly changing, and I want something predictable. The whole point is to create a workspace that you want to start with every time you start a certain task. When you select Manually Update, a new button called Update this Workspace Now is added to the window. When your workspace is properly laid out, click on this button to learn the new Workspace layout and feature set.

Let's create an Audio Workspace with settings that are linked by name.

1. Click on the Workspace setting in the Settings list and duplicate it. (Ctrl+D/Cmd+D).

2. Name the duplicated Workspace setting by typing in the space to the right of the word Workspace and to the left of the word "User."

3. Open all of the audio specific tools that you like to use. These should include the Audio tool and Audio Mix for sure. You could also open AudioSuite, Audio EQ, and Automation Gain.

4. Position all of the windows to best use your screen real estate. For example, for audio work, I didn't really need to see the video monitors, so I minimized them, leaving a source and record Timeline so I could easily edit. I also expanded the height of the Timeline because I like to use rubber-banding.

5. Customize other settings that can be linked to the Workspace. These could include your keyboard setting, Timeline views, and Bin views. I made the video tracks small and the audio tracks big. I also enabled Sample Plot in the Timeline. You can also hide tracks or enable other Timeline options that you think you'll use when working on audio. Changing keyboard settings wouldn't get you very far in an Audio Workspace, but for an Effects Workspace, you could add buttons for all the effects keys. In order to get the Timeline views, keyboard settings, and other items to link to the appropriate Workspace, you must name them the same as the Workspace.

6. When you have created your Workspace, double-click the Workspace button. This will call up the Workspace window. Select Activate Settings Linked By Name if you plan on linking other settings. Also select Manually Update This Workspace. Selecting this choice enables a button called Save Workspace Now. Click on this button whenever you want to save changes to your Workspace. Then click "OK" or hit return.

7. To speed launching these Workspaces, it is advisable to map the Workspace buttons to your keyboard, and maybe to your Timeline as well. The Workspace buttons are on the More tab of the Command Palette. For more information regarding mapping these buttons, see "Keyboard" on page 42 in this chapter.

 One linked setting you may consider using is the Interface Setting. You could create a custom Interface look that would help indicate which workspace you have active. The Digitize Workspace could be red, the Audio Workspace could be white, and the Effects Workspace could be blue (the color of unrendered effects).

Warning There is no return to normal button to get you out of a workspace. If this is something you feel you need, then you can create a basic or blank workspace to get you back to regular editing,

CONCLUSION

Settings are an incredibly powerful way to enhance your performance on Xpress Pro. A small investment of your time in setting these customized features now will pay off every single day for years to come. Keep an eye out for new features and try to incorporate them into your workflow as they become available. Also, engage other editors in discussions of how they customize their systems. Remember that settings can be traded and shared. This can be far more profitable than trading baseball cards ever was.

To reiterate a final important message that may have gotten lost in the shuffle earlier in the chapter: Save your settings someplace portable and incorruptible. After spending all this valuable time customizing your settings, burn them to a CD. Make a copy to a spot on a hard drive or network server. The other geek-chic thing to do with settings is to copy them to one of those little USB thumb drives and wear it around your neck or put it on your key ring with all your dongles.

Chapter 3

Capturing

The first step in getting your project started in Xpress Pro is capturing the media. This is also known as digitizing. Somewhere along the line, the term "digitizing" became an old school term, and "capture" was the buzzword. But it doesn't matter because whether you're digitizing, digitalizing, capturing, or ingesting, you're doing the same thing.

It may come as a surprise to you that capturing footage is one of the things that editors do not do well. As a consultant to several television series and motion pictures, I can usually find one or two little things that will speed up the process and make it more efficient. And as the late, great Alabama football coach Paul "Bear" Bryant once said, "It's the little things that'll git ya." So while it isn't the sexiest function of Xpress Pro, the Capture tool is important to learn if you want to make more time for editing.

SETTING UP THE CAPTURE TOOL

Opening the Capture Tool

Before you begin to capture media to a project, you have to open a bin where the clips are going to be stored, then, with the bin highlighted, choose Tools>Capture (Ctrl+7/Cmd+7). You can also choose Toolset>Capture to open the Capture tool. The screen will display the Capture tool.

A Quick Tour of the Capture Tool

The Capture tool provides you with all of the controls necessary to bring tape-based media onto your hard drives. You will find that the tool is divided into five basic groups.

1. Recording controls such as the Capture button, track selector, a deck button, and Audio tool are at the top.

2. Clip information, including the clip name and comments, are in the second section.

3. Storage information, including the chosen bin, storage drive, resolution, drive toggle, and remaining space window are in the third section.

4. DV-specific information is in the fourth section. This includes audio delay and frame offset.

5. The bottom section contains deck type, controls, marks, and tape names.

 There are twirl-down triangles alongside each of these five basic groups. If you don't need to see information in a specific group, and you're short on screen real estate, you can "twirl up" the triangle to hide the information.

THE RECORDING CONTROLS

Starting at the top of the Capture tool, you will see a number of icons, including a big red button, a black square, a trash can, a disk icon with the word "Cap" above it, a videotape deck icon and a trash can. Let's take a closer look at what each one does.

3.3   Recording Controls

The Capture Button

The red button at top left is the Capture button. You click it once to start capturing and click it again to stop. How do you know whether or not you're recording? The black box to the right of the Capture button indicates this by flashing on and off as you digitize. When it flashes red, you're capturing. When it doesn't flash, you're not. If it flashes any other color, either your monitor is messed up or the sixties were really, really good to you.

The Trashcan

Unlike the trashcan on a Mac or the Recycle Bin on a Windows system, the Trashcan in the Capture tool is used only when you want to stop capturing and you don't want to use

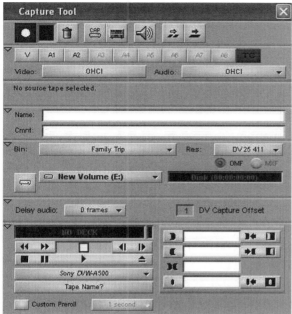

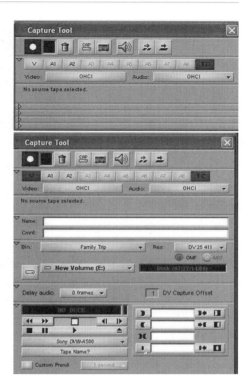

3.1 The Capture Tool
3.2 Twirl Down Menus, Open and Closed

what has been captured so far. For example, if you started capturing a clip and then realized that this material will absolutely not be used, you can click on the Trashcan icon.

Even though the Trashcan is obviously a way to abort capturing and to dispose of media, when you click on the Trashcan icon, it will still ask if you want to keep or discard the media that you digitized. This is, depending on how you look at it, a blessing or a pain. Avid created editing systems for the computer-challenged editor. These days, most editors know their way around a computer pretty well. Even so, the functionality of Avid systems extends across a very wide range of users. As a result, the "keep or discard" message stayed.

The Capture/Log Mode Button

Next to the Trashcan is a disk icon with the word "Cap" over it. This is your Capture/Log Mode button. Click on it. You will note that the interface changes somewhat, shrinking in height (There is no disk assignment during logging, which we'll cover later.), and the top row also changes. No more Capture button, flashing record light, or Trashcan. The system has switched from Capture mode to Logging mode. This is also indicated by a Pencil icon in the Record Button.

When you log a tape, you're only creating clips. No media is captured. As a result, there's no need to choose which media drive the media will go onto, because there is no media, or to misquote a David Lynch film, "No Hay Media!" Enough obscure quotes for now, let's move on to the Logging buttons.

Logging Buttons

When you go into log mode using the Log/Capture selector, the red Capture button is replaced by a button with a Mark In icon. This is done so that you can mark an IN point on the fly. You can also type in a timecode using the timecode registers below. If you enter a timecode in the register or click on the Mark In icon, the Mark In icon will switch, this time to a somewhat odd-looking combination icon. This icon, a combination of Mark Out and a pencil, allows you to mark out and log with the push of a single button. (The Pencil is a logging icon). If you prefer to use the timecode registers to type an OUT point, the icon will switch to a Logging (Pencil) icon. Click on this icon and a clip is logged. Before we proceed, click on the Log/Capture Selector and switch back to Capture mode.

The Deck Button

Continuing our tour of the Capture tool interface, the next button is a Deck button. Choosing this button determines whether or not a deck will be used online or offline.

What are online and offline? Not to be confused with the editing terms, this button selects whether Xpress Pro will control the deck or if the deck has no mode of external control. An example would be VHS. Most VHS decks, including some used professionally, have no RS-422 or FireWire connections. As a result, Xpress Pro cannot control them directly. We'll go over these two protocols a little later in the chapter. The important thing to know about the Deck button is this: if your source cannot be remote-controlled externally, you need to click on this button. This includes capturing from sources like microphones, CD players, and satellite feeds or straight from animation or motion capture cameras. When you click on the Deck tool, its icon changes from a Deck icon to the same icon with a red circle and a slash through it. This is, of course, the international symbol for "No!" One would think from this that there is no deck attached, which could be the case, but it usually is used for decks and other sources that are not controlled by Xpress Pro.

Warning If you choose to turn the Deck button off and are recording direct to the system, all of the rules of capturing apply. You cannot uprez from a lower resolution because there is no way for Xpress Pro to find the original source. Without reference points such as timecode and machine control, any data acquired could easily become data lost. Perhaps more importantly, any capturing errors that occur could prove devastating.

3.4   The Video Input Tool Selector on Capture Tool

The Video Input Tool (Optional: Mojo Only)

If you're familiar with other Avid systems, you probably know all about the Video Input tool, right? The Vectorscope icon normally opens a window that displays both Waveform and Vectorscope icons. The difference here is that you cannot do this on Xpress Pro. This is both good and bad. The good side of it is that Mojo has been calibrated to faithfully reproduce the picture and sound of your video elements, and besides, if you have analog video coming into the system and you're doing uncompressed online quality, you really need an external waveform/vectorscope combo or a rasterizer to measure the input signals.

The bad side of it is that there is no waveform and vectorscope.

So what does this tool do? Assuming that you are using Mojo, it allows you to choose the type of video that you will be recording. The choices are:

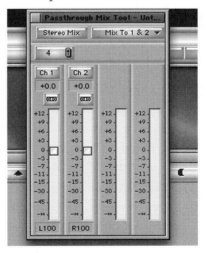

- *Composite:* Choosing Composite is the most objectionable choice. Composite video is video at its most basic. It has lower resolution and because the signal is combined into one simple BNC input, it's not the greatest quality.

- *S-Video (Also known as Y/C):* S-Video is a step up from Composite. The advantages are very simple. The chrominance in the picture (color information) is separated from the luminance information (brightness) and thus is a more faithful and accurate representation. The quality of this signal is good, but there are better options when available.

- *Component:* The addition of Component video to Mojo was a stroke of genius for Avid. When the original specs for Mojo were released, some users complained that the lack of component input made Mojo less than a value. Avid listened. When combined with an optional cable (which connects to both the S-Video and Composite inputs on Mojo) the system can receive analog component signals. Not all decks have the ability to output this higher quality signal, but those that do can produce very good pictures at much better quality than the previously mentioned inputs. For reference, Component is also referred to as YUV, Y Cr Cb, and R–Y, B–Y, Y. These terms really shouldn't be used interchangeably, but many people use them anyway. Check your deck operations manual to see if it has component output.

- *DV:* The DV input is the best possible choice for any DV source going into the system. The reason is simple: you keep everything recorded in the digital domain. What is the digital domain? Good question. This is the kind of question that could take hours to explain, but we don't have time, so here's the *Reader's Digest* version. For those of you who already know this information, skip ahead a paragraph, or just for fun, sense the squirm factor as I try to explain it briefly.

There are two types of signals, analog and digital. Digital signals are made up of binary encoded information, basically zeroes and ones (0, 1). Analog information is made of electronic signals, pulses made by electrons. When copying from one analog source to another, the signal can weaken due to the characteristics of electronics, i.e., the fidelity of the signal degrades as it passes through multiple processors. As a result, an analog original is always better than a copy of the same thing. The copy is said to be second generation, meaning one generation off of the original. With digital recording, everything remains the same, so long as the binary information is passed through a digital pipeline. Zeroes and ones remain zeroes and ones. If you should, however, play back a digital signal to the analog domain, where the signal is encoded as an electronic signal, it loses its digital fidelity. Digital-to-digital dubs (also called clones) are very, very close to the originals.

Okay, so when using a DV source, the signal is digital. It is best to keep it digital. You can even output it as digital and the quality will be superior.

Now let's move on to the next button, the Audio tool.

The Audio Tool

Before capturing audio, you will need to set up both your sample rate settings and input levels.

Setting Audio Project Settings

To set your sample rate for your project, go to the Project window, select the Settings tab and double-click on Audio Project. The Audio Project menu will appear.

At the top right of the Audio Settings Menu is the sample rate data. You can choose between three settings: 32kHz, 44.1kHz, and 48kHz.

The higher the sample rate, the better the audio quality. It is important to note that there is only marginal difference between 44.1kHz and 48kHZ. The default sample rate for Xpress Pro is 48kHz. The higher the sample rate, the more disk space is required, but note that, in this day and age of 300GB drives, either sample rate of audio does not take up a significant amount of space.

Note also that for most compact disc recordings, 44.1 is the normal sample rate. As a result, should you import any tracks from a prerecorded disc (assuming that proper permissions are obtained, of course), you will need to upsample or downsample accordingly to make that recording properly fit the audio sample rate for your project. 48kHz is the sample rate for many digital video- and audiotape formats, including DigiBeta. DAT can record and play back both sample rates from most players, but the typical DAT sample rate is also 48kHz.

You can play back different audio sample rates within the same sequence so long as the Convert Sample Rates When Playing setting is set to Always. This will perform a sample rate conversion on the fly when playing back mismatched samples. This selection is fine for offlining solutions, but the proper sampling must be adjusted before outputting any sequence. If you choose to not convert sample rates while playing, the audio that does not match the Audio Project sample rate will play back as silence.

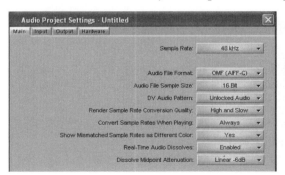

3.5 Audio Project Settings Menu

3.6 Convert Sample Rates Selection

Sounds of Silence: Occasionally an editor is confronted with the issue of "silent audio" playing back. When this happens, it is natural to look for media that has been deleted or taken offline. The first place to look is not on the media drives, but in the Audio Project Settings. If the Convert Sample Rates When Playing is set to Never, chances are that there is a sample rate mismatch and some of the media isn't playing because it was not sampled at the preselected project sample rate. To remedy this problem, select Always and try playing it again. Alternatively, if all of your media is a certain sample rate and your project is set to a different sample rate, you should simply reset your project sample rate to the sample rate of your media.

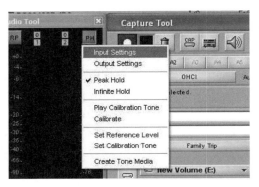

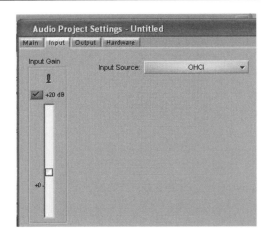

3.7   The Audio Tool *(above)*

3.8   Audio Tool Peak Hold Menu *(right)*

Setting Audio Input Levels

To adjust input levels, click on the Speaker icon in the Capture window. The Audio tool appears. To go to the input adjustments, click on the Peak Hold button (PH) on the right side of the Audio tool. A menu allows you to select Input Settings (see Figure 3.7).

When Input Settings is selected, the Audio Project Settings window will open. The Input tab is selected, and you can adjust the slider according to your needs. An added feature is the +20dB adjustment button. This is used for devices that need an extra boost, or +20dB pad (see Figure 3.8).

When monitoring audio input on the Audio Tool, keep in mind that the right side of the meter is analog VU and the left side is digital (see Figure 3.9). In the digital domain,

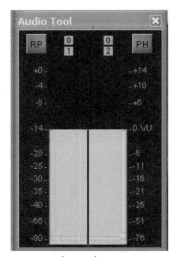

3.9   Audio Tool Meters

anything above 0dB (or approximately +14dB analog) becomes distorted. Therefore, when monitoring input, be sure that the gain is set properly so that it does not exceed 0dB digital.

The Audio Passthrough Tool (Optional: Hardware Dependent)

If you have Mojo attached to your Xpress Pro, you have an additional button at the top. This is the Audio Passthrough tool. The Audio Passthrough tool allows you to monitor, adjust, and pan audio coming from the source to your system without affecting the levels during capture. The advantages of using the tool are significant. If you are capturing media and want to get a sense of how the sound will be when mixed, you can use the Audio Passthrough tool to create a faux mix for monitoring while the media is captured. If you want to hear what a stereo pair mix will sound like when correctly adjusted, you can use the Passthrough tool. When capturing a source with narration on one channel and sound on tape on the other, you can pan the sound so that you get a feel of what it will sound like in the final mix (see Figure 3.10).

With the Passthrough Mix tool, you can choose between a direct mix to Channels 1 and 2 or a stereo pair. You can adjust the levels of sound appropriately for monitoring, or pan them any way you'd like. You can gang channels of audio together and adjust them as a group.

But anything you do will not affect capturing the media, which means that you can listen to the source in any way that you'd like, using this tool.

Choosing Recording Tracks

The Capture tool will capture information from the tracks that you select. Xpress Pro will automatically activate the tracks that were selected in the previous capture session. Before capturing, it is a good idea to monitor the tracks to ensure that they will be needed. For example, if you find that there is no audio on track two of a tape, there is no need to capture it. If you decide to capture it anyway, valuable drive space will be used. But then again, for every rule, there are good reasons to ignore it (see Figure 3.11).

3.10 Passthrough Tool

3.11 Capture Track Selection

Several years ago I was editing a documentary that involved a confrontation, off mic, between two men. This confrontation later proved to be central to the story line. The camera mic was running, as it always does, but the sound guy had disconnected the fish pole boom mic because they were just shooting B-roll that day. Like many documentaries, a lot was scripted in post, and the director inadvertently heard this off-mic conversation exclaiming, "Holy cow! Did you hear what he said?!" It wouldn't have happened if I hadn't made the mistake of digitizing both audio channels. My point? Sometimes a mistake is a good thing. If you have plenty of drive space, digitize whatever is there in documentaries. It may prove to be a key story device.

Xpress Pro will capture up to four audio tracks, video, and timecode information. To select or deselect tracks, simply click on the corresponding buttons to toggle them from their current state.

Okay, so now you've selected your tracks. What's next? Below each track (video and audio) is a selection of source types. Each source type will vary, depending on your hardware configuration.

Choosing Video and Audio Input Formats

The Video and Audio pop-up menus in the Capture tool show the current selected audio and video formats.

For video formats, we've already discussed the selection of these using the Video Input tool with an optional Mojo. If you are not using Mojo, your video format will default to OHCI (see Figure 3.12).

For audio, the inputs also vary, depending upon whether you have Mojo connected to your system. For those who do not have Mojo, the inputs are OHCI (default), MIDI, CD Audio, Line In, and Mic In. This also depends on your computer configuration (see Figure 3.13).

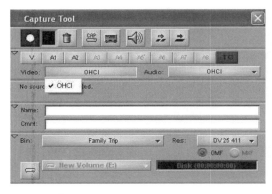

3.12 Video Input

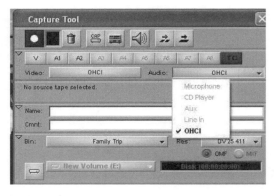

3.13 Audio Input

For those with Mojo, the audio formats are RCA (–10dBu) and OHCI. Because Mojo takes over your system, the other inputs are not available. When these are needed, you can disconnect Mojo (shutting down the computer first) and restart Xpress Pro.

One thing that I like about the RCA format on Mojo—it is what it is. Avid makes no bones about it. The signal is not coming in at line level. The disadvantage is the potential for lower quality of audio. So how do you address the issues of line level input going to RCA and RCA input going in at –10dB?

There are a couple of options to help. One is to adjust the signal of the source so that it reaches an optimum level as it passes through Mojo. The other is to adjust your Audio Project Settings Input tab from 0dB to +6dB, depending on your source.

The Message Bar

Just below the input buttons is a mostly blank area used to update you with the status of the Capture tool. The Message Bar will tell you what mode you're in (Capture versus Mark In for Logging), whether you are batch capturing, and so forth. I find this area extremely handy when the system isn't doing what I think I'm telling it to do (see Figure 3.14).

3.14 The Message Bar

3.15 Notes and Comments Boxes

Name and Comments Boxes

Somewhere along the line, you're going to want to name each clip. It's better for organizational purposes to do it during digitizing and get it over with. The Clip Name entry box allows you to do this before or during the capture of each clip. If you want to add information during capture, just start typing. To switch from the Clip Name entry to the Comments entry, use the Tab button on your keyboard. Any comments entered after tabbing will appear in the Comments column of your bin (see Figure 3.15).

It's a good idea to do some postproduction planning (pre-post—yes, it sounds silly) before naming clips and bins. The same conventions that apply to bin naming apply here. Come up with a method and stick with it. For example, films use Scene/Take, thus a clip named 15/11 is Scene 15, Take 11.

3.16 Target Bin Selector

Warning

If you choose not to name each clip as you digitize, that clip will be named after the bin. So if your bin name is "George Foreman," each clip will be named George Foreman.01, George Foreman.02, George Foreman.03, and so on. This could lead to a lot of confusion later in the project. This would be similar to the confusion at George's house, where all of his sons are named George Foreman.01, George Foreman.02, George Foreman.03, and so on.

Choosing the Target Bin

Any bin that is currently open can be selected as the target bin for captured clips. If you wish to capture to a bin that is not open, simply open it and it will appear in the list of open bins in the Target Bin pop-up menu. Once a bin has been opened or a new bin has been created and opened, you can select it from this menu.

Selecting Media Resolution

Xpress Pro has up to three different media resolutions:

- *1:1 (uncompressed) resolution.* This is available only with the optional Mojo. You can capture 1:1 uncompressed resolution using a number of methods: Composite video, S-Video (Y/C), or Component, with the optional component cable.

  The optional component cable uses the signal paths from S-Video and Composite inputs for the three required separate signals for R–Y, B–Y, and Y components. As a result, you can input a far superior picture through Mojo and gain uncompressed resolution.
  So which method of capture should you use? Start with Component. If the deck doesn't offer Component output (or if you don't own the optional component cable), try S-Video (Y/C). If the deck doesn't have that kind of output, you're stuck with Composite.

- *DV-25 (4:1:1) or DV-25 4:2:0 (PAL Only).* This compression uses standard DV codecs. DV video is compressed 5:1 in its native form. No additional compression is added when coming from a DV-25 source directly through FireWire. You can also use DV-25 as a compression scheme on any input source, including sources that originate as analog signals coming in through Mojo or a transcoder.

- *15:1s Compression.* Although the ratio for this compression sounds bad, it isn't. 15:1s compression is a great offline resolution and usually is clear enough to detect fine focus. Thus it can be used for any offline cutting. It is especially great because it uses far less drive space than DV-25 or 1:1. For those used to higher end Avids, 15:1s gives almost twice the space as 20:1.

15:1s shines when it comes to cutting documentaries, especially DV-based documentaries where the shooting ratios can be extremely high. Although one might figure that the compression ratio runs at about one-third the storage of DV-25, 15:1s doesn't use the same compression scheme. The "s" in 15:1s stands for "single field," meaning that only the first field of the video frame is captured. As a result, the storage is closer to one-eighth that of DV-25. So for a 100GB disk, which can store as much as 9.5 hours of DV-25 footage, one could get as much as 75 hours or more at 15:1s.

Warning

If you are not capturing your footage using timecode, do *not* use offline resolutions! In order for this workflow to be successful, you must be able to redigitize the final sequence with timecode accuracy at a higher resolution. I once did an offline using highly compressed material and then the producer lost the original tapes. We had no choice but to deliver the offline quality program (which was, thankfully, a VHS "master" for a temporary museum installation). So keep track of those masters!

You can choose your Capture resolutions directly in the Capture tool or select them in the Media Creation Dialog Box.

The Media Creation Dialog Box

The Media Creation dialog box allows you to set the video resolution and to select drives for capturing, creating titles, importing, performing audio and video mixdowns, and creating motion effects (see Figure 3.17). Because media files can occasionally be very large, you can also remove your system drive from the list of storage locations so that your media is stored on the proper drives that have more space. The Media Creation Settings also insure that all of your media for a project is created at the same resolution.

To use the Media Creation dialog box, double-click Media Creation in the Settings scroll list of the Project window. The Media Creation dialog box opens. You can also

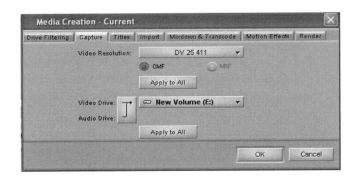

3.17 Media Creation Dialog Box

access the Media Creation dialog box through the menus by selecting Tools>Media Creation or by pressing Ctrl+5/Cmd+5.

OMF/MXF Selection

Just below the Resolution pop-up menu is a format selection for your media files. The two choices, which are selectable radio buttons, are OMF and MXF. MXF (Material Exchange Format) is the future for exchanging media between file servers, data streamers, and digital archives. OMF (Open Media Framework) is the file format used currently on Avid systems to store media. Eventually OMF will fade away and MXF will become the industry standard. MXF is a new format which allows you to exchange media information between Avid, Pro Tools and other Digidesign products, as well as any other systems which accept MXF import and export files.

Selecting Target Drives

The Capture tool will display the available drives on your system that can be used for storing media. To switch between available drives, click on the drive name in the Bin section of the Capture tool. A list of available drives appears. Note that one of the drive names is in bold type. This is the drive with the most storage space available.

3.18 Target Drive Selector

To the right of the Drive Selection tool is a time register. The time register will give you an estimate of how much time is left for digitizing at the chosen resolution using the chosen tracks on a specific drive. Note that the estimate is always slightly conservative.

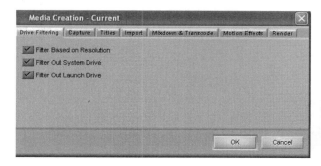

3.19 Drive Filtering Select on Media Creation Box *(left)*

3.20 Separate Drive Selector *(below)*

It's important to remember as you capture materials there will always be a need for space on the drives for your Media Database information. Media Database information is contained in two files in each OMF folder that catalog all of the media in the folder. Be sure not to overfill your drives because the media databases will continually need to rebuild as you edit. You can read more about this in Chapter 4, "Media Management" on page 101.

Which drive(s) should you select for capturing media? If you have a set of striped drives, you can choose it. If you have a spare drive for media, choose that one. It's not a particularly good idea to choose your system drive, but if you're on a laptop and it's all you have, go for it. Drive selection is located about two-thirds of the way down the Capture tool. To select a drive, click on the drive name icon. The list of available drives should appear.

If the selection is grayed out, there's a Drive Filtering Setting that needs to be changed (see Figure 3.19). Here's how to do it: Go to your Settings and select Media Creation, or optionally, select Ctrl+5/Cmd+5. The Media Creation box appears. Deselect Drive Filtering Based Upon Resolution. This will allow all available drives (except the operating system and launch drive) to be selected. If you want your system drive to be available, deselect these as well. When you return to the Capture tool and click on the drive selection button, the drives names will appear in black.

Digitizing Tracks to Separate Drives

On the left side of the Drive Selection register is a single drive icon (see Figure 3.20). Click on it and two drive icons appear. Cool, huh? The two icons represent the ability to place video and audio on separate drives. There are number of reasons to do this, for example, if the video files need to go out for special effects processing, or if the audio files are needed for mixing or creating a premix of your sequence. If you have two drives and one is running at a slower RPM or cannot cache data as quickly as the other, digitize the audio files to the slower drive and video to the faster one. Audio files are smaller and can be processed using lower drive speeds, but video, particularly at lossless resolutions, is more demanding for speed and data rates. Splitting audio and video can also help throughput and prevent audio underruns.

Warning   Be careful that you split audio and video onto two actually, physically different drives, and not just to separate partitions of the same drive.

The Drive Time-Remaining Display

To the right of the Drive Selection tool is a Time-Remaining display (see Figure 3.21). This tool will show the time remaining for each clip as you digitize. Alt-clicking/Option-clicking on the Single/Dual Drive Icon described previously will allow you to see the total time left for a chosen drive at the selected resolution.

3.21 Time Remaining Display *(left)*

3.22 DV Capture Offset *(below)*

DV Capture Offset

Although FireWire is a fairly reliable protocol for capturing, you might encounter some unexpected turbulence. For example, when processing pictures with any type of device through FireWire protocol, there is a chance that audio may precede video. This usually occurs when using a transcoder while capturing from a non-DV source through FireWire. As a result, picture and sound are captured out of sync (see Figure 3.22).

Note   Adjusting DV Capture Offsets deals solely with the issues of audio, video, and timecode being captured at the same time. If you experience a delay between your client monitor and the desktop playback, adjust the Play Delay settings.

Another possibility is that timecode information may arrive earlier than picture and sound. When using RS-422 for deck control and digitizing picture and sound through DV, there will possibly be a mismatch of the timecode versus picture information. The problem is that the two signals are not transmitting at the same time.

How can you detect these latencies? For video, it's fairly simple. If it looks out of sync and you're processing picture through a transcoder, try adjusting the audio using Audio

Delay. You can adjust this setting from 0 to 5 frames. If the latency is more than five frames, you have a bigger issue than a simple processing delay. Check your original to see that picture and sound are in sync. Another way of doing this is to digitize a sync pop.

You can create a sync pop using Xpress Pro. Create a sequence with nothing but a single white frame, which you can create in the Title tool. This white flash needs to be big so that you can see it. Insert a single frame of tone at the same point, and do a digital cut. What's a digital cut? Well, you'll have to read Chapter 3 "Output" on page 379 for that information. But if you need to check for latency right away, find a piece of video that has SMPTE leader or a sync pop on it and digitize it. If, when you play it back, the audio and video don't pop at the same time, you have a latency issue. If you're not using a transcoder, there's no reason to worry about this.

Timecode latency is very simple to inspect. Find a videotape with a timecode burn-in that matches the timecode on the tape or record from a tape with timecode, turn on the feature of the deck that displays timecode (on many Sony decks this switch is called "Character") and use the video output of the deck that includes the timecode characters. Digitize it. Look at the tracking menu and see if the V1 timecode matches the timecode displayed in the burn-in. If it doesn't, the timecode needs to be delayed using the DV Capture Offset window. If you're not digitizing picture through FireWire and using an RS-422 controller, you shouldn't have this problem.

3.23 Checking TC Latency Numbers

Warning

There are some cases where burn-in windows themselves are victims of capture delay. Before digitizing a timecode burn-in, make sure that the timecode on the tape and the burn-in windows match. Otherwise, you'll have a delay of a delay of your timecode and the problem will not be resolved immediately.

DECK AND TAPE CONTROLS

Continuing our tour southward on the Capture tool, let's take a look at the deck controls and configurations. We'll also look at the Tape Naming button and discuss some methods used to name your source tapes.

Selecting a Deck or Camera for Capture

There are two standards of control for decks and cameras. The first is IEEE 1394, more popularly known as FireWire. The second is known as RS-422. The manner in which the deck is controlled by the system depends largely upon the format of deck or camera that is used.

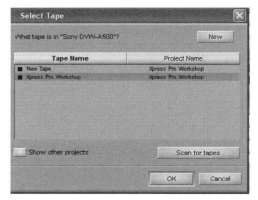

3.24 Deck Controls

If your deck has neither an RS-422 serial interface nor a 1394 FireWire control, you will have to control the deck manually during capture. Manual control of a deck works fine with Xpress Pro, but keep in mind that no timecode information from the tape will be stored. As a result, you will not accurately be able to redigitize the media should you either accidentally erase it or need to "uprez" it.

Identifying the Source Tape

When you begin to capture material, it is of extreme importance that you correctly identify the source tape name. Should you fail to do this accurately, you could find yourself in a number of quandaries, not the least of which is "Where is that shot?" If you are offlining material that is to be finished on another Avid or online system, tape identification could mean the difference between a smooth online session and a disaster.

While it is possible to name tapes with phrases such as "interview with Joe," it is much better to use alphanumeric names. This is kind of a holdover from the days of linear online edits, when the edit controllers could only use 6–8 alphanumerics as tape names, but it is also easier to sort and make sure that tape names are unique. Also, I see a lot of Avid Projects where all the tapes are named "Tape 01," "Tape 02," etc. Using the word "Tape" is redundant and unnecessary. Oftentimes, editors will create specific alternate numbering schemes for the offline to insure unique tape names. This is especially true in documentaries when you may get numerous tapes from different sources or crews, all with a different naming or numbering scheme.

If the deck is controlled by Xpress Pro and it is put in remote mode, every time that you insert a new tape, the Select Tape dialog box will appear. If you are controlling the deck manually, you can still change tape names by selecting the Tape Name button at the bottom of the Capture tool.

In the Select Tape Dialog box you will find the names of all of the tapes associated with the current project. If the project is new, the tape list will be empty. If your tape name isn't in the list, click on the New button, or press Ctrl+N/Cmd+N. A new tape entry appears at the bottom of the list. Type in the name of the new tape and press Return. The tape name appears in the list and can now be selected.

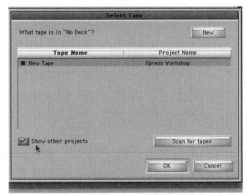

3.25 Deck Controls with Show Other Projects checked

Warning

If tapes were created in another project, for example, if they were logged on another system, then you will need to use the "Show Other Projects" option. This will let you see the tape names that were assigned in the other projects.

3.26 Deck Configuration
Settings Menu

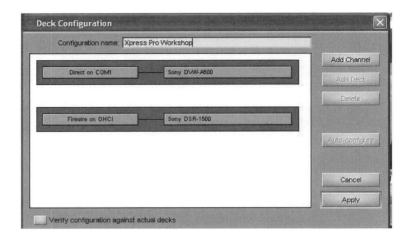

Tape Naming Quagmire: When entering new names for tapes, be careful! If, for example, you create a new tape name "001" and there already is a "001" in the existing name list, Avid systems will still add the new name to the list and "see" the tapes as two different entities. Although the tape names are identical, the system encodes them as being different nonetheless. This can be extremely frustrating when redigitizing, as you will get messages such as "Finished Digitizing 001. Please insert 001."

Configuring Your Deck or Camera

Xpress Pro allows you to establish deck configurations for every camera or deck that you own. The proper configuration of cameras and decks means total control of peripherals through the software interface. Therefore, it is essential that your decks and cameras be correctly identified and adjusted so that you do not have to work in more than one place when digitizing.

There are two different control interfaces that can be used in deck configurations which were discussed earlier, RS-422 (also referred to as Direct) and OHCI (IEEE 1394, or FireWire). With either of these protocols, the communication is two-way, and your Xpress Pro can poll the deck or camera to determine its model and make.

There are some times, however, when the Xpress Pro does not properly identify the deck or camera. Keep in mind that there are now many decks and cameras on the market, and although the protocols are common, the methods of implementation are not. So the best thing to do is to go to your deck configuration settings and do it yourself.

1. First, go to the Project window and click on the Settings tab.

2. Locate the Deck Configuration Settings and double-click (see Figure 3.26).

It may take a moment or two for the deck templates to load. The deck templates contain information about how to control the most commonly used decks. If your deck is not among the templates, you can still use a generic template and configure it for your deck.

3. If this is your first time using Deck Configuration, you will need to click on the Add Channel button. The Channel Options appear. You can choose between Direct (RS-422) and OHCI (IEEE 1394 or FireWire).

On Windows machines, usually an RS-422 to RS-232C adapter, such as Addenda's Rosetta Stone, is used for controlling the deck. The deck is therefore connected to one of the two RS-232C serial ports built into your system. On Windows systems, you must choose between the Com 1 and Com 2 RS-232C ports.

On Mac systems, RS-422 control can be established, but it requires either a third-party card, such as Gee Three's Stealth card, or an adapter from USB to serial, such as those made by Keyspan, and a Mac serial to 9-pin cable. The Stealth card (and many others like it) will allow direct connection between the RS-422 connector on the deck and the card on your Mac. The Keyspan adapter, which is a less expensive option, connects to any USB port and will control the deck directly through your Mac without dealing with any card installation. In Deck Configuration, this is shown as the Direct choice. If you are using a hardware codec or Mojo and want RS-422 control, you should choose either the Com 1/Com 2 selection (Windows) or the Direct selection (Mac).

If your deck has neither RS-422 nor OHCI capability, you'll need to control the deck manually. In cases such as these, there is no need to configure a deck, because the deck cannot be controlled by Xpress Pro (see Figure 3.27).

Once you've added your channel, it's time to add a deck. Click on the Add Deck button and the deck selection window appears. In order to properly select a deck, you must choose the manufacturer first. For example, if your deck is a Sony DSR-11, choose Sony. The list of Sony configured decks will appear (see Figure 3.28). Scroll down the list and select DSR-11.

If your deck is not listed under the manufacturer's name, you might be able to find the template on Avid's website. Avid frequently adds or creates new templates because new decks and cameras come out frequently.

Another option would be to select a Generic deck. A generic deck follows standard protocols for controls of OHCI and RS-422 controllers. It is not particularly sensitive to the full capabilities of a specific deck, but it can fulfill the needs of just about any deck.

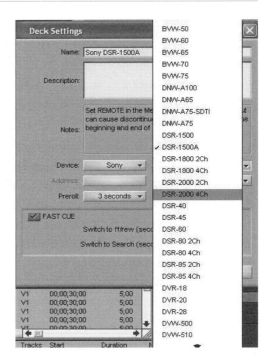

3.27 No Controlled Deck Selector *(above)*

3.28 Add Deck Selection Menu *(right)*

Deleting Deck Configurations

If you need to delete a previous deck configuration, do the following:

1. Go to your Project window and click on the Settings tab.

2. Select Deck Configurations.

3. Click on the deck and Shift-click on the channel. Or, you can lasso them both in the Deck Configuration tool.

4. Press Delete.

   The deck configuration disappears.

Selecting Decks through the Capture Tool

Another method of selecting a deck is to Auto-configure it through the Capture tool. At the bottom of the tool underneath the deck shuttle is a window that identifies the type of deck that the system believes is being used. If this is not the correct deck, click on it. A pulldown menu appears.

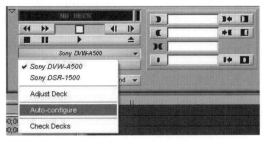

3.29 Capture Settings

From the pulldown menu, select Auto-configure. The system polls the deck to determine which template best fits it. In many cases, the Auto-configure might not present the best selection. This is because some DV devices do not respond to the Auto-configure command. In other words, some decks and cameras, when polled by the system, will not reveal their make and model. If you know that a template for your deck exists but Auto-configure did not select it, configure it manually as previously described.

Using Timecode

The Xpress Pro capture system works like any other good nonlinear editor. With specific information, it functions flawlessly. Without that information, however, your capture session can be tedious and laden with issues.

Timecode is a tool that is used for numbering video frames. It is nothing more, and nothing less. Without timecode, reference to any specific frames is lost. Most modern DV devices use timecode, including those that are generally classified as consumer or prosumer decks and cameras. For DV cameras and decks, the timecode usually begins at one hour (1:00:00:00) and cannot be changed to a specific hour. This is unfortunate, in the sense that it would be good to have the hour of timecode match the number of the tape (for example, Tape 1 timecode begins at 1:00:00:00, tape 2 timecode begins at 2:00:00: 00, and so forth) Nonetheless, *any* timecode is better than none, because it refers to a specific frame on the specific tape.

Warning Editors who are new to nonlinear systems frequently make the error of forgetting to change the tape number when capturing. It is much easier to change names when capturing than trying to discern which pictures came from which tape later on! Try to maintain an accurate database as you capture your materials. This is especially important if using source materials from mini–DV cameras with 1:00:00:00 timecode. Otherwise, you could have two very different clips with the same timecode and the same tape name in the same bin. This will undoubtedly cause problems with media management.

Although the Xpress Pro system is very reliable, there is nothing better than a feeling of security. If for some reason you lose media, you still have accurate timecode and tape names. Most of the time spent during capture is getting the numbers. So long as your bins still exist, recapturing takes little time and is very simple to do.

If your source is from a non-timecode device (such as VHS), it is advisable to bump up the material to a timecoded tape format. Doing this before capturing allows the flexibility of both using a controllable deck and timecode that can be entered into the system in case of data loss.

The Marks Registers

To the right of the Deck Control tools are the marks registers. These allow you to mark IN and OUT, enter timecode numbers directly, jump to specific points, and store a timecode number temporarily in a register.

Mark In

This button allows you to mark the beginning of the clip that you want to capture. With the tape rolling, click on it, and the timecode that occurred when you clicked on the button will appear in the register to the right. You can also use this register for direct timecode entry. To do this, click in the white space. If there is a number present already, be sure to drag across the number and press Delete to get rid of it. Alternatively, you can click on the button to the far right, which is the Clear Mark In button. Once this has been done, begin typing the timecode number and press return. Also note that to the right of this register is a Mark In icon with an arrow. This button allows you to cue the tape to that specific point, or "go to" the mark in. Each register, with the exception of the duration register, has this capability.

Mark Out

This button, directly below the Mark In button, denotes the last frame of capture. To use the button, you can use the same procedures mentioned above in the Mark In description.

 A little-known secret is that you can drag and drop a clip into the Mark In or Mark Out registers and the Mark In and Mark out for the clip will be automatically entered into the Marks registers. This can be convenient on multi-cam clips, where multiple clips from different iso decks share the same, or similar timecodes. You can also use this if you discover that your clip is corrupt or the deck didn't play back the clip correctly during capture. Just drag the bad clip into the Capture tool and recapture it without reentering the timecode info.

Go To Buttons

On both Mark In and Mark Out sections, there is a button just after the register with an arrow, pointing to a Mark In or Mark Out. When you click on this button, it will go to the timecode on the tape that is entered into the register on the left.

Duration

The Duration button has both a Mark In and Mark Out icon together. Actually, it isn't a button at all. This is Xpress Pro's calculation of the duration of your clip based upon the Mark In and Mark Out. If you adjust either the Mark In or Mark Out, the number in this register will change. You can also do direct entry of timecode in the duration register. For example, if you have a Mark In and you want the clip to be twenty seconds long, type in "20:00." The Mark Out will be calculated based upon your duration. You can also do this inversely to back-time a clip with the Mark Out already entered. In this case, enter the same number in the duration register and the Mark In will be calculated based upon the Mark Out minus the duration.

The last entry on the Marks register is a temporary storage place for a timecode number to be used later. You can mark this timecode using the adjacent Locator icon to the left of the register, or manually enter the timecode by clicking in the register and typing in the number.

METHODS OF CAPTURE

Capturing Using Non-Timecode Source Materials

Of course there are times when you are in a hurry to capture a few small items manually.

1. To do this, deactivate the Deck tool on your Capture window. The deck controls disappear and the deck icon has a red circle with a diagonal line through it, as shown in the right side of the graphic.

2. Cue up your deck using the controls on the deck locally to the material to be digitized. Be sure to allow plenty of extra seconds of media both before and after the needed material, as you may need to use some of the extra head and tails for transitions such as dissolves.

3. Press Play on your deck. Wait until the deck gets up to play speed and the picture stabilizes.

4. Click on the red Record icon on your Capture tool. The material is digitizing, indicated by the flashing red light above the Capture button.

5. To stop recording, press the Capture button again. The flashing red light above it will stop flashing and a new clip will appear in the bin.

Xpress Pro will assign a time-of-day timecode to the clip, based on the time of day you digitized it. If you want, this timecode can be modified. We have done offlines with Xpress Pro using VHS timecode window dubs. After they have been captured, you can use the Modify command in the Clip menu to make the burn-in numbers match the actual timecode of the clip itself. If you do not modify the clip, your offline edit timecodes will be meaningless.

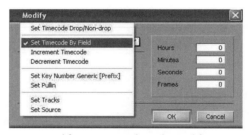

3.30 Modifying Timecode with Modify Command

Capturing Using Timecode Source Materials

When using timecoded source tapes, capturing can become much more automated and simple. There are three ways to capture from timecoded source:

1. Capturing using previously logged bins;

2. Capturing using mark in and mark out points; and

3. Capturing on the fly.

Batch Capturing Using Previously Logged Bins

If you already have logged bins and simply need to capture the media, all that you have to do is set the resolutions, assign the correct drives and tell Xpress Pro what to capture. The system goes into an automatic capturing mode that can be monitored, or in the case of offline editing, simply set and left to do its own work.

Before we begin this automated process, let's take a look at some of the Batch Capture Settings. To access these, click on the Settings tab in your Projects window and select Capture, then select the Batch tab.

You can optimize the Batch Capture process for speed and for disk space. The first two selections in the Batch settings allow you to do this. If you choose to optimize for speed, the system will determine the fastest way to digitize your footage and proceed accordingly. For example, if two clips are relatively close to each other on the tape, the system can choose to continue digitizing between the clips without stopping. Doing

3.31 Batch Capture Settings

this does waste disk space, but it also allows you to finish digitizing quicker. If you prefer to save disk space and are not in a particularly big hurry, you can choose to optimize for disk space. Even if two clips are close to each other, the system digitizes only what is needed.

The next setting is Switch to emptiest drive if current drive is full. When selected, this option allows the system to switch between drives rather than stop and inform you that the current drive has run out of space. This setting is a great way to prevent unexpected stops in your batch-digitizing session. Should you choose to do it, be sure to switch to the Media Creation Settings tab and choose the amount of drive space that is to be left before the system switches. Xpress Pro will not switch drives in the middle of digitizing a clip. It is "smart" enough to recognize whether or not a clip will be able to be digitized on a drive before digitizing it, so long as this option is selected. You can choose between 1 and 10 minutes of drive space left when the switch occurs. If you're using the optional Mojo and digitizing uncompressed footage, 1 minute of drive space is plenty. For offline or DV resolutions, consider switching at 5 or 10 minutes to ensure plenty of room on the drives for the Media Database.

The next two Batch Settings are intended for convenience. Rewinding the tape after digitizing is useful. It returns the tape to the front in case you need to view it again and prevents you from having to do it later. Ejecting the tape is good to prevent wearing out both the tape and the heads on your deck. Although modern decks are smart enough to pull the tape off of the heads after a specific amount of time, the drum continues to spin and wastes drum hours. Ejecting the tape prevents this from happening.

The final four Batch Settings allow you to either use the compression settings as logged in the bin or change them to your current settings for media creation.

Let's take an example of why you might want to adjust these settings. A director comes to you with what appears to be a very simple documentary and only 10 tapes. You log the 10 tapes and intend to digitize at DV resolution. No worries, you have plenty of space on the drives. Then the other shoe drops. The director comes in with 40 more tapes, explaining, "Here's the bulk of what we'll use." Has it happened to you? It has to me. This usually occurs when either the director is less organized and "forgets" or when he or she wants to keep information at a minimum. As a result, you will have logged all of your footage as DV compression, when in fact, you're going to need to do it at 15:1s in order to fit it on your drives (your actual mileage will vary, but let's just say this is the case of this particular scenario).

What to do? What to do?

Go to your Batch Settings and deselect the Use Video Compression Logged for Each Clip. Set your Capture tool for 15:1s and voilà! Problem solved. You can also use these settings to adjust for audio sample rate, for sample size, and for the tracks selected.

Capturing Tracks Logged is extremely useful. Oftentimes the logger has no clue of what should be captured and will log all of the tracks available for the clip. As you begin to familiarize yourself with the footage for the project, you may notice that some tapes have no sound and capturing sound will waste space. By deselecting this option and picking tracks in the Capture tool, you can save a lot of disk space.

To batch-capture using logged bins:

1. Choose your Batch Capture Settings as described previously.

2. Open the bin with the logged clips.

3. Select the clips to be batch-captured. Make sure that you have selected the correct drive(s), video resolution, and audio sources.

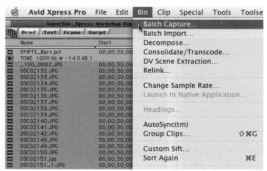

3.32 Setting Up for Batch Capture

Fun With Timecode!

There are two types of video timecode used with NTSC video: drop frame and nondrop frame. These two "frame code modes" determine how frames are counted. They do nothing more, but nothing less. Because NTSC video runs at 29.97 fps (frames per second), not 30 fps, the method of actually counting 30 frames to a second isn't quite accurate. What difference does it make? If you're not a broadcaster or overly anal retentive, not much. But if you need exact timing or are in a situation where any sort of automated equipment is used, you're going to need to use drop frame timecode. Drop frame timecode "skips" two frames every minute, except for every tenth minute, in order to keep the frame count correct with real time. Don't let this worry you though, if you aren't familiar with drop frame timecode, it doesn't actually "drop" any frames; it just renames them. This is kind of along the same thought process as high-rise buildings that never have a 13th floor. It's not that there's a giant space in the building. It's just that no one wants to live on the 13th floor, so they skip that name.

Nondrop frame timecode uses a count of 30 fps even though the video is still moving along at 29.97. While inaccurate in its timing, the advantage of nondrop frame is that the frame count remains sequential and there are no numbers "dropped" from the count. The difference in an hour-long show between drop frame and nondrop is about 3 seconds, with a "one hour" non-drop tape being a little more than 3 seconds longer than an actual hour.

So how do you tell the difference between drop frame and nondrop frame timecode? When playing back the tape, a 1 hour timecode will either appear as 1:00:00:00 or 1;00;00;00. If the timecode window displays numbers with a semicolon, it is drop frame. If the numbers are displayed with a colon, it is nondrop frame. The simple way to remember this is that a semicolon has a little part of it that "drops" down (indicating drop frame) while a colon does not.

It is important when logging to read the source timecode on the tape before starting. Indicating nondrop frame code on a drop frame tape will cause capturing errors. Better to correct this when you begin the log than having to do it after the logs are completed!

4. Ready for some automated fun? Under the Bin menu, select Batch Capture.

5. The system instructs you to load a tape and begins to capture material automatically. From there, follow the system prompts. When complete, it will tell you "Batch Capture Complete."

If you want to make sure that you have enough space on the drives to capture all of your logged shots, you can select them all in the bin (Ctrl+A/Cmd+A) and then hit Ctrl+I/Cmd+I ("I" stands for "info"). This will open up the Console and display the total length of shots that were selected. Make sure that no Titles or Sequences were selected, or it will add in those lengths for the totals.

Capturing Using Mark In and Mark Out Points

Capturing using marked points offers the convenience of doing two things at once: log and capture. While this once was prohibitive on more expensive NLEs (due to the cost per hour of renting or maintaining the system), it's pretty common on less expensive systems like Xpress Pro.

To capture using Mark In and Mark Out:

1. Find the first frame of the footage to be digitized and select the Mark In button on the Capture tool.

2. Find the last frame of the footage to be digitized and select the Mark Out button on the Capture tool.

3. Press the Capture button.

The system prerolls the tape to a specified point a few seconds before the IN point, then rolls it forward and begins capturing. Once the capture is completed, the system sends a message that the media has been digitized.

You can also digitize footage with no set OUT point. Simply Mark In and press record. When you're finished with the clip, press the Capture button a second time to stop capturing. Similarly, you can set an OUT point for your capture (for example, before a timecode break or the tape end) and not mark an IN point, just using the Capture button to capture on the fly wherever the tape is cued.

Another similar method is to Capture from a handwritten log, using specific times from that log. When I do this, I try to find a "barker," someone who works nearby in a particularly boring job that needs some time away. This person can call out the

Capture Keyboard Shortcuts

The Capture tool has plenty of buttons, but if you prefer to use the keyboard, the following shortcuts can be used:

Tab—Jumps from one time code entry to the next.

I—Marks In

O— Marks Out

Spacebar —Plays the Source Tape

F4—Begins Capture

J and L—Moves the source forward (L) or backward (J) in speed increments, with each press increasing the speed of shuttle.

numbers while you type them in. To enter the times, just type the number for the IN point next to the Mark In button and tab to the Mark Out entry and type that number in, then you can either log it by clicking on the Log/Digitize button at the top of the Capture tool or immediately digitize it and talk to your new friend, the barker. A note about barking and barkers: old-time editors like me prefer the number read in two digit cadences. Why? For some reason, a cadence helps you remember the numbers easier (it's a short number, after all) and it also appeals to an editor's sense of rhythm. Why two digits only? I haven't the foggiest recollection. So, for timecode 1:03:04:08, it would be read "01...03...04...08." Now that you've learned the black art of barking, you have something to fall back on.

On the Fly Capture

Capturing from timecode sources doesn't require typing or marking IN and OUT points. You can also capture on the fly, as the tape rolls forward. To do this:

1. Play the tape and find the footage that needs to be captured.

2. Roll it back so that you have plenty of preroll or footage adjacent to the beginning of the needed footage.

3. Play the tape forward, giving the deck plenty of time to get to speed.

4. Press the red Record button. You're capturing.

5. Press the red Record button again to end capture.

Typing Clip Names and Comments During Capture

As you are capturing the source material to your drives you may have noticed that the Clip Name space has an active cursor. During capture, you can type in a name for your clip. This speeds up the capturing process by not having to go back later to do data entry. There is also an entry for a clip description. To switch between the two, press Tab and begin typing.

DV Scene Extraction

Perhaps the best thing about nonlinear editing is its random access abilities. However, the randomness of access becomes glaringly apparent when you have long clips containing various subject matter. In fact, if the project is not carefully constructed, you could find yourself shuttling through long clips much as you would though linear videotape. To solve this issue, there is DV Scene Extraction.

The concept behind DV Scene Extraction is simple: divide and conquer. In a world where too much information is the order of the day, DV Scene Extraction allows you to choose smaller sections of a clip and create subsections (or subclips) then categorize them more specifically.

Let's say, for example, you shot footage at your local zoo. On a single recorded clip, you captured the penguins, an aviary, some alligators, a lion, and two tigers. If you wanted to go straight to the alligators, how would you do it? Wouldn't it be simpler to create a subclip for each?

When DV footage is shot, time of day (TOD) information is also recorded. DV Scene Extraction allows you to capture from the entire tape, but will create subclips and/or locators from each individual shot in a clip. This is distinguished through TOD information. Whenever the TOD changes between shots, DV Scene Extraction recognizes it and creates either a locator on the master clip or it can create a subclip of each shot, depending on how you've set it up.

Setting Up DV Scene Extraction Before Capturing

To set up DV Scene Extraction before digitizing footage:

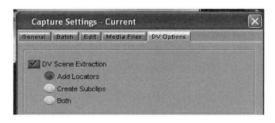

1. Go to the Project window and select Settings.

2. Choose Capture Settings.

3. Click on the DV tab.

4. Select Create Subclips, Add Locators, or Both.

The system will automatically extract each scene digitized as a subclip. Add a locator to the beginning of each scene, or both as selected.

Setting Up DV Scene Extraction after Capturing

To set up DV Scene Extraction after digitizing footage:

1. Click on the source clip or clips.

2. Select Bin>DV Scene Extraction.

3. Choose Create Subclips, Add Locators, or Both.

4. Choose a source bin for your subclips.

The system extracts individual scenes from the master clips, based on TOD information.

Capturing Directly to the Timeline

In some cases, your project may require that you capture footage straight into the Timeline. Xpress Pro can do this, even allowing you to patch tracks when necessary.

There are several reasons for you to want to do this. If your sequence is only a few shots long and relatively simple in nature, capturing to the Timeline directly prevents the need to load footage, mark it, and edit it across to a sequence.

Capturing directly to the Timeline also saves you time. No need to re-mark IN and OUT points. Just do it while capturing. If you're pretty confident of what you want, and it doesn't require a lot of tape changes, this is a fast way to get the job done. This capability was added from Avid's Newscutter where the need to get material into a sequence quickly is very important.

To capture directly to the Timeline:

1. Go to the Project window and select Settings.

2. Open your Capture Settings.

3. Select the Edit tab.

4. Select the Enable Edit to Timeline button.

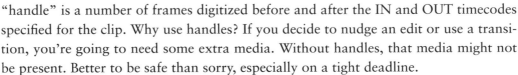

5. Choose the number of frames that you want captured as a handle to each clip. A "handle" is a number of frames digitized before and after the IN and OUT timecodes specified for the clip. Why use handles? If you decide to nudge an edit or use a transition, you're going to need some extra media. Without handles, that media might not be present. Better to be safe than sorry, especially on a tight deadline.

6. Select OK.

Before you begin digitizing, create a new sequence where the footage will be captured if you don't have one open already.

Patching Directly When Capturing to the Timeline

You can patch your tracks before you capture to the Timeline. There could be several reasons to do this. If, for example, you need ambient sound on audio track 2, but the best ambient sound exists on track 1 of your source, you can patch the track before capture.

To patch tracks before capturing to the timeline:

1. Click the track selector for the source track in the Capture tool.

2. Click and hold on the track selected. A pop-up menu of destination tracks appears.

3. Choose the destination track in the sequence for this source track (see Figure 3.33).

3.33 Choosing Timeline Destination Tracks in the Capture Tool

4. Once you begin capturing footage, the track is patched directly to its proper destination in the sequence.

Capturing across Timecode Breaks

One of the Capture Settings that is very useful is Capture across timecode breaks (see Figure 3.34). Created originally during the development of Avid MultiCam, Capture across timecode breaks is used for capturing entire tapes that have frequent start/stops, where the camera stops rolling and the timecode is not continuous. When selected, Capture across timecode breaks will enable the system to stop when the timecode stops, create a clip, then roll forward to find the next piece of timecode and sync. When the next piece is found, the system rolls forward to a point where sync is stable, then prerolls and begins recording again. There are only three caveats when using this option:

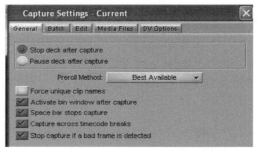

3.34 Capture across TC Breaks Setting

1. You must have plenty of preroll on your shots. If not, the system may go past the desired IN point and begin capturing later than anticipated. When shooting, it is a good idea to count to ten after the tape is recording and before beginning your shot. Without enough preroll, you will have to capture manually.

2. There must be very little space between start/stops. The system understands that there is no sync between shots and will roll forward. But if you have shots with, say, five minutes of blank tape in between, the system might not be able to find the next sync piece.

3. The system will capture everything that is timecoded with sync and on the tape. If you have need for disk space and there are plenty of outtakes on the tape, this might not be your best option.

LOGGING

Logging with the Capture Tool

The capture tool can also be used as a logging station. To the right of the Capture button is a small disk icon with the letters "DIG" on it (standing for Digitize). Click on this icon and it changes to a Pencil icon with the word "Log" on it. You have now successfully switched to Logging mode.

In Logging mode, you can still shuttle the machine and enter timecode just as you would during Capture. The difference is that the actual Capture function is disabled. When you log, the timecode and clip information go into a bin, but the media itself will not be captured on your hard drives.

There are plenty of reasons to use the Logging mode. If you are awaiting more drive space, if a client is doing the logging but is not familiar enough with setting up the tapes, if the tapes are not present but a list of numbers has been made—all of these are good reasons to log.

Logging the Correct Frame Code Mode

It is important when logging to know whether your source tape was recorded in drop frame or nondrop frame timecode. Otherwise the log will not match the tape. If this occurs, the system will prompt you that the timecode on the clips and the timecode on the tape are in different frame code modes; therefore, there is a problem. This is easily avoidable if you know the frame code mode of the tape when entering timecode information.

Importing Logs

If the logs were created elsewhere and they are in an Avid-readable format, they can be imported into a bin. To do this:

1. Create or open a bin for the logged clips.
2. Under File, select Import. The Import menu appears.
3. Select Shot Log under the type of import.
4. Navigate to your log and select it.
5. The log is imported.

Importing ALE Logs

Avid Log Exchange is an intermediary program that allows you to read from the most common log creation tools to an Avid-readable log, which can then be imported into a bin. The ALE program comes with the other installers (such as EDL Manager) on your Xpress Pro CD.

Avid Log Exchange will convert the following log types:

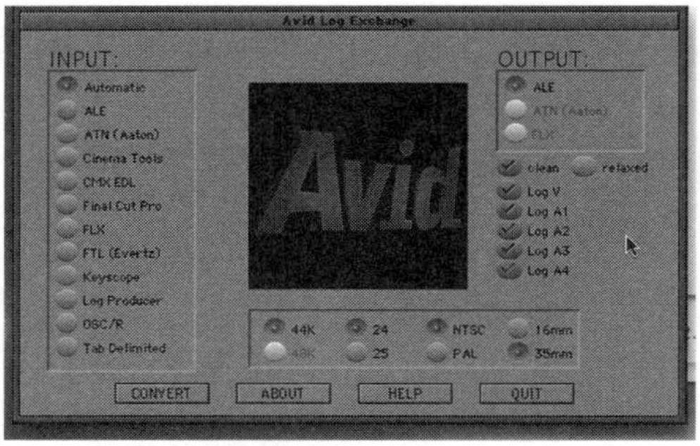

3.35 The ALEui Interface

- Avid Log Exchange
- ATN (Aaton)
- Apple Cinema Tools
- CMX EDL
- Final Cut Pro
- FLX (Flex files, from telecine)
- Keyscope
- Log Producer
- OSC/R
- Tab-delimited databases such as those from Filemaker Pro and Excel databases.

ALE will output ALE, ATN (Aaton), or FLX (flex) files.

You can drop an alias of ALE on your desktop and automate input. ALE will read your log files and convert them to Avid Log Exchange files.

USING THE CAPTURE TOOL

For many editors, the process of capturing is overlooked, because while we edit almost every day, capturing is a prelude to that process. As a result, proficiency on the Capture tool will be gained through time and experience. Oftentimes editors have little to do with capturing materials, leaving it to an assistant. But the knowledge of the tool can improve your ability to improve workflow and efficiency. Time in the postproduction process can be gained. If you can use Capture efficiently, you will have more time to edit. Isn't that the whole idea of modern day nonlinear tools? Try out some of the options and see which best fits your workflow.

Now that you've learned how to capture, we'll begin our edit.

Chapter 4

Media Management

One of Avid's strong points has always been media management. The way it manages files under the hood *and* the way it allows *you* to manage your media and locate clips are both part of this reputation.

This chapter will deal with two of the most important aspects of media management. One is how to access the footage you need quickly and efficiently during the editing process. The other is how to manage your media at the completion of a project to allow for the best use of disk space and to prepare you to deal with revisions and other aspects of the "after life" of your projects.

One of the major advantages of nonlinear editing is having nonlinear access to footage as you edit. Shuttling through your footage is not an efficient way to locate clips as you try to build your sequence.

Having immediate access to shots starts in the digitizing or logging process. Xpress Pro helps to automate this process as much as possible, but the lion's share of the work belongs to the editor or assistant editor. On large projects, or on projects that are shared by multiple editors working with the same footage, a plan must be developed to organize the footage and to create a labeling scheme that allows the right shot to be found at the right moment. Organizing and labeling is done in the project window and in the bins themselves.

Sparking Creativity

Although shuttling through footage in linear fashion is not an efficient use of your Xpress Pro, it sometimes serves an important creative purpose. A film editor once related the happy discoveries he used to make as he wound and rewound through reels of film. He used to edit using two KEMs. As he edited on one, he'd run footage on the other, with the monitor just inside his field of vision. Watching his footage, even peripherally, often sparked ideas and interesting juxtapositions of shots.

You can achieve a sense of this with an Avid by creating a sequence of all your footage in a single sequence, occasionally popping it into your source monitor and shuttling through it. This can help refresh your creative spirit by exposing you to shots that you might not consider because you are focused on finding a specific shot. Fighter pilots call this "target lock." When you know what you want, you sometimes forget to be aware of other possibilities. For fighter pilots this means they forget about other potential threats or hazards with their attention focused on one specific target. For an editor, sometimes being focused on a single solution for an editing dilemma may mean you're not open to the other creative possibilities.

Before discussing project management of media, we need to address the macro management of all the projects at a facility, even if the "facility" is just you and a single Xpress Pro.

I once consulted for a broadcast TV station that was having problems managing the media on their Avid systems, which were all linked by media stored on a LAN. This was before the days of Unity, when storage was still quite costly. They complained that they were regularly running out of storage space and couldn't figure out how to save the important "evergreen" media and delete what they no longer needed. I was horrified when I saw that—after months of having their systems—there were only two projects: "promos" and "shows." Inside of these two projects were all of the promos and all of the shows they had ever done. Each promo and show had its own bin, but there was no "project management."

Projects are an important organizational structure in the Avid universe. Without the distinction of having each project managed separately, there are several problems that arise. One is that project assignments are critical in creating a coherent scheme for deleting media. The other problem is that tape names are—unbeknownst the user—also assigned to specific projects. This is important because when you create a "Tape 1" for Project A, it is seen by the system as wholly different from "Tape 1" from Project B. The Avid software invisibly tags every tape with a project name. If an editor does not understand this important concept, a lot of media management mistakes can happen. You also want to be careful not to accidentally rename a tape you've already entered into the Tape Dialog box. Xpress Pro will only allow unique tape names, but if you call a tape "Tape 001" the first time you enter it and "tape 1" the second time, the system will consider it as two unique tapes.

MANAGING PROJECTS

Managing projects is the first step to getting organized. Sometimes the plan to do this must be fairly fluid as the facility changes and grows. I've worked at a number of facilities and been in charge of my own projects on my own personal systems. Trust me, the best choice is some kind of numerical system. Word descriptions are wonderful at a glance, but there has to be a root system of numbers. At one facility the numerical system was based on job numbers. When it came time for revisions months or years later, these job numbers were the only way to find the original projects. I've also worked on broadcast television shows and the project management in those cases centered on the numerical designation for a specific show. You can develop any method that suits you, but I urge you to have some form of numeric system, either based on the date a project is started or on a job number or invoice number or show number.

Organizing the projects themselves depends on how much of a packrat you are. If you like to keep all of your projects accessible (and I just mean the metadata, not the media), you will eventually have such a huge list of projects in your Select a Project list, that it will be unmanageable. If this method describes you, then you'll need to create a system right from the start that divides your projects into more manageable lists of projects. You can create separate project folders for each client or each month or each season. If you are more selective in what you keep on your computer, you don't need to develop quite as stringent a system as long as you archive projects off to a disk or something and then delete them from the current project list.

To create folders of projects, Xpress Pro has three categories of projects: Private, Shared, and External.

Private Projects can only be viewed and edited by the person who logged on to the computer. Shared Projects can be shared by anyone logged on to the computer. External Projects are shared projects stored outside of the Private or Shared folders of the Xpress Pro application. These projects are not necessarily on external drives. Shared Projects allow communal access to projects, but they do not offer any additional management capability beyond the basic list. Other Avid applications allow for the creation of folders

and subfolders within the Select Projects list. To gain this kind of control over project management in Xpress Pro, you must rely on External Projects.

It is possible to create organizational folders within the Shared Projects folder, but Xpress Pro does not see them, because they are not Project folders. These folders *are* visible with External Projects selected.

In the Select Projects window you can browse to a folder that contains projects. You browse to the folder you want by clicking on the open folder icon in the upper right corner of the window, to the right of the Folder path.

This ability to browse means that your project management can be done at the desktop level and can be revised continuously if necessary.

To try this out, create a folder on your desktop anywhere on one of your internal drives. I would keep it in the vicinity of the default Avid Projects folder. You can name this folder anything you want, but we'll call it "2004 Avid Projects." Inside of that folder, create 12 new folders and name them for the months of the year. Now you can browse to these locations with External Projects and create new projects in these monthly folders.

If you have another organizational scheme you'd prefer, do a quick test to see how it will work and how to navigate around in it. The trick with any of these schemes is that anyone should be able to find the correct version of a project without too much help. If you use a monthly system, there has to be a way for someone to clearly decipher which project would have been opened in a particular month. I call this the "hit by a bus" approach. What if a bus hit you? How would anyone else know where and how to access all of your projects? What is the most intuitive, foolproof approach? For this project-level management, I like a client-based approach. You always know which client is approach-

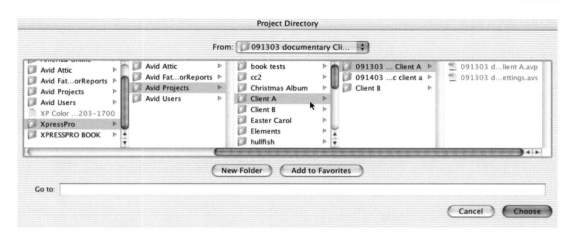

ing you for revisions. Also, it compartmentalizes information better. I have many clients that can't know about other clients' projects. Keeping each client in a separate folder minimizes the chance that they might see their competitor's project in the "Select Project" window.

Another important distinction to make is that renaming or altering Project folders causes havoc for media management in Xpress Pro, but changing and renaming these "project management folders" can be done anytime at the desktop level with no harm to the projects. If you start with project organization based on months and find that you need to move to some other hierarchy of folders, you can create the new system at the desktop level and copy and paste Project Folders from the old folder system into the new system. Something to watch out for is the number of folder levels that you have to plow through to get to the folder you want. Obviously, the fewer levels of folders and subfolders the better.

Warning

Whatever method you choose for project management, "back up early and back up often"— to paraphrase the old Chicago voting adage. The metadata you create while you are editing is a precious resource. I've never met a project that I didn't meet again somewhere down the line. You want to make sure that a hard drive crash or some other disaster doesn't wipe out this data that you struggled so long to create. Keep a copy of each project on-site and keep one off-site. Archive at least your current project off to some medium every single night. Buy one of those little USB thumb drives and put your current project on that at the end of every day and take it home with you. At the end of every week save all of your latest projects to a couple of CDs or DVDs. And don't forget to label everything thoroughly.

BIN MANAGEMENT

Now your projects are neatly organized so you know how to find last week's project should your client call for revisions. But what is more pressing in your mind is how to keep track of all the media for *today's* project.

The first line of defense as you draw up the battle plans for the day's work is to organize the bins themselves. Avid took the concept of Bins from film postproduction. Film bins are essentially metal square containers with lint-free cloth bags from which you can gently cascade your film dailies. You can organize your bins in whatever way best helps you find the things you want.

Some people—especially old linear tape editors—organize by tape or reel number, with every tape having its own bin. Others organize by the type of media, with bins for digitized footage, imported graphics, audio, titles, animation, stock footage, and sequences. Editors working on narrative films based on a script usually organize by scene, since footage from specific scenes rarely mixes with footage from other scenes. Documentary filmmakers often digitize things by subject or concept: interviews on topic A, interviews on topic B, B-roll for topic A, B-roll for topic B, stock footage, narration, temp score, final score, etc.

It is possible to have multiple organizational methods. You could use the tape-based method and the documentary method at the same time. Start out by using just the tape-based approach until most of your footage has been digitized and you have to start cutting. When you are ready to start cutting, you can duplicate your clips and use the duplicate clips to populate your documentary bins. These duplicated clips do not take up any extra space on your hard drive (well, not much) because the media of the clips isn't duplicated, just the metadata that points to the media. Now if you need to find a clip, you have two ways to track it down. If you know where the clip was, you can search based on the tape name, or if you need something in a specific topic area, you can use the "documentary" bins.

You can wait to create each of these organizational bins until after you've created the media that will go into it, or you can create all of the bins at the beginning of the project. Obviously you have to have at least one bin to capture the media in the first place, but Xpress Pro automatically creates at least one bin when you create a new project. I have used both of these methods. On long-form projects, I tend to create the bins at the beginning because the organizational demands for longer form projects are much greater. On short projects, I often just create a "Digitize" bin where I bring in all the media. If I need more bins, I'll move clips from this bin to other bins as needed.

Master Bin

Another organizational method that you can add to this mix is the Master Bin method. If you want a way to sort through all of the clips in all of the bins, the answer lies in the Media Tool. Go to Tools>Media Tool and choose Current Project, All Drives, Master Clips only, then click OK. This will call up the Media Tool filled with every clip from the current project. You can now create a new bin in your project and simply drag all of the clips from Media Tool directly into your new Master Bin. (If you have added footage from other projects in your current project, make sure to include it in your master bin.)

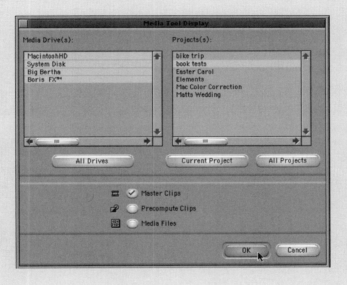

In either case you'll need to create at least two additional bins for sequences. Your Xpress Pro will run better and save faster if you keep your active sequence in a bin by itself. Then create another bin for old versions of your sequences or for partial sequences or for other sequences from the same project. Label these sequence bins well so that anyone will know which is the proper final version of any given sequence. It's often difficult to know which sequence is the final sequence if you go back months later into a project when all of the media has been deleted. Place old, or alternate, versions of sequences in a properly labeled bin and keep your final sequence or sequences in their own bin. Another trick that usually works for me is to wait

until I am about to lay-off a sequence to tape before adding bars, tone, and slates. That way I at least know when a sequence was laid to tape by seeing if it has that formatted media at the head.

Creating Folders to Organize Bins

Sometimes there can be so many bins in a project that it is necessary to organize the bins in some meaningful way. To do this, you can create folders and subfolders within a project to organize the bins.

To create a folder in a bin, you can use the Project window's Fast menu. One of the choices in that menu is New Folder. Choose that and then name the folder something useful. You can even create subfolders and sub-subfolders.

And if you're saying to yourself, "All of this organization may sound cool, but all it really does is make you click through more layers to get to the stuff you want," you'd be wrong, because in the Project's Fast menu, you can choose Flat View and all of the folders disappear, leaving nothing but your bins, even the ones that had been tucked away two or three folders deep.

Bin Navigation

If you are really trying hard to use your keyboard as much as possible, you'll be happy to know that there are a bunch of keyboard strokes for navigating in bins.

Tab moves from left to right through columns of a bin and Shift+Tab moves right to left. Return moves to the next clip down in the bin in the same column and Shift+Return moves to the clip up. The Up arrow moves to the previous clip in the bin, but only if you are in the clip icon column. The Down arrow does the same thing, except it goes to the next clip down.

Moving Media between Bins

Oftentimes, I will digitize or import media into bins that I know are not the final destination for that clip. Moving a clip from one bin to another is as simple as dragging it from one open bin to another. Or, in the case of Xpress Pro, you can even drag a clip from an open project to a closed project by dragging the clip to the bin icon for the bin you want in the Project window.

If you want to move a copy of a clip to another bin (so you have two of them), then Alt-drag/Option-drag the clip into the new bin. You should be aware that there is a slight difference between Alt-dragging/Option-dragging clips and actually making duplicates of a clip and dragging the duplicate to a new bin. When you Alt-drag/Option-drag a clip to a new bin, it makes a clone of that clip that is completely linked to the original clip. So if you modify the copy in any way, the original clip is also modified. If you make a copy of a clip (Ctrl+D/Cmd+D), the copy is given a ".copy" suffix. That ".copy" clip is a separate clip and can be modified without changing the original. This is an important distinction to make in certain instances: the main one being in the logging of multi-cam shows. One of the great ways to log and batch-digitize multi-cam shows is to log and digitize just the linecut or the four- or nine-way split. Then, duplicate the clips from that source and modify it to reflect all the different camera iso tapes. For example, if the line cut tape is called L1 and has a 8:00:00 timecode, then the four- or nine-way split is called S1 and has a 9:00:00 timecode, the first iso camera has a tape name I1 and a 1:00:00 timecode, and so on for each of the iso cameras. Now you can log from the L1 tape, finding the usable takes. Duplicate all of those clips and put them into a bin called "Iso1" then modify the timecode backwards 7 hours for each clip and modify the source name to I1. Duplicate again and put it into a bin marked "Iso2" and modify the timecode by six hours and modify the source to I2, and so on. Now all you have to do is batch-digitize all the isos. This would not be possible if you Alt-dragged/Option-dragged the clips, because modifying the clips in the new bins would also change the clips in the original bins.

OPENING OTHER PROJECTS' BINS

With a new project open, your options may seem limited to New Bin, but a whole world of options actually exists from the File menu pulldown. It is possible to open other projects' bins into your current project. I do this a lot. It allows me to grab elements that I have digitized or imported in other projects or to copy over effects that I have used in previous sequences or even color corrections in my current project.

To open a bin from another project:

1. Your Project window has to be set to the Bin tab (as opposed to the Settings tab).

File	Edit	Bin	Clip	Special
New Bin				⌘N
Open Bin...				⌘O
New Script...				
Close Project				⌘W
Save All				⌘S
Save a Copy as...				
Page Setup...				
Print...				⌘P
Get Info				⌘I
Reveal File				
Export...				
AvidLinks...				▶
Send To...				
Import...				
Refresh Media Directories				
Load Media Database				
Mount All				
Unmount...				

2. Then either choose File>Open Bin or Ctrl+O/Cmd+O.

3. This calls up the Open a Bin dialog box. Navigate to the project you want then the bin you want to open within that project and choose Open and the bin will open up into your current project. When you close the bin, it is saved in your current project in your Other Bins folder.

A very powerful use for this feature is to create a project to be used exclusively as a holding place for common elements. One of the first things I do on any new system I use is to create a project called Elements or Shared Elements. In this project I create bars and tone at each resolution and sample rate.

Sample rates are not mixable in any of the Avid products, so you should have tone or other multiproject audio at each sample rate. The DNA products add the ability to work in multiple sample sizes, so these should also be taken into account if you plan to use them. The two sample sizes are 16 bit and 24 bit; 16 bit is the common video bit depth while 24 bit has greater resolution and is more commonly used for interchange with Pro-Tools sessions.

Although creating bars and tone at each resolution and sample rate isn't really necessary with the Avid DNA products like Xpress Pro and Adrenaline, since they can mix resolutions, it is a very important media management method for weekly TV series or episodic projects. Before creating the projects for the individual shows, create a master project for the show to hold all of the show elements like opens, bumpers, credits, music, sound effects, location stock shots, etc.

With the Meridien and ABVB–based Avid products, they can only mix resolutions in "families." Uncompressed, or 1:1, is its own family. Note that 1:1 cannot play in a sequence with any other resolution in a Meridien system. But 2:1, 3:1, 10:1, 15:1, and 20:1 are all compressed resolutions in Meridien that can be interchanged. The "s" resolutions are single field resolutions in Meridien and can only be mixed with other single field resolutions. The "m" resolutions are multi-cam resolutions that can only be mixed with other multi-cam resolutions. When I work on these Meridien systems, I create bars and other multi-project media at the highest resolution in each of the families.

This Elements project is also a smart place to create and store various slates and editing elements that you may use over and over, such as countdowns or animations of show logos or client logos that are used over numerous projects.

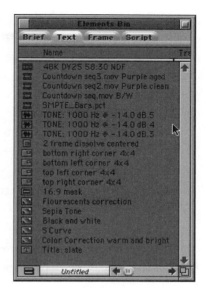

The reason that you want to create a brand new project for this media, instead of just creating an Elements bin in the first project you start, is because the easiest way to manage and delete media is on a per-project basis, so having this media in its own project isolates it from being easily deleted.

Eventually, this project is also an excellent place to save favorite effects or color corrections that you develop as you work on projects. (For more on saving color corrections, see Chapter 12 "Color Correction" on page 341. For more on saving effects, see Chapter 9 "Effects" on page 245.)

Opening bins from other projects is one of my standard workflows for many projects. If I haven't saved a specific Title, effect, or color correction to my Elements project, I will often go directly to the project, open the bin that contains the information and edit or copy directly from that bin.

I have used this technique to match the style of lower thirds between projects or even to help me remember the source tape or source file of a given clip. If I know I used a certain shot or imported a specific music clip that may not have worked for a past project, but would work perfectly for what I'm working on now, I'll open the bin from the old project and batch-digitize or batch-import the clip.

It is also possible to open all of the bins in a project at once, or just multiple selected bins, by using Ctrl+A/Cmd+A in the project window or using a combination or lassoing, Ctrl-clicking/Cmd-clicking or Shift-clicking to select the bins then using Ctrl+O/Cmd+O to open them or by double-clicking one of the selected bins.

Bin Settings

Before we get too in-depth with how to organize and label clips in bins, we need to discuss how bins are affected by two things: Bin Settings and Bin Views.

Bin Settings control how often your bins are saved. If you live somewhere where there are lots of power outages or something, you can set things to save very often. The frequency that you choose for these saves depends on how quickly you work, how often you crash, and how crazed it makes you when you lose important editing decisions. Most people use the factory-set defaults for this setting, but you should really take a moment and determine what it means to use these default settings. If you don't like to be interrupted by "auto-saves" every few minutes and you want to take the chance that nothing will happen during your edit, you can set longer auto-saves and longer force saves. I personally would not let the system go longer than 30 minutes without a forced save, but you can. Some people are not bothered by the persistent interruption of bins saving automatically, but they *hate* to lose any work, so they set saves at 2 minutes and force saves at 5 minutes. You can usually remember all of your edit decisions from the last five minutes. The other problem with saving very frequently is that it requires saving more versions of your bins in the Attic. If you use a very short "save" interval, you'll do well to keep the bins you have open fairly small, so they will save faster. Only keep one active sequence in a bin at a time. Old versions of sequences should be cataloged in another bin that is generally kept closed.

The first three entry panes in Bin Settings control the saving behavior of the bins themselves, while the second two control Attic behavior. Auto-Save interval is the length of time at which Xpress Pro will automatically save your bins. (You can always force a save using Ctrl+S/ Cmd+S at any time.) The Inactivity period setting is designed to delay the Auto-Save until you have finished

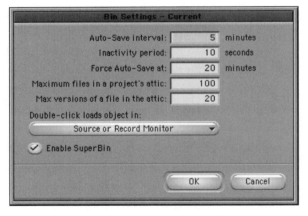

working. If you have this set at anything other than 0, it waits until you have stopped editing for the prescribed number of seconds before Auto-Saving. The Force Save setting is merely there to override the Inactivity period. No matter how frantically you're working, Xpress Pro will force a save at the interval set in the Force Auto-Save pane.

The next two panes determine how the Attic behaves. The Attic is a back-up folder of old versions of bins. It's great to have around when you accidentally delete something from a bin that you didn't mean to delete or if a bin becomes corrupted. I also use the Attic if I make changes to a sequence and later decide I want to go back to the original version. (Of course, the smart thing to do is to make a duplicate of a sequence before you start revisions to it, but you're bound to forget occasionally and a trip to the Attic is an easy way to get back to where you were.)

For the security of everything being available in the Attic, set the numbers of bins much higher than the default. With the rapidly decreasing cost of disk space and the relatively large size of internal hard drives, I'd set this very high. This figure is also dependent on how often you save. If you save often, you'll need to save more bins to maintain a longer history. I generally want to have at least 24 hours of bin history—or even 48. So if you figure the bins are saved every 15 minutes, and you edit for 10 hours a day, then you'll save about 40 bin copies of a specific bin in 24 hours. Probably less. So I might want 40 or 50 versions of each bin as an ideal. If my hard drive space starts getting eaten up too fast, I'd lower the number accordingly. Some questions to ask yourself are: How often do I use the Attic? How far back do I usually need to go? How many bins do I need to save to go back 48 hours into the past? How many bins do I have in a typical project? Those questions will help you set the Attic save numbers.

The two numeric entry panes for the Attic are "Maximum files in a project's attic" and "Max versions of a file in the attic." You need to figure how many bins you normally have in a project and multiply it by how many versions of those bins you want to have saved to determine the first number. (The first number pane always has to be at least as high as the second number pane.) The second pane is determined by how far you want to be able to go back to find an old bin.

You can save disk space by deleting dead projects from the Attic. When was the last time you cleaned out your Attic? The Attic is saved in various places depending on your OS. Do a Find or a Search on "Attic" to locate it. You should delete all the files for a project in the Attic every time you delete the media for that project.

Warning

The Bin setting is a user setting. If multiple editors use the same bins and projects, then copy the Bin Setting into your Site Settings or the Attic will wipe out bins based on the settings of the skimpiest User Setting. In other words, if one editor saves 50 copies of each bin, then another editor who only saves 5 versions uses that project, as soon as they save a bin, they will wipe out 45 old copies of the bins! If you have freelancers on your systems (or if you are a freelancer) make sure that their Bin Settings won't do any damage to your Attic.

The Bin Setting also lets you decide how clips can be loaded from bins. You can set "Double-click loads object in" so that double-clicking loads a clip into its own pop-up monitor or into the source monitor or that a double-click loads a sequence into the Sequence Monitor. This is a personal preference and often depends on the Avid product you edit with. I prefer to have a double-click load clips into my source monitor, but you may prefer individual pop-ups.

Xpress Pro also allows you to enable or disable a feature called SuperBin. SuperBin is a feature to help conserve screen real estate. With this feature active, a single click of a bin in the Project window launches the bin as a SuperBin instead of as a regular bin. Bins typically open into their own eponymous window, but with SuperBin, any bin launched with a single click replaces the bin inside the SuperBin window.

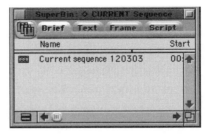

Double-clicking a bin in the Project window still launches the bin into its own window.

Bin View

One of the reasons bins are such a powerful method for media management is that each clip in a bin can have a huge list of identifying information associated with it. Much of this information is generated by the Avid as the clips are captured. Some of it can be customized, based on your project's needs. In order to allow users to view, sort, and sift through this clip information, Bins can have customized "headings" that can be organized and recalled. I hesitate to use such an uncreative word as "spreadsheet" to describe them, but that's basically what it is.

You have the clip icons down the left side and then usually the name of the clip, then you can place any other column or "heading" of information in any order you want. The headings can be accessed from the Settings list in the Project window or from the Bin View pulldown menu at the bottom of any bin that is displaying the text tab. Bin views can not be accessed when the Brief, Frame, or Script tabs are active, since these are essentially custom bin views themselves. You can't actually call up bins with certain views from the Settings list. They're only there so you can copy and trade them. (Double-clicking on the Bin View in

the Settings list will launch the Bin View window so you can change the headings in the View.) Having some custom bin views can definitely help you work more efficiently.

Determine the bin headings that you need to examine the most (i.e., Start Timecode, Tape Name, Comments) and make various bin views using those headings for specialized purposes during the editing process. I have a very stripped-down bin view with just name and start timecode. I also have a bin view specifically for conforming or up-rezzing a project. I have another for doing media management.

To check for wrong resolution video or wrong sample rate audio in a sequence, put the sequence in its own bin with no other clips. Then in the Bin Fast menu (sometimes called the Hamburger menu) select Set Bin Display from the pull-down menu and choose Show Sources. This will magically fill the entire bin with every source that feeds that sequence. If you have a bin view that includes the Video heading and the Sample Rate heading, you can then sort on those headings to see if there are any clips that do not match the others. This is a very good thing to do before laying off a show that has been up-rezzed, because you may have missed some short clips that are still at the old resolution. I will admit to having at least a few 10:1 shots make it to air before I learned this trick.

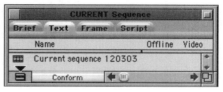

To create a custom bin view, you have to have a bin active and set to the Text tab. To call up the editable Headings list go to Bin>Headings. Xpress Pro gives you the option to quickly choose all or none of the Headings in a Bin View. You could start out by selecting

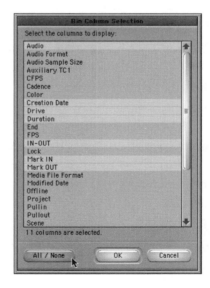

them all, then go through each column in the Headings and delete the ones that you don't use. For example, there are many film headings and if you don't cut film, then you never have to worry about any of them.

Here are some Bin Headings and an idea of what they're good for:

- *Name* is actually not a choice in the Bin Headings because you can't get rid of this Heading. It's required. I tend to be very descriptive with names (i.e., scene 12, WS talent crosses left, says "Say Good night Gracie!"), but some editors prefer to give simple consecutive names (i.e., wm105, wm106) to clips and save descriptive information for a custom column.

- *Audio* provides the sample rate of your audio. Sample rates can't be mixed, so this is an important Heading to check before you lay-off a sequence to tape or if some of your audio appears to be missing.

- *Audio Format* describes the type of audio files you chose to digitize or import, which is determined by the Audio Project Setting. This is most valuable when taking media to another system, like ProTools or another Avid product. Each audio format is helpful for a specific type of interchange. For more on Audio Format, see the Chapter 2 "Settings" on page 15.

- *Audio Sample Size* provides the sample size of your audio. There are only two choices, 16 bit and 24 bit. Sample sizes can't be mixed, so this is an important heading to check before you lay-off a sequence to tape or if some of your audio appears to be missing.

- *Auxiliary TC* allows you to use timecode from some alternate source. For example, you can digitize audio timecode from a source that may differ from the Longitudinal Timecode track.

- *Cadence* describes the type of pulldown used on NTSC source tapes in a 23.976 or 24p project. This is reserved for film projects. Cadence is the order of pulled down fields that converts from 24 to 30 fps so that it can be played back for video. For example, a normal film telecine would use a 2–3 pulldown, which means that the first frame consists of two fields, but the second is held for three—one extra field. Although you can use 24 fps media on Xpress Pro, the only media that you can create uses the advanced pulldown cadence of 2-3-3-2 that is recorded on the Panasonic DVX 100 and similar cameras. If you don't own or didn't shoot on this particular camera, you've nothing to worry about.

- *CFPS* is short for captured frames per second. This allows you to determine the frame rate for your project—24 fps or 30 fps. Also in older Avid systems, it was possible to set captures to 15 fps to save disk space. I cannot think of a real value in having this viewable on a regular basis.

- *Color* allows you to see a column with a color chip representing the assigned color of a clip. Clip Color can be assigned to help organize clips and can be set by selecting a clip and choosing Edit>Clip Color>[color choice]. Since clip color also changes the color of the text in the bin, the only reason to have this selected is to be able to sort based on clip color.

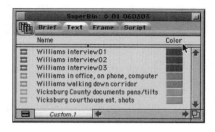

- *Creation Date* displays the date and time the clip was logged or captured. I use this to manage media when my drives get full or sometimes to locate a missing media file that I failed to label well. If I remember when I digitized it or imported it, I can find it with this Heading. I've also used it to track how long I worked on a project. Since I'm almost always rendering or creating media in some form or another even in the editing stages, I can check all my creation dates for a project to see approximately how long I worked on it.

- *Drive* shows the last known drive on which the media for that master clip existed. This is helpful in troubleshooting. I had a sequence that would crap out every time on the same few clips. I eventually found they were all on the same drive and, using that information, figured out I had a bad SCSI cable.

- *Duration* shows the length of the digitized clip. This is different from In/Out, which displays the duration between the IN and OUT point currently marked on the clip. In/Out can fluctuate, based on where the marks are set. Duration is a fixed number for any given clip. Sometimes I've used Duration as a troubleshooting technique. If a clip is not digitizing properly, I'll check Duration and sometimes I'll notice that it's dozens of hours long or at least much too long for a tape length. This happens when hand-logging is used.

- *End* is the OUT timecode of a digitized clip. This is helpful to have as a setting when producers are requesting specific timecodes for shots. By setting the Start and End headings, you can quickly ascertain which clip has the timecode they're looking for.

- *FPS* shows the actual frames per second of your clip. For video projects in NTSC-land, this is going to be 29.97 fps, for PAL 25, for NTSC film projects, 24 or 23.98 fps. Except for troubleshooting purposes, you can probably do without this heading.

- *In/Out* displays the duration of the clip between the currently set Mark In and Mark Out. This can fluctuate depending on where the mark in and mark out are set on any given clip. I rarely display this as a setting.

- *Lock* displays an icon of a padlock if the clip has been locked. If you are doing media management, this is a good heading to choose, because if clips are not deleting as expected, it could be because someone has locked them to prevent them from being deleted. To lock a clip, select it in the bin and go to Clip>Lock Bin Selection.

- *Media File Format* is generally OMF, with the option to be MXF. This is a fairly recent addition to Headings and I don't use it at all currently. This will probably be a heading that will be necessary to display as you prepare media to move to other systems that accept MXF files.

- *Modified Date* displays the time and date a clip or sequence was last modified. Many things can cause a clip to be modified, so this will change quite a bit. This is different from the Creation Date, which will remain stable.

- *Mark In* displays the current timecode location for the Mark In of a specific clip.

- *Mark Out* displays the current timecode location for the Mark Out of a specific clip.

- *Offline* provides the track names for any media files that are offline. I use this heading all the time for media management. It's useful to check before you lay off a sequence. It's also a handy heading to have up when you are up-rezzing a sequence to an online resolution.

- *Project* tells the project into which the media was originally captured. This is another great column for doing media management. This often helps me figure out which media to delete in the Media Tool. It also helps to identify the source project of footage brought in from another project. Generally, though, you don't need this heading when editing because most of your clips—if not all—will be from the same project.

- *Pullin* is used in NTSC-based film projects only. It indicates the pulldown of the first frame of the clip, which is called the pulldown phase. Pullin is either A, B, C, D, or in the case of matchback, X. Many film transfers come with a file that starts all clips on the A frame.

- *Pullout* is used in NTSC-based film projects only. It indicates the pulldown phase of the last frame of the clip. Pullout is either A, B, C, D, or in the case of matchback, X.

- *Scene* is used to identify a scene number. This can be used in film or video projects.

- *Sound Roll* is reserved for film projects. If you need to record and refer to this information to track a dual system sound project, you will want to view this Heading. This heading does not need to refer only to reels of tape; it can also be used to identify DATs or ADATs.

- *Sound TC* is generally reserved for film projects. If you need to record and refer to this information to track a dual system sound project, you will want to view this heading. Although primarily a film heading, multi-camera productions can also use this heading when sound is being recorded on a separate tape.

- *Start* displays the starting timecode of a digitized clip. This is different than the Mark In timecode, which can vary depending on where the Mark In is placed at any given time. Along with End, this is helpful to have as a setting when producers are requesting specific timecodes for shots. By setting the Start and End headings, you can quickly ascertain which clip has the timecode they're looking for.

- *Take* is used to identify a take number. This can be used in film or video projects.

- *Tape* gives the source tape name. The main time this is needed is during Batch Capture. I always decompose my sequences into their own bin before I up-rez, and I'll put the Tape heading to the far left so it's easier to lasso all of the clips from a single tape. Name does not have to be the first heading.

- *Tape ID* is an additional identifier for a tape. However, since the Tape ID is not requested when new tapes are digitized, it is probable that the Tape heading is more accurate than the Tape ID. I do not use this heading at all.

- *Tracks* displays the audio and video tracks that were digitized or imported for a clip. This is a good heading for up-rezzing or conforming a project.

- *Video* shows the resolution of the clip. This is good to check before you lay off a sequence. Sometimes, a low-rez clip can sneak by in a sequence of higher-rez material. To make sure all of your clips are at the resolution you want them to be, you can sort all your clips by Video to make sure.

Some of the most useful headings are the Custom Headings. Customized headings are very useful as a media management tool. To create a custom column, make sure you are in the Text tab of the bin, not the Brief, Frame, or Script tabs. Then simply click in the top of the bin to the far right of where the other headings are—like Name, Start, End, Tape—

and type your custom heading name. There are hundreds of specific uses for these custom headings, but the two primary uses are to write comments about a clip—kind of an extension of the Name description—or to "rate" a clip—keeper/safety/NG or using a "star" system of asterisks. I know many editors who use this star method, and when they're trying to figure out the next shot to cut in, they'll search through their clips using their Star column, looking for multiple ******. Many people also use custom headings to provide shot types like WS/MS/CU/XCU/2-shot/OS/POV.

In documentary-style work multiple custom headings can be used to create almost a spreadsheet of various categorizations for a specific interview bite or piece of B-roll footage. For example, specific, separate headings could tell you the speaker's name, the topic covered by the specific question, a reference to another speaker, the date, a subtopic, the direction the speaker is facing, the location of the interview, and the exact opening words of the bite. The value of having all of these items in separate headings is that they are easier to search, sort, and cross-reference when they are separate columns. Remember, the point of any of this categorization and labeling is to make it easier to find the right clip in the least amount of time.

One important tip to being able to successfully sort or sift any column for specific entries is having the entry groups be identical. In other words, if you are using a column to identify a character by name, you want to spell that name the same way every 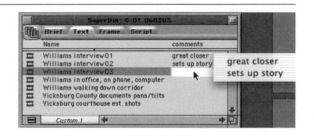 time or use the same nickname every time. The easiest way to do this is by Alt-clicking/Option-clicking the entry area for any column and clip for which you've already entered information. When you Alt-click/Option-click, it calls up a list of previous entries for that column, so you can simply pick the one you want instead of retyping it. If you do this, and the name you want is not one of the choices, then you can choose not to make a selection from the list, and type a new entry. The next time you Alt-click/Option-click on a clip in that heading, the new name will be there.

Most people rely on the same bin view headings for most of their work. But you should hone your bin views so that you get the most beneficial information organized in the best order with the least amount of "noisy" information. To cut down on noise—information that you don't need at a specific time—you should design several bin views based on specific tasks or procedures. For example: a bin view for logging or cataloging, a

				01 060303			

	Name	Start	End	Tape	comments	Audio	Video
▦	Williams interview01	01;06;05;12	01;07;12;15	01 060403	great closer	48000	DV 25 411
▦	Williams interview02	01;08;13;15	01;08;52;13	01 060403	sets up story	48000	DV 25 411
▤	Digitizing						

4.1 The order of the headings in this screen capture is not really the best. You may want to put comments immediately after the Name heading.

bin view for editing, a bin view for conforming or onlining, and a bin view for media management. Even separate bin views for the rough-cut process of building the story and another for the B-rolling or finishing of the project.

Bin headings will depend on both the editor and the specific project. But let's take the examples above and consider certain headings for each of them.

A bin view for logging or digitizing needs to be fairly inclusive. Name is a given. Start and End timecode would definitely be included, because if you get distracted, you may need to look in the bin to see where you left off. Tape should probably be included. It's obvious to you what tape you have in the deck, but I have logged multiple tapes under the same tape name by accident, so having this heading staring at you as you digitize can alert you to the fact that you need to change your tape name. Comments can be very important, depending on how much information you put in the clip name. The less information in the clip name, the more important the Comments heading is. Video Resolution and Audio are really only important for the same reason that Tape is: to act as a flag in case you are digitizing at the wrong sample rate or resolution. Other than that, though, it's fairly superfluous. Custom views that allow your clips to be categorized are very useful while digitizing or logging. Creation dates and Modified dates are completely useless at this stage. While digitizing or logging, you won't need Mark In, Mark Out, or In/Out, since you aren't doing any editing yet, so all of these will be blank. Project is pointless since you know what project you're in. Tracks are only useful if you are changing tracks a lot between clips; otherwise, if you're digitizing all of your clips with VA1A2 or VA1A2A3A4, then this only acts as a flag if there are missed tracks.

A bin view for editing is going to be heavy on headings that help you categorize, sort, sift, and search. These headings are obviously Name, Tape, Start, End, Comments, and any other Custom Headings. Sometimes, I will include creation dates at the far right of the headings if I can remember what day or time I digitized something. Audio, Audio Format, Audio Sample Size, Media Format, Tracks, FPS, CFPS, Modified Date, Drive, Duration, Mark In, Mark Out, In/Out, Offline, and Video are all more for media management and troubleshooting than for editing, so I'd leave them out. If you are editing a video project, obviously all of the film headings can be left off. Keep tabs on the things you look at as you search for clips. The most frequently examined items need to be to the left side of the bin and the least frequently used items can go to the right. Color is a good heading to have if you color-code your clips, because it allows you to sort based on clip color.

Name	comments	Color	Start	End	Tape
Williams interview01	great closer		01;06;05;12	01;07;12;15	01 060403
Williams interview02	sets up story		01;08;13;15	01;08;52;13	01 060403
Williams interview03			01;09;14;20	01;19;37;12	01 060403
Williams in office, on phone, computer			01;16;14;15	01;22;12;19	01 060403

A conforming or onlining bin view is a very specialized application of bin headings. The left-to-right order of these headings, especially the first few to the left, is very important. I start with Tape, because after decomposing a sequence to up-rez it, I will sort the bin in order by Tape for the best efficiency. Next can be either Video or Offline. Either of these will help you identify which clips you've already digitized. The Video column will change from the offline resolution to the online resolution as you progress. The Offline column starts out listing the video and audio tracks that are offline next to each clip. As you digitize them, the Offline column becomes blank. Start is a good heading to have next because it allows you to sort each tape in timecode order. End and Duration aren't really necessary, because you can see the timecodes in the Digitize window and know how long you have left on each tape or clip. When I conform, I never redigitize audio, so I don't have any audio-related headings in my Conform view at all. If you aren't working on a film project, you won't need those settings. If you *are* working on a film project, then you still don't really need any of the film headings, since you're doing a video conform. The film conform will come later and you can worry about film-type stuff later. The film conform should be coordinated with your negative cutter, who will explain exactly what they need to accurately cut your project.

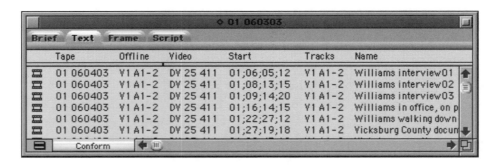

Tape	Offline	Video	Start	Tracks	Name
01 060403	V1 A1-2	DV 25 411	01;06;05;12	V1 A1-2	Williams interview01
01 060403	V1 A1-2	DV 25 411	01;08;13;15	V1 A1-2	Williams interview02
01 060403	V1 A1-2	DV 25 411	01;09;14;20	V1 A1-2	Williams interview03
01 060403	V1 A1-2	DV 25 411	01;16;14;15	V1 A1-2	Williams in office, on p
01 060403	V1 A1-2	DV 25 411	01;22;27;12	V1 A1-2	Williams walking down
01 060403	V1 A1-2	DV 25 411	01;27;19;18	V1 A1-2	Vicksburg County docun

Depending on the way you edit, you may do a "radio" or "skeleton" cut or whatever you like to call it. Basically this is assembling all of the sound bites and narration into a rough version of the show before you start adding B-roll and determining the final look and timing. If this is the way you work, then you could have two different views for each stage of the project. One stage would provide you with only headings that provide information about audio content. You can strip away any Custom Columns that provide visual cues. When you move to the next step, you can do the reverse.

It is possible to do media management in the bins themselves, but I almost exclusively perform these tasks in the Media Tool. For many years, the Media Tool could not be customized in any way. Then Avid reorganized it and added some headings so that at least the noncustomizable headings were more useful. Recently, they've allowed full use of bin-style headings to customize the Media Tool.

The most important heading during media management is probably Project. It's especially important if you are looking at *all* of your media, trying to decide what should stay and what should go. Sometimes you'll spot media from projects that are *long* dead. Resolution is very important. You may want to keep certain resolutions and discard others. Date is fairly important, allowing you to delete the oldest media. Tape is often an important part of media management if you know you have tapes that are non-timecoded, you may wish to archive that media in some fashion before deleting it. Drives are usually fairly important, especially if you are trying to consolidate a project, or to clear specific drives that will either be taken offline or so that a new project can be assigned exclusively to a set of drives.

MANAGING DRIVE SPACE AND DELETING MEDIA

While we're discussing media management headings, let's also jump past the digitizing and editing stages of a project and discuss managing drive space.

I have seen a lot of approaches to managing media and the main description that I would use for most of them is "firedrill." Clients have an uncanny knack for waiting to ask for revisions until five minutes *after* you've deleted all the media for a project—even if you call them before you delete it. Because of that, everyone wants to leave the media on their drives as long as they can, meaning that each new project always begins with a frantic, last-minute search for the one "safe" project that can be deleted. Here are some tips for attempting to save as much valuable media as possible.

First, delete all of your rendered media. The Avid refers to these files as "precomputes." The good thing about deleting precomputes is that if the client does call five minutes after doing this, all you need to do is re-render. That could be a long task in some instances, but at least it's fairly foolproof and doesn't require tapes or files that have been shipped to some distant outpost.

The process of deleting precomputes is fairly simple. Deleting *unused* precomputes should actually be performed throughout a project's life and definitely after laying the first version of it to tape. As you figure out the effects and transitions in a sequence, each time you render an effect, that creates a media file that remains on the disk until you delete it. Obviously, many of these renders don't result in an effect that ever becomes part of the edit, so you definitely want to get rid of it as soon as possible. These renders that are not part of your final sequence are referred to as "unreferenced precomputes." Here's how to delete them.

1. Open Tools>Media Tool.

2. Select All Drives, Current Project, and Precompute Clips only. Make sure that Master Clips and Media files are *not* selected (see Figure 4.2).

3. Open all bins with final sequences. Do not have bins open with old versions of sequences or you will leave "orphaned" precomputes on your drives.

4. Select Bin>Select Unreferenced Clips (see Figure 4.3).

5. This highlights all of the clips in your bins and in the Media Tool that are not referenced by the sequences in the active bin. These are all precomputes that are associated with old sequences, or that were replaced with revised renders before the final sequences were complete.

6. Delete any of your unreferenced precomputes by simply activating the Media Tool and hitting the Delete button.

7. This calls up an additional dialog box explaining the number and type of files you are about to delete. Check or uncheck any of the boxes. Chances are at this stage you can delete all of the files without worry.

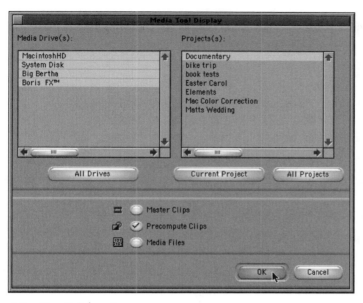

4.2   Step 2 *(above)*

4.3   Step 4 *(right)*

If you maintain a regular schedule of deleting your precomputes, you'll keep the media object (MOB) counts down on your projects, which is good for the overall speed of your system.

If you have never done this before, do a check of all the media on your drives.

1.   Open Tools>Media Tool.

2.   Select All Drives, All Projects and then select Precomputes, Master Clips, and Media files. Then hit Return.

3.   If your drives are very full and you have a good deal of storage, it could take a minute before the Media Tool opens.

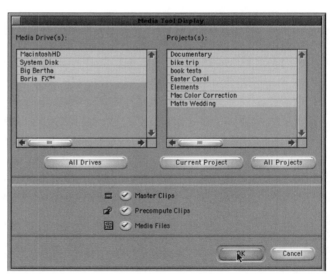

4. With the Media Tool window open, find or add the Projects heading and sort on it by clicking on the word Project near the top of the Media Tool and pressing Ctrl+E/Cmd+E. This sorts the media in the Media Tool alphabetically according to Project.

5. Make a list of all of the projects that have media online.

6. Go into each project and at least delete the unreferenced precomputes using the method just described. You may also find entire projects that you can't believe still have media on the drives. For those projects, simply select all of the media files pertaining to that project and delete them with the Delete key.

Once you've cleared out the huge number of fairly small precompute files, you may be looking for more ways to make space on a crowded hard disk. There are several ways—short of deleting projects "wholesale." Which way is best depends on what you might think will happen with revisions to a project.

Consolidating

If you have enough extra drive space and you think the changes will be minor things, like removing sections, changing Titles, or making minor revisions to effects, you can consolidate your project. Consolidation is Avid's term for copying just the footage used in a particular sequence (plus some handles) and then deleting the original, longer clips. So if you digitized a 30 minute tape, but only used four :05 second shots from it, the consolidation would save the four shots, plus some handles, creating :36 seconds of new media, but allowing you to delete the original 30-minute clip. After you consolidate, if your client needs to add other shots from that 30-minute tape, you'll need to redigitize, but you can still trim the original shots a few frames here or there and even add transitions. You can consolidate if you think you won't need any of the unused footage you digitized. Or if you think any additional footage needed will be minimal.

To consolidate, you need enough free hard disk space to copy all of the new media created in the consolidation. To determine this, take the length of the sequence and add 2–4 seconds of extra media for every edit, to account for media in dissolves and handles. Don't forget any areas that have multiple tracks. Select the sequence you want to consolidate. You can even consolidate multiple sequences from a single bin at the same time.

Then select Bin>Consolidate/Transcode. This calls up the Consolidation window.

Your options here include the ability to simply consolidate the media or Transcode it. Transcoding is similar to consolidation, but allows you to change the resolution of the clip. This is useful if you digitized your media 1:1 but you want to continue your edit on a laptop system that may not have the drive space to accommodate the 1:1 media. You can use transcode to transform the large, uncompressed files to smaller DV-quality files. In this case, we are simply consolidating the media.

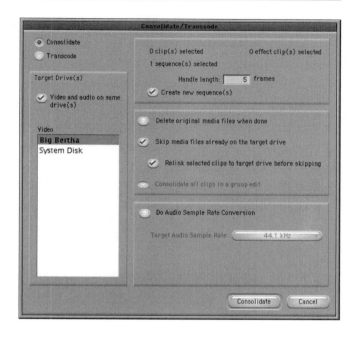

You have a check box to decide whether you want to send the audio and video media to separate drives. Sometimes this helps throughput.

You are also provided with the option of how much "handles" you want your media to have. The default is 60. I tend to go with 30. If you thought you might want to do a lot of trimming or have the ability to add long transitions, you might want to go for a longer "handle" length.

You are given the option to create a new sequence. This links the newly created media with a new sequence. If you deselect this option, your current sequence will be linked to the new media. I think that it is much safer to have a new sequence created, so that your original sequence is left unaltered. However, another smart workflow would be to make a duplicate of your original sequence before consolidating. In that case, there would be no reason to automatically create a third sequence.

You can check "Delete original media files when done." This is the correct option if you are Consolidating to save drive space. You can also consolidate to create new media to transport to another system. For example, you can consolidate your audio media to a CD so that it can be sweetened in a ProTools session. In that case, you would choose *not* to delete original media.

"Skip media files already on the target disk" is another option. This option is used if you are trying to consolidate all of your media to a single drive or drive set. Oftentimes, with removable drives, projects are consolidated so that all of the media is on a set of drives that can be moved to a different system. If that is your intent, then you could skip the files that are already on the system. However, this will not "shrink" those files. If you want to Consolidate to conserve space, then do not use this option.

"Relink selected clips to target drive before skipping" allows you relink the skipped media to the target drive. Otherwise the clips will become unlinked from the skipped media.

"Consolidate all clips in a group edit" allows you to have access to the other grouped clips (usually used in multi-camera editing) in the portions of the clips that were used in the show. This will allow you to still switch camera angles after consolidating, but it will take up a lot of extra disk space. Depending on the project, I would either not consolidate it if I thought there were going to be a lot of additional changes, or I would not choose this option because the show was pretty much locked and I wanted to save disk space.

Finally—just as you can transcode the video—you are given the option of converting the sample rate, in case there are multiple sample rates in your sequence. Hopefully all of your footage was brought in at the same sample rate, so you can avoid this option, but if you do have multiple sample rates, this is probably a good time to convert them, since you may not be able to convert them later, and while you're re-creating the media anyway, you might as well re-create it correctly.

Once you've chosen all your settings, pick a target drive or drives in the Target Drive(s) area and hit Consolidate. This process will take some time. It's pretty much real-time, but you've got to read and then write every piece of media in the sequence. For lengthy sequences this can obviously take quite a while, even with high-speed disks. You do *not* want to interrupt this process once it starts.

Deleting Unused Media

Another approach is to delete the media from clips that never got used. This is similar to deleting precomputes. The decision here is to delete files that you think your client won't use if revisions are needed. This approach can still leave a lot of unused media on your drives, because even if a 30-minute clip only got used for a :03 second bite, the whole clip will be saved.

To delete all unreferenced clips:

1. Select Tools>Media Tool.
2. Choose All Drives, Current Project, Media files. Then hit Return.
3. This calls up the Media Tool with all of the Media Files associated with your current project.

4. Select all of the sequences for which you want to save the media. (They'll all need to be in the same bin.)

5. Select Bin>Unreferenced Clips. This will highlight all of the media files in the Media Tool (and all of the clips in your open bins) that are not referenced by the sequences you selected. That means that it's safe to delete them.

6. Hit the Delete key. This calls up an additional dialog box explaining the number and type of files you are about to delete. Check or uncheck any of the boxes. Hit Return to execute the deletion of the files.

Survival of the Smallest

The final concept to use is when you know you need to make space fast but there's nothing that you feel you can delete. Then, the best option is deleting the largest, easiest files to recover. This buys you a lot of space at a small cost in effort down the road. For example, if I created a :60 promo by digitizing an hour-long show, plus a bunch of graphics, animations and music files, I'll delete the large hour-long file and try to save all of the smaller files. Then if I need to do further editing on the promo, I know I can easily either redigitize the single, lengthy file, or decompose the sequence and just digitize the specific shots that are in the promo. This is faster than almost any other option and can possibly save you time because you don't have to try to recover a project that was created from dozens of tapes, and files could take much longer to track down than one or two major tapes.

Archiving

Archiving a project involves saving the media files and the project files to another drive or storage media. Some people have old hard drives that they use for this purpose temporarily. Or you could use DVDs if the project isn't too big.

The best way to archive a project would be to save all of the digitized and imported media in its OMF form, but even with the low cost of most removable media, this is beyond the financial abilities of most editors. Another choice would be to save the consolidated media to a removable medium such as DVD or DAT or DLT.

Here are the steps for consolidating a project to a low-speed medium.

1. Go to the Media Creation setting and turn off Drive Filtering. Drive Filtering is an option that is designed to ensure that your hard drives are capable of sustaining the throughput necessary for playback. However, in this instance, we merely want to archive the media, so playback throughput is not required. (If you want to restore the media that you archive to a DVD or CD or DAT or DLT, you need to copy it back to a high-speed hard drive before working with it again.) With filtering off, even floppy drives will show up as potential media target drives.

This is one of those "school of hard knocks" tips that should not be ignored. On the desktop level, create a new folder, call it Imports and drop it in your current Project folder. Then, whenever you import any kind of files into Avid projects, you should first move them (or copy them) at the desktop level to that Imports folder inside of your Project folder for that project. This will not harm the project in any way. Then only import files from inside of that folder. This makes it much easier to archive that job when it is done, because all of the files used to create the project are inside of the project already. It also makes any batch importing much, much, much easier down the road. *Not* heeding this tip has almost bitten me in the butt enough times for me to do this consistently. Maybe it'll sink in now that I've written it down…

2. With the final sequence selected, go to Clip>Consolidate/Transcode. (You can also consolidate complete master clips that you may want to save, if you have room.)

3. From the options in the Consolidate window, choose not to relink the media to the new target drive. And if you don't want to delete the original media at this time, don't choose the Delete after copying option. Then hit Return or choose OK.

    There is no way to copy to multiple disks, so you may need to break up your sequence into more digestible bites.

4. Drag a copy of the Project folder for the project to the same drive, or at least drag the bin with the sequence to the drive, so there's no way that the sequence gets separated from the media. If you have some extra space, include the Imports folder that I mentioned in the tip on this page. Another good thing to put on the disk are any bin views that contain customized headings for the project, so if you need to find clips to redigitize at a later date, it's easy to find the right clips without having to load up the tape first.

If your project is even too big for that, try saving just the OMF media for non-time-coded tapes. Look through the Media Tool for your project, examining the tape names. If you recognize any tapes that you doubt are timecoded, consolidate the entire clips to DVD or other media using the same process as for consolidating your sequence, only instead of selecting your sequence, select the appropriate clips.

 As you digitize, if you use media from non-timecoded sources, it's a good idea to note this in the tape name (i.e.: 01 NTC VHS). That way you have some kind of warning when you are later doing media management that it will be difficult or impossible to re-create the edit if any media from that tape is deleted.

One of the best ways to organize and find things for edits is not even an Avid tool, but your word processor. If the script or transcript is in a Word file or some other form, simply search the file for the word or phrase that you need. This has saved me vast amounts of shuttling time. This is very handy for transcribed projects when you're trying to make a sentence or thought from various words or sentences from an interview. So when I'm saying to myself, "If he just said 'In my opinion' it would bridge these two thoughts perfectly," I call up the transcript in Word, and run a Find on the phrase.

One of the fastest ways to search for footage that you've recently already used is to call up the Source Monitor list (see Figure 4.4). It's a pulldown that you access by clicking on the name of the currently loaded clip above the Source Monitor. The list contains the names of the last 10 clips you've loaded. This list is alphabetical, which doesn't actually help too much, if you know that you can't remember the name of the clip you're looking for, but you know you saw it in your Source Monitor in the last few clips. If you want to see a list of the clips you've loaded into the Source Monitor in the order in which they were loaded, with the most recent at the top, then Alt-click/Option-click on the Source Monitor pulldown. Sometimes, if I know I'm going to need a certain group of clips at a certain time, I'll load them all into the Source Monitor at once, just so I can access them quickly from the pulldown instead of going to the bin.

Finding, Sorting, and Sifting Clips

So we have enough drive space for our projects and we have good bin views. But what we really want to do with this Xpress Pro system is *edit*. So how do you find the right clip from this huge mass of media on the drives?

There are a lot of tools for finding the right clip. To start with, you don't have to use the custom text bin views. You can use one of the other bin views that are set up as tabs for each bin. These preset views are Brief, Text, Frame, and Script.

The Brief tab (see Figure 4.5) gives you a very pared-down text view. This is a good view if all you are looking for is a clip name or timecode. For serious searching though, this is only going to be useful if you don't need much information.

Warning

You are able to "customize" this Brief View of your bin, but any customization done in the Brief tab is not saved. So you can add custom columns, and various headings, but as soon as you leave this bin or tab of the bin, these new columns—and any information you've stored in them—will disappear.

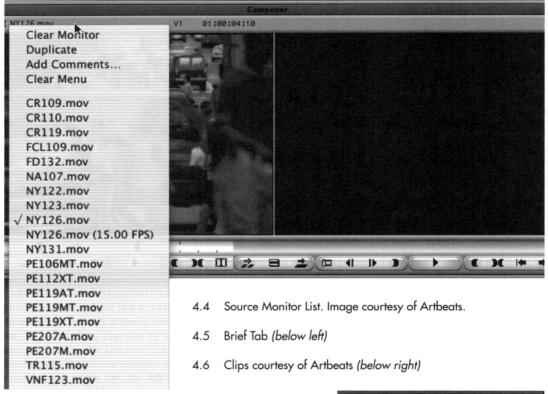

4.4   Source Monitor List. Image courtesy of Artbeats.

4.5   Brief Tab *(below left)*

4.6   Clips courtesy of Artbeats *(below right)*

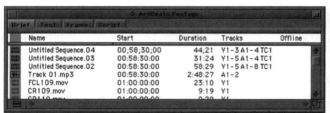

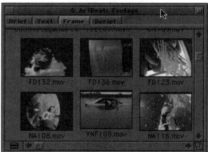

The Text tab is the tab used for all of the high-level bin view customization that we've been discussing.

The Frame View is basically best used for finding clips visually. Sometimes this is the best way to get inspired when you're trying to cover a sequence with B-roll. For sorting and sifting and finding clips in any other way than simply seeing the image you want, this view of your bin is very limited.

There are some pretty cool ways to use Frame View, however. This tab allows you to drag your clips around freehand, creating storyboard views of your clips (see Figure 4.6).

Once you have created an order for a sequence by dragging your clips around in the bin, you can select them and drag them into the Timeline, where they create a kind of instant edit.

I use Frame View sparingly when I edit, because of the amount of screen real estate this view takes up and the redraw times for the windows when there are a lot of clips. Usually, I reserve this view for select bins where the best way to find a clip is visually. Basically this would be B-roll that is broken up into subclips. If you have long strings of many B-roll shots in a single clip, Frame View can actually hinder your efforts to find the right clip, because you are only presented with a single frame of the clip, so you aren't reminded of all the other shots in the clip that are *not* represented by that single frame.

There are several organizational tools at your disposal in Frame View. You can resize the frames in the bin by selecting all of them and using Ctrl+K or L/Cmd+K or L. Like all the other uses of this key combination elsewhere in Xpress Pro, K shrinks the frame and L enlarges it. You can go to the Bin Fast menu to fill the window or sort the window.

One of the ways to make the best use of Frame View is to make sure that the Frame that is used as the representational frame for the whole clip is the most representational frame from the clip. The default frame that is displayed to represent the clip is the first frame in the clip, But if you were digitizing on the fly and wanted to make sure you got all of a certain shot, you may have actually started digitizing a few seconds of the previous shot, so your representational frame wouldn't even really be for the right shot. There are two ways to remedy this. The easiest way for a short clip is to click once on a shot in the bin to select it (but not to launch it into the source monitor), and then use the JKL keys to play or shuttle through the clip to find the frame you want. The other way (learned by the old-guard editors) is to double-click the clip to launch it into the Source Monitor, then navigate to the frame you want using any of the traditional methods you would use in the Source window, then mark the frame you want with the Mark In button. Now click back just once on the clip you want and hit the Q button (Go To In) and the representational frame will change to the same frame where you marked your IN point on your source clip.

Script View is one that I rarely use, but that shouldn't deter you from seeing how you can apply its unique display of clip information to help you edit. Script View is primarily useful for delivering a greater quantity of textual information than even the Text View can offer. For me, entry of that much text takes too much time away from editing. But for many people, having script or transcript dialog attached to their clip could be a critical way to sort and find the right clip.

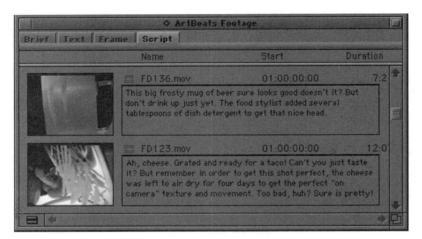

4.7 Images courtesy of ArtBeats

There is one very cool tip that can only be done in Script mode. If you would like to have a certain clip in a bin appear at the top of the bin, so that it is easy to find and use again and again, Script View can help you. In Script View, it is possible to drag clips into a custom order. This is great to be able to put room tone, or a narration track or a piece of animation that you use time and time again, at the top of the bin for easy access. Once you drag it into place in your Script View, the Text View will maintain that order—at least until your next sort. (So, sort your bin first, then use this script tip.)

Sorting

The way I most often search for footage is by sorting on bin headings. The basic sort of a bin is done by selecting a bin heading and hitting Ctrl+E/Cmd+E. You can also reverse sort by using Ctrl+Shift+E/Cmd+Shift+E. If you are looking for a clip name, sort on the name heading, for timecodes, sort on the timecode heading.

You can also do multilevel sorts by selecting more than one heading. The heading with the most importance should be placed to the left. So, if you want to sort based on tape and timecode number, you probably want all of the timecodes from a certain tape to be together (see Figure 4.8). To force the tape to the dominant position, place it to the left of the Start Timecode heading (just drag the heading to a new position in the bin), click on the Tape heading, then Shift-click the Start Timecode heading. Ctrl+E/Cmd+E will then sort by tape with the timecodes of each tape in order. If the column order was reversed then the timecodes would all be in numeric order and any that were identical would be sorted secondarily by tape name.

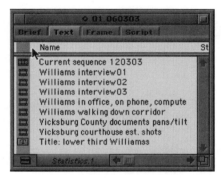

4.8 Sorting by Timecode

When you have finished dragging your bin headings into the order that you want them, you can Ctrl+T/Cmd+T to tidy the bin. This moves all of the columns as close together as they can get.

One of the very useful sorts that you can perform is one that many people do not even consider: sorting on the clip-type icon. This is the column that is always farthest left. I have watched editors scroll through lengthy bins searching for any sequences in the bin. The easiest way to find a sequence is to sort on the icon column. Sequences get sorted—like cream—to the top of the bin, with master clips and subclips and motion effects and titles and other various types of clips organized accordingly. This is also a useful operation if you want to move all of the titles or motion clips or audio clips into another bin. By sorting on the icon column, all of these items are neatly grouped together for easy dispatch.

You can also sort on the clip color of a clip. I find this very useful for organizing groups of clips. As you look through your clips, maybe you will decide on all of the ones that would be useful in an opening montage. As you identify these shots, select Edit>Set Clip Color>[color], assigning a single color to all of the opening montage clips (see Figure 4.9). Later you can sort all of the clips you identified for the opening montage by selecting Clip Color as a bin heading, then sorting (Ctrl+E/Cmd+E) on that heading.

Sifting

Sifting allows you to find a specific clip by doing a database-like search through your bin.

When you perform a Custom Sift—which is accessed from the Bin menu—the bin only shows clips that meet the search parameters (see Figure 4.10). When you perform a

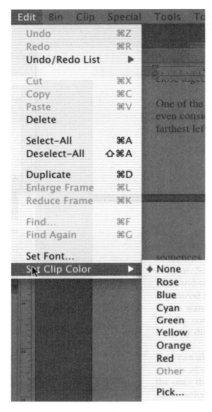

4.9 Assigning a Color to All of the Opening Clips *(left)*

4.10 Choosing Custom Sift from the Bin Menu *(right)*

4.11 Custom Sift Specifications *(below)*

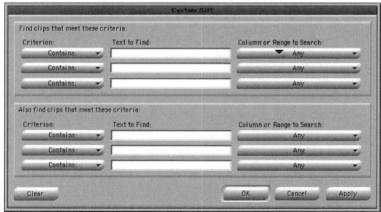

Custom Sift on a bin, a dialog box appears, providing you with two panes, each providing three levels of criteria with which to perform your search (see Figure 4.11).

There are three rows of information in the top pane and three in the bottom pane (see Figure 4.11). There are also three columns. From left to right, these columns allow you to set whether the text entry in the next column to the right either Contains, Begins With, or Matches Exactly with any clips in the bin. The second column from the left is for entering text for the search. The third row is to designate which columns in the bin should be searched. Your choices here are Any, None, then a group that includes every individual bin heading name. There are also four very powerful search headings at the bottom: Auxiliary TC1 range, Mark In to Out TC Range, Sound TC Range, and Start to End Range. We'll cover how to use these "Range" options in the step-by-step instructions for performing a search.

At the bottom of the dialog box are your options for executing or aborting the search: Clear, OK, Cancel, and Apply. Clear is used to clear the information from the text panes. OK is used to execute the search and close the Custom Sift dialog box. Cancel closes the Custom Sift dialog box without performing a search. Apply executes the search (the same as OK) but keeps the dialog box open.

How to Perform a Sift

1. Choose Bin>Custom Sift to open the Custom Sift dialog box.

2. Type your search text in the Text to Find text box. It's even possible to sift clip color; just type in the name of the clip color using the correct spelling and capitalization.

3. Depending on how sure you are of the text you typed, or what kind of a search you want to perform, you need to set the search criterion—the button in front of the text box—to Contains, Begins With, or Matches Exactly. I usually use Contains but there are certainly times when you'll want to be more selective.

4. Use the Column Or Range To Search pop-up menu—immediately following the text box—to select a Bin Heading or Range to use for your search.

5. If you want to expand or narrow your search, use the additional text boxes, criterion, and Columns or Ranges.

6. Click OK or Apply. OK will do the search and close the Custom Sift Dialog box, while Apply keeps the box open so you can do another search.

The bin will only display the clips that met the search parameters, with the word "sifted" added in parentheses to the bin name. You can toggle the bin to display the sifted clips or the unsifted clips until you perform another search.

Sometimes I'll add an additional step after a sift so that I have faster access to the sifted information. I'll add a new custom column that briefly describes the search, then I'll put an "x" in that column on any clips that came up in that sift. That way, to find those clips, I can just do a sort (Ctrl+E/Cmd+E) to find those clips much later in the edit. For

If your producer is looking for a specific timecode, you can do a Custom Sift to find it. If this is something you do a lot, then I would map the Custom Sift menu selection to a keyboard command. Once you have set your Column or Range to Search menu in the Custom Sift dialog, it maintains that selection as the default every time you open the Custom Sift, until you search using another range or Bin heading. Most of my searches use Start to End Range, but you may have reason to use one of the other types of timecode ranges. And for a special tip within a tip—the headings that are displayed in the "Column or Range to Search" pulldown menu are limited to the actual bin headings that have been currently selected in your bin, so it's faster to find the right heading if your bin doesn't have every single heading displayed. So if the Brief tab of the bin gives you enough information to work from, choose that before you sift. Finding exact timecodes in a bin becomes as fast as hitting the Custom Sift button mapped to your keyboard, typing the requested timecode number, and hitting Apply or OK. The bin then displays only the clips in the bin that contain that exact timecode somewhere in its duration. Then load the clip into the source monitor, click on the source monitor and type the timecode again to jump to it. I can be parked on any given timecode in an entire project within seven seconds using this method in conjunction with the Master Bin concept discussed earlier in this chapter in the sidebar on page 107.

example, let's say I did a search for all of the clips with "bloopers" in the comments column. When that sift was complete, I could then create a Bloopers heading and put an x in that heading column for every clip in the sifted bin. Once I Select Unsifted, I can still find those clips without sifting, by just sorting on the Bloopers heading.

After you have sifted the clips in a bin, you can display the bin in a sifted or an unsifted state. Just toggle back and forth by going to Select Bin>Show Unsifted or Select Bin>Show Sifted. And as I mentioned earlier, if you use this a lot, you can map Show Sifted and Show Unsifted to your keyboard to make it faster to toggle back and forth.

CONCLUSION

When it gets right down to it, the whole point of any of this organization process is to allow you to find the shot you want to cut in as quickly as possible. Organizing and viewing your media also provides you with a way to be inspired by the possibilities of the editing choices presented to you. With the knowledge you have gained from this chapter, you need to find your own way. What works best for you and the specific project on which you are working? Use all of these tools as a means to an end.

Chapter 5

Basic Editing

APPROACHES TO NONLINEAR EDITING

Through years of training editors, we've learned one thing: everyone learns a little differently. So in this chapter, we're going to learn some basic editing on Xpress Pro. For some people (ourselves included), there is an air of impatience when learning what should be a simple process. For those, getting through the process of making that first edit is more important than learning how to edit. If you're like us, just follow these five easy steps.

1. Assuming that you have gone through and captured some footage during the previous chapter, start up Xpress Pro and open your project.

2. In your menus, select Toolset>Source/Record Editing. Open a bin and double-click on a clip, any clip. It doesn't matter. The clip loads into the left Source Monitor on the interface.

3. See the Play button directly in the middle underneath the Source Monitor? Click it to play back the footage.

4. On either side of that Play button are your Mark buttons. Click on the left button to mark an IN point for the edit. Continue playing back the footage and click on the button to the right of Play to mark an OUT point.

5. Click on the red button near the center of the interface.

Congratulations, you are now an Avid editor, meaning only that you have successfully made an edit on an Avid system. Please go and tell everyone that you know that you are an Avid editor so that established editors will send us hate mail.

On a more serious note, you can spend a lot of time deconstructing what we just did, or you can go through it step by step in the following paragraphs. Either way, you'll learn the basics of editing on Xpress Pro.

The Nonlinear Advantage

When nonlinear technology was introduced, Avid came up with a catchy slogan: "Change Your Mind Without Losing Your Mind." And this was true. Any transitional effects could be added at any time. You could create multiple versions of any sequence with just a few mouse clicks. You could add new shots to the beginning of a sequence without starting over. All of this could happen because a computer was controlling the media and sequencing the playback through random access.

Our point is this: learn to think in a nonlinear fashion when using these tools. Every first draft of your cut will probably be awful. One of the differences between an amateur and a professional editor is that the professional editor knows this. The process of honing the cut, of refining it, is one of delight to most editors. Laying down the basic track is rudimentary, an almost Zen-like experience. Your brain doesn't even begin to do the tough work until you've laid it all out.

The ability to create so quickly and re-create is nothing less than blissful. But it does have its drawbacks. The biggest one to avoid is the tendency to ignore footage that might help you create a better cut. When digitizing, many editors pay little attention to the material being captured. They don't get to know the material as well as they should. My advice: know your material. You may very well find solutions to problems during edit sessions just by remembering a shot that wasn't digitized. The more you know, the better the session.

One other piece of advice: cut everything loosely. "Out of sight, out of mind" works best here. If you don't get everything that you're considering into that first cut, chances are that you will forget about those key shots entirely. Even if it makes your first cut look awkward or bulky, who cares? At least the shots will be there to remember. Don't force final decisions on your first cut. Take advantage of the nonlinearity of the system and perform multiple cuts, each one narrowing down the focus and excluding shots that you've deemed unnecessary. If you get stuck with too little, go back to a previous cut with more footage in it and start from there.

XPRESS PRO INTERFACE

Nonlinear Workflow

When working with nonlinear editing systems, the basic workflow is, well, basic.

1. *Capture media.* This generally means capturing media with the Capture tool but can also involve importing graphics and QuickTime movies, PICT sequences, or other required materials for your sequence. Also known as digitizing or "ingesting." Why are there so many names? Who cares? Just call it capturing.

2. *Edit your project.* In Avid's terms, the final edited piece is known as a sequence. Again, there are different terms. Some editors call it "my cut" or "the cut." Lots of editors like to refer to it as "the final cut," but this is rarely so.

3. *Output your project.* It used to be that outputting a project simply meant transferring it to videotape. Avid's term for this is "digital cut." But with Internet, DVD, CD-ROM, and other delivery methods, outputting can also include Exporting.

So, assuming you followed the instructions in Chapter 4 and have your bins ready, let's take a look at the editing interface.

Desktop Real Estate

If you have configured your system with two monitors using a video card capable of such monitoring, you'll have a very easy time navigating the Xpress Pro tools and interface. If you have a single monitor system, a certain amount of organization is necessary due to the limited amount of "screen real estate." Some of this organization involves the implementation of the proper toolset.

Choosing a Toolset

There are two ways to set up the interface for editing.

1. Use the Basic interface, which is standard on all Avid Xpress products (see Figure 5.1).

2. Use Source/Record interface, which is standard on all Avid Media Composer and Symphony products.

Xpress Pro automatically defaults to Basic mode, but you can change that by going to Toolset>Source/Record.

You can also enter the side-by-side Source/Record mode by dragging the lower right corner of the Basic Monitor so that a wide rectangle is created instead of a TV-shaped square.

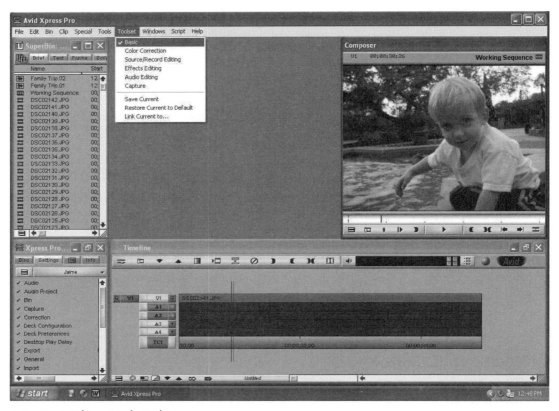

5.1   Basic Editing Mode Toolset

The only real difference between the Source/Record and Basic interfaces is that with Source/ Record, the Source Monitor is stationary and not a pop-up monitor as it is in the Basic interface. When using Basic mode, for each source that you double-click in the bins, a new pop-up monitor will appear. With Source/Record, every clip that is double-clicked in a bin appears in the Source Monitor.

If you prefer to edit with fewer pop-up monitors, use Source/Record. If you like lots of windows on the screen and can manage it, you might prefer Basic mode. For purposes of clarity, I prefer Source/Record. No bones about it, this is the same toolset on every Avid except for Avid Xpress.

Basic Toolset Overview

The Basic toolset consists of three major areas:
1. The Composer Window or Monitor
2. Pop-up windows or monitors
3. The Timeline

The Pop-Up Monitor

To access a pop-up monitor, double-click on any clip in your bin. Be sure not to double-click on a sequence, as this will load it into the Composer window.

The pop-up monitor appears.

The title bar at the top of the monitor should show you the name of the clip.

The buttons adjacent to the clip name allow you to resize or close the monitor.

Now that we've defined the pop-up monitor, we'll look at the Source/Record toolset and the rest of the interface.

Source/Record Toolset

To switch to the Source/Record toolset, select Toolset>Source/Record (see Figure 5.2).

5.2   Source/Record Mode Toolset

5.3   Source/Record Setup on a Single Monitor

Now the editing interface has two stationary monitors and a Timeline. We're going to start by doing basic editing, which uses the top monitors and buttons. In the next chapter, we'll go into more depth and cover the Timeline, along with sync-related issues and other issues.

Let's start with the Source Monitor. The Source Monitor, unlike a pop-up monitor, remains in one place. However, you can still create pop-up monitors while in Source/Record mode by Alt+double-clicking /Option+double-clicking on a clip in a bin.

To load a clip into the Source Monitor, select a clip in the bin and double-click on it. The source should now be loaded into the monitor. You can also drag the clip from the bin into the Source Monitor, but this takes longer than a simple double-click. Most editors avoid repetitive stress injuries and the potential for carpal tunnel by double-clicking. The more you drag, the more likely you are to create stress on your wrists.

It is also possible to load sequences into the Source Monitor by dragging them into the Source Monitor. (Double-clicking the sequence loads it into the Sequence Monitor, where it will replace your current sequence.) Once a sequence is loaded into the Source Monitor, portions of the sequence or all of the sequence can be cut into your current sequence, just as if it were a single clip. This works great for creating shorter versions of a previous cut.

Loading Footage

Now that you know how to capture, organize bins, and set up projects, it's time to edit.

The first thing to do is load source material. To do this, open your project; then open a source bin with clips. Choose a clip to be loaded and double-click on it. The clip loads into the Source Monitor.

The Source Monitor

You'll notice that below the source footage in the monitor is a mini-Timeline. This Timeline gives you instant access to any place that you want to go in the clip.

Below the Timeline is a set of buttons. These buttons are the standard configuration for Xpress Pro. In the center of the buttons is a Play button. You can use this to play back the media, though you should really be using the keyboard. If you are using the default keyboard buttons, the L key will play. To the immediate left and right of the Play button are Mark In and Mark Out, respectively.

 Mark In and Mark Out: When you're new to Avid, remembering all of the icons and their meanings can be difficult, and similar icons sometimes are confusing, such as Mark In and Mark Out. To help you remember, consider the resemblance between the two icons and two human faces looking at each other. In your Timeline, the two marks should face each other, so that they are "looking" at the media.

Now, play the source material back. As you play, you can stop anywhere to Mark In and Mark Out. Choose your points and we'll proceed with the edit.

If you edit using the keyboard, there is no need to actually stop playback to set your IN and OUT points. Marking INs and OUTs with the keyboard allows you to choose your points without any interruption in playback. This is a much better way to determine your marks. It also follows the ideal of preventing excess stress on your wrists from using the mouse too much.

Creating a Sequence

Now that you have some new material to start your sequence, we need to create a new sequence to be edited. If the Record Monitor is empty, Xpress Pro creates a new sequence automatically. But there are reasons to create the sequence manually as we will see.

First, let's create a new bin for the sequence. By placing your sequences in separate bins away from the clips, your project will remain well organized. In your Project window, select the Bins tab and click on the New Bin button. Name the new bin "My First Sequence." Note that when you create the new bin, the name is already highlighted, so all you have to do is start typing the new name.

In your menus, select Clip>New Sequence. If you'd like to use the keyboard, select Shift+Ctrl+N/ Shift+Cmd+N.

If you have more than one bin open, Xpress Pro will ask you which bin the sequence should be in. Select the My First Sequence bin that you created.

The sequence is created, but you need to name it. We'll call it Edit Version 1. Now you're ready to begin the edit.

Normally edits require three marked points. This is called *three-point editing*. The points needed are:

1. A Mark In on the source or record side,

1. A Mark Out on the source or record side, and

2. An additional Mark In or Out on the source or record side.

5.4 A Typical Three- Point Edit

At first, it might seem strange that three marks make an edit, when in fact, you would actually have four. But remember that we're using a computer here. It can figure out how long the edit should run on the side that's missing a mark.

So far you've marked an IN and OUT on your source side. Now we need to mark an IN on the record side. But when a sequence is new, there is no need for this, because there is nothing new in the sequence, so it has nowhere for the mark to be made. However, as we add more edits, this will become necessary.

Making the First Edit

Now that we've defined our points and created a new sequence, let's make the first edit. Click on the yellow or red arrow to the left of center just below the monitors. If you'd prefer using the keyboard, the red arrow is B and the yellow arrow is V.

Notice that your Timeline now has a clip in it and you see the last frame of your edit in the Record Monitor.

Splicing versus Overwriting

As more material is added to a sequence, more options are presented. For example, you might want to put material between two existing edits, or you may want to cover an existing edit with new material.

In the first example—the splice—adding new material between two edits will extend the duration of your sequence by the length of the clip that is added. This recording technique is called *splicing*. By putting material between the two edits, it is as though you are electronically splicing it in. The yellow Splice arrow is located to the left of center below the two monitors in the Composer interface. Splicing also has the potential to knock your sequence out of sync after the edit, because the splice only adds length to the tracks that are enabled in the sequence unless special measures are taken.

5.9   Splice vs. Overwrite, Two Sequences Shown

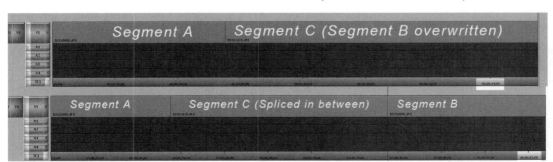

The Three-Point Rule

Three-point editing is determined by certain needs. While some of this may seem elementary, it's important to understand when and why to make the marks.

A mark IN and OUT on the Source side and a Mark IN on the record side is best used when your source material dictates a specific IN and OUT point, such as the beginning and ending of an interview bite that is marked on the source. Then a mark is made on the sequence side where you want that interview bite to start on the sequence. This kind of edit is used where you know that a certain section of a clip needs to *start* at a certain place in the sequence. This is the typical edit used when building a rough cut of your sequence.

5.5   Source-Dictated Three-
Point Edit

You can also mark a IN and OUT on the source and mark an OUT point on the sequence. This is called a backtimed edit, because in the linear days, the only way to figure out how to have an edit end at a certain point in the sequence was to do the math and subtract the timecodes so that the Mark OUT would be correct. This kind of edit is used with a sequence that is more or less complete. You use this edit when the out of the source needs to *end* at a specific part of the sequence. Secondary to the importance of those two OUT points is the IN point on the source.

5.6   Sequence Backtimed
Three-Point Edit

The next type of edit is to mark an IN and an OUT on the sequence and an IN on the source. Choosing to mark an IN and an OUT on the sequence side means that the sequence has to be completed to some extent. A common reason to do this kind of edit is that you are trying to cover a specific part of your sequence with cover video or B-roll. For example, you have rough-cut an interview together, then, based on the content of the interview, you decide to lay some video over a specific portion of the interview. So you would mark an IN and an OUT to define the part of the interview that was to be covered, then mark an IN point on the source clip that you want to cover that portion.

5.7   Record-Dictated
         Three-Point
         EditSource Backtimed

The final type of three-point edit is to mark an IN and an OUT on the sequence and an OUT point on the source side. This is similar to the previous type of edit, except that in this case, the end of the source clip is more important than the beginning. For example, you want to cover the same portion of the interview in the above example, except that it is important for a certain movement—such as a zoom—to be completed before the cut back to the interview is completed.

5.8   Source Backtimed
         Three-Point Edit

If you decided to cover an edit with a new edit, you would be *overwriting* the existing edit with the new material. The existing edit or edits would be covered by the new material, and the sequence would, under normal conditions, remain the same length. This recording technique is called *overwriting*. The red Overwrite arrow is located to the right of center below the two monitors on the Edit interface. If used at the end of a sequence, both the Splice and Overwrite buttons can be used interchangeably, executing the edit identically.

Which color is for which method? An easy way to remember the color for each method of recording is this: Splice is normally a film-editing technique, and film editors use yellow grease pencils to mark edits on workprint. Overwriting is frequently done by video editors, who had always used red recording buttons and frequently used the term *make it red* when performing an edit. So splicing is with the yellow arrow and overwriting uses the red arrow.

The Replace Edit

The Replace Edit is a unique function that allows you to replace a shot in a sequence based upon a key event. Replace Edit uses no marks IN or OUT as a reference, just the existing cut in a sequence and the location of the blue position indicator on both the Source and Record monitors.

That's probably pretty hard to visualize, so let's go with an example. You've shot and edited a music video. At a key point in the video, there's a cymbal crash. Using the video provided, you've filled this spot with the drummer, in sync, hitting the cymbal. But it's not very exciting. In fact, it's downright boring.

So the director goes for a reshoot, this time with the cymbal loaded with a bunch of sparkly material. This time, when the drummer hits the cymbal, stuff flies everywhere and it looks more like an explosion than percussion.

Kewl.

So now you want to replace the shot quickly. Here's how you do it.

1. Find the point in the sequence where the cymbal crash occurs and just park your blue position indicator on it.

2. Find the place in the new source material where this same point occurs and park the source blue position indicator there.

3. Click on Replace.

The new video is inserted in the exact same place where the old shot was located, and if you parked the source and record in the right places, it looks in sync and totally fabulous.

The Fit-to-Fill Edit

Fit-to-fill makes life really simple for those who need coverage of narration, and this is its most common use. Again, let's use an example:

You're cutting a news piece on a new fighter jet being developed by the government. The piece is mostly talking heads, but you get just a sliver of footage of the jet, taken from a distance, that is cleared by the government. Problem is, the footage is only 6 seconds long, and the narration for it is 8.5 seconds. How do you solve the problem?

Exceptions to the Three-Point Edit Rule

While most edits require the three points we just mentioned, it is possible to make edits without any marks at all, though this is usually only possible in the rough-cut stage.

When editing without marks, Xpress Pro uses the Timeline locator (the vertical blue line in the Timeline) as the IN point on both the source and the sequence side. The end of the source clip dictates the OUT point. Linear editors call this a "sloppy tails" or open-ended edit. This means that you don't really care what the OUT point is because you'll end up covering part of it with the next edit.

Other variations of the no-mark edit include single-mark edits and two-mark edits. A single-mark edit is similar to the no-mark edit, except that on either the sequence or the source clip one mark is made. By and large, it makes sense for that single mark to be an OUT point, because an IN point can always be indicated simply by the Timeline locator.

Two-mark, or dual-mark, edits can be made with the basic variations of the three-point edit, using the Timeline locator as the third mark, or you can backtime edits by using one OUT point in both the source and sequence side, then allowing the IN point be determined by the starting point of the clip. Placing Mark INs in both source and record would be very similar to doing a no-mark edit. The other variations either place both marks on the source side or both marks on the sequence side. These would be similar to three-point edits. There is also the possibility of doing a two-mark edit with an IN on the source and an OUT on the sequence or vice versa, but these would be fairly unusual choices.

The key to consider with any of these edits is to understand how Xpress Pro will determine the INs or OUTs that are not specifically marked.

Mark every frame of the new jet footage. Mark only the narration that it will cover on the record side. Click on the Fit To Fill button. The footage is slowed down enough where it will fit the narration perfectly.

We'll discuss motion effects like this a bit more in Chapter 9, Effects.

The Fast Menu (or "Hamburger")

Throughout the Avid interface, you will see Fast menus. The icon for the Fast menu is two gray flat rectangles sandwiching a black flat rectangle. During the first days of the Avid Media Composer, someone dubbed this "The Hamburger" and the name stuck.

You will note that on the Xpress Pro interface, there is a Fast menu in each window. The Project window, SuperBin, Bin, Source/Record, and Timeline all contain Fast menus. Each Fast menu relates to its assigned window and will contain options that relate only to that window.

For example, in the Bin Fast menu, you will note that the options are identical to the Bin menu. But in the Timeline Fast menu, different options appear.

Xpress Pro Help

If you right-click/Option-click on any button on the interface, the words "What's This?" will appear. Selecting this option launches Avid Xpress Pro Help, which will explain the function of that button. Xpress Pro Help can also be accessed directly through the Help menu. It contains a table of contents, a searchable database, an index, and a

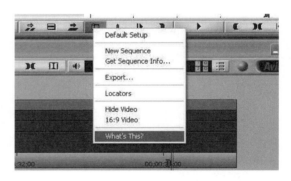

place to put your favorite topics. Avid Xpress Pro Help is indeed helpful for exploring many of the less used functions on the system. You can access Xpress Pro Help by going to the Help menu at the top of your screen as well as contextual access mentioned earlier (see Figure 5.10).

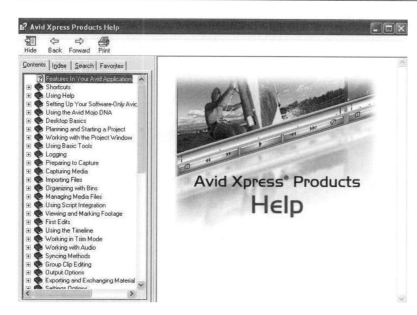

5.10 Xpress Pro Help

The Clip Name Menu

Above the source picture you will see a clip icon and the name of that clip. Click on the clip name. A menu appears.

Most of the stuff in the Menu Monitor is pretty straightforward. For example, Clear monitor clears out whatever clip or sequence is currently displayed and the monitor contains nothing. Duplicate allows you to duplicate the clip currently in the source monitor. Add comments will let you place comments with a particular clip. These com-

ments are saved in the Comments heading in your bin. Clear menu clears out any previously loaded clips from the menu. This is especially helpful when you are switching from one section of editing to another and you don't want to see any other clips located in the source monitor. At the bottom is a list of clips—up to the last 20—that you've loaded into source. These clips can be accessed directly from this menu instead of finding them in the bins. This can be helpful for frequently used clips.

Not everyone uses the Clip Name menu. I personally have little need for it, save for identifying names of clips when they appear in the Source Monitor.

You may have noticed that the Record Monitor, to the right of the Source Monitor, also contains a Clip Name menu. This menu is a duplicate of the Source Monitor's, except that it refers to the last 20 sequences loaded into the Record Monitor rather than the last 20 clips loaded into the Source.

The Tracking Menu

To the right of the Clip Name menu is a Tracking menu. This menu allows you to track information about the clip as it plays back. This information could refer to time-code location, frame counts, and other vital information. Both Source and Record sides have one Tracking menu each.

Here is a quick rundown of what the Tracking menu can display:

- *Mas:* Master Timecode. Displays the Master Timecode of a sequence (not source timecode) but will remain blank if the source is a clip. I generally use this to mark time on the Record Monitor. Most of my sequences begin at 1:00:00:00 timecode, so it's easy to track durations.

- *Dur:* Displays the duration of a clip as digitized from beginning to end.

- *I/O:* IN to OUT marks. Displays the duration between a marked IN point to an OUT point. If no IN or OUT points are made, it will display the duration from your blue position indicator to the end of your clip.

- *Abs:* Absolute time. Measures the time from your current location in the source Timeline (below the monitor) backward to the beginning of the source clip.

- *Rem:* Remaining Time. Measures the time from your current location in the source Timeline (below the monitor) forward to the end of the source clip.

- *TC:* Timecode. This displays the number values of your clip where it is currently located. You can display video timecode, audio timecode (normally the same in a video clip), or key code information (KC) if the clip originated from film. When doing video projects, I will usually monitor the V1 track timecode as a reference.

- *Timecode:* Shows numbers in the tracking display as timecode (i.e., 1:00:45:02).

- *Footage:* Shows numbers in the tracking display as running footage (i.e., 10008+12).

- *Frames:* Shows numbers in the tracking display as frame counts (i.e., 309).

- *None:* Displays nothing in the tracking info display.

Extracting   ✂

One of the great features of nonlinear editing is the ability to quickly remove unneeded or wanted segments from a sequence. In the case of Xpress Pro and other Avid products, there are two methods.

The first method, Extracting, works much like the opposite of splicing. When you extract material from a sequence, you remove it, joining the media on either side of it together. Keep in mind that when you extract material, the sequence will shorten by the duration of the material that is extracted. Again, like splicing, extracting works like film. If you were to remove a piece of film from a sequence, it would become shorter.

The Extract button, which looks like a pair of scissors, is mapped onto your default keyboard, but it is not on the default on-screen interface, so for now, we'll use the keyboard. Refer to Chapter 2, "Settings," to see how to map the Extract button to your on-screen interface.

The location of the Extract button is easy to remember on the Xpress Pro keyboard. It is the letter X, as in "X-tract."

First, select a section of the sequence that you want to be removed. Just mark an IN point and an OUT point in the sequence, then select the tracks that you want removed in the Timeline. Once you've done that, press the X button on the keyboard.

The material is extracted, shortening your sequence and joining the material before the Mark In with the material that was after the Mark Out. As with the Splice button, the Extract button has the potential to introduce sync problems, since the only change in the length of the sequence occurs on the tracks that were selected.

Lifting   ⬆

The second method of removing material from a sequence is Lifting. Lifting allows the material to be removed from the sequence without changing the duration of the sequence. When you lift material out of a sequence, filler or a "black hole" is put in its place. Therefore, when lifting, the Timeline will not shift. This is especially convenient for removing unwanted audio that will need to be filled with other material or pulling out a single shot that can be replaced with another shot. Using the Lift function is similar to removing items from a master videotape. The length of the tape will remain the same, but the item will be erased.

The Lift button on your default keyboard is the Z key. To lift, mark an IN point and an OUT point on your sequence, select the tracks that you want lifted in the Timeline, and then press the Z key.

The material is lifted from the sequence and filler is inserted in its place, maintaining the length of the sequence and the sync of all tracks.

Extract versus Lift

Let's take a moment to discuss reasons why you would want to use Lift and Extract and the advantages of each. Here is an example:

You're editing a corporate piece for ABCD, Inc. It talks about a revolutionary new product called the Kruxmeyer Capacitor. The Kruxmeyer Capacitor uses new technology from EFGH, Inc., which has supplied ABCD with a Holtzenjammer Cog. Are ya with me so far?

Somewhere along the line, ABCD discovers that EFGH has been stretching the truth a little, and the Holtzenjammer Cog isn't quite up to spec. The zinger is that you've already edited the piece about the Kruxmeyer Capacitor, with information about the Holtzenjammer Cog included.

Fortunately for everyone, the IJKL Corp has developed an item similar to the Holtzenjammer Cog, which they call the Capable Cog, or C2. Your job is to insert new narration and pictures into the piece, replacing all that stuff about Holtzenjammer.

How would you do it?

The fastest way would be to mark the sections of info about the Holtzenjammer and extract them. Then insert the new pics and narration for the C2 by splicing them in, making sure that the narration and pics were of the same length so that your sequence doesn't go out of sync. While it's true that in theory you could lift these sections out and replace them by overwriting the new material, you need to be realistic. The narration for a product called C2 will almost inevitably be shorter than for a similar product called a Holtzenjammer. It's harder to fit things this way, and with nonlinear technology at your fingertips, this sort of fitting-to-fill method is unnecessary and tiresome.

But let's take the same scenario with one major change. It seems that EFGH actually improved the Holtzenjammer. As a result, all you have to do is replace the old Holtzenjammer video with new pictures. The pictures are coming tomorrow, but the ABCD execs want to see the video today. Keeping the old pictures will create a ruckus among the suits, so you don't want to show them these pictures. But the narration is fine, and all you have to do is put up a title that says "New Pix Come Tomorrow." For some companies, this could mean the difference between seeing nods of approval versus the editing equivalent of an "I Love Lucy" skit.

How do you do it?

The best way would be to lift the old pictures, keeping everything in sync and the narration intact. You can add a title, or if you prefer, explain it during the screening. Either way, the material minus the new pictures would be intact.

As you become more accustomed to editing with Xpress Pro, you will increase your ability to determine which method—lift or extract—works best for each specific purpose.

Adding Filler

Once you've made a few edits, you might want to add some filler at the beginning of your sequence. Before you do this, you may want to set a default duration for your filler.

1. Go to your Project window and select the Settings tab.
2. In the Settings tab, double-click on the Timeline Settings.
3. In the Timeline menu, click on the Edit tab and type in the duration for Filler.

Once you've set the filler duration, you can add filler to the start of the sequence. To do this, right-click/Option-click anywhere on the Timeline and select Add Filler at Start (see Figure 5.12).

Adding Filler Anywhere in Your Sequence

In some cases, you may want to add filler in the middle of a sequence, for example, if you fade between scenes and want to give it an extra beat, or if you have segments of a pro-

5.11 Filler Settings

5.12 Contextual Add Filler At Start TL Menu

gram where a duration of black needs to be inserted for commercials. In cases such as these, Add Filler is useful. To add filler anywhere in a sequence, choose Select Clip>Load Filler.

A 2-minute piece of filler loads into your source monitor. From there, you can make your marks and splice or overwrite it into your sequence in the same way that any other source clip is used.

Undo and Redo

Previously we defined the Xpress Pro and other nonlinear systems as proactive. They also have the ability to undo any mistakes made along the way. With Xpress Pro, you have the ability to undo as many as 32 tasks. For example, assume that your extraction of material was a mistake. To undo, press Ctrl+Z/ Cmd+ Z. By pressing these two buttons, the last task that you executed is undone. In the case of an extraction, the material is restored in the sequence as if it were never extracted.

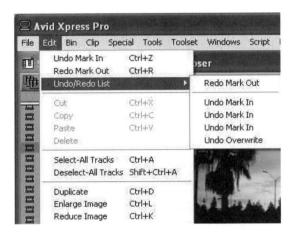

Now, for sake of example, we'll pretend that you actually *did* intend to extract the material and that *undoing* it was a mistake. In this case, you want the system to redo what was undone. To redo, press Ctrl+R/Cmd+R. The material is again extracted as it was previously.

To view the list of tasks that were undone and redone, go to the menu and select Edit> Undo/Redo List. The tasks are displayed. Note that the Redos are listed first, with a line between them and the Undo list.

 Undoing and Redoing from the List: Note that when using Undo and Redo from the list, the list or "buffer stack" is like a house of cards. You cannot undo a single item that was done several tasks ago without undoing all the tasks done after it. Therefore, when you recognize that a mistake has been made, undo it or redo it immediately.

A Word about Commands and Settings

As we continue our exploration of the Xpress Pro interface, it is important to remember that Avid interfaces were built not for a single editing style, but for many. In other words, you're going to find more than one way to do the exact same thing through keystrokes, menu commands, and peripheral controls.

As a result, some people think that Avid interfaces are harder to learn. Nothing could be farther from the truth. The difference to keep in mind is that one way of performing a function may seem unnecessary to you, while another editor may deem it absolutely imperative. As a result, some editors who are new to Avid systems might find themselves overwhelmed with options. Which one is right for me? Only experience will tell you. In only a few cases is there a better way to perform any one function.

Other nonlinear editing systems may appear to be easier to operate because there are fewer methods for performing a function. While this can hold true during initial learning stages, it later proves frustrating to the experienced editor.

Advanced Navigation

Now that you've done some edits, lifts, extractions, and undos, let's take a look at some of the better ways to navigate through media.

Jogging and Moving

If you're the type of person who likes to jog forward and backward through your media frame by frame, jogging is easy. There are several ways to jog (see Table 5.1).

Table 5.1   Jogging

	Right and Left Arrow Keys: Use the right and left arrow keys on your keyboard. First, click on the material that you want to jog through in the Source or Record Monitor, then press the left arrow to go backward and the right arrow to go forward. For each press of the button, the media moves one frame.
	Step Backward One Frame: This key moves the media backward a single frame for each keystroke. You can hold down the key to repeat the action several times, but be careful— it will take time to catch up with your commands.
	Step Forward One Frame: This key moves media forward by a single frame. Again, for each press of the button, it moves one frame and you can hold down the key to repeat the action.
	Step Backward 10 Frames. This key steps the media backward 10 frames for every keystroke. If you hold the button down, it will continuously step back through the media in 10 frame iterations.

Table 5.1   Jogging (Continued)

 Step Forward 10 Frames: This key steps the media forward 10 frames for every keystroke. If you hold the button down, it will continuously step through the media in 10 frame iterations.

 Go To In: Moves the position indicator to the marked IN point of the media.

 Go To Out: Moves the position indicator to the marked OUT point of the media.

 Go To Audio Mark In: Moves the position indicator to the marked audio IN point of the media.

 Go To Audio Mark Out: Moves the position indicator to the marked audio OUT point of the media.

 Go To Start: Moves the position indicator to the first frame of the sequence or source media.

 Go To End: Moves the position indicator to the last frame of the sequence or source media.

 Go To Previous Edit: Moves to the previous transition from the location of the blue position indicator that contains the currently selected tracks in the Timeline. To move to the *nearest* previous transition regardless of track selection, use this button with the Alt/Option key.

 Go To Next Edit: Moves to the next transition from the location of the blue position indicator that contains the currently selected tracks in the Timeline. To move to the *nearest* next transition regardless of track selection, use this button with the Alt/Option key.

 Rewind: "Rewinds" to the nearest locator on the selected track. To rewind to the nearest locator regardless of selected tracks, use this button with the Alt/Option key. This key works exactly like the Go To Previous Locator key mentioned below. Note that rewind can be customized on other Avid systems, but not on Xpress Pro.

 Fast Forward: "Fast forwards" to the nearest locator on the selected track. To rewind to the nearest locator regardless of selected tracks, use this button with the Alt/Option key. This key works exactly like the Go To Next Locator key mentioned below. Note that fast forward can be customized on other Avid systems, but not on Xpress Pro.

Table 5.1   Jogging (Continued)

 Step Forward One Field: Steps the media forward by a single field. In the video world, frames are interlaced. Each scan of the monitor includes every other line of video resolution. Two of these scans, called *fields*, equal a single full-resolution frame. Stepping forward by a single field moves from one field of a frame to the next one. I use field jogging to look at problem areas of video, for example, if there is some distortion or drop-out in the picture, I will try to isolate the location of the problem by jogging through fields, then look at my original source to see if the problem exists there as well. Oftentimes the problem occurred in capturing the media, with a failure of the deck to play the video correctly. Whatever the reason for the failure, the bottom line is that if it doesn't exist on the source, you need to redigitize.

 Step Backward One Field: Steps the media backward by a single field.

 Go To Previous Locator: Moves the position indicator to the previous locator.

 Go To Next Locator: Moves the position indicator to the next locator.

JKL: The Media Movement Kings

At this point, you're probably wondering where the shuttle knob is on Xpress Pro. With all of the marvels and innovations of nonlinear technology, did Avid forget to put a shuttle knob on its latest system? The answer is yes...and no.

Over the years, Avid has tried a number of outboard peripheral shuttles with varying degrees of success. First there was the Multi-User Interface, or MUI. Then came the Steenbeck controller, designed by Steenbeck. This was followed by the Avid Droid. Now there are jog shuttle controllers that use MIDI which can control Xpress Pro. There are also jog/shuttle controllers that use the USB bus, much like a glorified mouse.

So far, none has emerged as the best system for media control. They all have (or in some cases, *had*) various advantages and disadvantages, but none has overwhelmed the consensus of editors.

Why not?

Because Avid has a method of shuttling built into the keyboard itself. This method uses the J, K, and L keys. The JKLs are used in various combinations to play, rewind, fast forward, jog, and slow motion through media. For those who have edited film, the JKLs operate much like the KEM flatbed editing systems.

If you look at your keyboard preferences, you will notice that the J key is a reverse play button, the K key is a pause key, and the L key is a play key. Note the differences between the L key and the 5 and tilde (~) keys? The L key is a play key with a notch in the back. The same is true for the J key, only it is reversed. This signifies that both the J and L keys have other functions, as we will see.

If you press the L key once, it will play back the media at normal speed. If you hit it again while media is playing, the media plays back at double speed. And for each consecutive keystroke, the media speeds up until it reaches 8× normal play speed. Audio will continue to play back at high speed through 3× speed before it mutes.

The same is true for the J key. Press it once, and the media plays backward at speed. Press it again, and the backward speed doubles. For each consecutive keystroke, the speed increases until it reaches 8× backward speed. There is a new JKL ratcheting feature in Xpress Pro 4.6.

The K key, when pressed, pauses the media.

The use of the JKLs in combination produces even more methods of media movement. When J and K are pressed and held at the same time, the media moves backward at 1/4 normal speed. When K and L are pressed together, the media moves forward at 1/4 speed. If you hold three fingers over the JKLs and practice a little, you can rock and roll through an edit, analyzing it for continuity, eyeline, or any other number of reasons.

If the K key is held down and the J key is tapped, the media jogs one frame backward. If the K key is held down and the L key is tapped, the media jogs one frame forward. So you can see that the combination of keystrokes with JKLs produces a number of desired methods of playing, analyzing, and jogging through media. These variations are even greater with the new JKL ratcheting feature implemented in Xpress Pro 4.6.

Marks and Movement

So far we've shown you how to create marks. Let's take a moment to show you how you can delete them and play only marked media (see Table 5.2).

Table 5.2   Marks and Movement

▐▌	*Clear In Mark:* This button clears your Mark In.
▐▌	*Clear Out Mark:* This button clears your Mark Out.
▐▐▌	*Clear Both Marks:* This will remove both IN and OUT marks on the selected side (Source or Record).

Table 5.2 Marks and Movement (Continued)

 Mark Clip: This is definitely a handy button. It will mark a clip in its entirety. If you use it on the Source side for a clip, it marks IN at the first frame and OUT at the last frame. If used in a sequence, it will mark a clip based upon which tracks are selected in the Timeline. (Track selection is discussed in full in Chapter 6 "The Timeline" on page 165.) No need to search for beginning and end frames of a shot in the sequence. Just choose the tracks you want to mark and press this button. I use it primarily for removing or moving clips around in the Timeline.

 Play In to Out: This will play the media from your Mark In to your Mark Out. If clicked with Alt/Option, it will play the media in a continuous loop until it is stopped.

 Play to Out: Plays back the media from your current location to the Mark Out point.

Editing by the Numbers

As you can see from the examples above, Avid systems have all kinds of ways for navigating through media, but one rarely escapes the need to occasionally use precise numbers.

You can navigate at any time using numbers. With the Source window highlighted, type in a number with a + or – symbol and the media will move forward or backward that many frames. When you type in numbers of 100 frames and beyond, the system will assume that you are referring to seconds and frames. In other words, an entry of 100 is seen as 1:00, or one second. If you intend to type numbers of frames rather than seconds and frames, type a lower case *f* after the numeric entry and the system will recognize your command as a frame count, not a seconds and frames command.

 Warning If this technique does not seem to work, it is possible that there is no tracking information (timecode info) above the Source or Sequence Monitor. Moving forward or backward by set numbers, or jumping to specific timecodes is only possible if you have tracking information available.

Any number typed into the numeric keypad is stored in a cache. If you want to use the same number again, you don't have to type anything. Just hit the Enter key. So if you want to move forward +5 frames numerous times, just type "+5" then Enter once. Then each subsequent occasion where you want to move forward five frames, just hit Enter.

Direct Timecode Entry

Many times editors work with timecode notes or with an associate director, a director or producer who gives out timecode information for specific cue points. You can enter timecode numbers to navigate to specific points.

1. Make sure that your tracking menu is set to Timecode so that the numbers entered will be followed correctly.

2. Enter the timecode number. Don't worry about the colons or semicolons. The system will enter them for you. Typically, producers and directors call out timecodes only down to the accuracy of the nearest second. If so, you need to add two zeroes to the end of the number to indicate the frames. For example, if someone says, "Please go to one hour, 17 minutes, 45 seconds," you should type 1174500.

While leading zeroes are not necessary, you do have to enter the proper frame numbers. Instead of always typing "00" to go to an even second, you can type a period at any point. So if you want to go to "01:00:00:00" you can type "1. . . ."

3. Press enter, and the system will navigate to that timecode.

4. You can always verify that the system did indeed go to the right spot by checking the location in the Tracking menu.

Timecode Short Cuts: An editor only has so many keystrokes in him or her before it is time to retire. You never have to enter any leading zeroes when typing in timecode numbers. For example, if you want to go to 00:00:02:05, enter 205. The system understands that there are zeroes at the front of this entry and there is no need to type them. You can also shortcut through redundant numbers. For example, if you are parked at 03:05:22:23 and want to go to 03:05:31:03, simply type in 3103. The system assumes that you will be remaining at hour 3, minute 5, and moves to 31 seconds and 3 frames without delay.

Chapter 6

The Timeline

The original Avid Timeline was just a chronological graphical display of your sequence. Trimming was accomplished through the use of the editing interface. There were no methods for juxtaposing shots or replacing shots through the Timeline. You could not digitize directly to the Timeline. You could not drag clips directly from the bins to the Timeline. You could not nest effects or autonest. You might not know what any of these terms mean, and they will be explained in other parts of the book, but suffice it to say that now the Timeline does all of that and more. In fact, you can use the Timeline as an editing interface without even using the Source/Record interface described in the previous chapter.

With Xpress Pro, the Timeline takes on an even greater level of maturity with the addition of audio metering and increased interface options. But before going into these new methods, let's learn to navigate through our sequence using the Timeline.

6.1   The Xpress Pro Timeline

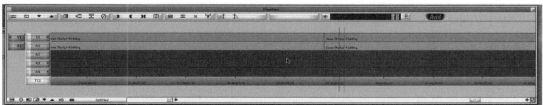

TIMELINE NAVIGATION

Xpress Pro contains several methods to navigate the Timeline. In this section, we will take a look at these different methods and their capabilities.

The Position Indicator

The blue position indicator (often referred to as the Timeline locator or "playhead" in similar applications) allows you to drag or click in the Timeline to navigate to a specific point. When navigating the Timeline to a specific point, there is no need to drag the position indicator across the Timeline. Just click on the desired Timeline destination and the position indicator will update its position. Dragging the position indicator is a good way to view contents and "roll over" your cut to inspect edits. As you move the position indicator across the Timeline interface, Xpress Pro updates the picture in the Record Monitor.

Timeline Scroll

The Timeline Scroll bar at bottom right is like any other scroll bar. Scrolling forward will move the expanded Timeline forward in the sequence. Moving it backward will move it backward to previous portions of the sequence. Although the scroll bar may seem redundant to the Timeline, it can be especially useful when skipping over large portions of your sequence, especially when the Timeline is expanded and only a small portion of the sequence is visible.

Timeline Scale Bar

The Timeline Scale bar was first introduced with the Avid MCXpress system many years ago. When presented with this option, editors were told that it would be available only on lower-end systems. We protested, "We *like* it!" and it was added to every system in the Avid line. The scale bar allows you to expand and contract the Timeline with a simple click and drag motion.

Scaling the Timeline with the Keyboard

You can also use the keyboard to expand, contract, and focus on areas of the Timeline. Ctrl+[/Cmd+[will contract, Ctrl+]/Cmd+] will expand, and Ctrl+/ or Cmd+/ will show the entire sequence.

Timeline Movement Controls

Certain modifiers can be used when dragging through the Timeline to advance in specific increments. These modifiers can also be used for moving clips using Timeline editing, which we'll cover later in this chapter on page 185.

- *Snap to Head Frames:* To snap to the head frame of the next transition, Ctrl-click/ Cmd-click and drag the mouse. The position indicator snaps to each first frame of each edit on the selected track(s).

- *Snap To Tail Frames:* To snap to the last frame of each segment, press Ctrl+Alt-click/Cmd+Option-click and drag the mouse. The position indicator will snap to the tail frame of each edit on the selected track(s). This is useful if you want to mark an edit that includes the last frame of a segment, but doesn't include the first frame of the next segment.

- *Frame by Frame:* To move in single frame increments, hold down the Alt/Option key and drag through the Timeline. The system will slowly jog in increments as small as a single frame.

A TOUR OF THE TIMELINE

Starting at the top of the Timeline, you'll see a toolbar, a Speaker icon for monitoring audio, an Audio meter, an Audio menu, a Real-Time button, and the Avid Logo.

The Toolbar

The toolbar in the Timeline is used for placing additional function buttons used for editing. Not every editor likes this many buttons on the interface, and the Toolbar can be turned off by going to the Project window, selecting Timeline, and deselecting Show Toolbar.

All of the default function buttons in the Toolbar relate to the use of the Timeline or different editing modes. Some of the buttons are Timeline-specific and are only used in the Timeline. Buttons used for editing modes and effects will be discussed in later chapters.

Monitor (Speaker) Icon

The Speaker icon in the Timeline allows you to monitor or mute input or output sound. If you click and hold on the Speaker icon, a volume slider will appear. You can use this to adjust the monitor volume in the room, but it will not affect output from Xpress Pro.

Audio Meters

The Audio meters in the Timeline make it convenient for you to monitor sound coming in to the system during capture or to monitor sound going out during playback and/or digital cut. The meters are used in conjunction with the Audio menu to the right. The icons to the right of each track can be switched from I (input) to O (output) with the click of a mouse.

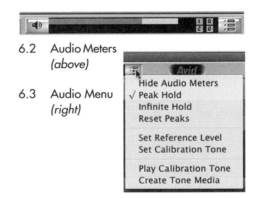

6.2   Audio Meters
(above)

6.3   Audio Menu
(right)

Audio Menu

The Timeline Audio menu controls the function of the meters. You have a number of options on this menu. Many of these options are also discussed in Chapter 8 "Audio" on page 217. Let's take a look at those options.

- *Hide Audio Meters* will clear the Audio meters from the Timeline toolbar and add four new icons. If you're not particularly interested in the Audio meters but need the extra functionality, this is the way to get it. The four icons can be mapped with functions from the Control Palette or the menus. However, we are firm believers that to be a better editor—not just a faster editor—you should be using the keyboard as your primary interface with the Avid, not the buttons on the screen, so we'd suggest leaving the Audio meters if you bother with the toolbar at all.

- *Peak Hold* displays audio peaks and holds them long enough for you to notice if the audio has exceeded peaks. The best reason to use Peak Hold is this: if the audio fluctuates wildly, you might not notice if it has exceeded its peak. When the peak is held, the Audio meters denote it by showing you the highest or "hottest" level. As audio continues through the meters, other levels will also show, but the peak will hold and stay for a short duration so that you can monitor the audio for higher peaks and avoid distorted audio input and output.

- *Infinite Hold* allows you to hold the peak until the peaks are specifically and intentionally cleared. This is a great setting for digitizing. If you're doing an offline and step away from Xpress Pro during a batch-digitize session, you can return and see whether the peaks were exceeded. If so, then you'll have to redo the clips that have hot audio, so using this tool provides you with peace of mind.

- *Reset Peaks* will release the Infinite Hold peak levels. If you use Infinite Peaks, it is a good thing to reset this often, so that you know which peak level pertains to your current clip.

- *Set Reference Level* allows you to set the standard for reference audio. Different facilities use different standards. For example, –14dB is a standard used by many postproduction facilities, but others use –20dB. Why the difference? Headroom. Digital audio that reaches 0dB will distort. As a result, when setting your input reference level, you will have to determine which works best. If you're preparing a tape for broadcast, it's best to check with the broadcaster and ask about their standard level. The same holds true for an audio mix facility. The problem frequently encountered with footage is that, if hotter levels occur that go beyond your reference point, you'll need the headroom to maintain fidelity of the audio. If you need more headroom, setting the level at –20dB is best. If you need less headroom, –14dB is acceptable.

- *Set Calibration Tone* allows you not only to adjust the level of tone on your system, but also to set the tone frequency. For most projects, the tone is set at 1000Hz (1kHz). But some audio facilities ask you to use different levels so that they can monitor your audio at different frequencies. Again it is best to check with the audio facility or broadcasters first.

- *Play Calibration Tone* will play back the calibration tone as you have set it and will allow you to monitor it on your meters.

- *Create Tone* will create a media file and a clip for your reference tone as set. If you intend to use tone at several different frequencies, you will need to create a media file and clip for each frequency. You can also create different tones for different audio sample rates.

Warning

Perhaps you're thinking that this creation of tone media is a waste of time. Please reconsider. Without reference tone, no one can set up the audio and optimize playback of your sequence. This would be akin to sending a black-and-white picture to a photo processor and saying, "make it color." You cannot guarantee audio fidelity without some sort of reference. References such as tone and color bars allow us to properly calibrate playback and monitoring devices. When in doubt, be professional. There is not a television program in existence that doesn't use some sort of reference. Even some DVDs use color bars and tone for set up.

Toggle Digital Video Out (Non-Mojo Systems Only)

Next to the Audio meters is a small button icon. Depending on how you've set up your system, it's either blue or green. Note that when you click on it, it changes from one color to another.

Cool, huh?

Upon further inspection, you will note that the green mode has an outer glow or "aura" to it. That's because the green mode of Digital Video Out allows for the playback of Real-Time Effects.

Real-Time Effects are discussed in detail in Chapter 9 "Effects" on page 245, but it should be mentioned here that this is a major capability and feature of Xpress Pro. The playback of Real-Time Effects prevents you from having to stop editing to render an effect. Rendering is the process of creating a digital file for something that you have built, or composited, using one or more effects.

To help, Xpress Pro allows you to play back these effects in real time if the green mode button is displayed. If the blue button is displayed, the Real Time mode is turned off. But you can use a client monitor on your system if blue mode is selected. Otherwise, the system will not display in an NTSC monitor. However, it should be noted that only DV video can be played through a client monitor. In other words, 15:1s media cannot be displayed on the monitor, but it will play back on the Xpress Pro interface.

When the optional Mojo is connected, 1:1 video can play back and be displayed on an external monitor. The Toggle Digital Video Out button does not appear on the interface at all when Mojo is connected. Without Mojo, 1:1 (uncompressed) video playback is not supported.

Now that we've taken a look at the top row of buttons, let's swing down to the Track Selector panel, where we will see an incredible amount of versatility and flexibility in a very small space.

The Track Selector Panel

The Track Selector panel is deceiving. On the surface, it appears to be a simple panel for patching and editing tracks. But over the years, Avid has added additional controls that make for an elegant yet versatile tool.

The Track Selector panel is used to select, delete, lock, manipulate, patch, monitor, and maintain sync with all of the different tracks that you create and use.

Adding Video and Audio Tracks

As you continue making edits, there will be need for more audio and video tracks. Video tracks usually are reserved for effects. Audio tracks can be added for music, sound effects, narration, and so forth. To add an audio track, press Ctrl+U/Cmd+U. To add a video track, press Ctrl+Y/Cmd+Y.

There are other ways to create tracks as well. To create a new video or audio track, you can right-click/Shift+Cmd-click in the Timeline and select New Video Track or New Audio Track. Additionally, you could also select Clip>New Video Track in the menus (see Figure 6.4).

6.4   Timeline Contextual Menu—Creating New Tracks

 Adding Tracks: Normally when adding tracks, Xpress Pro goes in order. For example, if you already have A1 and A2 in your sequence, the next track to be added would be A3. But what if you have already designed assignments for the tracks and want to make an edit on A6? One option would be to continue adding tracks until A6 was reached, but this makes for an unnecessary amount of space in the Timeline. If you want to add a higher track by name, Alt-click/Option-click the Clip menu and select New Audio Track. A menu will appear where you can select the name of the new track. It's easier than managing empty tracks in your Timeline and it takes up a lot less space.

With Avid Xpress Pro, you can use up to 24 video tracks and 24 audio tracks. For average-sized projects, this is usually enough, but there are also other tools that allow you to expand the existing tracks, such as audio and video mixdowns.

Deleting Tracks

To delete existing tracks of a sequence:

1. Select the tracks that you wish to delete on the right side of the Track Selector panel.

2. Make *sure* you want to do this—consider the consequences. Okay, you can always undo (Ctrl+Z/Cmd+Z), so it's not that big of a deal.

3. Take a deep breath and press Delete. The tracks disappear, along with everything on them.

The Track Selector Panel Buttons

The Track Selector panel consists of Source and Record Track Monitor buttons, Source and Record Track activation buttons, Sync Lock and Lock Track buttons, Timecode button, Sync Lock All Tracks button, Video Track Monitor button with Monitor icon, and Audio Track Monitor buttons with black or gold speaker icon.

The Track Selector Panel Sides

There are two sides to the Track Selector panel.

The source side of the panel displays only those tracks available for the clip that is currently loaded. For instance, if you loaded a clip that was digitized with video only, only the V1 track would appear on the source side of the panel. A clip with Audio on channel 1 only would appear as A1 on the source side.

When you create a new sequence, V1, A1, A2, A3, and A4 tracks are created automatically on the *record side* of the Track Selector panel for the sequence. When you add more tracks, they appear on the record side of the Track Selector panel. Even if you "create" a new sequence by making an edit to a blank record monitor, V1, A1, A2, A3, and A4 tracks are created automatically on the *record side*. I mention this only because I tend not to use the New Sequence command when creating a new sequence.

Track Selection Rules

To understand exactly how the Track Selector panel works, there are specific rules. At first inspection, these guidelines may seem tedious, but they save you lots of time and energy. These three rules are very simple.

You cannot edit deselected tracks from the source side into the sequence, regardless of what is selected on the record side of the Track Selector panel. In other words, if you do not select a track from your source, it will not be edited into the sequence. Simple, huh? You'd be surprised how many times this happens. Select the source tracks so that they are highlighted (purple on the Track Selector panel) and you can edit them in. If you deselect the tracks (where the Track Name icons in the selector are gray), they won't go in the sequence.

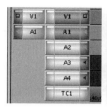

6.5   Deselected Tracks on Source= No Go

6.6   Deselected Tracks on Record= No Go

The second rule is complementary to the first one. You cannot edit deselected tracks on the record side into the sequence, regardless of the tracks you select on the source side of the Track Selector panel. In other words, if the "input" to the sequence (the Record panel selector) is turned off, nothing will go into the sequence.

6.7   Uff Da— Tracks misaligned

You must "patch" the selected tracks so that they are in line with each other. Unless the selected tracks are patched to the same track, they will not edit into the sequence.

Track Selection Methods

There are many ways to select tracks. Like most Xpress Pro functions, the fastest way is through the keyboard. The standard keyboard has selectors for Video tracks 1–2 and Audio tracks 1–4. Pressing Shift with these keys will select Video 3–4 and Audio 5–8. However, it is important to remember that the track cannot be selected unless it is created first.

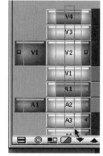

6.8   Lassoing Tracks on and off

The Track buttons on the panel selector toggle on and off. You can click the Track button of any inactive track with your mouse to select it. (To deselect the track, click the Track button of any active track.)

If you're selecting multiple tracks, you can lasso them with the mouse. Drag a lasso around the tracks you want to select. Don't forget that the Track buttons toggle on and off, so any selected tracks become deselected and any unselected tracks become selected.

You can also use Xpress Pro's menus.

1. With the Timeline window active, select Edit > Select-All Tracks to select all tracks on the record and source sides.

2. Click the Cycle Picture/Sound button in the Edit tab of the Command Palette to cycle among selected video tracks, audio tracks, and all tracks.

3. With the Timeline active, press Ctrl+A/Cmd+A to select all tracks. Press Shift+Ctrl+/Shift+Cmd++A to deselect all tracks.

> Some of the fastest methods for selecting and deselecting tracks take advantage of combinations of these methods. For example, if you have several random tracks selected and you want to only have V1 selected, then use the keyboard shortcut to deselect all tracks, then hit the V1 button.

As you can see, there are a great many ways to select and deselect tracks. Avid designed the system to suit a number of editing styles. Some editors are clickers, some are button pushers, some like to lasso, and so on. As a result, there are a great many ways to do some of the most common functions on the interface.

Track Patching

When you work with multiple tracks and sources, there will be occasions when you will need to patch from the source to a track in the sequence that is not parallel to those tracks. For example, if you decide to put all graphics on V2 of your Timeline, the imported graphics will appear as a V1 source and the resulting clips will be placed parallel to V1 of the record side of the Timeline. In order to patch the V1 source to V2 of the Timeline, you must create a new V2 track (assuming one hasn't already been created) and patch V1 of source to the new V2 record track.

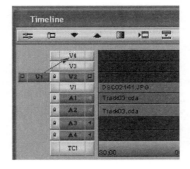

Here's how you patch it: once the track is created, click on the V1 track selector of the source and drag your mouse over to the V2 track on the record side of the track selector.

Notice the little gray arrow that points to your target track? This shows that you intend to make the patch. When you release the mouse, the V1 source track moves parallel to the V2 record track. The patch is complete.

To patch the track back, simply click on the V1 of the source and point it back toward V1 of the record side.

While attempting to patch, if you were hesitant before dragging the mouse, you may have noticed that a pulldown menu appears with all of the available tracks for patching. This is another way to patch without dragging the mouse. For example, if you just click and hold on the V1 track of the source, a menu will pop up with the two available tracks, V1 and V2. Choose the correct track in the menu and it will make the patch. Keep in mind that if there is only one video track present on the record side, the only option that will appear in the pulldown will be V1.

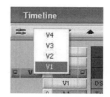

Track Monitoring

Now that you know how to select and patch tracks, let's discuss track monitoring. The track monitoring features of Xpress Pro allow you to choose and isolate specific tracks that you want to see and hear.

Track monitoring selections are made in the monitoring column. This column is located on the right of each track on the record Track Selector panel and on the left of the source Track Selector panel.

To activate or deactivate the Audio and Video monitors on the source or record sides, click on the Monitor column next to the desired track. Each type of track, video or audio, has distinct monitoring characteristics.

Video Monitoring

The video monitoring on Xpress Pro works vertically from the top down. For example, if you choose to monitor V2 (video track 2) but there is nothing on V2, the monitor reads whatever is beneath on V1. In other words, you can only monitor one track at a time, but if there is nothing on that track, it will read the track below.

Normally when monitoring video, it would seem wise to choose the topmost track so that you could see the end results of your sequence. However, in some cases, you may not want to monitor all of the tracks. When viewing a sequence, for example, you may want to disable playback of graphics on V2.

You might want to turn off video monitoring altogether. This is useful for mixing audio. To turn off video monitoring for your sequence, click on the monitor in the Monitor column next to your video track on the record side. The record monitor turns black. You can do the same thing on your source monitor. Load a clip with video into the Source Monitor and click on the Monitor column to the left of the Track Selector button. The Source Monitor turns black. To turn the monitoring back on, click on the Monitoring button again. The icon in the column and the video in the monitor will reappear.

You can also "solo" or isolate individual video tracks. There are a number of reasons to do this. If you have a multiple track effects sequence, for example, soloing tracks allows you to isolate problems from within an effect. You can also use this feature to play back only certain elements of a sequence. For example, if you built your sequence on V1 and placed all of your graphics on V2, you could solo V2 to check the graphics without the V1 backgrounds. To solo video tracks, Ctrl-click/Cmd-click the Monitor icon on the track. The Monitor column icon should turn green. To deselect track soloing, click the icon twice. On the first click, the icon completely disappears and the Monitor turns black. On the second click, the Monitor returns to its normal track monitoring state. You can also Ctrl-click/Cmd-click the Solo icon to return to the normal state.

Audio Monitoring

With Xpress Pro, you have the capability of monitoring all of your tracks at the same time, but you can also scrub tracks and solo them as well. This added versatility gives the editor better ability to refine audio edits. For example, suppose you edited a scene with multiple tracks that will be later mixed together. Somewhere along the line, you notice during playback that there is some noise or other unwanted audio in your sequence. You might not be able to tell which track has the bad audio. In this case, you can solo tracks to isolate the problem area, then remove it.

Before monitoring audio tracks, you might need to adjust your pan settings so that both tracks are center panned. By default, Xpress Pro pans odd numbered tracks to the left and even numbered tracks to the right. If you want to change this, you can choose All Tracks Centered from the Audio preferences in the Project Settings window.

Audio monitoring is somewhat similar to video monitoring. You can turn individual tracks on and off by clicking on the monitor icon (the speaker icon) next to the track. The monitors for the source track are located to the left of the track buttons and the monitors for the record side are located to the right. Click once to turn monitoring off. Click again to turn it back on.

Like the Video Monitoring tool, you can choose individual audio tracks for soloing, but with audio, you can solo out as many tracks as you like. The selection procedure for soloing audio tracks is the same as for video tracks: Ctrl-click/Cmd-click the Monitor icon. The Monitor icon turns bright green. At this point, when the sequence is played back, only the solo tracks will be audible. Again, to deselect, click the Monitor icon twice or Ctrl-click/Cmd-click it once to return to a normal Monitoring mode.

Perhaps you're wondering what the difference is between soloing a single track versus just turning all of the other track monitoring off. The answer is: nothing. But soloing can reduce the amount of mouse clicks that it takes to turn off the other tracks. And if you're working with 24 tracks of sound, that's a lot of mouse clicks.

Xpress Pro audio can also be "scrubbed" or sampled as it is jogged through. This term *scrubbing* comes from the old days of audio, when a tape was jockeyed back and forth to listen for a specific cue. When doing this, the audio engineer was said to be scrubbing the audio heads. Xpress Pro has a digital equivalent of this method.

Before determining which audio tracks will be scrubbed, you'll need to activate audio scrubbing. To do this, turn the Caps Lock on your keyboard. To turn scrubbing off, turn Caps Lock off. Most keyboards have an LED indicator that tells you whether this function is enabled.

There are two different types of scrubbing on the Xpress Pro. Digital scrubbing is what occurs when the position indicator is dragged across the Timeline or the media is jogged through with the Caps Lock on. Digital scrubbing has a distinctly digital sound to it and plays back precise frames, specifically determined by your settings. Analog (also called smooth) scrubbing will be discussed in Chapter 8 "Audio" on page 217. The Track Monitoring column selects tracks that will be digitally scrubbed.

When a new sequence is created, there are four audio channels on the record side of the Track Selector panel. Note that two of the icons in the monitoring column are gold (A1 and A2, the lighter ones) and two are black (A3 and A4). The gold icons indicate the tracks that are enabled for digital scrubbing. Only two tracks can be scrubbed at a time, so the first two tracks are selected by default. Let's enable scrubbing on A3. To do this, Alt-click/Option-click on the A3 monitoring icon. It turns gold. The
A1 monitoring icon turns black, due to the fact that you can only scrub two tracks. Now you can scrub on A2 and A3.

Here's a handy thing to remember. When you select a new track to scrub, the system will deselect the first scrub-enabled track in order to allow for two scrubbed tracks. In the case of new sequences, A1 will be selected.

 RAM Munching: Digital Audio scrub can be a very useful tool, but it is also a RAM eater. If you find your system is running sluggishly and could use a little more responsiveness, turn the audio scrub off by deselecting the Caps Lock key. Normally the difference will be significant. Likewise, with effects-intensive sequences, you may find the audio scrubbing more sluggish than desired. To improve the effectiveness of scrubbing, bring your video monitoring down to a lower track to avoid on-the-fly rendering of complex effects as you jog through the Timeline. This will increase RAM to be used for scrubbing and improve responsiveness of the system.

Locking and Unlocking Tracks

If you've been editing on digital nonlinear systems before, you probably understand the value of locking and unlocking tracks of your sequence. The number of mix-ups that can occur boggles the mind. As a result, Xpress Pro has a method for locking and unlocking tracks.

To lock tracks, select the tracks in the Track Selector panel that you want to lock. Right-click/Ctrl+Shift-click anywhere in the Timeline. The Timeline Options menu will appear. Select Lock Track. A tiny padlock should appear in the box to the left of each selected track in your sequence.

Once Lock Tracks is selected, no further editing can occur on the selected track(s). To unlock the tracks, select them in the Track Selector panel, Right-click/Ctrl+Shift-click the mouse in the Timeline and select Unlock tracks. The padlock icon goes away and the selected tracks are unlocked.

Keep in mind that locked tracks will prevent any kind of editing, including segment editing, which will be discussed later in this chapter on page 185.

CUSTOMIZING THE TIMELINE

The Timeline displays a lot of information that can help you as you edit, and customizing how that information is displayed can make editing much more intuitive. Not only do dif-

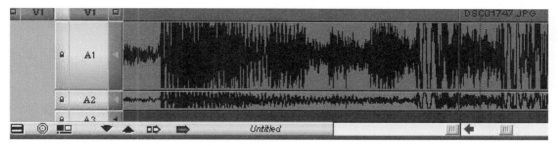

6.9   Expanded Audio Track with Waveform

ferent editors want different information, but even different projects or phases in a project require different customization of the Timeline. The key to getting the information you want is in the Timeline Fast menu.

Enlarging and Reducing Track Sizes

Enlarging and reducing the sizes of your tracks will help you in certain situations. For example, when viewing an audio sample plot, enlarging the track will provide more detail (see Figure 6.9). By enlarging and expanding an audio track, you can search for specific audio cues visually in addition to the scrubbing methods described previously.

To enlarge a track:

1. Select the track or tracks that you want enlarged.

2. Press Ctrl+L/Cmd+L.

3. The track becomes vertically larger.

4. To continue enlarging the track, continue to press Ctrl+L/Cmd+L.

Another method of enlarging a track is to move your mouse to the space in between tracks on the Track Selector panel. You will notice that the pointer switches from the standard arrow to two vertical arrows pointing up and down. Click with the mouse and drag downward. The track will enlarge.

To reduce the track:

1. Select the track(s) that you want to become reduced in vertical size.

2. Press Ctrl+K/Cmd+K.

3. The track becomes vertically reduced in size.

4. To continue reducing the track, continue pressing Ctrl+K/Cmd+K.

Reducing and Enlarging: The Keystrokes: Most keyboard options use a letter that is easy to remember. For example, to open a file is Ctrl+O/Cmd+O in most applications. To close a Window is Ctrl+W/Cmd+W. For track enlargement, think of Ctrl+L/Cmd+L as "Larger" and Ctrl+K/Cmd+K as "shrinK" or "Kibosh" (or, if you prefer, "Krunch").

If the sample plots in your Timeline are very small because the audio is faint or is so loud that you can't see the peaks of the samples because are cut off by the top of the top of the track—which is common for music imported from CDs—you can shrink or enlarge the Sample Plot without shrinking or enlarging the track itself. To do this use Ctrl+Alt+K/Cmd+Option+ K to shrink or +L to enlarge the selected tracks.

Saving and Replacing Your Timeline Views

To save your view of the Timeline, click on the current named view. If you've never saved a Timeline view before, this is usually called Untitled and is located at the bottom

middle of the Timeline window. When you click on the name, the dialog "Save as..." appears. Select it and name the view. Your display settings for the Timeline will appear every time this view is selected.

If you want to replace your existing Timeline view with a new one but keep the same name, Alt-click/Option-click the view name in the Timeline window. A list of saved views appears with "Replace" in front of each. Choose the view that you want to replace. The previously named view will be replaced with your current view of the Timeline.

Restoring Default Timeline Views

Every editor is different, and that's why there are specific user settings with Xpress Pro. In some cases, you may find the Timeline views available as unacceptable. There are enough color schemes and mismatched options that can be included to make any Timeline appear confusing. As a result, Avid placed an option in the Fast menu to restore the Default View Settings (see Figure 6.10).

To access the default Timeline view:

1. Click on the Fast (Hamburger) menu of the Timeline.

2. Select Default Setup at the top of the menu.

6.10 Timeline Fast Menu with Default Setup Selected

3. The default settings are applied.

OTHER TIMELINE FUNCTIONS

Finding Flash Frames

In some cases, you may have inadvertently placed some stray frames in your sequence. For purposes of definition, a flash frame refers to a clip that has an extremely short duration. This is as opposed to say, a clip that has a camera flash at the end of it, for example, a film clip that has a white flash at the end where an assistant checked the gate or any other longer clip where something occurred that was not intended as part of the shot.

In any case, Find Flash Frames can assist you in locating particular elements that were placed in your sequence, but need to be deleted.

To set up Find Flash Frames:

1. Go to your Project window and click on the Settings tab.

2. Double-click on the current Timeline settings

3. In the Timeline Settings menu, click on the Edit tab.

4. In Find Flash Frames less than ___ frames long, enter the maximum number of frames that you are searching for. In other words if you know that you have used edits with 20-frame durations in your sequence, you might type in the number 20 or lower, just so you can avoid hitting those edits.

5. The system will now detect flash frames of 19 frames or lower.

To use Find Flash Frames:

1. Click on the Timeline.

2. Go to the beginning of the section where you want to search for flash frames and park your position indicator there.

3. Right-click/Shift+Ctrl-click on the Timeline.

4. From this menu, select Find Flash Frames.

5. The blue position indicator moves to the first flash frames detected.

6. To continue searching for more flash frames, repeat steps 3 and 4.

Now let's look at some of the functions of the Timeline that are located to the right of the Fast menu.

Focus

The focus button is a quick way to expand the Timeline to show 100 frames on either side of the point where you are currently located. Click it once to expand so that it can show the details. The second time you click it, it will return to the previous view.

Video Quality

The Video Quality button chooses a specific quality of video to display as the sequence is played back. Video Quality is only available when real time is selected via the green button on the top of the Timeline next to the Avid logo. If the button is blue, select it and the Video Quality icon will appear. This button will allow you to choose system performance or picture quality as the priority. There are four settings for Video Quality, shown in Table 6.1.

Table 6.1   Video Quality settings

	Full Quality (Green on Green) is available only with the optional Mojo interface. Full quality always shows the best frame possible during playback.
	Best Quality (Yellow on Green; called "Draft Quality" on systems with Mojo) is $1/4$ resolution single-field playback. Draft quality allows better playback of complex effects.
![icon]	Best Performance (Yellow on Yellow) displays $1/16$ resolution single fields. Best performance, while somewhat blurry on most average systems, virtually guarantees playback of complex effects, provided they do not go over the five-stream real-time limit.
	When the blue Toggle Digital Video Out button is displayed (non-Mojo systems), full-quality dual-field DV-25 video can be played back, but all effects must be rendered in order to see them play back. Note that only DV-25 is supported in this mode. 15: 1s video cannot go out to an external monitor and thus is not supported in this mode.

 Choosing Video Quality: For software-only Xpress Pro users, Draft Quality is sufficient to detect fine focus. If you're just checking content of the sequence, Best Performance works fine. But if you're playing back for a client to review, it might be worthwhile spending some time rendering all of your effects and switching to Non-real-Time (blue dot) mode on the Timeline.

Rendering Faster: The first rule of rendering is "do it as little as possible." Rendering goes faster when it is done with the green dot (real-time effects) enabled. So, before switching to Non-real–time (blue dot) mode, render all of your effects in Real-Time mode. This seemed to be a mysterious attribute. After consultation with a number of Avid specialists and engineers, it was discovered that because the rendering "pipeline" is different in Real-Time Preview versus Non-Real–Time, the effects, when rendered, go through a few extra steps that delay rendering. According to Avid, this does not affect the quality of the rendered effects, but is more related to how the effect is fed to the rendering queue. Thus, the important thing to know is that Real-Time Preview should always be on, because it speeds up the process.

Show Source/Record

The Show Source Record Timeline button gives users the options of looking at their current sequence Timeline or looking at the source Timeline. While at first this may not seem like a very useful tool, consider the following scenario:

You are given 26 hour-long sequences and have to cut them down to 52 30-minute programs. You take the first sequence and load it into the source monitor. Finding your first cut point, you jog to the very last frame

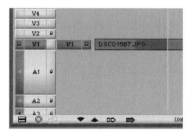

6.11 Viewing a Source Timeline

before making the cut. You continue to do this on each and every edit. Wouldn't it be simpler to just see the Timeline for the source and make the cut in the appropriate place?

Show Source/Record is also excellent for evaluating content, particularly when developing multi-groups for multi-cam. Often when playing back filmed multi-cam shows, we would find issues with the groups. A piece of tape would be added to the clip list that wasn't necessary or that posed a question. Using the source Timeline view, we could see the issues associated with the groups and delete them.

EDITING WITH THE TIMELINE

Timeline editing is uniquely nonlinear and computer-oriented. Through this tool, individual segments can be moved, swapped, deleted, dragged from the beginning to the end of a sequence, and moved to other tracks. Individual segments can be moved or entire sections. Individual video clips can be moved, or they can be moved with their audio counterparts. It is indeed a marvel that comes only with the advent of the computer.

Avid systems use two functions for Timeline editing. They are:

- *Extract/Splice:* Extract/Splice is indicated by the solid yellow arrow at the bottom of the Timeline window. When a segment is selected using Extract/Splice and moved along the Timeline, it performs an extraction in the place where it previously had been, thus pushing the two adjacent segments together, and then performs a splice where it ends, separating the two segments where it is placed. As such, it could be referred to as a noninvasive form of editing.

- *Lift/Overwrite:* Lift/Overwrite is the solid red arrow located at the bottom of the Timeline window. When a segment is selected using Lift/Overwrite and moved along the Timeline, it leaves a blank space or "black hole" in the area from which it was lifted, and overwrites on top of any segments that reside where it is placed. As such, we could say that Lift/Overwrite is destructive editing in that it will eradicate any segments on which it is placed and leaves a black hole behind.

Normally, this sort of editing might seem limited. However, there are some instances in which it can be used more effectively than Extract/Splice.

In addition to moving horizontally through the Timeline, segments can be moved vertically. For example, you may want to move a segment from V1 to V2. Or, for the sake of audio sweetening and creating discreet tracks, you might want to isolate certain segments of audio onto a different set of tracks. In cases such as these, you'll still need to maintain sync and leave the rest of the Timeline unchanged. Lift/Overwrite is the best way to do this.

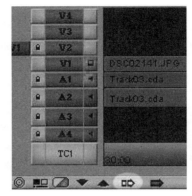

6.12   Extract/Splice Button in Timeline

6.13   Moving Segments with Timeline Editing Functions

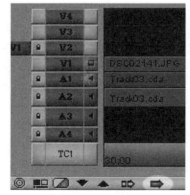

6.14 Lift/Overwrite Button In Timeline

6.15 Vertically moving a Timeline segment

To move tracks vertically and maintain sync:

1.   Select the Lift/Overwrite (red) button.

2.   Select the segment that you want to move.

3.   While holding down the Ctrl key, move the segment vertically up or down to an open (empty) track. The segment should move without slipping.

Now that you've learned the two functions, let's see how they work.

Moving Individual Shots

We'll start with an example where a montage has been created. In this montage, you have placed various shots, but recognize that two would be better if swapped with each other. To do this:

1.   Click on the Extract/Splice (yellow) arrow at the bottom of the Timeline.

2.   Click on the first segment to be moved.

3.   Drag it to the area in the Timeline where you wish to move it.

4.   To ensure that you are placing it in the correct space, hold down the Ctrl/Cmd key. In doing this, the segment will "snap" to the beginning of each edit. (You can also use Ctrl+Alt/Cmd+Option to drag things to "snap" things to the tail of the segments.)

5.   Once you've found the correct place to "land" your segment, let go of the mouse. Be sure to continue to hold down the Ctrl/Cmd key until the mouse is released, otherwise the segment could slip and create flash frames.

6.   Now select the segment that will replace this shot and, using the same technique, move it to the place where the previous shot resided.

Voilà! You've switched two shots in a relatively short amount of time.

Moving Segments

In some cases, you may find yourself in need of moving entire segments of your sequence. Although it may sound absurd, there are occasions where segments of dramatic sequences are switched to increase impact. In cases of informational programs, modules are often switched.

Moving an entire segment of a sequence seems both dangerous and difficult, but it is actually fairly foolproof. Remember, with the Undo function (Ctrl+Z/Cmd+Z), there is nothing to worry about.

You begin by selecting the entire segment in Segment Mode editing. Usually you would want to use the Extract/Splice (yellow) arrow for this. Using the Lift/Overwrite (red) arrow would leave a black hole and cover existing material, and we certainly don't want to do that.

Start by lassoing the entire segment. Be careful not to miss any segments. Lasso both audio and video segments at once. Always lasso from left to right. Doing it backward will put you into a trim mode called *slipping*, which we'll discuss on page 212 in Chapter 7. If this happens to you, you will see two pink rollers on the screen. Hit the Escape button and try again.

Once the segment is selected, make sure that the correct arrow (yellow) is selected. Drag the segment to wherever you want it to be moved and let go of the mouse. It lands in place.

Warning

Using this method can cause sync errors if all the tracks aren't exactly the same length.

The first thing to do after moving a segment is to play it back. Make sure it appears in the right order and in its entirety. If you made a mistake, Undo and try it again.

Another way to move segments is, with the Yellow arrow selected, to click on the first clip and Shift-click on each additional clip. This normally works fine, but be forewarned: if every clip is not adjacent, the segment cannot be moved. In other words, if you missed a quick flash-frame edit, the system will beep at you if you try to move the segment. Lasso-ing is easier, because that way you know everything is selected.

You can also lasso, then Shift-lasso additional segments.

Turn off the Arrows! After segment editing, you might have noticed that the segment-editing arrow stays turned on. Click on it again to turn it off. Not doing so can cause all kinds of confusion. On many occasions, editors have complained that their system is broken, only to have a technician come in and turn off the segment editing arrow. Technicians refer to this as PEB-CAK or "Problem Exists Between Chair and Keyboard." Some rather cruel technicians call this an ID-10-T issue, or ID10T. Don't let it happen to you!

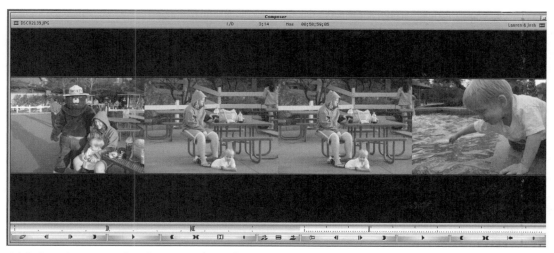

6.16 Four-Screen Display during Timeline Editing

The Four-Screen Display

You have no doubt noticed while you are happily segment-editing that the monitor display changes from two screens to four.

The four-screen display shows four different pieces of crucial information:

1. The first frame of video that will appear before your segment

2. The first frame of video of the selected segment

3. The last frame of video of the selected segment

4. The first frame of video that will appear after the segment

You can suppress the four-screen display using your Timeline Settings. Why would you want to do this? In some situations, particularly when working with effects-laden sequences, dragging through the Timeline can be an arduous task. The four-screen display has to update itself, and that can really slow down your system response.

Using Segment Mode Editing for Quick Deletion

You can also use segment mode editing for quick deletion of unwanted segments in the Timeline. If you use Extract, it will delete the unwanted segment(s) and close the gap between the adjacent edits in the Timeline. If you use Lift/Overwrite, the Timeline will leave filler in place of the segment(s).

To do a quick deletion:

1. Select the segment-editing mode, either Extract/Splice or Lift/Overwrite.

2. Click on the segments to be deleted.

3. Press Delete or Backspace.

4. The segments disappear from the Timeline.

6.17 Segment Selected for Deletion

Keep in mind that if you accidentally delete the wrong segments, you can always Undo.

Warning

> **Deleting Auto Gain:** Using this method on audio tracks that have Auto Gain (rubber-banding) enabled does not delete the segments, but the Auto Gain. In order to delete segments with Auto Gain, you have to delete twice: once to delete the Auto Gain and again to delete the segment. This also holds true for deleting video segments with effects. The first deletion will erase the effect; the second deletion will remove the video.

MAINTAINING SYNC IN THE TIMELINE

How Sync Is Lost

Xpress Pro has a variety of different tools for editing and trimming your sequence. As a result, maintaining sync requires some thought.

The most common ways to lose sync are:

- Adding material on a single track at the beginning or middle of any sequence with multiple tracks of audio or video

- Trimming on one side of an edit to extend a sequence

- Splicing in materials instead of overwriting, which can throw audio out of sync.

The Rules of Maintaining Sync

There are a few common rules that can be remembered to avoid breaking sync:

1. When trimming a single track (e.g., just the V1 track) always use center trim. (Trimming will be explained in Chapter 7.)

2. When removing from a single track, always use Lift.

3. When adding to a single track, always overwrite.

Like every set of rules, there is always an exception, but following these three simple rules can prevent the most common sync-breaking errors.

Unfortunately, you may find that these rules limit your ability to perform the editing or trimming that you need, so when you want to break these rules, there are a number of tools that can help you maintain sync.

Sync Locks

The blank column in between the Source and Record Track Selector panels in the Timeline can be used to turn on Sync Locks. This is the same panel used for indicating locked tracks. Sync locks make it easy to maintain sync during editing. For the novice nonlinear editor, sync locks can prevent the usual mistakes that might occasionally occur. However, a number of experienced editors use them as well.

Sync Locks versus Sync Breaks

The sync locks are governed by a very simple principle: make sure that track durations remain the same length, and the sequence will remain in sync. When a situation occurs that adds or subtracts frames on a single track, sync locks will adjust durations to the other sync-locked tracks so that all tracks maintain the same duration. In order to maintain sync, sync locks will not allow some adjustments to a sequence, as we will soon see.

There is a common misperception among even experienced editors that using sync locks will guarantee that a specified video source remains in sync with its accompanying audio. This is not the case. The Sync Locks feature only maintains the same durations between enabled tracks. In many cases, this is sufficient to maintain sync. However, in some cases, you will want to maintain the relationship between captured audio and video tracks. This is achieved using the Sync Breaks indicator in the Timeline, which is discussed later in this chapter on page 191.

Using Sync Locks

To apply sync locks, click the button to the left of the desired tracks to be locked in sync. A forward slash (/) appears and the button is highlighted. You can lasso the sync lock column with your mouse to toggle between enabling and disabling sync locks for multiple tracks. To toggle between enabling and disabling the sync locks on all tracks, click on the Sync Locks column next to the Timecode track.

It's important to remember that in order to maintain sync, all of the tracks must be sync locked together. Only those that are sync-lock–enabled will maintain sync. So, for example, if you select only audio tracks and inadvertently extend a video shot, the relationship between audio and video will change.

When the sync locks are enabled, they will automatically protect you from breaking sync in most instances. In the previous examples, we examined ways to avoid breaking sync. Now we'll take each example and show how sync locks prevent sync from being broken.

One-Sided Trimming on a Single Track

Let's start with a sequence that needs to be trimmed. You want to add video only to the head or the tail of one shot, but leave the other shots the same. Normally, this is accomplished through trimming, which is explained in Chapter 7 "Trimming" on page 197. Logically, if you're adding video frames to one shot and not removing frames at the same time, the video track will become longer and thus out of sync. With sync locks enabled, what happens? In cases such as this, the audio is opened up and the frames are added so that the rest of the video shots remain in sync. Both audio and video tracks are lengthened by the number of frames that you added to the shot, and thus, sync is not broken. For the audio track, empty filler frames are added. Although this might not be the desired choice, you've indicated that maintaining sync is a priority by activating sync locks, so the system does what it needs to in order to fulfill that request.

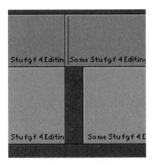

6.18 Before and After. A track trimmed on one side maintains sync by opening up with sync locks enabled.

Now let's try a different scenario. Same sequence as before, but this time, you're removing head or tail frames from video only using Trim mode and with the sync locks enabled. In this case, nothing will happen. If your system is set to emit a default beep, you'll hear it. Why? If you remove frames from the video track only, you shorten it. Shortening the video track throws it out of sync with the audio track. In this case, the only way to maintain sync would be to remove frames from the audio track. Sync locks will not allow this to happen during trimming. As a result, the trim is not made.

Extracting from a Single Track

Let's take a look at another common way to break sync. When you remove video from a track by extracting it, how will sync locks react when enabled? In this case, the video is extracted and the audio that is in sync with it is removed as well. Xpress Pro assumes that you know what you're doing and will maintain sync by the removal of the other tracks in order to keep the track durations the same as they were when sync locks were enabled.

Splicing to a Single Track

If you were to attempt to splice to a single track, sync locks will open the other sync lock–enabled tracks and insert filler of the same duration in the same place as the clip which was spliced into the sequence. So, for example, if you were to do this with a video clip, the audio track would open at the same point in the Timeline as the splice and filler would be inserted.

Using Sync Locks with Segment Editing

Segment editing, discussed earlier in this chapter, involves the moving of segments within the Timeline to eliminate, juxtapose, rearrange, or otherwise move a shot or a contiguous group of shots within the Timeline. Segment editing has unique characteristics. As a result, enabling sync locks with segment editing may produce different results than what one might expect.

The Lift/Overwrite segment mode works the same whether Sync Locks are turned on or off. Using this powerful feature, Xpress Pro can lift a segment from a single track, such as video, and overwrite it anywhere you want to move it in the Timeline. One might think that with sync locks enabled, this would not occur because it moves the video segment away from its accompanying audio segment, but again, so long as audio and video tracks remain the same length, Sync Locks will allow it.

Like Lift/Overwrite, the Extract/Splice segment mode works the same whether the sync locks are enabled or not. Extract/Splice will extract a segment from its original place in the Timeline and splice it wherever you choose to drag it on the Timeline.

When selecting either form of segment editing, deleting clips from the Timeline will not change whether Sync Locks are on or off.

There are ways to adjust the behavior if you are segment editing with Sync Locks turned on. Go to your Project window, Settings tab, and select Timeline. Click on the Edit tab and select Segment Drag Sync Locks. When this option is selected, the Extract/Splice segment-editing mode will lift a segment out of the Timeline (leaving filler in its place) and splice it to wherever you move it, inserting filler on all other Sync Lock–enabled tracks.

Sync Breaks

As you can see, Sync Locks performs specific functions to prevent you from breaking sync. But in some cases, more information is needed to maintain sync.

Sync Breaks is a feature that shows any broken relationship in the Timeline between the audio and video tracks of a digitized clip. Thus, if you were to inadvertently extend or shorten the video track of a clip that contained both audio and video, the Timeline could display the segment with a white negative or positive number indicating the number of frames that the segment is out of sync with its audio counterpart.

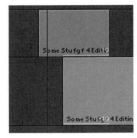

6.19 Sync Breaks indicate when sync is lost.

Here's how Sync Breaks works: when a track is short by a number of frames and is out of sync, it has a negative number. When a track is long and has thrown the sequence out of sync, it shows a positive number. That's simple enough to understand, but what happens when you're not sure which track should be adjusted? Usually this can easily be determined. Turn off video monitoring and listen to the audio. If the audio sounds correct, then the video needs to be adjusted. You can extend or shorten the video by the number of frames indicated by sync breaks. If it is a negative number, add frames to the sequence. If it is a positive number, subtract frames.

Of course, the easiest solution is to Undo whatever was done to cause the sync break to appear in the first place.

There are some occasions where sync breaks will be indicated but there isn't really a break in sync. For example, there could be a case where you captured a clip that included a pickup shot or a cutaway at the end. If you insert the cutaway portion of the clip over the original clip in your sequence, you'll get a sync break indicating it is out of sync, because the video from the same clip has been inserted from a different audio segment. As a result, Xpress Pro thinks that you've broken sync where the cutaway is used.

Warning Other important sync relationships are *not* accounted for by sync breaks. For example, stacks of effects, titles, and music tracks that have been carefully synced to the action of your sequence, do *not* have sync relationships that are recognized by the Sync Breaks function.

CREATING SYNC RELATIONSHIPS USING AUTOSYNC

You might have the need to create a synchronous relationship between audio and video from different sources. Creating this "faux sync" relationship would allow you to maintain sync using the Sync Breaks feature. This can be achieved through the use of Xpress Pro's Autosync function.

To create a new clip with a faux sync relationship, you'll first need to edit together a sequence using the different clip sources. There are specific rules that apply to Autosync. Ignoring these rules will inevitably create undesired results. In order for Autosync to work correctly, there must be one clip only on each source track of the sequence. The audio and video segments should be equal in length. If they are not, Autosync will convert only the portions of the sequence where both audio and video exist. Any sections at the head or tail of the sequence where there is audio or video only will be eliminated in the resulting clip.

Here's how you do it: create a new sequence and edit the video and audio together from their different original clips. Be sure to adjust the resulting sequence so that the desired sync relationship exists between sources. Click on this new sequence in its bin and select Bin>Autosync. When the sequence is converted through Autosync, it maintains its original name, but the icon in the bin changes from a sequence icon to a subclip icon. Once this is achieved, the resulting autosynced clip can be loaded into the source monitor and edited into a sequence.

USING ADD EDIT FOR MAINTAINING SYNC

In some cases, in order to trim a multi-track sequence you can use Add Edit. For example, if you trim the audio and visual of a shot preceding a title graphic on V2, how do you keep the V2 track in sync with the rest of the sequence? Shortening just your V1 and audio tracks would make the title come later in relationship to the edit. Lengthening it would make the title appear too early.

The solution is to place a "false edit" or Add Edit on the V2 track and trim it while trimming V1 and the audio tracks. To do this:

1. Go to the transition where you want to begin trimming.

2. Select the track(s) where the edits must be added in order to trim in sync.

3. Press the Add Edit button or click on it in the interface.

An edit is added to that track. Now you can select all of your tracks and trim them accordingly.

The Add Edit Function

The Add Edit function allows users to place a false edit in between the frames of any clip. The advantages of Add Edit are numerous. For example, if you wanted to apply an effect to one portion of a clip and dissolve out of it to the same clip without the effect, you could place an Add Edit at the transition point, apply the effect to the first portion of the clip, and add a dissolve between the two.

Add Edits can be used to isolate a portion of a clip for any kind of manipulation so that it does not affect the rest of the clip. You can place an Add Edit on a single track or multiple tracks all at once. And, as we pointed out earlier in this chapter, Add Edits can be used for trimming.

To add an edit:

1. Move the blue position indicator to the point where the edit is to be added.

2. Select the tracks where the edit is intended to go using the Track Selector panel.

3. Click on the Add Edit button. It is located in the Command Palette under the Edit tab and can be mapped directly to your keyboard, placed under the Record Monitor buttons, or mapped to the Timeline button bar.

To remove an Add Edit:

• Undo after immediately adding the edit, or

• Go into Trim mode at the edit point and press Delete. The added edit goes away.

C'mon, Everybody! Let's Add Edits! Editors pride themselves on their timing abilities, and using Add Edit can be fun. If you are editing a sequence with music, you can add edits accordingly, and then fill them with picture. It's also fun to try when doing action sequences where the rhythm of the scene follows a logical pattern that you previsualize. To do this, map the Add Edit key to your keyboard, select the video track where the edits will be placed, and play back the music, pressing the Add Edit button where you think it would be appropriate. When you stop the sequence from playing back, the edits are already precut for you in the blank space. All you have to do from there is mark each clip and fill it in with picture. You can also hold down the K and L keys to slow down the music and listen for specific beats, adding edits as you go.

USING LOCATORS TO MAINTAIN SYNC

In some cases, you may find that true sync that you have established between picture and sound does not come as the result of digitizing picture and sound together. For example, when editing a cut to music, you may want a visual event to occur to match an aural event, such as a cymbal crash.

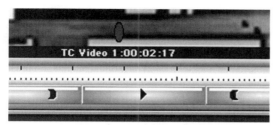

6.20 Locators show a sync relationship where no previous relationship existed.

In cases such as these, there isn't a defined relationship between audio and video, except for the one that you have created. Through the process of editing, there is always the chance that you may lose that relationship and will need to reestablish it.

Locators are pointers that can be made to make notes, make comments, or mark certain events. In a sense, they are the bookmarks for clips. In the case of the event described above, we have a cymbal crash that should occur in time with a visual event. To maintain sync, you can place a locator on the audio track and the video track where the cymbal crash takes place. To do this:

1. Find the point on the audio track that you want to reference.

2. Select the audio track *only,* and then add a Locator button at an audio cue (like the cymbal crash). A locator appears in the audio track of the Timeline.

3. In the Tracking menu above the Timeline, select V1. Click on the locator in the Record Monitor and copy the timecode number from the Tracking menu into the Locator window.

Now, whenever you think that sync might be slipping, go to the locator and look at the V1 timecode. If the numbers do not match, you will have to move the picture backward or forward to reestablish sync.

Rendering & Real-Time Effects

To explain what is happening during real-time effects and rendering, I use the analogy of doing math in your head. When Xpress Pro is playing back straight video or real-time effects, it is doing the math in its head. In other words, all of the complex calculations that are needed to be able to know where every pixel should land on the screen and what it should look like can be done as simply as you can add 2+2 in your head and quickly answer "4." However, if someone asks you to multiply 7623 ×247, you could figure it out eventually with a calculator or a pencil and paper. And if someone asked you the same question again, you could just look down at the answer on your paper without re-multiplying it. Renders are the same way. When Xpress Pro is rendering, it calculates the exact appearance and location of every pixel in an effect and writes that answer down somewhere on the drive. The next time you ask the system to play back that answer it plays it from the drive instead of trying to figure out the equation again.

An alternate method would be to add locators across all of the tracks, noting if any of the locators failed to line up correctly on the Timeline. Either way, it works.

Now that we've covered the basic use of the editing and Timeline interfaces, let's take a look at how we can fine-tune sequences using Xpress Pro's Trim function.

Chapter 7

Trimming

WHAT IS TRIMMING?

One of the more popular concepts of editing these days is that the editor is the storyteller. While it is true that in most cases, the editor is the writer of the final draft, we are rarely the tellers of the original story. Some documentary and magazine editing is an exception to this rule, with an editor left to create a story from the raw footage, without a script at all. The feature film/documentary "Comedian" with Jerry Seinfeld was one of these rare, editor-told films.

But in most cases, what does an editor do? We control the pacing, the presentation, the timing of images. We find the exact point when new information sometimes determines whether it is to be revealed at all. We pace the sound and image to fit the story. We determine the order of events within a story. Many times we reverse or alter that order.

Which brings us to the Trim mode, considered by many to be the most powerful tool in an editor's arsenal. When an editor trims, he or she is determining the exact point at which an edit should take place. Editors rarely create images, lighting, or dialog; give art direction; or manage set construction. But we always create transitions. The Trim tool controls those transitions.

The Trim mode is powerful and versatile, particularly on Avid systems. In fact, there are so many different ways to Trim that some editors never completely learn them all.

Others never really use trimming to its full potential, mostly because the Trim mode has so many options and may appear at first glance to be difficult. But actually, the many Trim mode options were created to suit the needs of individual editors.

Once learned, you will see that Trim mode is the heart of any nonlinear system, particularly on Avid systems like Xpress Pro.

Keep in mind that for editing purposes, there are three different modes on Xpress Pro:

1. *Source/Record,* where rough cuts are built and reviewed.

2. *Trim,* where rough cuts are refined.

3. *Effects,* where special visual and audio effects can be added and adjusted.

There are some who might think, "Why should we have different modes?" The answer is simple: every creation goes through the mode of roughness, of refinement, and then of decoration. The three modes on Xpress Pro were created to match these different aspects of creation and intend to help you follow a true creative model as you work.

The modality of the user interface also helps simplify the interface, because it allows for simple clicks and drags and other basic interaction to mean something different in each mode. If there were no modes, these simple interactions would have to be more complex to indicate to the computer what action the editor wanted to take place. For example, in Trim mode you can move a trim one way or the other with a simple drag of the mouse. Yet in Edit mode, this simple drag simply moves you to a new location in the Timeline. If there were no modes, one or the other of these simple operations would need to be more difficult because the system would need to know if you wanted to move in the Timeline, or whether you wanted to drag a trim. Also, this allows the monitors to serve multiple purposes, which wouldn't be possible without modal operations.

USING TRIM MODE TO ANALYZE YOUR WORK

When we discussed laying down the first cut of your sequence, I suggested that you do it in a rather loose fashion, leaving plenty of places to cut and trim later. During the rough cut, playing back and analyzing is discouraged, as the goal of the first cut is based more on completion than refinement.

Now that we've done a first cut, the trimming begins. With trimming, you'll need to get used to bouncing in and out of Trim mode. Go into Trim mode to make adjustments, then switch back to Source/Record mode to see how those adjustments look in context. If you remain in Trim mode and simply go from edit to edit, trimming all the while, you might find that the cut lacks rhythm or fluidity. It's better to trim, then look at it in context, then return to Trim mode. This takes a little getting used to, but once you get into the habit of zooming in and zooming out of each transition, you'll find that your cut moves along in a more orderly fashion.

Remember that while trimming is an analytical function, it can also be creative. Be sure to try trimming to create L-cuts, change timing of a scene, and create or emphasize specific areas of your sequence. With the Trim tools, you are the master of space and time. Do everything that you can to make the sequence better through trimming.

Entering the Trim Mode

To enter the Trim mode, you can press the [key (left bracket) on a standard keyboard or select Trim mode from your Command Palette. You can also select Trim mode from the palette above the Timeline. The Trim icon resembles a roll of film. (Originally, this was intended as a trim roller with frames on the side of it.) When the system enters Trim mode, it focuses on a specific transition, based upon the position of the blue indicator in the Timeline. Find a transition you'd like to alter, choose the tracks that are to be altered, and click on the Trim mode button.

An alternate way to enter Trim mode is to lasso a transition (be sure not to lasso more than one transition) from upper left to lower right (see Figure 7.1). The interface will change and the pink rollers appear in the Timeline.

Exiting Trim Mode

If you find yourself in Trim mode at an inappropriate moment, press the Escape key or click anywhere on the timecode track in the Timeline to return to Source/Record mode. You can also click on the Trim mode button ([) to toggle Trim mode off.

Between all of the easy and very fast ways there are to get in to and out of Trim mode, using a separate mode for trimming really isn't all that big of a deal.

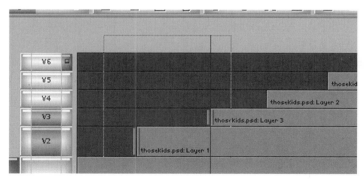

7.1   Lassoing to Enter Trim Mode

7.2   The Trim Interface

THE TRIM INTERFACE

Once you're in the Trim mode, you will notice that the interface changes slightly.

Under the Source and Record windows, the icons change—more under the source side than the record side. Two purple number windows appear underneath the monitors in the center. On the Timeline, a pair of purple rollers appears for each track selected.

In the Source and Record windows, the images have changed. The former source side monitor is now the outgoing side or A side of the transition. The record side monitor is the incoming or B side of the transition. The system has adjusted itself so that you can focus on this particular transition. You can play it, trim it, and adjust it until it meets your specific needs.

The Trim Loop

Let's start by examining the Play button. Notice that the Play button underneath the Record Monitor has a straight vertical line running through the center. This is actually not a Play button, but a Play Trim Loop button.

Warning

Using the actual Play button while in Trim mode can cause you to actually Trim the transition instead of reviewing it if you have J-K-L Trim mode selected in the Trim Settings. J-K-L trimming is the default setting for most Avid products, because it is a very intuitive way to trim an edit by playing through it or jogging through it instead of dragging it or typing in numbers to adjust the trim point.

The Trim Loop is a section of the transition that plays back when you examine it. The default Trim Loop is two seconds of preroll (before) and two seconds of postroll (after) the transition, but you can alter this by adjusting your Trim Settings. Select your Trim Settings in the Project window; then select the Play Loop tab. Your Play Loop Settings appear. From here, you can adjust the preroll, postroll, and intermission Settings. The Intermission is by default set to zero frames so that the Trim Loop will play continuously. In some situations, this can be problematic. For example, when trimming a fast-cut montage, one can frequently find oneself overwhelmed with the number of transitions that take place during the loop. If you set an Intermission time, the loop will play back, then switch to black for the intermission duration, then begin play again. This will continue until you tell the loop to stop.

Some editors, and even more producers, can't stand the trim playback loop. Remember that it is only a tool to gauge how well the transition plays. If you'd rather not use it, you can always switch back to Source/Record mode and play it back normally within the context of an entire scene.

Selecting Trim Sides

When trimming, you first must determine what needs to be trimmed. By default, the system enters the Trim mode with Center Trim enabled. This selects both the A and B sides of the transition. When Center Trim is selected, whatever you do to one side will conversely affect the other. For example, if you add three frames to the A side of the transition, it takes away three frames from the B side of the transition. You can also choose A-side trimming or B-side trimming. To select trimming on one side only, click on that side in the Video Monitor. When you click on the A side, you will notice that the pink roller in the Timeline switches to the A side of the transition. The same is true when you click on the B-side Monitor. To return to center trimming, click in between both Monitors.

UNDERSTANDING HOW TRIM WORKS

It can be somewhat taxing to determine how each form of trim (center, A-side, or B-side) will affect your sequence. Let's start with the easiest to understand, Center Trim.

Center Trim

Consider this: a carpet salesman is trying to sell you a spare roll of carpet. The roll of carpet is laying with its tail out, adjacent to a green roll of carpet, whose tail is also out, facing in the opposite direction. In order to show you more of the red carpet, the salesman kicks the two rolls one way. In doing this, the red carpet moves so that it reveals more of its tail. The green carpet conversely rolls up, so that its tail is less revealed.

This is how Center Trimming in a transition works. By rolling forward and adding frames to the A side (red carpet), we take frames away from the B side (green carpet). The two shots remain the same in total duration, because whatever is added to one is subtracted from the other.

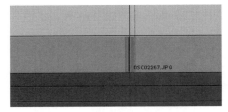

7.3 Center Trim. One side conversely affects the other.

When making an L-cut (also known as a delay, overlap, or split edit), you center trim the video. If you want the B-side video to come in late, center trim it forward. If you want the B-side to enter early, center trim it backward.

I find that, when cutting dramatic sequences, I rarely have the visual and audio cuts happen at the same time. This is because I like to wander through the scene and show the audience some reactions of the characters. In some cases, I'll want to hold on a particular character while the dialog continues. In other situations, I may want to show a character react while another character is speaking. Using center trim allows you to do this easily. In almost every case, I will experiment with center trim on each cut, just to see if there are elements that need to be focused as the dialog transitions.

Using L-cuts is also an effective way of softening a transition without resorting to a dissolve. By having the audio for the next scene precede the video by several frames, the audience is subconsciously expecting a change in the video as well, so when it comes, it seems less harsh.

7.4   Trimming +2 frames on the A side of a transition extends the length of the sequence.

Center trim is also the easiest way to keep your sequence audio and video in sync, because it never makes the sequence longer or shorter in duration. But there are reasons not to use this method, as we will see.

Trimming Single Sides of a Transition

If a scene is up cut, if you need to hold a few frames longer, or if a reaction isn't held long enough, you'll need to trim a single side. Basically, any time one side of a transition needs to be "fixed" while the other side is perfect, you will need to perform a single-sided trim. Another example would be in an interview, where two bites are intercut. If the second interview bite starts perfectly, but there is too much space at the end of the first bite, then you will need to do an A-side trim. Trimming a single side can be tricky, because if all tracks are not selected when doing this—or you don't employ some other method of keeping your sequence in sync—you can throw the sequence out of sync. We'll discuss methods to maintain sync while trimming in a moment.

Assuming that you're just beginning to trim a rough cut, you will probably find yourself analyzing each cut at both entry and exit. A common mistake made by editors who are new to trimming is to center trim as an overall solution. This rarely works because the overall effect is to adjust the duration of a scene.

Let's take an example. You enter Trim mode on the first transition of your sequence and notice, much to your chagrin, that the outgoing side is up cut a bit (meaning that the end of the shot is cut too tightly). You want to continue the scene for a beat longer before proceeding to the next scene. If you choose an A-side Trim on all tracks, you can extend the scene and not worry about going out of sync. Just be sure to remember that all tracks should be selected, or you'll lose audio sync. Upon inspection, you find that the B side of the transition begins just fine. If you center trimmed this transition, that extra beat that

7.5   Trimming +2 frames on the B side of a transition shortens the length of the sequence.

you added to the A side of the transition would have been taken away from the B side of the transition and the results would have been less than desirable. So when you're trimming for timing, you'll want to do it one transition side at a time.

Trimming single sides of transitions is a method of lengthening or shortening scenes. When you control the pacing of a sequence of shots, you'll find yourself doing single-sided trimming frequently on all tracks in order to find the rhythm of the scene.

MAINTAINING SYNC WITH MULTIPLE VIDEO TRACKS

If you have a sequence with multiple video layers, you have to be careful when trimming. Even if you follow the basic rules of maintaining sync, added titles and effects can be accidentally slipped out of sync with the rest of your visual elements. Although this is technically not a sync issue, the elements will not occur where you originally intended them to be. This can be especially treacherous with multiple-layer effects that have been rendered. One bad trim could cause the entire effect to slip out of sync, requiring you to reposition layers and re-render your results.

The easiest method to prevent this is to add an edit on every video track at the trim point when trimming the video. In other words, if you need to add frames on V1, be sure to add just as many frames on each additional video track. Not doing so will make the other video tracks shorter, and the effects on those tracks that occur after your V1 trim will appear sooner than originally intended.

To prevent this, select all of your video tracks before entering Trim mode and add an edit. Then, when trimming, make sure all active tracks are selected. Then trimming those Add Edit points will add filler on the blank tracks to match the length of the trim that was done on V1, preventing you from losing sync.

This method of adding edits also holds true when trimming audio. For example, if your narration is on A1 and A2, and you've added some occasional sound effects on A3 and A4, you'll need to make sure that any adjustments to the track length are made on all of the tracks by adding edits to the sound effect tracks as well. So, if you wanted to shorten one piece of the narration by a few frames on A1 and A2, be sure to add edit to A3 and A4 and trim using all tracks so that the sound effects occur at the correct place. Failure to do this will result in the effects slipping out of sync with the rest of the audio.

Maintaining Sync: Here is a cool way to maintain sync on multiple tracks. If you are at a transition point and you want to do a single-sided trim, but you also want to be able to trim a track with filler at the exact point where the transition is, you can Alt+Add Edit/Option+Add Edit and it will only add edits to filler. Cool! So now you can select all of your tracks for the trim and the sequence stays in sync.

 Trim Detective: Occasionally you may find yourself in a situation where some anomalous audio or video enters the frame and it appears to be right in the middle of your transition. You can jockey through the transition using the regular Source/Record navigational tools, but you may still find it difficult to determine on which side (A or B) of the transition that the sound occurs. To remedy this, Xpress Pro allows you to play the Trim Loop as a single side, looping only the one side to determine where the stray audio or video frame is located. To isolate the sides during Trim Loop, play back the Trim Loop as you normally would, then select the Q button to loop the A side of the transition only. Select the W button to loop the B side of the transition only. By isolating the sides of the transition, you should be able to find the bad frame. This will only work if you have retained the default keyboard mapping of the Go To In and Go To Out buttons. If you have not, instead of using the Q button on your keyboard, hit the key that you have assigned for Go To In. Instead of the W button, hit the key that you have assigned for Go To Out.

Adding or Subtracting Frames

While we're on the subject of single-side trimming, let's clarify something that might be confusing if you're new to trimming: "When is a trim adding frames and when is it subtracting frames?" For example, if I am trimming the A side of a transition and move forward +6 frames, I am adding frames to the track. But when I am trimming the B side of the transition and move forward +6 frames, I am removing frames from the track. Why? It goes back to our earlier carpet analogy. When you are trimming the B side or incoming video, in order to add more frames to this side, you must roll it backward (in this example, –6 frames) in order to reveal more frames and lengthen the track. Conversely, if you are trimming the A side or outgoing video, you add frames (in this example, +6 frames) in order to extend the track and make it longer. It takes a little getting used to, but once you've committed this to memory, the amount of time spent trimming will decrease significantly.

Methods of Trimming

Now that we have thoroughly discussed the types of trimming, it's time to show you how to actually do it.

Xpress Pro was created after many generations of the Avid Media Composer. One of the key components of this system for editors were the methods with which trimming could be done. Every editor is different. As a result, there are many different methods of trimming. Some like to click the mouse. Others like to click and drag. Some prefer buttons. I prefer the keyboard, which is almost always faster. You may use some or even all of the methods described herein. The important thing is to find a method or methods that best suit your needs.

Grabbing the Rollers

Once you've entered the Trim mode and have selected which side of the transition is to be trimmed, you might have noticed some pink rollers at the transition point in the Timeline. These rollers can be clicked and dragged to adjust the Trim interactively with your mouse. Although not as accurate as numerical entry or the Trim buttons described below, grabbing and dragging the rollers will update the monitors, providing feedback as you trim. You can also add and subtract rollers by Shift-clicking on additional tracks.

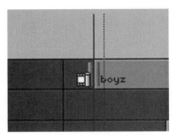

7.6 Trimming by Grabbing Rollers

The click-and-drag method with rollers is used primarily for shorter trims, where only a few frames need to be added. When Caps Lock is activated, the system will scrub audio as you move along, so that you can listen for audio cues.

Table 7.1   Navigation Buttons

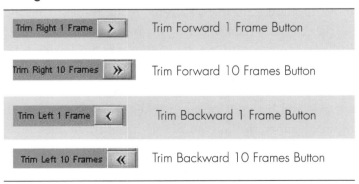

Trim Right 1 Frame **>**	Trim Forward 1 Frame Button
Trim Right 10 Frames **»**	Trim Forward 10 Frames Button
Trim Left 1 Frame **‹**	Trim Backward 1 Frame Button
Trim Left 10 Frames **«**	Trim Backward 10 Frames Button

Button Trimming

The Trim interface uses buttons for adjustment of a transition, both on the interface and on your keyboard. These buttons are mapped to the interface under the source monitor. They are also mapped on the default Xpress Pro keyboard. The four buttons include Trim Forward 1 Frame, Trim Forward 10 Frames, Trim Backward 1 Frame, and Trim Backward 10 Frames.

Button trimming is normally used as a nudging device, where each frame advance or reverse can be monitored and played back immediately. Some editors use the 10 frame buttons as a means to move forward in larger increments, although it can be done much easier using JKL trimming or by dragging handles.

Trimming by Numerical Entry

Some editors can determine, based upon their experience, the approximate amount of frames needed to be trimmed in a transition. If you prefer to directly enter a number of frames to be trimmed, enter Trim mode, select the A side, B side, or Both and type the amount of frames to be trimmed with a plus (+) or minus sign (−) (see Figure 7.7). The transition adjusts appropriately. One thing to note about numerical entry: once you've entered a number higher than 99, the system assumes that you are referring to seconds and frames, therefore an entry of 106 would result in a trim of 36 frames, or 1 second and 6 frames. If you want to enter higher numbers in frames, enter the number and follow it with a lower case "f" before pressing the Enter key. This lets Xpress Pro know that you intend for this entry to be expressed in frames, not seconds and frames.

Trimming on the Fly

Trimming on the Fly is a simple yet elegant way to adjust a transition based upon timing with real-time playback. When you trim on the fly, the transition loop will play back and you tell the transition where to move based upon a Mark IN or Mark OUT point. It doesn't matter which type of marked point is used, so long as it is done on the keyboard. The keyboard equivalents on a standard Xpress Pro are the E, R, I, and O keys.

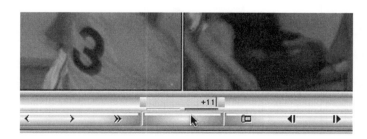

7.7   Trimming by Numerical Entry

To trim on the fly, enter the Trim mode and select the transition side(s) to be trimmed. Play back the Trim Loop. Before trimming on the fly, you might want to let the loop play back a couple times so that you can get a feel for the transition. As the loop plays continuously, select the point at where you want the transition to move by pressing the E, R, I, or O key. The transition point moves accordingly. If you did not select the appropriate point, let the loop continue to play back and reselect, or press Ctrl+Z/Cmd+Z to undo and then continue playback.

7.8   Changing Loop Duration in Trim Settings

If you need to trim past the loop, change your Trim Settings to reflect a longer preroll or postroll. By doing this, you will give yourself more space in which to make the trim. It also gives you more "breathing space" to look and select the proper trimming point.

Trimming on the fly is normally used for trimming to a precise moment in music or in action. Although it could be said that there are more precise methods, most editors pride themselves on their sense of timing. Trimming on the fly is a great exercise in creative freedom, and when an editor has good reaction time, it produces great results.

Practice, Practice, Practice: Trimming on the fly takes a little practice before you get used to it. A common mistake when trimming on the fly is to trim too far, obliterating almost all of either the A- or B-side clip. Sometimes Undoing the trim is better than spending time trying to bring back the partially missing clips. Don't waste time! Undo the trim and try again.

JKL Trim

JKL trimming is one of Xpress Pro's best features. The ability to dynamically trim media and view it as the trimming takes place makes trimming simple and precise. Using this method, you can trim and maintain continuity all at the same time, adjust your trimming to maintain action, establish a proper eyeline between characters, and adjust for camera movement, audio cues, and so on.

7.9   Activating JKL in Trim Settings

On Xpress Pro, JKL trimming is an option. In order to activate it, select the Settings tab in your Project window. Double-click on the

Trim Settings. The Trim Settings window Appears. Click on the Features tab and select JKL Trim.

To JKL trim:

1. Enter the Trim mode.

2. Use the JKL keys to move the transition point (see Table 7.2).

Remember, as you use the JKL keys, the transition point moves with you. JKL trimming, like trimming on the fly, is very powerful. It takes a bit of getting used to, but it can be very useful. The keys work the same as they would normally work during Source/Record navigation, save for the fact that they are actually trimming as the media moves.

Table 7.2   The JKL Keys: How They Work

Key	Action	Result	Audio Scrub
J	Pressed Once	Moves at 1× Reverse Speed	Yes
J	Pressed Twice	Moves at 2× Reverse Speed	Yes
J	Pressed 3X	Moves at 3× Reverse Speed	Yes
J	Pressed 4X	Moves at 5× Reverse Speed	No
J	Pressed 5X	Moves at 8× Reverse Speed	No
J	Tapped	Jogs One Frame Backward	Yes
J & K	Held Down Together	Moves at 33% Reverse Speed	Yes
K & L	Held Down Together	Moves at 33% Forward Speed	Yes
L	Tapped	Jogs One Frame Forward	Yes
L	Pressed Once	Moves at 1× (Normal) Forward Speed	Yes
L	Pressed Twice	Moves at 2× Forward Speed	Yes
L	Pressed 3X	Moves at 3× Forward Speed	Yes
L	Pressed 4X	Moves at 5× Forward Speed	No
L	Pressed 5X	Moves at 8× Forward Speed	No

JKL Trimming: Keep in mind that the designers of the system recognized some of the pitfalls of using this method. As a result, you can never completely get rid of an entire segment through JKL trimming. If you want to delete an entire segment, use segment mode editing. If you find yourself confused by the amount of trimming you've done during a JKL trim, Undo.

When there is a need to trim, you will almost always find yourself using JKL trimming. The reason is that you can use it for small and larger trims. For example, if you are extending the tail of the video on shot A to cover some of the dialog on shot B, you can click on the L key and play it to the point where the shot is to be extended, then press the spacebar. The trim is made instantly. For more close up and shorter trims, you can use the K and L keys to roll forward and the J and K keys to roll backward. If you place your middle finger on the K key and then alternate the motion using the J and L keys, you can rock and roll through the media until you find the point where the trim looks best.

THE EXTEND FUNCTION

Extending an edit is a way of trimming without actually entering Trim mode. In some cases, you may want to extend a single track or tracks forward or backward to a specified point. For example, if cutting a news story, you may add an on-camera sound bite, which in turn can have video extended backward to backtime the viewers to the sound, which is fairly common. It is easier to select the video track and extend it backward to a cue point than to enter Trim mode.

Not everyone uses Extend for these quick trims. But if you'd rather not bother with going into Trim mode, it's an easy way to get the job done.

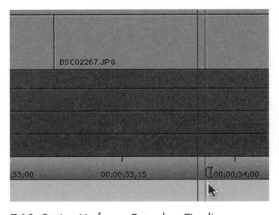

7.10 Setting Up for an Extend on Timeline

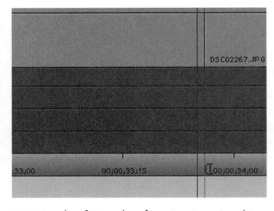

7.11 Results of Extending from Previous Graphic

To extend, select the track(s) you want to extend. Find the point in the sequence to where you want to extend the clip. If this point is before the edit, mark an IN point. If it is after the edit, mark an OUT point. Click on the Extend button. The edit is extended in the Timeline.

Extend edit is an excellent way to perform split edits of L-cuts. Once the edit is made on all three tracks, select the track you want to Trim, mark your point and Extend. This is very fast and intuitive.

Warning

Dangerously Extended: Extend can be dangerous, because if you have both an IN point and an OUT point marked, Xpress Pro uses the IN point as the higher priority. Why is this dangerous? Because if you mark an OUT point near the transition you want to Extend, and you don't notice that you have an IN point marked at some far-flung location on your sequence, when you hit the Extend, the transition that you want to Extend will not be extended and some transition that you aren't even paying attention to—and which might have been perfect—gets extended by accident. To prevent this, you can always hit the Clear Marks button before marking an edit for an Extend.

Advanced Trim Functions

Now that we've covered the basics of how to operate in Trim mode, let's look at some advanced functions that might come in handy for specific scenarios.

Dual-Directional Trimming

You can trim in two different directions at the same time. This can come in handy especially for sound overlaps where the sound department wants to feather in and out segments of sound, or where you need to cover an MOS shot with some sort of presence or ambience.

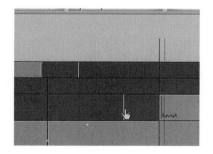

For example, let's take a dramatic scene. A big battle is taking place, with bombs, machine guns, and explosions heard everywhere. Somehow in the midst of it all, two lovebirds find each other to say goodbye. Then the Lieutenant calls the soldier back into action, causing him to depart from his loved one.

Pretty corny, huh? Let's dissect this a little more. The battle scene has plenty of background noise, with ack-ack-ack and explosions. The scene with the lieutenant has plenty of the same. But the scene with the two lovebirds was shot without any presence. In order to add the sounds of the battle in the background of shot B, we'll take shots A and C and trim the audio inversely so that they overlap scene B of the lovebirds. By overlapping the two audio tracks, the presence of the battle continues throughout the sequence. To do this, enter Trim mode and select only the outgoing audio of shot A and the incoming audio of shot C. Then grab either of the rollers. The two audio tracks will extend toward each other until they meet. If you placed the audio on separate tracks, they can even extend over each other, should the amount of media permit this.

SLIPPING AND SLIDING

Two methods that are frequently used by film editors are known as slipping and sliding. These methods allow you to trim shots in ways that previously took much more time. In both cases, they are methods of trimming that would normally take two or more steps. Although they still can be done using conventional trimming methods, the ease in which they can be done makes it more desirable to use these methods.

Slipping

Slipping can be defined as the process of adding and subtracting frames proportionately to a chosen shot. So, for example, if we want to add three frames to the head of a shot, we would also subtract three frames from the tail to maintain duration of the shot. Whatever is added to one side (the head or tail of the shot) is subtracted from the other. Thus, we are "slipping" the frames within a specific duration or window of time.

This is more easily pictured by thinking of the shot inside of a window. Slipping allows you to look at a different part of the shot without changing the size of the window. An example of this would be that you have three shots: A, B, and C. A and C are perfectly trimmed and the B shot is the perfect duration, but the portion of the shot that you can see during that duration is wrong. Maybe a character doesn't get a chance to get off set before the cut. So you slip the shot backwards so that the character exits before you cut to C.

Another example would be that you're editing a piece where a window of time—say, six seconds—is given to identify a product. You've found the product shot and the timing seems to work just fine. It starts close and then zooms out, revealing a wide shot of the product. You put it in your sequence. The producer looks at the shot and asks if there is any way you can make the zoom happen later. Because the narration only lasts six seconds, you have two choices: either extend the duration of the program, which you decide not to do, or slip the shot so that more head frames are added and tail frames are inversely removed. You enter Slip mode, type in –8, then play it back. Problem solved.

To enter Slip mode, lasso from right to left covering the entire segment to be slipped. If you want to slip a series of shots, such as in a montage, drag the lasso around the end of the last segment to be slipped and continue until it is around the beginning of the first segment to be slipped. You can control slipping using all of the Trim methods described previously, including J-K-L.

An alternate way to enter Slip is through the Timeline menus. While in Trim mode, place your cursor over the segment that you want to Slip and right-click/Shift+Ctrl-click to reveal the Timeline menu. You can Select Slip Trim or Select Slide Trim using the menu.

 You can switch from Slip to Slide by Alt+double-clicking/Option+double-clicking on the segment.

7.12 Contextual Slip/Slide Trim Menu

You may have noticed that, upon entering Slip mode, the interface uses four screens instead of the usual two. This is because two separate transition points are being affected when you slip. Thus, the first monitor contains the last frame of visual before the slipped shot, the second contains the first frame of slipped shot, the third monitor contains the last frame of slipped shot, and the fourth monitor contains the first frame of the next shot following the slipped shot. As you slip the shot forward or backward, only frames 2 and 3 will update, because the first and fourth frame are not changed through slipping.

Sliding

Sliding does just the opposite of slipping, affecting adjacent scenes. Assuming that we have three shots placed together, we can move the position of shot B by sliding it—adding frames to the tail of shot A, and subtracting from the head of shot C. In this case, the content of shot B remains unchanged, but its relative position is moved forward or backward in the Timeline. Using this tool, the tail of shot A and head of shot C are the only adjustments being made. This will, however, affect the position of shot B, which is in the middle of the two.

Like slipping, slide trimming will display four monitors. The first is the tail of the outgoing scene, which is adjusted in slide mode. The second monitor is the first frame of the scene being slid. The third monitor is the last frame of the slid scene and the fourth monitor contains the first frame of the next incoming scene. When you slide, the first and fourth monitors are affected. The second and third monitors, which contain the clip that is sliding in the Timeline, do not change.

Here's an example of where sliding can be used: Let's say you put together a program where, in the middle, you created a pretty slick little fast-cut montage. Somewhere along the line—you're not sure how, where, or who, and it really doesn't matter—the montage slipped so that the music was about three frames behind picture. Rather than try to reconstruct the sequence, you can enter Slide mode and slide the visual of the entire montage forward three frames. The correction can be made in about half a minute and everything will look great again.

There are other reasons for sliding, including moving visuals to match narration or music, adjusting a shot for continuity, and so on. As you gain experience using the Slide form of trimming, you'll find more reasons to use it.

ADDING FILLER WHILE TRIMMING

In some cases, you might want to trim on one side of a single track and keep everything in sync. The best way to do it is to add filler while trimming. To add filler while trimming, go into Trim mode and select one side (A or B) of a transition. While clicking and holding on the pink rollers, hold down the Alt/Ctrl key. This adds or subtracts filler on the unselected tracks so that sync is maintained.

Another way to maintain sync while adding filler is to turn the Sync Locks on. Whenever you trim a single side, it adds filler on the tracks to maintain sync.

Going to Last Trim: Here's a neat trick that comes in handy. If you performed a trim and later realize that you need to go back to the Trim mode on that same transition, Alt+Trim mode/ Option+Trim mode will bring you back to your last trimmed transition. You can use this on occasion where there are hundreds of cuts in the sequence and just locating the transition point would take a considerable amount of time.

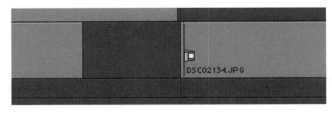

7.13 Adding Filler while Trimming in Timeline

The Trim function is the heart of any Avid system. Xpress Pro's modality allows you to focus specifically on Trim and hone your craft as an editor. While it may seem a bit overbuilt and intense at first, Trim mode alters the interface enough so that you can focus on one very specific part of your work—finding the exact frames to start and end each cut.

Your precision as an editor depends on a tool that lets you examine every frame carefully. It's not enough to look at each transition once or twice in real time. Xpress Pro's expanded trimming features let you examine each cut along with adjacent cuts.

For the fledgling editor, it takes time. You must examine your work up close with the trim tool, then from a distance, by playing back your sequence and examining it as a whole. The ability to micro focus, then macro focus doesn't come easy.

If you were to follow editing like any other form of art, we could say that Source/Record mode is the rough draft. Trim mode is where the precision and refinement of the talented editor can be exhibited.

Now that we've covered how to build and adjust sequences, let's enter the mysterious world of effects and learn how to spice up your sequences.

Noir Trimming

One of my first editing experiences was with the late Edward Dmytryk, the film noir director and editor. Dmytryk had our class look at a scene from an old Phillip Marlowe private detective movie that he had directed in the 1940s. It was classic noir, with Marlowe interviewing a suspect in his cheesy office, located in a rundown slum area of the big city. (Everyone was a suspect in those movies, except Marlowe himself.) Outside of Marlowe's office was a flashing neon sign, which shone on the faces of the two men as the intensity of the scene gripped the audience. Dmytryk's challenge, which focused on trimming, was: How do you approach the editing of this scene? Should you become a slave to the neon sign and trim each line of dialog so that the sign flashes at regular intervals, or is there something more important here?

In hindsight, I see the wisdom of the exercise. To a fledgling editor, cutting is microscopic—make every transition fit perfectly, every nuance and every piece of continuity must work correctly, or the editing is wrong. There is a tendency to behave like what Dmytryk would call a mechanic. What we were unknowingly taught was that, if you cut the scene so that the neon sign *did* flash at regular intervals, all of the snappy dialog that was the hallmark of any good private eye movie would be followed by irregular pauses so that the sign could flash on and off at the right intervals. And this is why it is important not only to use the Trim mode for its precision, but also to step back and look at the scenes after you've trimmed.

What is the difference between Dmytryk's mechanic and an intuitive, precise editor? The ability to trim, and to trim well.

Chapter 8

Audio

Most of us consider ourselves picture editors, but I can't remember the last time that I edited picture only, without audio. Audio is an integral part of the job and an integral component of the Xpress Pro's editing capabilities.

Before reading this chapter, please see the section "Audio Setting" on page 23 in Chapter 2. The Settings related to audio are the Audio, Audio Project, Timeline, and Media Creation Settings. These Settings will establish certain parameters for how the audio in your project is created and treated. That chapter also explains the basics of audio sample rate and sample size.

This chapter will discuss some of the basic concepts of editing and mixing audio with good craftsmanship. If you are interested in a deeper understanding of recording and editing digital audio, there are two excellent books from CMP Books by Jay Rose: *Producing Great Sound for Digital Video* and *Audio Postproduction for Digital Video*.

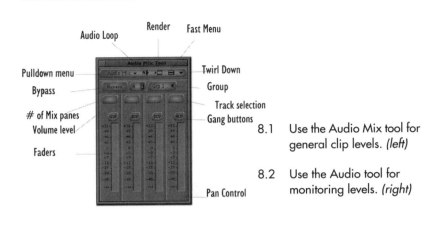

8.1 Use the Audio Mix tool for general clip levels. *(left)*

8.2 Use the Audio tool for monitoring levels. *(right)*

TOOLS OF THE TRADE

When I am mixing audio, I generally use just a couple of tools: the Audio Mix tool for general clip levels; the Timeline window with Auto Gain for keyframed level changes; and the Audio tool for monitoring. I generally don't use the Auto Gain Faders, but there are those who like that method.

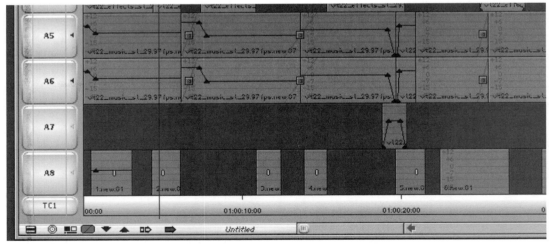

8.3 Use the Timeline with Auto Gain for keyframed levels. Sometimes referred to as "rubber-banding."

AUDIO MIX TOOL

Let's take a look at the most obvious of these tools, the Audio Mix tool. It can be called up from the Tools menu, or mapped to the keyboard for quick recall. (Check out "Keyboard" on page 42 of Chapter 2 to learn how to do this.)

8.4   Audio Mix Tool
      Pulldown Menu

Starting at the top left of the tool is a pulldown menu that gives you access to the Audio Mix tool, Auto Gain tool, EQ tool, and AudioSuite (see Figure 8.4). All of these tools are also available separately in the Tools menu.

The next button is the Audio Loop Play button. This allows you to play back audio in a continuous loop in the Timeline while adjusting the faders in the Audio Mix tool. This can be an extremely useful tool, giving you almost real-time feedback on levels, *if* your computer is fast enough to give you good response time. On slower computers, you won't notice a change in the level until after the audio loops back.

 You will get better response from most of your audio tools, including the Audio tool, Audio Mix tool, EQ tool, and Auto Gain tool if you turn off video monitoring in your Timeline.

The next button to the right is the Render button. This allows you to render audio effects without leaving the Audio Mix tool. Unlike previous Avid products, Xpress Pro audio dissolves are real-time effects. As a result, this button has lost some of its usefulness.

At the far right, along the top is the Audio Mix Fast menu. The menus inside this Fast menu allow you to set levels and pans globally, or between marks.

Warning In order for these menu selections to be active, you must select the audio tracks you want to be active by using the track selector buttons—which are the buttons labeled A1, A2, etc.—above the faders.

These menu selections are very useful for things like bringing up the gain of an entire audio track across all of the edits, or in switching the pan, so that all of the clips on a particular track are centered, for example. You can also remove pan and level settings from

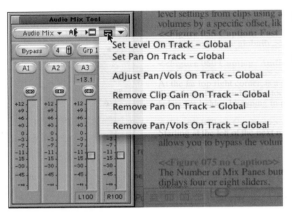

8.5 Fast menu controls allow you to set levels and pan between marks or globally. (left)

8.6 Audio Mix tool with faders hidden. (below)

clips using a Fast menu selection (see Figure 8.5). You can also adjust pans or volumes by a specific offset, like lowering all clips between marks by −3dB (see Figure 8.6).

At the far top-right corner, is a small twirl-down triangle that allows you to hide the faders of the Audio Mix tool. You can still make level adjustments while the faders are hidden by typing numbers into the volume level display text boxes.

Starting at the left of the next row of buttons is the Bypass pulldown menu. This allows you to bypass the volume settings created using the Audio Mix tool.

The Number of Mix Panes button allows you to select whether the Audio Mix tool displays four or eight sliders.

Warning

The Audio Mix tool only displays faders for tracks that are being monitored in the Timeline. If you are missing a fader for a track that you want to adjust, check the Timeline tracks to make sure that the track has a little monitor speaker next to the track number.

The Group button allows you to switch between faders for tracks 1–8 and tracks 8–16.

The next row has the track selector buttons. These buttons are used to activate the tracks for modification by the selections in the Fast menu. You activate the tracks you want by clicking on them.

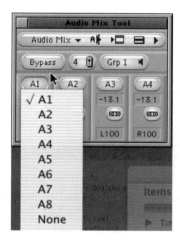

 You can Alt-click/Option-click on the track selector buttons for a pulldown of all the available tracks. This makes it possible to enable tracks from the Audio Mix tool, if they were not being monitored in the Timeline. Or if you didn't want to open up the Audio Mix tool to show eight sliders, you could simply switch the four available sliders to control any track you want by Alt-clicking/Option-clicking on a track and choosing the track you want.

The next row is the Volume level display. This is a text box that allows you to see the current volume level for the track. You can also type entries into this text pane to adjust levels numerically. For fine control, you can also use the up, down, left, and right arrow keys in this pane to adjust by tenths of a dB.

The next row down is the gang row. By clicking on these gang buttons you can gang tracks together so that a change to one of the ganged tracks affects all of the tracks equally. Clicking on a gang button again toggles it off.

Below the gang buttons are the faders. The most common way to adjust these faders is using by dragging the fader up and down. You can also use the up, down, left and right arrow keys. Typing numbers while the fader is active will also adjust the level the same way that it did when the Volume Level Display pane was active.

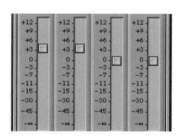

At the bottom of the Audio Mix tool is the Pan control. The alphanumeric display indicates the direction of the pan with L being left and R being right. The numeric entry describes how far the track is panned from 1 to 100. If you want to center the pan of a track, you can drag the pan slider to the center, type a 0 on the numeric keypad and hit enter, or you can Alt-click/Option-click on the pan slider.

Warning If you are unable to change the pan of a track, the most common cause for this is that you have your Audio Project Output Setting on either Mono or Direct output. Obviously both of these settings ignore pan information entirely. So if you want to adjust pan, you need to have your Audio Project Output Setting set to Stereo.

Audio Tool

A lot of people miss out on many audio features because they only perceive the Audio tool as meters. For the Audio tool, being "just meters" is like being Clark Kent for Superman. Hidden behind those meters is a superhero looking for a handy pay-phone booth. (And when was the last time you saw a pay-phone booth that you could change in?)

The Audio tool can be called up from the Tool menu or with the default keyboard command Ctrl+1/Cmd+1. I have the Audio tool mapped to my F11 key, just to save pushing that one extra modifier key. As I mentioned before, I've got the Audio Mix tool mapped to F12, so I generally hit them both at the same time, since I rarely mix audio without looking at levels.

At first glance, this is a tool without a lot of information to provide and even fewer options. If you're more of a Superman fan than a Clark Kent fan, let me show you the way to the phone booth, although for you veteran Avid editors, the handle to the phone booth door has been moved. Don't worry, I'll show you where they moved it.

To access the tools that are left, check out the controls along the top. The buttons are RP and PH, with two small alphanumerics in between. To understand what the RP button does, you need to know what the PH button does, so let's start there.

Clicking on the PH button calls up a pulldown window. Your pulldown options are shown in Figure 8.7.

Input Settings calls up the Input Setting tab of the Audio Project Settings (see Figure 8.8). This allows you to change the input source to RCA or DV (if you have Mojo) or adjust the input gain to 0dB or +6dB. You also have access to the Passthrough Mix Tool. The Passthrough Mix Tool allows you to adjust pan and volume of the way the

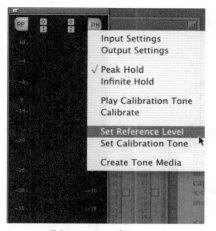

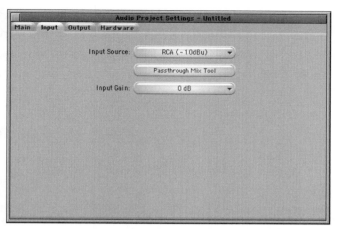

8.7   Pulldown menu from PH button

8.8   Input Setting tab of the Audio Project Setting

incoming audio is *monitored*. This Passthrough Mix does *not* affect the actual captured levels of audio in any way (see Figure 8.9).

 Note   The Passthrough Mixer is only available with Mojo attached.

Output Settings calls up the Output Setting tab of the Audio Projects setting (see Figure 8.10). This allows you to set the Output Gain (which allows you to calibrate the global output level) and the Master Volume (which allows you to make global output-level adjustments). Confused? I was too, but play back some audio when adjusting these

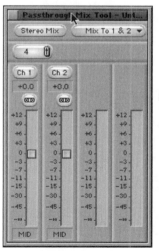

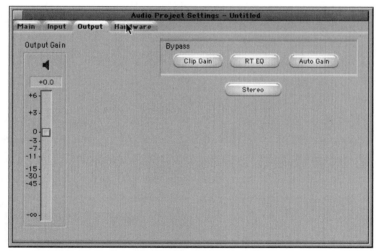

8.9   The Passthrough Mix Tool only adjusts the *monitoring* of the incoming signal. *(left)*

8.10   Output Setting tab of the Audio Projects Settings *(right)*

two levels. Output Gain actually changes the output level, so if you are playing back tone, the level of the tone in the meters changes as well as the sound volume. But changing the Master Volume leaves the levels on the meters the same, while lowering the volume of the audio reaching your headphones, speakers, and output devices. You can also affect the bypass controls—which let you bypass Clip Gain, RT EQ, or Auto Gain—and whether your output is stereo or mono.

Peak Hold momentarily displays the peak level on the meters.

Infinite Hold displays the peak level on the meters for an indefinite (infinite) amount of time. This indefinite amount of time can be ended by clicking on the Reset Peaks button on the Audio tool.

Play Calibration Tone plays a reference tone at 0dB analog. This reference tone can be calibrated to equal any digital audio scale. Normally, the digital reference for 0vu on the analog side is –14 or –20. This can be set to correspond to the headroom of your audio output device. –20 allows for more headroom. While digital decks tend to use a –20dB signal, conventional analogs have a +12dB to +14dB headroom. As a result, many who have decided to set their peaks at –20 (thus allowing +20 headroom when monitoring audio) will get completely blown out audio when outputting.

Calibrate magnifies the meters, allowing you to see very fine increments in the meters for calibrating incoming tone from a deck or other source. This shows you only a single dD scale on either side of reference across the entire meter (see Figure 8.11).

8.11 Note the markings on the scale of the Audio tool in Calibrate mode.

Set Reference Level allows you to determine the digital reference level for tone, corresponding to 0vu. The digital scale on the left is fixed and the vu scale on the right can slide so that 0vu corresponds to any digital reading. Generally people like to match these settings to the scales of their predominant output device. For example, a DigiBeta deck has meters that display 0vu at –20dB. The default is –14, but –20 and –12 are also popular choices. If you aren't sure what to set this at, leave it at –14.

Set Calibration Tone allows you to determine the level of the tone as well as the frequency of the tone. The default is –14dB and 1000Hz. The tone referred to is the one played back when you Play Calibration Tone, not the one created when you Create Tone Media.

 Amaze your friends! You can set the Hz of the tone to two very interesting "easter egg" settings. If you'd like a tone sweep, type in *–777* for the frequency. And if you'd like "pink noise" (static), try 0. This tip applies to both Set Calibration Tone and Create Tone Media.

Create Tone Media allows you to determine the level of the tone as well as the frequency of the tone. The default is –14dB and 1000Hz. This is similar to Set Calibration Tone, but Create Tone Media creates tone that can be cut into a sequence. Setting Calibration Tone creates no media; it only plays the tone to the outputs.

So, knowing all of that, the Reset Peaks (RP) button allows you to reset the peaks if you use Infinite Hold.

 There's another reason for using Reset Peaks. If you want to find out the highest peak level (that's kind of redundant, I guess) in a section of a sequence, or in an entire sequence, hit Reset Peaks, then go to the beginning of the section you want to examine and play to the end of it. Now, call up the console (Ctrl+6/ Cmd+6) and type DumpMaxPeaks in the small text pane at the bottom. This will call up some text in the console that tells you the peak audio level of each audio track. Cool, huh?

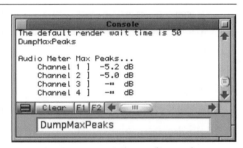

8.12 Typing "DumpMaxPeaks" in the Console displays the peak audio levels on each track since the peaks were reset with the RP button.

Also, there are two tiny alphanumeric readings in the top center of the Audio tool. The top row displays either the letter I or O. These indicate whether the Audio tool is displaying the Input or Output levels. Generally these are set to O and indicate the sum of level changes made with Clip levels, Auto Gain levels, and any other level changes made to the original clip. The I indicates that the Audio tool is displaying the level of the clip as it came into

the system, whether it was digitized or imported. You can toggle between these by clicking the alphanumeric displays. The numbers below them correspond to the numbers of your output channels.

Finally, since the small meters just above your Timeline are simply a miniaturized version of the Audio tool that is available from the Tools menu, you can execute all of these commands from there. All of the options that normally reside under PH are available on the Timeline version of the Audio tool under the little Options icon to the right of the meters. Also, you can Alt-click/Option-click on the speaker icon to the left of the meters for access to the master volume control slider.

8.13 Audio Tool in the
Timeline toolbar

AUTO GAIN OR RUBBER-BANDING

Many old-guard Avid editors resist using Auto Gain, or rubber-banding. I resisted it myself for a short while, until I saw the error of my stubborn ways. Rubber-banding offers many advantages to the traditional method of setting levels and adding dissolves. The main reason is that rubber-banding doesn't get "lost"—even after trimming. If a clip has dissolves on either end—to fade up and fade down—then you move that clip up or down the Timeline or onto different tracks, the dissolves will disappear. With rubber-banding, however, when you move those tracks, the keyframed level changes remain with the track. The one bad rap that rubber-banding deserves is that if you are planning to take your sequence to ProTools, the rubber-banded changes do not translate over. This is basically a bad thing, but you could also say that the reason you're going to a ProTools session in the first place is to take advantage of the ProTools editor's mixing and editing knowledge and advanced skill set as well as the advanced tools that ProTools has to offer, so you might as well let them do their job from scratch.

Some people resist rubber-banding because they think it takes too much time. That may be true for people who don't have the Add Keyframe button mapped to their keyboard. (The same Add Keyframe button that puts keyframes in special effects puts keyframes in rubber-banded tracks.) The other thing that speeds up rubber-banding audio is saving several Timeline views with and without Auto Gain selected. Having Auto Gain enabled in your Timeline does not place a huge screen refresh strain on the system, like Sample Plot does, so you can leave it on most of the time.

Warning One good reason for disabling Auto Gain in your Timeline is so that you do not casually or mistakenly change audio levels or move keyframes when you don't mean to.

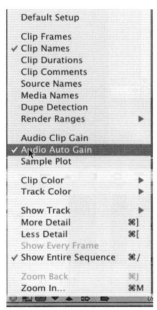

To rubber-band audio in the Timeline, in the Timeline Fast menu, choose Audio Auto Gain. It is also helpful to have your audio tracks "enlarged." With your audio tracks selected in the Timeline, hit Ctrl+L/Cmd+L to enlarge the audio tracks. On my 20" monitor, I have each of my audio tracks about 3/4" to 1" high. From their smallest possible size, that's about 30 clicks of Ctrl+L/Cmd+L. I like to get the audio tracks big enough that I can see the dB markings for +12, +6, 0, −7, −15, and −45. The more enlarged the track is, the more levels you'll see in the scale. Save this Timeline view as Auto Gain, if you want to be able to access it quickly. Also, make sure that you have the keyframe button mapped to the keyboard. On the default keyboard, it is on the N key.

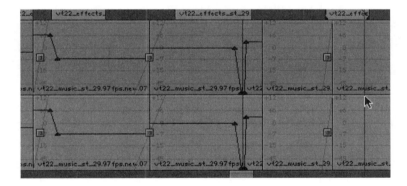

Alt+Ctrl+K/Option+Cmd+K and +L. These modifiers plus the letter K in the Timeline will shrink the Sample Plots inside the audio tracks. The modifiers plus the letter L enlarges the Sample Plots inside the audio tracks. This is useful if the Sample Plots are so loud that they appear as a solid block, then they can be shrunk to see level detail, or if the plots are so faint that it is hard to see them, then they can be enlarged to better discern individual waveforms. This does *not* change the audio levels themselves: just their graphical representation in the Timeline (see Figures 8.14 and 8.15).

Rubber-banding is very simple. Adding keyframes to audio only works on the tracks that are selected, so you need to have one or two tracks selected. Then, if you add a single

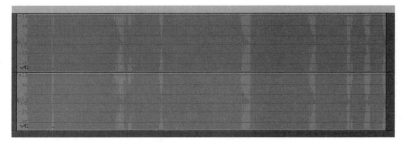

8.14 Sample Plots too large inside the tracks to see detail.

8.15 Sample Plots shrunk to see detail.

keyframe to a clip in the Timeline, and click and drag up or down on that keyframe in the Timeline, you will adjust the volume for the entire clip. If you add two or more keyframes to a clip, you only adjust that single keyframe on any selected tracks. If you want to adjust a group of keyframes, you can mark an IN and an OUT with standard editing tools, and all keyframes between those marks will go up or down by the same amount when you drag a single keyframe from between those marks.

Warning

If you segment-select any clips in the Timeline that have Auto Gain, and attempt to delete the clips, it will take two "deletes" because the first delete just removes the Auto Gain and the second delete actually deletes the clip.

Sometimes I completely bypass the Audio Mix tool and set all of my levels using Auto Gain in the Timeline. You don't quite have the control with rubber-banding that you have with the Mix tool, but it is very fast. For more control while rubber-banding, make your tracks larger (Ctrl+L/Cmd+L). The wider the track, the greater finesse you can achieve with rubber-banding.

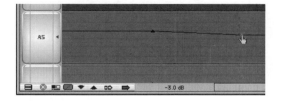

When you are rubber-banding audio levels, check out the bottom of the Timeline to the left of the segment selection arrows. The Timeline View button switches to display the dB gain level while you are dragging the rubber-banding up or down.

The most common use that I have for rubber-banding in the Timeline is putting fade ups and fade downs on clips. Add a keyframe at the very beginning of the clip, and another keyframe perhaps 20 frames later. Then put a keyframe at the end of the clip and another around 20 frames earlier. Drag the first keyframe and the last keyframe down as low as they'll go. The little dB designation at the bottom of the Timeline should read "negative infinity dB."

Listen to the way the audio fades up and down. Does the ramp up or down seem too abrupt? You can drag the keyframes to new positions by Alt-dragging/Option-dragging the keyframe left or right. Sometimes I will use this in conjunction with the display of Sample Plot in the Timeline, so I can see exactly where a note or voice comes in. For example, one of the reasons that many audio fades seem abrupt is not because they are too short, but because of a note that is heard just before the music fades out. So if you can see that note in the Sample Plot, you can drag the keyframe so that the fade ends just before the note hits. I generally don't use Sample Plot to help with editing and mixing decisions, but this is an exception. But usually, when working with audio, your ears are a better tool than your eyes.

Another excellent use of rubber-banding is trying to blend two pieces of music. Many people will try to segue between two pieces of music using a dissolve with the music tracks all on the same two stereo tracks. This is rarely an acceptable way to transition between music. The best way is to place one stereo track of music on—for example—A3 and A4—and the other stereo track of music on A5 and A6. This method has several advantages. The most important is that it allows you to gradually fade out the outgoing

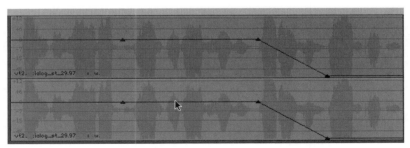

8.16 The keyframe is moved so that the audio is completely attenuated by the time the next beat in the music comes in.

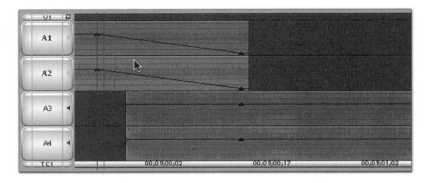

8.17 This is an example of music gradually fading away in one stereo pair, while the other stereo pair cuts in. This edit sounds very natural.

music while cutting in directly on the incoming music. That is a natural sound for music. Think of striking a piano note. It comes in hard and percussive, then trails out. If you hit another piano key shortly after, that note also cuts in while the previous note is still dying away. If you try this by placing a dissolve between two pieces on the same track, it softens both the end of the outgoing piece and the beginning of the incoming track. With most music—string sounds being the possible exception—this does not sound natural. There are very few musical sounds that have a beginning that is as soft as their end. Also, by adding your keyframes to make the dissolves, instead of using dissolve effects, you can segment-drag the two pieces in relation to each other until you get the rhythm and pacing just right.

 When I try to set this kind of pacing between two musical cuts, I either pretend to be directing the musical score, or I tap out the rhythm in time with the first piece and make sure that I don't lose a beat or pick up a beat on the transition to the second piece. I use this same technique when I time a music cue before or after dialog. I pretend that I am directing an orchestra or band and I sense whether they start playing too early or too late.

Rubber-banding is also useful to make seamless dialog edits. Often times, I am asked by a producer to drastically cut interviews. Sometimes this means pulling words from other sentences to create grammatical segues from one thought or another. Oftentimes, this results in strange inflections on certain words. To make those inflections more transparent and believable, I punch them up or lower them with rubber-banding. For example if a word has too much emphasis, I'll lower the volume on that word, or even just a syllable of a word, in order to make it seem more conversational.

I also use rubber-banding as a kind of poor man's compression. One of the ways that radio stations make their station sound louder than their competitors is to strongly compress the peak volumes out of the music and their DJ's voices. That way they can crank up

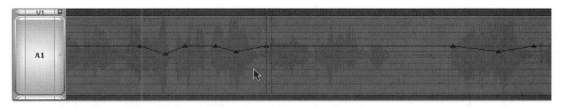

8.18 At the point in the clip where the levels are rubber-banded down for a brief time, the talent's voice got much louder than the rest of his levels. Rubber-banding was used as a kind of "poor man's compression" to even out the reading

the overall volume without going over the volume limit. If you are trying to lay something to tape and you don't want to distort your levels by having anything too high, you can get a greater overall volume by minimizing a few big peaks. For example, you've probably worked with an interview where the speaker was fairly soft-spoken, but every once in a while, he or she would take a deep breath and seem to shout the next few words before returning to their soft-spoken ways. In this case, I crank up the volume of the clip so that I get the average reading that I want, then rubber-band down the levels of the few loud words. The same is true in the reverse for someone that speaks at a normal volume, but then, at some crucial moment, barely whispers a word or two or "swallows" a word. In this case, I'll rubber-band up the volume of the lost words. The trick to doing this success-fully is to be very aware of the increase or decrease in room tone or presence as you do these quick level adjustments. You do not want to bring up the level so much that the air conditioning noise or something becomes apparent all of a sudden. It's less noticeable when lowering the volume for a short moment, but you want to use some finesse. Ask yourself, does it still sound natural?

Another thought about Auto Gain is that you can bypass them. In the Audio Project Set-ting's Output tab, there are three Bypass but-tons: Clip Gain, RT EQ, and Auto Gain. This

can be very useful if you are laying a sequence to tape for someone else to do the audio sweetening. Usually, in this day and age, you would transfer your audio files to the audio sweetening house in some digital audio file format. But if you are going to lay to tape, then you could do all of your rough mixing with rubber-banding, so your client could get an idea of how the audio would sound, but then, when you laid off your audio tracks to DAT or ADAT, you could choose to bypass those level adjustments, so that the audio sweetening house got them fairly clean at full level.

Before I move on from Auto Gain, we should discuss using the Auto Gain tool to set levels. Operationally, this is different from using Auto Gain in the Timeline, but in the end, they both put keyframes in the Timeline and adjust them.

Call up the Auto Gain tool from the Tools menu. The faders in Auto Gain tool look very similar to the faders in the Audio Mix tool. The primary difference is the addition of a Record button. This Record button records the slider positions while you play through your sequence. If you attempt to use this on tracks on which you've already done some Timeline Auto Gain—for example, fading up at the beginning of a track—you'll notice that the Auto Gain tool faders will "fly" in response to the Auto Gain that is already in the track. So put your Timeline locator at the beginning of a sequence—or even in the middle if you want—and hit the record button on the Auto Gain tool. The audio will begin to play. Now, you can drag the faders of the Auto Gain tool up and down during playback and

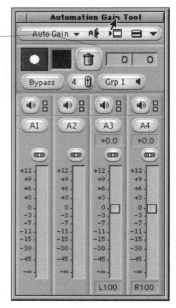

8.19 Auto Gain tool

you will hear the levels of the tracks change in response. When you stop playback, the tracks will have keyframes added and adjusted in response to the way you moved the faders. If you simply play back this section again, you can watch the Auto Gain faders "fly" in response to the keyframes you added to the tracks. If you don't like some of your level changes, you can record over them again. If you don't move the faders, then the keyframes will stay the same. They aren't just erased by recording over them.

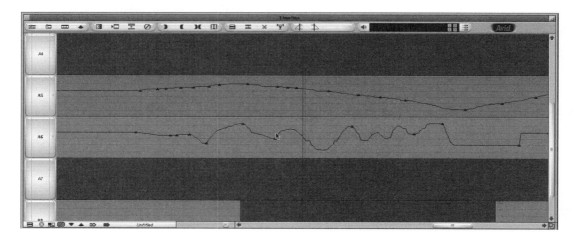

There are quite a few additional features of the Auto Gain tool that are worth discussing. Most of the features are identical to the regular Mix tool (see Figure 8.19). In addition to the Record button, there is also the Record Status light and the Cancel Recording button with the Trashcan icon. Next to the Cancel Recording button are two text panes that allow you to set preroll and postroll times for the Auto Gain recording.

Also, the speaker icons above the track numbers have color identifiers. Purple indicates that the track is selected, gray indicates that the track is muted, and green indicates that the track is soloed. It is possible to solo more than one track at a time.

To switch between solo and active, click on the Speaker icon. To mute a track, Alt-click/Option-click the speaker.

The Fast menu in the Auto Gain tool provides a lot of control. All of the commands in the Fast menu are grayed out until a track is selected by clicking on the Track Selector button in the Auto Gain tool. Some Fast menu selections will slightly differ if there are marks present in the Timeline. In addition to the options that are the same in the Audio Mix tool, Auto Gain also lets you delete Auto Gain keyframes between marks—if they are set—or globally. You also have the option, if there are Auto Gain keyframes, to Filter Auto Gain on Track. This removes about half of the keyframes. When you use the faders or an external device like a JLCooper FaderMaster or a mixer that has been qualified for use with Xpress Pro, like the Digi002 unit in Avid Studio, you can add a lot of unnecessary keyframes, so the filtering process helps to cull these keyframes down to the essentials. You can use this function as many times as you want on a given area until you're left with just the crucial keyframes. If you hold down the Alt/Option key when picking this menu selection, you will remove all of the keyframes except for the minimum and maximum peak keyframes. Deleting these unnecessary keyframes helps lighten the processing burden on your CPU, so it's good to keep these to a minimum. Alt-click/Option-click on the level fader to set to 0vu.

Ctrl+./Cmd+. stops redrawing the Timeline when Sample Plot is enabled. This is handy because sometimes redrawing with Sample Plot on can be lengthy. This tip allows you to stop the redraw and deselect Sample Plot in the Timeline Fast menu.

If you want to call up more than one Audio tool from the Effect Mode Selector pop-up menu, hold down Alt/Option when selecting it. To see how this works, call up the Audio Mix tool, then hold down Alt/Option and click on the Audio Mix button in the top left corner. This calls up a pulldown with Audio Mix, Auto Gain, EQ, and AudioSuite as selections. The normal behavior when selecting one of these options without holding down the modifier key is to replace the current tool with the new selection. With the modifier, you will call up the new tool in addition to the original.

You can use the Audio Mix tool to set levels of sources before they get edited into the sequence. This is very useful for clips that you are going to use several times in a sequence, like a lengthy interview clip. Call the clip up in the Source Monitor or a pop-up bin and call up the Audio Mix tool. Set the levels and pan. Now whenever you cut that source into the sequence, those levels will already be adjusted. One of the biggest reasons to use this tip is with imported music from CDs. CD music usually imports at a very loud level, so immediately lowering their source volume keeps you from blowing out your speakers and your ears. Generally, I use music as a bed—not at full volume—so I'll often set the source level on CD music to −30dB as soon as I import it. When using this tip, remember that you can type in the level, so it's very easy to call up a dozen files, gang the left and right tracks, type −30, and call up the next track.

EQ TOOL

EQ is something that takes a fairly well-trained ear. Music training definitely helps. As a matter of fact, experienced sound mixers and engineers often refer to setting an EQ as tuning EQ; just as you would tune an instrument. You have to understand the basic ranges of sounds to help get you in the ballpark when starting to tune an EQ. The basic concept of EQing a track is that you select a tonal range of a clip, for example, the high end, midrange, or low end of a sound (sometimes referred to as treble, midrange, and bass), and either attenuate (lower the volume of) just that range or raise it. Sometimes this helps eliminate an annoying tone or hum that only resides in a certain frequency range of the audio spectrum and sometimes it is to enhance a deficient range. For example, adding some high end (boosting the level of the upper range or frequencies) can help make a somewhat muffled voice more understandable by increasing the sibilant sounds that help make speech clear.

The biggest trick in EQing something is finding the frequency range. If you wish that you were better at EQ then you need to practice. One of the easiest ways to do this is to try to eliminate a pitch or tone or at least reduce it using EQ. The best way to practice is with real-world examples, such as voices or music or natural sound. But if you are just looking to first understand the basic concept of what is possible or how to do it, then let's attempt to apply EQ to some test tones on the DVD. This is kind of cheating, because these tones are very pure. Most tones have harmonics, or appear over a range of frequencies, but we're going to just try to figure out what frequency the tone is and how to lower it. Then we'll up the ante and try to eliminate just one of three tones, while leaving the other two unaffected.

The tones in these examples were created using the Create Tone menu selection in the Audio tool. I specified a specific frequency when I created them. Your job is to figure out approximately what that frequency is. To start, the default tone that most people put under color bars is 1000Hz, or 1kHz. The tone that is used for a concert violinist or orchestra to tune to is 440Hz, or concert A. Compare the 1kHz tone to the tones on the DVD in the Audio Chapter's EQ tutorial folder. Is the tone lower or higher that 1kHz?

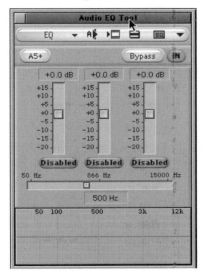

In the EQ tool, there are three faders. They are not labeled as low, mid, and high because the frequency ranges that they affect can be changed. But in general you can think of these three faders as adjusting low, mid, and high. The left fader—called the "low shelf— allows you to select one of three specific frequency ranges: 80, 120, and 240. You pick the frequency range by clicking on the button with the frequency number in it, directly below the fader. The center fader, called the parametric midrange, allows you to select a frequency range using the horizontal fader in just above the graphic EQ display. By dragging that fader left or right, you can select a frequency range that covers the entire spectrum from low to high (50Hz–15,000Hz). The range of human hearing is roughly 20Hz to 20,000Hz. Obviously this range is very different from person to person and changes as we age. The center fader also allows you to choose whether you want to affect the selected frequency in a very narrow 1/4-octave band, or a wider 2-octave band. This option simply lets you either specifically target a precise range of frequencies, or affect more frequencies with your

Default EQ Settings

One of the features of the EQ tool is that you can access several factory-default EQ Settings from the EQ tool Fast menu. These are preset effects that you can apply to any audio you want. If you have an EQ setting that you'd like to be able to access from the Fast menu at any time, you can make your own factory preset.

1. Create the EQ effect on a piece of audio, and then drag the EQ effect icon from the top of the EQ tool into a bin. Now name the effect something descriptive.

2. Then go to File>Open Bin and navigate your way to your Program (for PC) or Applications (for Mac) folder>Xpress Pro folder>Supporting Files>Site Effects. Inside the Site Effects folder is a Site EQs bin. You should be able to just open it from there. You may need to choose "All types" as the file type instead of just Bins.

3. Once the bin is open, your can add your effect to the bin. I had some trouble getting this to work on a Mac and discovered that dragging the Site EQ bin to the Desktop, then opening it from that location allowed me to get this to work.

4. Once you've closed the Site EQ bin, your EQ effect should be selectable from the EQ tool's Fast menu, just like the factory effects.

adjustment. If the sound you want to affect is spread over a broader range of frequencies, then use the 2-octave selection. If it is a narrowly focused hum or buzz, then use the 1/4-octave range so that your correction does less damage to nearby frequencies that you do not want to affect. The right fader, called the high shelf, allows you to select 6000, 8000, 12000, or 150000Hz. The faders themselves work just like volume faders, increasing or decreasing the level of audio, but only in the specified frequency range.

To make things easy, the tones are very pure, and I have limited them to the specific frequency ranges that are in the EQ tool—usually. I included the very highest and lowest frequencies that Create Tone Media would allow.

To start, play Tone.I. I will start out by telling you that this tone is 1000Hz (1kHz). Cut this into a sequence and mark an IN and OUT a few seconds apart on the tone clip in the sequence. Marking an IN and an OUT point allows us to use the audio looping button at the top center of the EQ tool, so that audio keeps playing over that area as we adjust the levels. Before you adjust any of the levels or frequencies, hit this button so that the signal is playing while you make adjustments. Depending on the speed of your computer, it may take several seconds for you to hear the changes that you make in the EQ

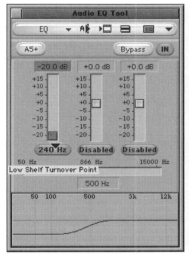

8.22 Center fader

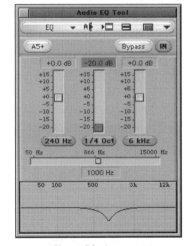

8.20 Left fader as low as possible

8.21 Attenuated right fader

8.23 Horizontal fader at 1000

tool. Definitely turn off video monitoring when attempting these exercises. Do them slowly, so you understand what effect each change has.

Let's see what happens to the volume of this tone if we set the left EQ fader to the highest frequency it can select, 240Hz, and attenuate that frequency as far down as the fader will go (see Figure 8.20). Nothing happens. Why? Because that fader is only going to affect things in that specific frequency range. Let's go to the right fader at its lowest frequency range, 6kHz, and attenuate it (see Figure 8.21). Still nothing happens. Now let's try two different things with the center fader. Click on the button directly below the center fader and select 1/4 octave (see Figure 8.22). Now drag the horizontal fader to 1000Hz (see Figure 8.23). You can also click on the fader and type in a number with the numeric keypad. With the specific frequency selected, this narrow frequency range, or notch, selects the tone and allows it to be lowered or raised (see

8.24 Effect of fader at 1000

Figure 8.24). You can see in the graphic area below the horizontal fader that if you drop the volume all the way down at 1kHz, it makes a sharp "v" with 1kHz at the bottom, but that it's also affecting frequencies from about 500Hz up to 3kHz. Now let's slide the horizontal fader down to 400Hz and see if the tone is affected. It's not changing in volume, is it? Now, let's change the 1/4-octave range on the center slider to a 2-octave range. As you can see by the graphical representation in the EQ tool, the range now affects a much broader area. So even without the exact tone specified, it will still have some affect.

To test out your skills with the other tones, cut them all into a sequence and set the center fader to 1/4-octave range. Loop a small section of each tone and try to isolate it by lowering the center fader to –20dB and then slowly sliding the horizontal fader to the position you think will isolate the tone.

Now comes the single tricky test. I have three tones and your goal is to lower only one of them. Use the 1/4-octave range and lower the center fader all the way to isolate it from the others. Try to find all three tones. Just slide the horizontal fader along slowly from left to right. At a certain point, you will hear the lowest tone drop away, leaving only the middle and high tones. Keep sliding to the right slowly and you'll hear all three tones again, then the middle tone will drop away, leaving only the high and low tones. As you continue to the right, you'll get back all three tones for a while, before finally losing the high tone, leaving you with just the two lower tones.

So how does this help you? If you can identify the frequency range of a sound you want to either enhance or diminish in the mix, and it can be isolated from other sounds that are in different frequencies, then you can target it with the EQ. In the real world, it is a little harder to do, because naturally occurring sounds—unlike these electronic tones—exist over a range of tones because they are made up of harmonics that provide richness and color to the sound.

Most human speech is in the range from 60–200Hz for a male and 150–350Hz for a female. Naturally, there is great variation in these figures. If you are trying to eliminate a hum in a dialog track, make sure that you do not alter the color of these speech frequencies too much if you want a voice to sound normal. Similarly, if you are trying to influence the EQ of a voice, these are the ranges you will need to affect.

The EQ tool in Xpress Pro is pretty fundamental and somewhat limited. There are much more powerful EQ tools accessible through AudioSuite (DAE) that include parametric equalizers.

AudioSuite Plug-ins

AudioSuite plug-ins allow you to access third-party audio filters and effects from within Xpress Pro. Some of these effects are quite complicated and require a fair amount of specialized audio engineering knowledge. Some basic AudioSuite effects are provided by Avid while others can be purchased from your local audio reseller or from the web.

The most prominent developers of AudioSuite plug-ins that are compatible with Xpress Pro are Arboretum (www.arboretum.com), Avid's own DigiDesign (www.digidesign.com), and Waves (www.waves.com).

The web sites of these manufacturers are great repositories of information on the individual capabilities and operation of the dozens of plug-ins manufactured by each developer. You should note that the music industry is very Mac-centric and many of the plug-ins only work on Macs. Some plug-ins have poor—or nonexistent—performance on anything *but* Wintel machines. So, caveat emptor. These plug-ins are constantly being revised and updated. Be sure to do your research before you buy.

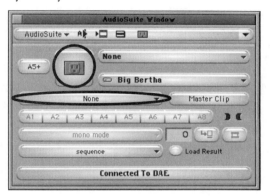

The basic operation of an AudioSuite plug-in is just as simple as adding any effect elsewhere in Xpress Pro. Call up the Audio-Suite tool from the Tools menu or from the Audio Mix tool. The button on the left, which either says None or indicates an audio channel, allows you to select the tracks on which to apply the effect. The large plug-in button (called the Activate Current Plug-in button) calls up the AudioSuite plug-in interface so that you can edit the effect (similar to going into Effects mode). The button that says None or that indicates the name of an AudioSuite effect is the Plug-in Selection menu that pulls down to reveal the names of all of the AudioSuite effects that are loaded on your system. Use these buttons to assign the tracks that you wish to affect, select the plug-in of your choice, and call up the AudioSuite plug-in interface. AudioSuite plug-ins can take more memory and horsepower than standard audio, so while adjusting the parameters, I recommend that you turn off video monitoring and mark a fairly small area with an IN and an OUT. Then use the audio looping button. Each time you adjust a parameter, you should be able to hear the adjustment during the next loop.

The Xpress Pro Help menu has complete information about the operation of the individual AudioSuite plug-ins that ship with Xpress Pro.

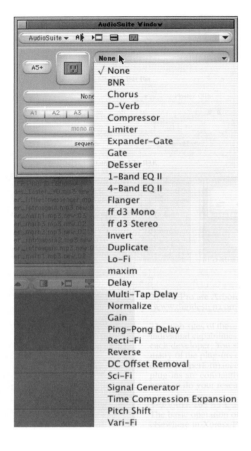

AUDIO CRAFTSMANSHIP

Audio is one of those places where an editor's sense of craftsmanship really shows. A lot of the artistic stuff an editor does happens with video, but the craftsmanship really shows with audio. This is like fine cabinetmaking. You make sure that everything is sanded smooth and all the corners join seamlessly and that the angles are all square. That's a lot like audio editing. I am constantly shocked by the poor craftsmanship of so much of the editing I hear. I have a couple of pointers to turn you into a Master Craftsman. Maybe you already follow these guidelines. If so, pat yourself on the back. You're a pro.

I see a lot of editors who cut in both tracks of audio from a field tape and leave them there. Why? Listen to each track "soloed." Which track sounds better? Use that track by itself. Make sure, if you're doing a stereo lay-off, that that track is center-panned. I have run into a few instances where the best sound was actually achieved by mixing the two tracks of field audio, but usually one track is superior to both. If you can, choose this track by listening in a couple of ways. You may like the bassy, rich sound of the lavalier microphone, but if you listen on a small TV-set speaker, you'll hear that the crispy high end of the boom mic cuts through the mix better and makes the speaker easier to hear.

EDITING DIALOG

The next big mistake that many editors make is that they leave holes in their audio sequence from interviews, using filler to make the space between bites. This is bad. There is a big difference in the sound of total electronic silence, like filler, and the silence created by recording a room where no one is talking. You *can* edit using just filler to determine the initial pacing of your dialog edits, but you should not leave the filler between the bites.

You need to find presence—sometimes called room tone or ambience—to cut in between the bites. Most good crews and producers remember to shoot 10–30 seconds of "presence" after an interview, running both mics, while the talent just sits quietly for a moment. But even if you don't get this luxury, you can usually go through the interview or dialog and find between 20 and 60 frames of relative silence to use as presence. Be careful not to use a section where the talent is taking a breath, and listen for sounds in the background. Once you've found your "sounds of silence" you should subclip it, label it, and put it in your sequence bin, or some bin that will remain open for as long as you're cutting dialog. I'll use presence to pace my dialog edits and allow for smooth transitions between thoughts. I also use it to get rid of things like double breaths, lip licks, "ums," and tongue clucks. Often when editing together two sound bites, you end up hearing the talent take a breath at the end of one bite, then another at the beginning of the next bite. This does not sound natural. Use presence to remove the breaths. If you only have one breath between comments, this is usually a pretty natural sound and I tend to leave those breaths in, but sometimes, I'll eliminate as many breath sounds as I can, by replacing them with presence.

A word of caution when cutting in presence: make sure that the presence is from the same audio track as the track you chose for the dialog and make sure that the pan and volume is the same as that set for the rest of the dialog. This is easy to mess up if you add presence at the end of the dialog-cutting process. An easy way to help yourself do this correctly is to only subclip the dialog track you chose and to set the pan and volume on the subclip, so that it's the same each time you cut it in.

The most crucial thing about editing dialog is that the pace and rhythm of the dialog is natural. When I am cutting together an interview or dramatic piece, I try to speak the line of dialog bridging the edit. So if I was editing together a sentence of someone saying "Xpress Pro is a great little box. Editing on it keeps my breath minty clean," but the first sentence was from one take and the second sentence was from another take, I'd make a first rough cut, then play it back and read along with the video. If my read matched across the edit, I'd be done. But if I naturally started to speak the second sentence before or after the video version, I'd adjust the edit so that it matched the way I was speaking the sentences. You may need to use a bit of presence to make this happen without stray audio between the bites.

As I'm cutting dialog, one of my guideposts to being able to get in and out of edits cleanly is to watch the mouth of the speaker. Understand the shapes the mouth makes forming certain syllables. Vocal coaches and speech therapists use all kinds of fancy words for the sounds and mouth shapes that go along with them, but all you need to know is "Where does one word end and the next word begin?" Editing dialog visually can be very precise. That "b" sound or "p" sound or "w" or "m" sound can't start until the lips part, for example. Or the "f" or "v" sound can't happen until the lip touches the teeth.

One of the exceptions to the rule of cutting dialog at a comfortable pace is when you are editing promos or commercials. In general, promos and commercials still follow this rule, but since the time is so compressed in these forms, sound bites are often pulled up so tightly against voiceover that they sometimes overlap. When I cut promos I often "checkerboard" my audio clips, alternating between track one and two, so that I can use segment mode or "slip and slide trimming" to slip the clips tighter and tighter to each other after my initial rough timing. If the clips were on the same track, you'd usually clip the endings or beginnings of adjacent words.

On the subject of commercials and promos, I'll pass along this cool tip that I learned from one of my colleagues, Jeff Schwartz. Jeff cuts a lot of car spots for J. Walter Thompson out of Chicago and he often beefs up his mono announce track by putting it on two different tracks. Then he sets the pan, level, and even the EQ of each track slightly differently to give it a meatier presence and more "life" in the stereo field.

Too often, we leave the pacing of the speakers to their natural rhythms. Often this is truthful and correct, but sometimes a good editor needs to alter these rhythms to fit the story. If one actor finishes speaking and another starts too soon after, you can use presence to add a dramatic pause between the statements to draw out the tension or suspense or even alter the meaning and intent of the actual words that are spoken.

EDITING MUSIC

Music has structure. Editing music requires that you understand the structure of the music. Editing so that the beats match is not good enough. In fact, it is frequently discouraged. You also need to be aware of where you are in the measure ("and a one and a two and a three and a four") and what part of the song you're cutting to and from. Imagine that the music had words, you wouldn't just cut from "Twinkle, Twinkle, little star" to "wonder what you are." People would hear the jump and wonder where the missing words are. Another example would be if you edited from the middle of a chorus to the middle of a verse. These things will cause the audience to subconsciously be taken out of the story you're trying to tell.

There are times when I have the perfect IN point for a piece of music, but then I also need to be able to "button up" the ending at a place that requires me to do a "nasty" musical edit somewhere in between. When this happens I try to find a loud noise or piece of "nat sound" that I can put up, that covers up the bad edit. If this is not an option, then try to take the audio down to such a low level that the audience will temporarily lose their place in the music so you can fade up after the bad edit. Sometimes you can hide these bad musical edits by adding a cymbal crash or some other sound effect or brief atonal musical cue over the edit—like a cymbal roll or big drum beat. When that doesn't work, you can just do what generations of editors have done: cough every time you get to the bad edit when the client is reviewing it...

Music editing is one of the few times that I find it helpful to be able to see the Sample Plots in the Timeline. You need to do the editing by ear, but you can easily spot exact position of the sample waveforms as you get down to the critical trimming.

Editing music is much easier if you use the playback and mark IN and OUT keys off of the keyboard instead of mousing. That will allow you to keep playback going as you edit. It is also much easier to "tap" a mark IN or OUT on the keyboard, almost like you're playing a keyboard. When I use this method to mark my points, I rarely have to trim them.

When cutting music, you naturally make edits on the beats, but often the best sounding transitions happen if the edit is off the beat. It is a good idea, once you have determined that your music edits maintain the rhythm of the piece correctly, to go back and use double-sided trimming or the Extend key to alter the edit point slightly without changing the timing of the beats. And as usual, a short dissolve is usually helpful.

Sometimes, if you have a slight click on an audio edit, you do not have to use a short dissolve to get rid of the click. Sometimes, trimming the cut by a frame or two one way or the other will eliminate the click.

Editing craftsmanship really shows up when you're editing audio. Hopefully these tips and tricks, along with the ones you've learned from experience, will help you make flawless edits so that nobody even realizes you had to do anything. One of the highest compliments I ever received for a music edit was when somebody told be I'd picked out a good piece of music for the edit. What they didn't know was that it was 12 different cuts of music, joined seamlessly.

I wrote a whole article on music editing on Avid's web site (www.avid.com). Check it out if you're interested in further information.

Chapter 9

Effects

The effects on Xpress Pro can range from very basic to extremely intricate. For most editors, the array of effects might seem a bit overwhelming. But while the specific parameters of a given effect will vary, they all have similar traits.

Many of the effects on Xpress Pro can be self taught—with a little bit of experimentation, you'll be able to master most, if not all of the parameters. This chapter shows you how to use the Effects Palette, define the different types of effects, and adjust their parameters. You'll learn how to save templates, apply and remove effects, and differentiate between the different types of effects on the palette.

There is also a whole separate category of very powerful effects created by third party companies called AVX effects. These effects can almost bring your humble Xpress Pro up to the power of a Symphony. There is an appendix on page 421 in the back of this book that describes the many AVX packages that can be used to enhance the effects power of your Xpress Pro. There are also many demo versions, example movies, and PDF files concerning these AVX effects on the DVD-ROM.

9.1 Typical Transition Effect

9.2 Typical Segment Effect

EFFECT TYPES

Every effect can be placed into one of two categories: transition effects and segment effects. Transition effects are effects that are used or applied at the transition point between two separate clips. Examples of transition effects can be wipes, fades, and dissolves (see Figure 9.1). Segment effects are specific effects that are applied to the segments of your sequence. Examples of segment effects are masks, picture-in-picture, and resizes (see Figure 9.2).

Vertical versus Horizontal Effects

An additional way to define effects can be whether they are horizontal in nature or vertical. A horizontal effect would take place on a single track. A vertical effect could be seen as a layered composite of several different effects on multiple tracks. However, the two frequently intersect each other—transitional effects, normally considered horizontal can be vertical, and layered effects, normally considered vertical, can be horizontal. For purposes of discussion, we'll stick to the segment and transition types.

USING THE EFFECTS PALETTE

Every effect available in Xpress Pro can be accessed through the Effects Palette. The Effects Palette can be accessed in two ways:

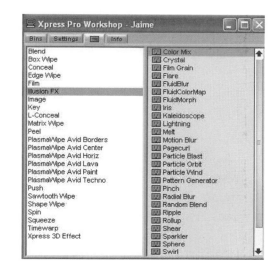

1. Select your Project window and click on the Effect tab.

2. Choose Tools>Effects Palette (Ctrl+8/ Cmd+8)

The Effects Palette has two columns. In the left column is the Effect category. In the right column is a list for each category of effects, as selected in the left column.

So, for example, if you were interested in looking at different types of Blend effects, you would first click on the Blend category in the left column. The right column would display the different types of blends available on your system: Dip to Color, Dissolve, Fade From Color, and so on.

Applying Effects

Applying effects to your sequence is a simple drag-and-drop operation.

9.3   Dragging and Dropping an Effect on the Timeline

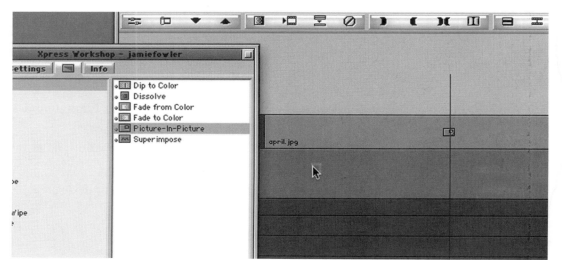

To apply an effect:

1. Open the Effects Palette and choose an effect category from the left column.

2. Choose a specific effect from your category on the right column.

3. Click on the effect and drag it into the Timeline to its desired location. The effect is applied.

When an effect is applied through drag and drop, it has certain default settings:

1. If the effect is a transition effect, its duration is one second long. (30 frames NTSC or 25 frames PAL).

2. The effect is centered so that its midpoint occurs at the original cut point. In other words, in NTSC systems, the effect begins 15 frames before the cut and ends 15 frames after the cut. In PAL systems, the effect occurs 12 frames before the cut point and ends 13 frames after.

Removing Effects

To remove an effect:

1. Place the blue position bar on the effect in the Timeline. Make sure that the track where the effect is located is selected.

2. Click on the Remove Effect Button under the Record Monitor. The effect disappears. Since removing effects is fairly common, you should consider mapping the Remove Effect button to your keyboard to reduce "mousing."

 Removing Effects: Occasionally you may encounter a situation where Remove Effect doesn't seem to work or where clicking on the Remove Effect button removes the wrong effect. To increase accuracy, make sure that the Timeline is spread out enough so that you can see that the blue position bar is placed on the right effect, and always choose the correct track(s). There may be cases where multiple effects occur on different tracks. Be sure to disable those tracks before removing any effects.

You can also remove a segment effect by using the Timeline Segment Editing modes. To do this:

1. Select either Extract/Splice or Lift/Overwrite (the yellow or red arrow buttons at the bottom of the Timeline).

2. Click on the effect—or even Shift-click multiple effects—that you want to delete.

3. Click on the Delete button. The effect or effects are deleted.

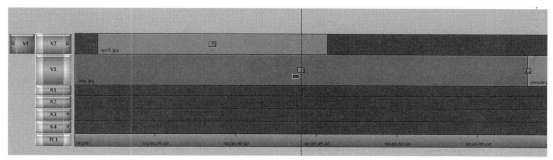

9.4   Removing Effects through Segment Editing Tools

Warning

Doing this to a transition effect will delete the media underneath the transition. Use this method only for segment effects.

REAL-TIME PLAYBACK OF EFFECTS

Real-time playback is one of the by-products of the ever-increasing speed of CPUs. Almost all of the Avid effects in your Xpress Pro system can be played back in real time, right after you apply them. However, third-party AVX plug-ins must be rendered in order to enable playback of the effect.

Xpress Pro has the capability of playing back up to five real-time effects simultaneously. Your system's playback abilities will vary depending on its configuration. While it would seem pointless to have the ability to enable or disable real-time effects, there are some trade-offs to be considered.

When you enable real-time effects:

- You cannot output an NTSC video signal, and

- Your external NTSC monitor (if you have one connected) will be blacked out.

So in some cases, real-time effects might not be desired.

It boils down to this: real-time effects are perfect for editing situations where either you or a client needs to judge the results of applied effects. Once that is done and the effects are all approved, you will still eventually have to render them before outputting a digital cut to video.

To enable or disable real-time effects, click on the Toggle Digital Video Out button on the Timeline. When the button is green, real-time effects are enabled. When it is blue, real-time effects are not enabled.

Using Mojo

When the optional Mojo box is connected to your Xpress Pro, the Toggle Digital Video Out Button is not available on the interface. This is because real-time effects are always enabled and digital video out is also available.

TRANSITION EFFECTS

A transition effect creates an effect between two clips in the Timeline. This can be one of many different effects, including dissolves, wipes, and pushes. The effects are all different, but they have many common characteristics, including the duration of the transition and the position of the transition relative to the two adjoining clips.

When referring to a transition, the outgoing clip is commonly referred to as the A side of the transition and the incoming clip is referred to as the B side. When working with transitions, you have four choices for the positioning of the effect.

1. Beginning at transition

2. Ending at transition

3. Centered on transition

4. Custom

9.5   Transition Point Pulldown Menu

Beginning at Transition

When Beginning at Transition is chosen, your transition effect will begin at the cut point between the A and B sides. Thus, a 30-frame transition starts at the cut point, and ends 30 frames into the B side. If you've worked with linear video editing systems, Beginning at Transition is probably what you're used to.

Ending at Transition

Ending at transition allows the effect to begin before the cut point. The number of frames in the transition is the determining factor as to when the effect will occur. For example, a 30-frame transition starts 30 frames before the original cut point, and ends at the cut point.

Centered on Transition

When an effect is Centered at Transition, it uses equal sides of both A and B and is centered at the cut point. For example, a 30-frame transition effect will overlap 15 frames on the A side and 15 frames on the B side. The actual center point is located at the original cut point. Traditionally, film editors have used centered transitions.

Custom

A Custom transition effect is neither centered on nor begins at or ends at the cut point. Custom transitions use an unequal number of frames from the A and B sides to complete the transition. There are a number of reasons for creating custom transitions, including insufficient source media on either the A or B side of the transition and undesired frames adjacent to the transition on the A or B side.

SEGMENT EFFECTS

Unlike transition effects, which are applied to the transition between two clips, segment effects are applied to entire clips in a sequence. Segment effects affect the picture for the entire duration in the Timeline.

To apply a Segment Effect, open the Effects Palette and drag the segment effect to the clip in your Timeline. Notice as you drag the effect, the entire clip becomes highlighted. Once the effect is added, an effect icon appears in that clip in the Timeline.

9.6   A Segment Effect in the Timeline

EFFECT EDITOR BASICS

Each effect in the Effects Palette has parameters—characteristics that are integral to the effect that can be adjusted and customized. Those parameters are controlled by the Effect Editor.

To open the Effect Editor, click on the Effects Mode button or change your toolset (Toolset>Effects Editing) (see Figure 9.7). Changing to Effects Editing will not automatically switch to Effects mode unless your blue indicator is parked on an effect in the Time-

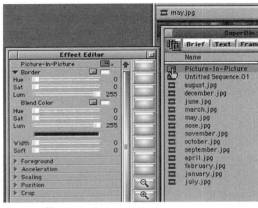

9.7   Effects Mode Button

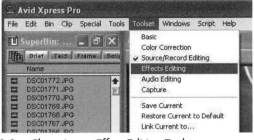

9.8   Changing to Effect Editing Toolset

line (see Figure 9.8). However, you can enter Effects mode by selecting the Effects Mode icon.

The contents of the Effect Editor will differ for each effect. However the editor layout is always the same (see Table 9.1 and Figure 9.9).

Table 9.1   Contents of the Effect Editor Window

Item	Function	Location
Effect Name	Identifies the Effect being Edited	Top of Effect Editor
Effect Icon	When dragged to a bin, stores an effect template of the edited effect	Top right of Effect Editor
Effect Parameters	Various adjustments that can be made to each individual effect, usually indicated by a twirl-down triangle menu that reveals more adjustments in each parameter category	Below Effect name. The central portion of the Effect Editor
Render Button	Renders an effect	Bottom left of the Effect Editor
Path Button	Does not apply to all effects. Used for defining the type of path (Smooth or Linear) of an effect	To the right of the Render Button
Transition Location Button	Determines the transition location for transition effects only	To the right of the Path Button
Duration Entry	Allows manual entry of the effect duration	Right bottom of the Effect Editor

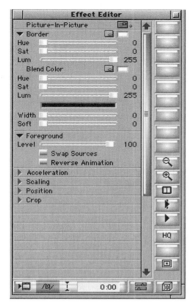

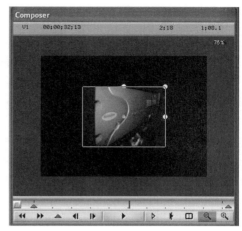

9.9   The Effect Editor *(left)*

9.10   Zooming in and Out of the Effect Preview Monitor *(right)*

Optional Buttons in the Effect Editor

In addition to the standard contents of the Effect Editor, several optional buttons are located on the right side of the Effect Editor. Each effect contains different optional buttons (see Table 9.2 and Figure 9.10).

Table 9.2   Common Optional Buttons

Item	Function
Zoom In	Zooms into the picture, thus increasing image size in the monitor. Each iteration increases magnification by 1×. Maximum: 8×.
Zoom Out	Zooms out of the picture, thus reducing image size in the monitor. Each iteration reduces the image by 25%. Minimum size is 25%.
Split Screen	Provides a split screen to examine both before and after the effect is applied.
HQ	Renders the effect in High Quality 16-bit mode. High Quality rendering is not available for every effect. Grayed out when not available.

Zooming In and Out: When working with effects, Ctrl-clicking on an image in the Effect Preview Monitor will cause it to zoom in. Using Shift-Ctrl-click will zoom it out.

ADJUSTING PARAMETERS

The Effect Editor lists different groups of adjustable effect parameters in collapsible twirl-down menus. A twirl-down menu is indicated by a triangle icon pointing at each specific parameter. When clicked, the triangle twirls down to reveal specific parameter sliders of each parameter group. If you click the triangle again, it twirls back to its original pointing position at the parameter group, and the individual parameters disappear.

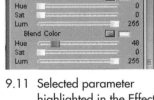

9.11 Selected parameter highlighted in the Effect Editor

Each adjustment of a parameter is controlled by a slider. You can control the adjustment of each parameter using three different methods:

1. Click on the slider and move it to the right or left.

2. Click on the slider, type in a numeric value for the adjustment, and press Enter.

3. Click on the slider and adjust it in increments by using your left and right arrow keys on your keyboard.

Adjusting Parameters: When adjusting parameters, you can move 10 increments by holding down the Shift key when pressing the left or right arrow buttons. You can also move from slider to slider by using the Tab key. Tab moves to the next parameter. Shift+Tab moves to the previous parameter.

The result of changing a parameter is WYSIWYG. The Record Monitor should update to the resulting image. If you cannot see the effect in your record monitor, select Clip>Render On The Fly, so that Xpress Pro will display the results.

Common Parameters in Xpress Pro Effects

Each individual effect has adjustable parameters. The number and type of parameters will vary greatly, from the simplest wipe, which may only contain a few parameters, to the most intensive AVX plug-in effect, which can contain dozens of parameters.

While it would be impossible to cover all of the effects that are available for Xpress Pro, many of the parameters work and operate the same. Here is a review of some of those parameters.

Border

Many effects, such as wipe, conceal, squeeze, shape, and 3D effects, contain a Border parameter (see Figure 9.12). The Border parameter allows you to adjust the color, blend color, softness, and width of the border of an effect.

Border Color

The Border Color and Blend Color parameters let you set the color for the border. Adding a blended color allows you to create a gradient border. There are three values that create the border colors. They are:

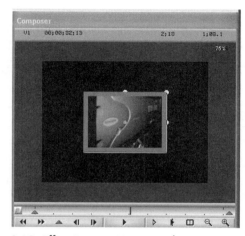

9.12   Effect Preview Monitor—Placing a Border on an Effect

- *Hue:* The shade of color as defined in value ranges between 0 and 255.

- *Saturation:* The intensity of color. The value range is again 0 to 255, where 0 represents no saturation (color) and 255 is fully saturated color.

- *Luminance:* The brightness of the border. Values are 0 to 255, where 0 represents black and 255 represents white.

There are three ways to adjust border colors:

- Parameter Sliders
- The Eyedropper
- The Color Selection tool

Note   Before you begin adjusting the colors of the border, adjust the width and then move in the Effect Timeline, which is located underneath the effect monitor on the right of the interface, so that you can see the border as you edit the effect.

Parameter Sliders

By clicking on and moving individual sliders, the parameters will change. Adjust the hue, saturation, and luminance to the desired color. You can preview the color of the border either by looking at the color preview box to the right of the parameters or by previewing the effect.

The Eyedropper

The Eyedropper tool is a great way to "sample" a color from the existing images in your effect. To use the eyedropper, click and hold the mouse over the Color Preview box. Slide the mouse over to your image in the Effect Preview Monitor and release the mouse on the color you wish to select. The color register box changes to the sampled color.

Eyedroppering: In some cases, the color may be too small in the picture. You can zoom in and out of the picture and resize the Effect Preview Monitor to more accurately choose a color from the monitor.

The Color Selection Tool

The Color Selection tool allows you to pick colors using standard Windows and Macintosh color selection. To access the Color Selector, click on the icon next to the Color Preview box. When you find the color that you like, press the OK button (see Figure 9.13).

Border Blending

You can add and adjust the border blend color in the same way as the border color, using the Parameter Sliders, Eyedropper, and Color Selection tool. Keep in mind as you select your border colors that the gradient will contain colors in between the primary border and border blend colors as well. A good mnemonic is ROY G BIV. These are the colors of the spectrum, represented by each letter in the name. Red, Orange, Yellow, Green, Blue, Indigo and Violet. Thus, if your border color is yellow and the blend color is violet, the gradient will contain all of the colors in between those two in the color spectrum, i.e., green, blue, and indigo will also be displayed in the gradient.

Border Blending: When using the Eyedropper tool on your border color, both the border and blend colors change to the selected color. To prevent this and allow the system to keep the existing blend color, hold down the Alt/Option key while selecting border color with the eyedropper. The system does not change border color when the eyedropper is used to select a blend color.

Acceleration

The Acceleration parameter determines the type of motion and fluidity between keyframes of an effect. It has nothing to

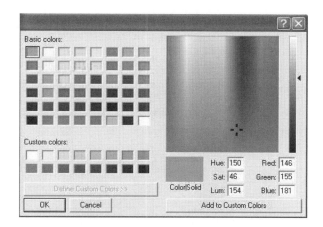

9.13 The Color Selection Tool in Windows

9.14 Border Blending in Effect Editor (top)

9.15 Effect of Border Blending in Effect Preview
       Monitor *(bottom)*

do with the speed between keyframes, which is determined by duration between keyframes.

Linear acceleration moves at a constant speed and motion and is indicated in the Acceleration parameter as 0 Acceleration. The opposite of this is Smooth acceleration which eases in and out of motion between keyframes. This is indicated in the Acceleration parameter as any number between 1 and 100. Thus a smooth acceleration starts at the keyframe and gradually accelerates, then slows as it arrives at the next keyframe. A linear acceleration does not change speed as it leaves one keyframe or arrives at the next. Smooth acceleration is much more natural and linear is much more mechanical.

There are cases where you could use each of these. An example of linear use might be where you have several images moving across the screen at once. If smooth acceleration was used, their speed and proximity to each other will vary. Using linear acceleration allows you to keep the images uniform in motion, provided that proper keyframing is used.

Smooth acceleration can be used when zooming in a picture to cover another. The acceleration increases as the image comes closer, then slows down to rest at its full screen position.

Above the Acceleration parameter is a graphical representation of the fluidity of the effect over time. This graphic is intended to assist you in determining how the acceleration works in its current configuration.

Although Acceleration can change the motion of the effect overall, you cannot vary the Acceleration parameter between keyframes. Only one acceleration mode can be used throughout a single effect.

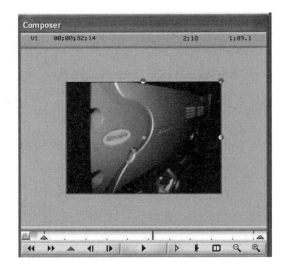

9.16 Background Parameter in Effect Editor *(above)*

9.17 A Background Adjusted in the Effect Preview Monitor *(right)*

Background

The Background parameter is used to determine background colors when used with Resize, Mask, Picture-in-Picture (PIP), and other similar effects where the image is scaled and a background source is needed to fill the screen. The Background parameter can also be used with transitional effects such as Dip to Color, where a color needs to be defined as a source.

Much like the Border parameter, Background uses Hue, Saturation, and Luminance parameters. It also uses a Color Selector tool and an Eyedropper.

Scaling

When the Scaling parameter group is present, the foreground image can be adjusted in size using X- and Y-axes. The X-axis (width) controls the horizontal size of the image. The Y-axis (height) controls the vertical size of the image. The image scale can be adjusted between values of 0 and 400, where 0 is infinitesimally small and 100 is 100 percent of normal image size. Keep in mind when scaling images that you are working with video, so any enlargement of the image will cause serious degrading of the overall picture.

Below the X-axis and Y-axis adjustments is a Fixed Aspect button. When selected, the Fixed Access button will maintain the aspect ratio between horizontal and vertical axis, so that the image maintains its original shape and is simply scaled down or up in size.

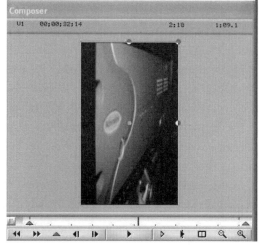

9.18 Scaling Parameters in Effect Editor *(above)*

9.19 Scaling in Effect Preview Monitor *(right)*

Thus, when the horizontal (X) axis is adjusted, the vertical (Y) axis follows when this feature is selected.

Note Although both Scaling and Position parameters use different terminology, it is a good idea to get used to the concept of X-, Y-, and Z-axes when discussing effects. Those terms are used here, despite the names used on the effect, to clarify for those users who are more effects savvy.

Here's a mnemonic device to help you distinguish X from Y. Think of the top of the Y as a downward-pointing triangle and the sides of the X as sideways-pointing triangles. So Y goes up and down and X goes sideways.

Scaling Adjustments: You can override the Fixed Aspect button by holding down the Alt/Option key and directly adjusting the handles in the Record Monitor in Effects mode. You can also scale the image in increments of 25 percent by holding down the Shift key when directly making adjustments. If you want to return to the normal aspect ratio, click the Fixed Aspect button twice. The normal aspect ratio will return.

Position

The Position group of parameters allows you to position the image from top to bottom and left and right in the screen. The parameter values vary from −999 to 999, where a 0 value is center screen. The horizontal position (X-axis) is H Pos. The vertical position (Y axis) is V Pos.

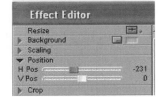

For horizontal positioning, negative values of H Pos move the image to the left of center. Positive values of H Pos move the image to the right of center.

For vertical positioning, negative values of V Pos move the image up from center screen. Positive values of V Pos move the image down from center screen.

Note At first it may seem confusing that positive numbers move the image down and negative numbers move the image up.

Positioning Adjustments: To adjust the image position on a single axis (X or Y), hold down the Shift key before you drag and continue holding it down as you drag. This limits the move to a single axis. This tip works in many areas of Xpress Pro and is a common computer software modifier used in many other programs.

Controlling Position and Scale Using the Effect Monitor

In addition to using the parameter sliders, Position and Scale parameters can be directly adjusted by clicking and dragging the image in the monitor. Scale handles are indicated by white dots on the top and side of the image. To position the image, click in the middle and drag it to the desired location Figure 9.20.

Crop

The Crop parameter is useful for removing unwanted elements from a picture such as a boom microphone or other nuisances. Using

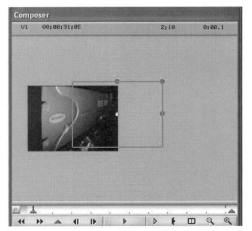

9.20 Position Adjustment Using Effect Preview Monitor

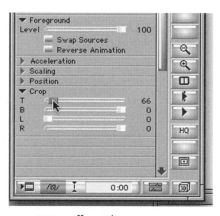

9.21 Cropping out Vertical Interval on Effect
      Preview Monitor

9.22 Cropping Using Effect Editor

Crop reduces the size of the picture, and it is usually used when creating a multilayered effect such as a picture-in-picture (PIP).

The Crop parameter can be of great assistance when substandard images are used. For example, when VHS or U-Matic tapes are captured, there can be muddled elements in the bottom of the picture (often called *flagging*). In some cases, the vertical blanking may show at the top of an image when it is scaled down for an effect. In cases like these, the Crop parameter is a necessity.

Crop values range from 0 to 999, where 0 is no cropping and 999 crops the entire image. The Crop parameters are T (Top of the image), B (Bottom of the image), L (Left side of the image), and R (Right side of the image).

Slowing Down the Sliders: Cropping can be an exacting task, and the parameter sliders aren't always as cooperative as you might want them to be. To move the sliders in smaller increments, use Shift-Ctrl/Cmd when clicking on and moving the sliders. You will notice that as you adjust the slider, it is not moving to the same position as your cursor arrow. This is because it is actually slowing down the movement increments. You can also use the right and left arrows on the keyboard to move sliders in increments of a single unit.

EFFECT TEMPLATES

Saving

Every good editor has an arsenal of effects that they have saved and can drop into their sequence. Once you've created an effect with elaborate keyframes and parameters, you can save the effect as a template to be applied to other segments and Timelines.

9.23 Effect Templates in a Bin

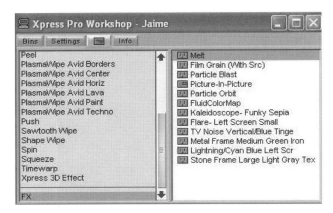

9.24 Effect Bins Shown in Effects Palette

To save an effect template:

1. Create a new bin for the template. This is optional of course, but a good idea organizationally speaking.

2. In the Effect Editor, drag the effect icon from the right top corner of the window into the bin. This saves the effect.

Once you've saved all of your keyframes and effect parameters and you've dragged the effect template into the bin you should name it (see Figure 9.23). By default, the template is given the name of the type of effect, for example, Picture-in-Picture or Dip To Black. Give it a descriptive name so you'll be able to identify the clip later, when you need it.

In addition to the listing of templates in your bin, the name of any bin that contains effect templates is listed at the bottom of the Effects Palette (see Figure 9.24). Xpress Pro does this so you can easily find any templates in your project that may have been misplaced.

Applying Effect Templates from a Bin

To maintain effects continuity, you can apply an effect template directly from a bin to your Timeline. You can also apply a template directly from the Effects Palette, much like you would any other standard effect in Xpress Pro.

Warning

Sometimes applying effect templates straight from the Effects Palette can cause a bug which causes your effect to come up as "WRONG FORMAT." Putting the effect in a bin first can fix this problem.

To apply an effect template from a bin:

1. Drag the effect template from the bin to the segment or transition in the Timeline where you want to apply it.

2. As you drag the template into the Timeline, note that each segment and transition that it passes over is highlighted.

3. When you find the correct location in the Timeline, release the mouse. The effect is applied.

 It is also possible to use the segment arrows to select a segment or segments in the Timeline, and then double-click on the effect in the bin to apply that effect to all of the segments in the Timeline. This can also work with transition effects if a transition effect is first chosen in Effects mode.

With segment effects, the effect will vary based on the duration of the effect, so it might move faster or slower than it did when previously applied. You can always go into Effects mode and adjust the keyframes to make the effect more to your liking. Adjusting the effect in the Timeline in no way affects the template.

Applying a Single Parameter from an Effect Template in a Bin

In some cases, specific parameters of an effect might be needed. For example, if you want to maintain continuity of a background color in all of your effects or a border color in your transitions. In cases such as these, you can apply just a single parameter from an effect template. When you apply a single parameter, Xpress Pro uses only the first keyframe in the template as a guide. The target effect, which should already be in the Timeline, is only affected on selected keyframes.

To apply a single effect parameter:

1. Select the effect in the Timeline and go into Effects mode. The Effect Editor appears.

2. Twirl down the parameter menu for the desired effect parameter to be replaced.

3. Select the keyframes that you want to change. If you click in the Effect Timeline, you can use Ctrl+A/Cmd+A to select all of the keyframes.

4. Select the effect template in the bin, and drag it to the parameter pane of the parameter that you wish to change.

5. The effect is applied to only that parameter on all selected keyframes when you release the mouse.

Saving an Effect Template with Source

In addition to saving just the template, you can save the effect template with source material included. To do this, Alt-click/Option-click on the Effect Template icon and drag it to a bin. When the template is saved with source, it will indicate it in the template name, i.e., Picture-in-Picture (with Src).

Some effects actually work in exactly the opposite way, for example, matte keys and Title effects. To save these effects with the source, you simply drag them to a bin, while to use them without their source, you Alt-drag/Option-drag them.

TIMECODE NAVIGATION IN EFFECTS MODE

You may have noticed that in effects mode, the Timecode display window above the record window changes. Two new elements are added:

1. Effect Duration
2. Current Position

The position number is particularly noteworthy, in that it not only refers to frames, but also fields. Thus 18.2 would be the 18th frame, 2nd field. You can navigate by typing frame numbers in Effects mode much as you would navigate by timecode in Source/Record mode. Type a plus (+) or minus (–) followed by any two-digit number, and the frame will move forward or backward by the number of frames that you indicate.

KEYFRAMES

Keyframes are the backbone of any effect. The keyframes define the principle moments of any effect. Normally, a simple effect such as a wipe would have only two keyframes: a beginning and an end. In Xpress Pro, all effects have a beginning and ending keyframe—these cannot be deleted. But you can also manually define other keyframes.

9.25 Effect Preview Monitor with Keyframes in Timeline

Each keyframe allows you to adjust or change effect parameters. Wherever you feel the parameters need change, you can add a keyframe. Xpress Pro determines what needs to be done between keyframes to make the effect flow properly. The process of adjusting or "in-betweening" from keyframe to keyframe is called interpolation. At first, adding keyframes may seem a bit challenging, and you might not get exactly what was intended. Over time, as parameters are learned, your ability to use keyframes effectively will improve.

Keyframe indicators are shown in the Effect Timeline underneath the Record Monitor. The indicators are small triangles. The Active keyframe—the keyframe that is currently being adjusted in the Effect Editor—is indicated by a bright pink color. Inactive keyframes are grayed out.

Adjusting the Right Keyframe: When adjusting a keyframe in Effects mode, it is important to notice which keyframe(s) are active. Often the blue position indicator under the Record Monitor is placed close to a keyframe, but that keyframe is not selected. If this is the case, you could be adjusting another keyframe "blindly" by moving the parameter sliders but seeing little or no results. Always be sure to check for the active keyframe before adjusting parameters.

Adding Keyframes

When you add keyframes, the effect will not change. The effect is altered only when that keyframe is selected and parameters are changed. You can select a keyframe in the Timeline by clicking on it. To add a keyframe:

1. Move in the Timeline to the position where you want to add the keyframe.

2. Click on the Add Keyframe button below the Record Monitor.

   You can also use the Add Keyframe key on the keyboard. The default keyboard uses the N key.

Selecting Multiple Keyframes

To select more than one keyframe:

1. Click on the first keyframe that you want to select in the Timeline underneath the Record Monitor.

2. Ctrl-click/Shift-click on any additional keyframes. Multiple keyframes are selected. You can also use Ctrl+A/Cmd+A to select all of the keyframes in an effect. You cannot deselect all of the keyframes of an effect, but you can click on a single keyframe to select that keyframe and deselect all others.

Deleting Keyframes

To delete keyframes:

1. Click on the keyframe you want to delete in the Timeline underneath the Record Monitor. The keyframe is highlighted. You can also Shift-select or Ctrl/Cmd-click multiple keyframes for deletion.

2. Press Delete on the keyboard. The keyframe is deleted.

Moving Keyframes

In some cases, you may need to move the position of a keyframe in the Timeline. To move a keyframe:

9.26 Moving Keyframes in the Effect Timeline

1. Select the keyframe to be moved in the Effect Timeline.

2. Alt-drag/Option-drag the keyframe to its new position. The keyframe is moved. On some slower systems, you'll want to make sure that the keyframe has updated to the correct position before you release; otherwise you will only have moved your keyframe part of the way to your desired location.

You can also use this technique for moving multiple keyframes, using the method for selecting multiple keyframes previously discussed.

Copying and Pasting Keyframe Parameters

Once you've defined your keyframes, you may want to copy and paste the same parameters from one keyframe to another. To do this:

1. Select the source keyframe on the Effect Timeline by clicking on it.

2. Press Ctrl+C/Cmd+C to copy it.

3. Select the target keyframe on the Effect Timeline by clicking on it.

4. Press Ctrl+V/Cmd+V to paste it. The keyframe parameters from the source keyframe are pasted.

Advanced Keyframing

One of the disadvantages of the keyframing tool in Effects mode is the inability to control keyframe parameters independently of each other. For example, when flying a Picture-in-Picture effect across the screen, it might be advantageous to add more scaling parameter keyframes while not affecting positioning keyframes.

Enter Advanced Keyframing, a new capability on Xpress Pro and other Avid systems. Advanced keyframing allows additional keyframes to be set on single parameters, thus many keyframes can be added to the Scaling parameter without affecting the motion path or any other parameters.

Most effects have no need for Advanced Keyframing. It is available on Picture-in-Picture, 3D, and Resize effects.

To enter Advanced Keyframing mode, click on the Advanced Keyframe button on the bottom right of the Effect Editor in a picture-in-picture, Resize, or 3D effect. The Advanced Keyframe icon is symbolized by a vertical double pink Timeline.

The Effect Editor expands to display several parameter rows with individual Timelines and keyframes. You can use the twirl-down menus for each parameter to show the sliders. As you work your way down the menus, you will notice that for each parameter

Adding Keyframes on the Fly

There may be situations where you want to add keyframes as the effect plays back. For example, you might want keyframes to occur at key moments of a music track. To do this:

1. Press play.

2. Press the N key on your keyboard. For every keystroke, a keyframe is added.

I used this technique to do a "follow the bouncing ball" sing-along video. As the music played, I hit the keyframe button on the beat of each syllable. Then I moved the position of the ball over the right syllable on each of my premarked keyframes. Finally, to get the ball to bounce, I added a keyframe in between each of the keyframes that I had marked on the fly and raised the ball up slightly on each intermediate keyframe.

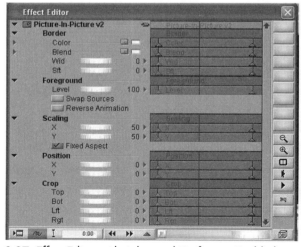

9.27 Effect Editor with Advanced Keyframes Enabled

9.28 Dual Split in Effect Preview Monitor

slider, there is a mini-Timeline to the right. To select a parameter, click on the slider or the mini-Timeline for that parameter. At the bottom of the Effect Editor is an Add Keyframe Button. With a parameter selected and the blue indicator in the middle, try clicking on the Add Keyframe button. You'll notice that the keyframe is added to only that parameter!

Over time you will find many situations where advanced keyframing is beneficial. The control over individual parameters can make for more exacting effects quality.

The Dual Split Button

Selecting the Dual Split button will display a "before" and an "after" image of your effect in the Record Monitor. The "before" image is indicated by white corner brackets. To remove the Dual Split display, press the button again. The white corner brackets can each be dragged to a new location if it is more important to see the split horizontally instead of vertically.

While building your effects, you may find it useful to zoom in and out of the Effect Preview Monitor for a more through examination of your effect. To zoom in, Ctrl-click/ Cmd-click in the Monitor. To zoom out, Shift+Ctrl-click/Shift+Cmd-click in the monitor. You can also map the Reduce and Enlarge buttons onto your interface. You'll especially find the zoom tools helpful as you use the Outline Path button. For effects that move on a path across the screen, the Outline Path selection will allow you to see the movement of the effect from keyframe to keyframe. Each gray dot in the path represents a keyframe.

And while we're speaking of keyframes, you can probably imagine how difficult it is to navigate your way from keyframe to keyframe through com- plex effects using the small Timeline underneath the Effect Preview Monitor. Just to the left of the Monitor is a very handy Zoom tool. Using this tool, you can zoom in on the Effect Timeline and see all of the keyframes. In the regular configuration, key- frames can easily get lost. Zooming the Effect Preview Timeline allows you to analyze the keyframes more effectively.

The Fast Forward and Rewind keys are also helpful. Normally these keys function so that you can jump forward and backward between each locator on your track. If you hold down the Alt/Option key and use these, they would normally jump from transition to transition in your Timeline. However, when you map these underneath the Effect Preview Monitor (and they must be under the monitor, not on the Timeline buttons, in order for this to work) they will jump forward or backward to each keyframe so that you can see and examine the parameters for each one.

While you are busily creating effects, you may have to determine whether elements are within the title-safe or action-safe areas. Using the Grid button will allow you to turn on and off a grid over the monitor so that you can see these areas. For the uninitiated,

9.29 A Multiple Layer "Vertical" Effect

title safe is the inner grid. No titles should extend beyond or over this area. Action safe is the outer grid, which covers most of the video image. In general, no significant action should take place outside of this area, as it isn't going to show up on some video monitors and televisions.

BUILDING VERTICAL EFFECTS

In the Chapter 5 "Basic Editing" we covered how to add video tracks (Ctrl+Y/Cmd+Y) and how to monitor video tracks (by clicking the monitor button next to the track name).

Previsualization

Building vertical effects such as multiple picture-in-picture tracks, keys, resizes, and titles is fairly simple, at least in theory (see Figure 9.29). The key to building vertical effects is a concept referred to as previsualization.

The people who specialize in designing and building effects will usually plot out some kind of road map before the actual effect building starts. This is a good idea, whether you have real-time effects or not. The reason is simple: if you don't know where you're going, you'll never get there.

Prior to creating any type of complex effect, it's a good idea to sketch it out on a piece of paper. Try to determine which effects will be used, how each track will be assigned, what sources will be needed and what resources will be required. Sketching out an effect can be as simple as drawing on a cocktail napkin or as complex as doing a spreadsheet with a storyboard visual reference. It's up to you, the effect designer, to determine which tools are necessary.

Previsualization is mentioned here only because so many picture editors can become overwhelmed with 24 vertical video tracks. The effect in itself is a fairly simple thing. Manipulating an effect and understanding its interaction with other effects is entirely different. When you previsualize, try to break down your effect design to its most simple elements and draw it on the page. When you attempt the effect in Xpress Pro, you can add each element step by step, then preview it to see if it works.

REAL-TIME PLAYBACK

Xpress Pro is a powerful software package. When integrated with state of the art hardware, it is quite capable of playing back quality images in real time. But like any system, it has certain limitations. Fortunately, the engineers who designed Xpress Pro understand the need for information and control of the application. As a result, several adjustable settings and information indicators are available.

Your System's Performance with Effects

The performance of your individual system will determine how well Xpress Pro can play back multiple layers of images in real time. While the software is designed to work with most current computer configurations, there are several factors to be considered. The primary factors are:

1. CPU processing speed
2. RAM configuration and speed
3. Bus speed
4. AGP processing speed
5. Graphic card performance
6. Hard drive performance.

CPU Processing Speed

Xpress Pro is a host-based editing system. This means that your host computer and, in particular, its central processing unit (CPU) will affect the performance of the software. There is no replacement or workaround for processing speed: the faster, the better. Xpress Pro has been qualified on several existing systems. The latest list of approved systems is located on Avid's web site.

The bottom line is this: a 2.0GHz CPU will run, render, and play back less favorably than a 3.0GHz CPU. Dual CPUs can be used, and the second CPU performance will vary, but the software will use the second CPU to boost performance, sometimes as much as by 75–90 percent. The chosen platform (PC versus Mac) will affect performance.

The CPU has two primary functions in Xpress Pro. They are:

1. *Compressing and decompressing images.* This obviously does not apply to uncompressed media using optional Mojo.

2. *Compositing effects.* The CPU must mix the layered tracks together as a composite and output the result. The only effects compositing not controlled by the CPU is compositing 3D effects, which are primarily controlled by your graphics card and OpenGL software and hardware.

As of this writing, Apple Computers has several qualified systems that work at approximately the same speed as PCs. The speed factors of Macs versus PCs will continue to vary through time. Your best bet is to choose the platform that suits you and can perform reliably.

RAM Configuration and Speed

Your system's random access memory chips are very important in determining the performance of Xpress Pro because the software relies on RAM-buffered playback. The RAM buffer preloads frames before it begins to play back images. As a result, faster RAM means faster preloading. Faster preloading means quicker playback.

Specific functions on Xpress Pro are RAM-intensive. A good example is audio scrubbing, which allows you to sample the audio as you scrub in the Timeline. The faster the RAM can preload and empty the samples from the RAM buffer, the more accurately you can scrub the audio. This is also true when moving the position indicator across the Timeline to view images. If Render on the Fly is selected under the Clip menu, the system will try to update the picture as you move the position indicator, even over the most intensive vertical effects. As a result, the RAM must preload and dump information very quickly.

While it is true that more RAM is always better, there are other factors to consider. The speed of your RAM is crucial to loading the buffer. The faster the RAM speed, the faster the buffer can load and unload.

There are several different types of RAM available. It is recommended that you do some research before choosing a CPU and motherboard configuration for your computer. The Motherboard determines some key elements, which are:

- The number of RAM slots.
- The maximum RAM size.

- The type of RAM that can be used.
- The number of RAM channels.

While the number of slots and RAM size are important, the actual type of RAM used with your CPU is also important. For example, your CPU might use DDR RAM or RAM-BUS RAM, depending on the platform of your host computer. There are some speed differences between these two types of RAM. Try to pick the one with the best performance.

RAM also interacts with the host CPU. The front-side bus speed of a CPU can, in some cases, be determined by the speed of RAM.

Some systems allow for dual-channel or interleaved RAM. The advantages of dual-channel RAM are significant. Dual-channel RAM allows for RAM chips to work much the same as striped drives. Two chips work in tandem to deliver faster performance. It is important to recognize that not all RAM chips work in or are approved for dual-channel performance. In some cases, a reseller may suggest that the RAM has not been tested but "will probably work." Many times, this simply is not true. Better to use prequalified RAM than to take your chances. Of course that ultimate decision is up to you.

Bus Speed

The bus speed of your computer will determine how fast information can be transferred in your host computer. Bus speed can be affected by a number of factors, including RAM speed. It is better to purchase a CPU with a faster front-side bus. The speed of your PCI bus will also affect performance when using different hardware, including FireWire (IEEE 1394) cards and audio cards. The faster the bus, the better the performance.

AGP Port Speed

We highly recommend that you purchase a system with an 8× or faster AGP port. The AGP port determines the speed of graphic information, which is integral to Xpress Pro's performance on your system.

Note　All of these parameters, particularly the AGP and Bus speeds, are difficult to determine with normal testing software. That's why it is so important to look at the prequalified configurations on Avid's web site!

Graphic Card Performance

Your graphic card must be OpenGL compatible in order for 3D effects to work properly. The performance of your card will affect system performance dramatically. Very few OpenGL graphic cards qualify for use with digital video. Again, Avid's web site has a list of prequalified cards. As of the writing of this book, only certain nVidia graphic cards qualify for use with Xpress Pro. As always, you can determine which graphic card suits you best, but good performance will not be guaranteed in every case. Be sure that whatever card you choose, it must be OpenGL compatible or 3D effects will not work in real time. While many cards are approved for other graphic applications and may be considered state-of-the-art for other programs, this does not guarantee that they will work just as well with Xpress Pro.

Hard Drive Performance

The type and speed of drive used with Xpress Pro can make all the difference between uncompressed real-time playback and rendering hell. Here is a list of the types of drives and their performance levels:

SCSI

SCSI drives offer the best performance on Xpress Pro. That performance can be enhanced significantly when the drives are striped together so that they work in tandem. Avid recommends a dual SCSI card with a four-way stripe.

IDE/ATA/SATA

IDE, ATA, and Serial ATA (SATA) drives will vary considerably in performance. Be sure to check their speed (in RPM) and the cache (in MB) The minimum speed recommended for these drives is 7200 RPM. The recommended cache size is 8MB. These drives can also be striped, which will enhance their performance. Avid does not recommend these drives for uncompressed media, but in some cases they can work. They will easily handle DV and 15:1 media. The relatively low cost of these drives makes them more desirable for most users, but you will want to test them extensively before purchasing them for uncompressed video. Internal IDE/ATA drives on laptop computers are generally not very good for use, primarily because their speed is usually between 4800–5400 RPM. While this speed should process 15:1 images, even this is not guaranteed. Better to use external FireWire drives or even USB 2.0 drives with your laptop.

FireWire (IEEE 1394), USB 2.0

For those who aren't familiar with these drives, they are actually IDE drives in a box using different modes of transfer. They are not recommended for uncompressed video. Like internal IDE drives, the faster RPMs and more memory cache, the better.

Demystifying Real-Time Effect Playback

The better your understanding of Xpress Pro, the easier it is to determine how your system will perform using vertical layers of real-time effects. In order to play back a sequence, Xpress Pro will do three things:

1. Build the pipes,

2. Load the RAM buffer, and

3. Begin playing back.

Building the Pipes

When you press the Play button, the system immediately begins a process known as building the pipes. This is the function of "reading" the sequence and determining what media it will need to play back, what effects will need to be preloaded, and so forth.

In many cases, it will take an insignificant amount of time to build the pipes, so that the process goes unnoticed in the background. But in cases where a large amount of media is accessed, where there are many cuts, or where the effects are fairly extensive, the time between pushing the Play button and the media actually playing can be extensive and frustrating. In cases such as these, the Play Length Toggle button comes in handy.

The Play Length Toggle switch allows the system to only build the pipes for one minute. This way, it will take a shorter amount of time to build the pipes and play back the sequence.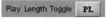

Xpress Pro will indicate that Play Length is active by switching your Play button from its normal color to white. When Play Length is toggled again, the system returns to normal playback mode and the Play button resumes its usual characteristics.

Loading the RAM Buffer

Although one might assume that Xpress Pro reads media directly from the drives, this isn't the case. The system will normally preload 20 frames into a temporary RAM buffer before beginning playback. This RAM buffer allows Xpress Pro to "catch up" with itself, should it have difficulty reading media, as opposed to some other systems, which, when difficulty is encountered, will often drop frames.

In some cases, the RAM buffer will get behind because of a system bottleneck. As mentioned previously, system bottlenecks can be common based on a variety of factors, including video card, bus speed, RAM speed, and CPU speed.

Should you encounter a situation where Xpress Pro is having difficulty playing back a stream of real-time effects, you can give the system more time to fill the RAM buffer.

1. Go to the Project window and select the Settings tab.

2. Double-click on the Video Display Settings

3. Under the Pre-filled Frames selection, type in 10.

4. The system will spend an extra 10 seconds pre-filling the buffer.

Playback Stress Indication

When Xpress Pro has difficulty playing back effects sequences, it has the ability to indicate exactly why and how the system is encountering difficulties. These stress indicators are located in the Timecode track of your Timeline, and they will show you what to do and how to remedy playback problems.

After playing back your sequence, take a look at the Timecode track. You may notice some tiny colored bars just above the Timecode numbers. These bars will indicate problem areas of the sequence. The color of the bars determines the problem encountered.

Red Bars: Indicate a taxed system. In these areas, Xpress Pro dropped frames in order to play back your sequence. Generally speaking, Red Bars indicate that your CPU isn't working fast enough to play back the problem-affected area. The only solution is to render this area. We'll touch on rendering later in this chapter on page 276.

- *Yellow Bars:* Indicate areas where the system is stressed to its limit, but it did not fail to play back all frames. You should consider making some kind of adjustment to alleviate the problem. Pre-filling frames, freeing up extra memory by exiting from other applications, and other methods to free up your CPU can be used. If you're concerned about playback performance and the edits in this area are pretty well locked in, it might be wise to render.

- *Blue Bars:* Indicate that the drives on your system reached a high stress level, but that everything played back okay. You might consider using a faster drive or

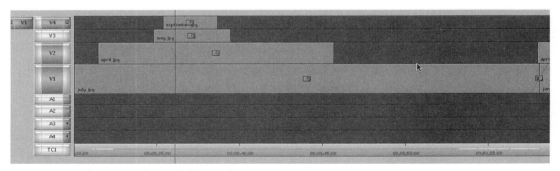

9.30 Stress Indicators underneath the Timeline

reconfiguring the drive in some manner to assure faster access to media. One solution, if you don't have a lot of captured material, is to stripe your drives and recapture, so that performance will increase. This isn't available on every type drive and you may not have the time to do it. Like other stress types, you can always render the media to alleviate the playback stress.

Using ExpertRender

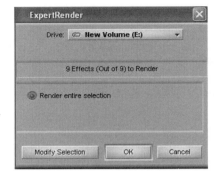

If you just played back a sequence that dropped frames, you can have ExpertRender "fix" your problem areas. ExpertRender is Xpress Pro's "thinking" render engine. It knows the rules of rendering and will only select those items that need to be rendered to ensure playback for different situations.

To fix dropped frames, play back your sequence and immediately choose Clip>ExpertRender. When the dialog box opens, you have three options:

1. *Render Entire Selection.* This will typically do the most rendering. It follows the rules of rendering and will assume that no effect can play in real time.

2. *Render for Digital Cut.* This method assumes that one or two stream effects will be able to play back in real time. Far less rendering than the first option, in most cases.

3. *Render Recommended Ranges.* This uses the stress indicators on the Timeline to determine what must be rendered. This third choice will only show in the dialog box when stress indicators are present in the Timeline. It takes into account only the dropped frame indications on the Timeline and will only render those affected areas.

Modifying ExpertRender's Selections

In some cases you might want to add additional effects to be rendered in addition to the selections that ExpertRender makes. Occasionally, you might also want to deselect some of those choices. To do this:

1. In the ExpertRender dialog box, choose Modify Selection.

2. Shift-click an effect to add or deselect it from the render queue.

3. Click the Render Effect button to render the selected effects.

Video Quality Toggle

In Chapter 6 "The Timeline", we briefly discussed the Video Quality Toggle. Using Video Quality is a good way to alleviate stress on your system and the drives. There are three quality levels:

1. Full Quality (available only with Mojo).

2. Best (Draft) Quality, which plays back only one field and reduces the image by half.

3. Best Performance, which scales the image by 25 percent in each direction.

The concept behind the Video Quality toggle is this: play back as many real-time effects as possible. The Video Quality toggle will only affect the quality of playback during editing. Once the sequence is completed, rendering must occur to ensure full quality of output.

Maximum Video Streams

Xpress Pro is designed to output a maximum of five video streams. A video stream is defined as a single video element being played back. For example, a Picture-in-Picture effect could be called a two-stream effect, because one picture is placed on top of another element. Any transitional effects are usually two-stream effects, because the transition involves two different sources.

You can adjust the Maximum Video Streams in your Video Display Settings. In some cases, you may want to lower the maximum streams due to poor drive or CPU performance.

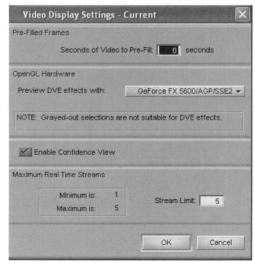

9.31 Maximum Video Streams set in Video Display Settings

Should you exceed the maximum limit, the system will drop streams based on the following rules:

1. The V1 track is always attempted.

2. Additional tracks are played, up to the maximum number, from the top down.

For example, if you had six video tracks playing back at once, Xpress Pro would play back V1, then from the top down, including V6, V5, V4, and V3. Playback of the V2 track would be dropped because the maximum stream limit would be exceeded.

The Laws of Rendering

Rendering is a pain. The whole concept of random access nonlinear computerized editing is that it takes less time to do and is more fun. Rendering can take the fun out of editing, create a break in the creative flow, interrupt your train of thought, and eat up your precious life. Most editors prefer not to render their lives away. Here, then, are a few tips to help you in your everyday workflow with regard to rendering.

1. *Render as little as possible.* This seems simple enough, but you might be surprised by how few actually do this. When you've added a non-real–time effect and already know it will work, render it when you're done with the sequence. You can always adjust it later if necessary. If you have a choice between using a real-time effect or a non-real–time effect and it doesn't matter which is used, choose the real-time effect. If you're building a multilayered effect that exceeds your maximum streams limit or contains non-real–time effects, don't render until all of the layers are added. If you can wait until the sequence is finished before doing a render, wait.

2. *For multilayered effects, rendering the top layer will also render the effects below it.* For example, let's say you're building a multilayered Picture-in-Picture effect with 10 boxes flying across the screen at once. As you build the layers, try to avoid rendering each one individually. You can use the Clip>Render on the Fly setting to preview once you've exceeded the stream limit. Continue adding all of the layers and then just render the highest track. This saves both space and time. Should you need to make an adjustment, go to the track, enter Effects mode and adjust it. Then re-render the highest track again. This is much less time consuming than rendering each individual track. It was previously mentioned that Xpress Pro plays back the V1 track, then will play back from the top track down until it reaches the maximum number of streams. This is the reason why. You should be able to monitor playback of each track as you build it. Monitoring is one thing—rendering takes much more time.

3. *Let Xpress Pro do the work for you.* Whenever possible, use ExpertRender.

MOTION EFFECTS

A motion effect is an effect that changes the speed at which a clip would normally play. Xpress Pro can create three distinct types of motion effects. They are:

1. *Timewarp Effects:* Timewarp effects are applied to segments in the Timeline directly from the Effects Palette. The rate of motion is determined by the effect.

2. *Freeze Frames:* Freeze Frames are applied to clips in the Source Monitor and create a new clip that must then be edited into the sequence.

3. *Motion Effects:* Motion Effects are applied to clips in the Source Monitor. Each motion effect plays at a consistent speed that is determined by the user or is fitted to fill a required space. Like Freeze Frames, once the motion effect has been applied to the source clip, a new clip is generated and must then be edited into the sequence.

Motion Effects Interpolation

Each motion effect can be interpolated in different ways. Interpolation determines how frames and fields will be blended, combined, or displayed in the motion effect. Interpolation can determine how good a motion effect will look when played back. There are six different modes of interpolating motion effects (see Figure 9.32). Some, as indicated, are not available for every type of effect. They are:

9.32 Selecting Interpolation Options

1. *Duplicated Field:* A duplicated field interpolation method consists of taking one field of a frame and duplicating it. Using Duplicated field will halve the resolution of the image. This method is not recommended for broadcast, but works fine for single field projects that are intended for the web, or in some cases, CD-ROMs.

2. *Both Fields:* Selecting Both Fields uses both fields of the video frame. In some cases, this method will work fine, but not for fast moving action. Often there are artifacts that develop from interfield motion. As a result, this type of interpolation could appear jittery.

3. *Interpolated Field:* Interpolated Field uses both fields and blends them. To be more precise, it uses field one for the first field of video, then blends field one with field two for the second field of video. Rendering an Interpolated Field motion effect is more

time consuming, but it works better for shots with interfield motion. However, when used with Freeze Frames, Interpolated Field may result in a softer image.

4. *VTR Style:* VTR Style interpolation is used only on Timewarp and Motion Effects and is not available on Freeze Frames for reasons which will be obvious. A VTR-Style method of interpolation emulates slow motion playback on VTRs by shifting field information by a scan line so that the fields are aligned. This results in a smoother motion without detail reduction, which would be noticeable in a Duplicated Field mode. VTR-Style interpolation renders slightly faster than Interpolated Field but can in some cases create some noticeable jitter at slower speeds because of the line shifting.

5. *Blended Interpolated:* Only for use on Timewarp motion effects, the Blended Interpolated method is very similar to Interpolated Field, but uses a more complex field-rendering technique using fields of adjacent frames to create even smoother motion.

6. *Blended VTR Style:* Blended VTR Style interpolation processes much like a VTR Style, but, like Blended Interpolated, it uses a more complex field rendering technique using successive fields to create a smoother motion.

Freeze Frames

Freeze Frames in Xpress Pro are clips that contain a single frame of video that can be displayed for a set duration that you choose (see Figure 9.33).

To create a Freeze Frame:

1. Load the master clip or subclip containing the image that you want to freeze into the source monitor.

2. Find the frame that you want to freeze in the Source Monitor.

9.33 Freeze Frame Menu Selection

3. Choose Clip>Freeze Frame. A menu of preset durations will appear. Choose a duration or Other to set a customized time for the Freeze Frame.

4. Choose a method of interpolating the Freeze Frame from the drop-down menu that appears.

5. After making your selections, Xpress Pro will ask where you want to store the media for the new clip. Select a volume and click OK.

6. Xpress Pro will ask which bin the Freeze Frame clip is to be stored in. Choose the bin or create a new bin, then select OK.

7. The Freeze Frame appears in the bin and is also automatically loaded into the Source Monitor for editing into your sequence.

Motion Effects

Motion Effects play back clips at a nonstandard nonvariable rate. They can also use a strobing effect, where a frame is frozen and held for a predetermined amount of time.

To create a Motion Effect:

1. Load the master clip or subclip with the media you wish to manipulate into the source monitor.

2. Mark an IN and OUT point for the media that will be used to create the Motion Effect.

3. Choose the Motion Effect button under the Source Monitor or from your Command Palette (Ctrl+3/Cmd+3), or map it to your keyboard or the user interface. The Motion Effect menu appears.

4. Under the Variable Speed heading, select the duration or the speed (Rate) of the Motion Effect.

5. If you want to strobe the motion, select the Strobe Motion option and select the number of frames between strobes.

6. Select an interpolation method for the effect.

7. Choose Create. The Bin Selection Dialog Box appears. Select a bin and click OK. The Motion Effect is created and stored in the bin.

Using Fit-to-Fill Motion Effects

You can create motion effects using the Fit to Fill button on your Command Palette. Understanding Fit to Fill is relatively simple: you have X amount of footage that needs to fill Y amount of space.

For example, let's say you're doing a corporate video and you have some footage of a product. The footage is 15 seconds long. In the video, the narrator talks about the product for 20 seconds. In this case, you could use Fit to Fill to slow down the existing footage, or fit it, to run long enough to cover the narration, or fill it.

Here's how to use the Fit to Fill function:

1. Load your source footage in the Source Monitor.

2. Mark IN and OUT points in the source footage of the footage that is to fit in the sequence.

3. Mark IN and OUT points in the sequence where you want the footage to fill.

4. Click the Fit to Fill button. The motion effect is placed in the sequence and stored in the bin of your choice.

 Motion effects usually look best when they are easily divisible by the original frame rate of the source clip. So for a standard NTSC video clip, which is 30 fps, the best looking motion effects are 15 fps, 10 fps, 6 fps, and 5 fps. High-speed clips are less affected by specific frame rates but are best done in multiples of the original frame rate like 60 fps, 90 fps, and 120 fps. If your Fit-to-Fill indicates that it is an odd frame rate, like 17 fps, it may be wise to lower the frame rate to the closest divisible frame rate, which in this case would be 15 fps.

Timewarp Effects

Timewarp effects work much like Motion effects, with the exception that they are applied directly from the Effects Palette to your sequence. These effects emulate VTR-like functions, gradually slowing down or speeding up the playback speed over the course of the clip in your sequence.

The Timewarp effects have specific characteristics and are essentially prefab or canned effects. There are no parameters that can be adjusted in the Effect Editor. In

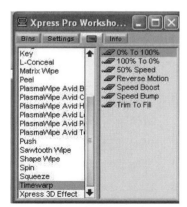

9.34 Timewarp Effects in Effects Palette

fact, if you try to go to Effects mode to adjust a Timewarp effect, it won't acknowledge the effect by highlighting the Timewarped segment.

There are a number of different reasons to use Timewarp, but the most common one is to isolate or highlight a specific portion of a continuous clip. Integrating Timewarp effects into sequences isn't too complex, though you will have to follow certain specific rules.

Besides the duration of the affected clip, Time-warp has only one additional parameter, which is the method of interpolation. To change the interpolation of a Timewarp effect, open the Render Settings in your Settings window. Select **Timewarps Render Using** and select the desired method of interpolation.

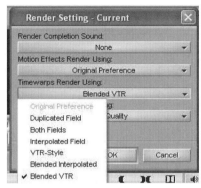

9.35 Render Settings for Timewarps

Almost all Timewarps are real-time effects, so you can apply them and play them back. The only exception to this rule is the Reverse Motion Time-warp. Reverse Motion is a little bit more difficult for Xpress Pro to maintain. The playback pipeline is based on forward motion and the media files themselves are meant to play forward, so as you can guess, playing it in real time might cause some errors.

Trim to Fill

Let's take an example of how you can use these effects. Pretend you have a clip where a specific incident occurs that you want to highlight or isolate by slowing down the playback speed. During this isolated part of the clip, you're not exactly sure of how much it should be slowed down, so you want to do a little experimentation.

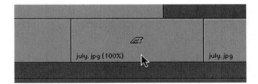

9.36 Trim To Fill in Timeline

First, you'll need to edit the effect into your Timeline. Once that's done, find the place where you want the effect to start. Effects editors usually refer to this as the "region of interest." Use Add Edit to separate this part of the clip from the beginning of your clip.

The next step is to find the ending point where of this region of interest. Once you've found it, add an edit there as well. You should now have three separate segments. Now the fun starts!

Find the Timewarp effect called Trim to Fill. Drag it to the region of interest. Trim to Fill is a very simple yet elegant solution. By trimming the region of interest to make the segment longer or shorter, Timewarp calculates the speed of the effect required to make it begin and end at the same frames that were originally edited into the segment. As a result, the beginning of the clip plays at normal speed, the affected segment plays at slower or faster speed, depending on if you've lengthened or shortened it, and the last segment picks up at the next frame, maintaining visual and timecode continuity.

But Trim to Fill is just one of the Timewarp effects. Let's look at the other six.

0 percent to 100 percent   0% To 100%

This effect begins with a freeze frame and gradually accelerates until 100 percent normal speed is achieved. Like all Timewarp effects, the ramping speed and duration depends on the length of the clip. If you apply this effect to an entire clip, it will take the duration of the clip for the speed to reach 100 percent. This rarely produces the desired results. In most cases, you'd want the video to ramp up to 100 percent speed, then continue on at that speed by making an additional edit from the original source, using the next contiguous frame of video from the clip as your in point. So if, for example, the effect ended at source timecode 1:32:18:05, the source timecode in point for your next edit should be 1:32:18:06.

100 percent to 0 percent   100% To 0%

This effect works much like the 0 percent to 100 percent effect, except that it does exactly the opposite. Normally this Timewarp effect would be used at the end of a video segment, where you wanted to stop the motion and perhaps even create a freeze frame to hold on before the next clip begins. But like all effects, the creative editor will find other uses.

50 percent Speed   50% Speed

The 50 percent speed Timewarp effect does exactly what it says—plays back the clip at half speed. You might be wondering why this particular effect is a Timewarp effect when you can easily create a Motion Effect to do the same thing. There are two reasons: first, the effect is drag-and-drop, so you can save yourself the trouble of going through Motion Effect dialog. The second is that Timewarps are added to sequences, not source clips.

Speed Boost   Speed Boost

The Speed Boost effect starts out at around 50 percent, then ramps up to a little under twice speed, then ramps down at the end. If you were to graph the speed against time, the shape would look something like a tall thin hill. You can use this effect for a variety of different reasons. One would be to draw attention to video at the beginning and end of clip, with the middle speeding through quickly, a method of "zooming ahead" on an unimportant portion of the clip.

Speed Bump   Speed Bump

Speed Bump could be considered the inverse of a Speed Boost effect. The video starts at full speed, slows to around half-speed in the middle, and then ramps back up, ending at normal playback speed.

NESTED EFFECTS OR SUBMASTERS

Now that we've explored many of the effects in the Effects Palette, let's take a look at a method for building them. Effect nesting is a powerful feature of Xpress Pro that uses its ability to build an effect within an effect.

Before we go too far into this heavily structured world, let's discuss one of the most common problems associated with vertical effects: transitions.

Here's a common issue: you build a really nice bed of video and need to create a title to identify something. So you create the title on video track 2. Now, your producer wants you to dissolve into and out of the title while at the same time dissolving in and out of the shot where you've placed it. So you're looking at four separate transitions: fading in and out of the title on V2, and dissolving in and out of the video clip on V1. If the duration of your title or the frame rate of your transitions isn't correct, it looks a little hinky. Plus there's all of those transitions to manage.

The easy way is to use the Collapse tool. Collapsing will conserve tracks as well as allow for clean transitions on a single track. Collapse can be used

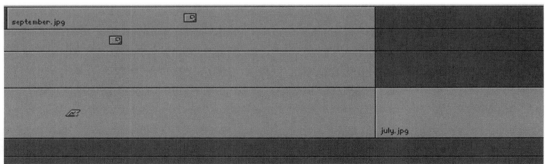

9.37 A multiple layer effect that needs to transition to a lower track

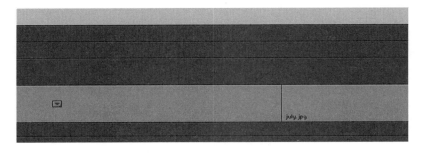

9.38 Tracks Collapsed, Transitions can be added in Timeline

on simple two-track titles with backgrounds or complex 20-track effects that need to transition to a single adjacent clip.

Here's how to collapse tracks: Using either of your segment mode buttons, select the clip on V1 and the title on V2 (or if you're using several tracks, click on all to select them). Click on the Collapse Tracks button and voilà! You've collapsed all of your selected tracks into a single track. Now all you have to do is add the transitions to the clips on either side (see Figure 9.38). No worries about matching the timing and durations between the two tracks, because they're all rolled into one track now.

But where did those tracks really go? When you collapse tracks, they become sub-nested. That is, both tracks still exist separately, but they are nested underneath a submaster effect. You can access these tracks by entering the nest, which we'll describe later in this chapter on page 285.

The Submaster effect is a great tool. You can add a submaster effect and nest inside of it by using Collapse, or you can add it to a higher track to create an effect that can be used over several clips.

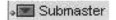

For example, let's say you have a piece with a recurring dream sequence. Each time the dream occurs, it is slightly changed. You want to maintain the same look over each of these sequences. The scene needs to be tinted blue, with a letterbox over it. For the first occurrence, you create tracks with the blue tint on V2 and the letterbox on V3. Now you can collapse the tracks into a submaster and save the effect as a template. That way, you never have to recreate your effect for each reoccurrence of the scene, and you've collapsed it into one tidy effect that can be placed over the video as many times as you require it.

You can do this same type of effect on higher tracks for simple snappy transitions. For example, you can create a gate flash effect on filler above your video tracks to transition from one scene to another. Rather than incorporate it on the same tracks as your clips, you can place this filler effect on a higher track and save it in an effect bin that can be used anytime. Be sure to check out our effect bins on the DVD.

Now that we've shown how you can collapse tracks and inadvertently build a nest, let's explore how you can build one manually, and why you would want to do it.

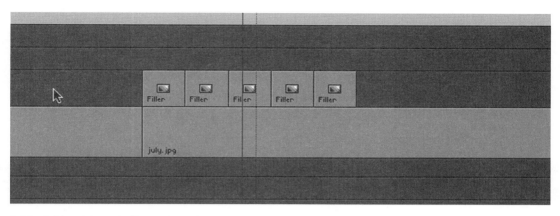

9.39 Adding Vertical Effects above Source

Step versus Expansion Nesting

There are two different methods of working with nested effects. The first method is called Step or Simple Nesting. Step Nesting allows you to focus and isolate a single effect, "stepping" inside of that effect to its core. The second one, Expansion Nesting, expands the Timeline to reveal the inside of the nest, as well as the rest of your edited sequence. Although they basically do the same thing, there are advantages to each method.

Step Nesting allows you to monitor inside of the effect where you are nesting. So, for example, if you are adding something to the inside of a picture-in-picture effect, the monitor shows you the video that is inside of the picture-in-picture, not the result of the effect. This inner view is important for placement and adjustment of parameters of any added effect.

Expansion Nesting shows you the tracks within a nest, but keeps the monitoring the same. With expansion nesting, you still monitor the entire Timeline with effects added, so it isn't particularly good for close-up work within the nest. On the other hand, expansion nesting allows you to monitor audio, patch source tracks to tracks that exist outside of the nest, view all levels of a nest, and see the entire Timeline, not just the element that is being affected in the nest.

All of these descriptions may sound a bit complicated, so let's take a look at an example of each method and how it can work.

Step Nesting

Here's a simple example of a step-nested effect: Suppose you have a picture-in-picture effect in your sequence. This effect uses two tracks of video, one for the background, a wide shot of a newscaster, the other for a graphic, a map.

In this scenario, there are parts of a map that need to be identified. You decide to add a title on track 3. So you add a track of video and build your tile, and everything is going just great. You might even get done early tonight, for a change. You edit the title onto track 3 and start playing back your finished sequence. Just when it looked like a walk in the park, the sinking feeling of impending doom enters as you realize that you created the picture-in-picture effect transition over the shoulder of the newscaster as a zoom from infinity to its normal size.

Again, not a particularly big deal. You enter Effects mode and scale the first keyframe of your title back to infinity and leave the second one in the final resting position. Another playback, another problem. When played back, the title doesn't exactly emulate the path of the picture-in-picture effect, because it was created originally off-center, resulting in an effect that begins off axis but lands in the right position.

You could continue chasing your tail, creating a new title in the center of the frame and again emulating the motion of the picture-in-picture effect, but life is short. And this is a great opportunity to nest.

If you could place the title inside of the picture-in-picture effect, it would track just fine.

Here's how to do it. Build the picture-in-picture as you normally would, but before building the title, select the video track with the picture-in-picture effect. Be sure that your blue position indicator is over the effect.

9.40 The Picture-in-Picture Built

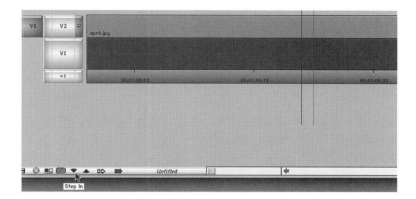

9.41 Stepping In to the PIP

9.42 Adding a Track to
the Nest

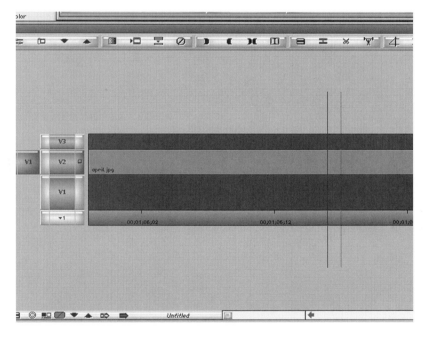

Now, click on the Step In button on the bottom of the Timeline (see Figure 9.41). The button is a downward facing arrow, indicating that we are going down into the effect, spelunking our way through it. The Timeline changes to reflect the picture-in-picture clip only. The Sequence Monitor image will also change to reflect the source of the effect in full-screen mode.

From here, you can add another video track inside of this nest and create the title, editing it into the nest as you would any normal sequence (see Figure 9.42). When you're inside of a nest, all of the normal sequence rules apply. You can build 24 tracks of video in this nest, just as you can with any sequence. In this example, the source clip of the effect is in full-screen mode while you are in the Step In mode, so you can position the title more

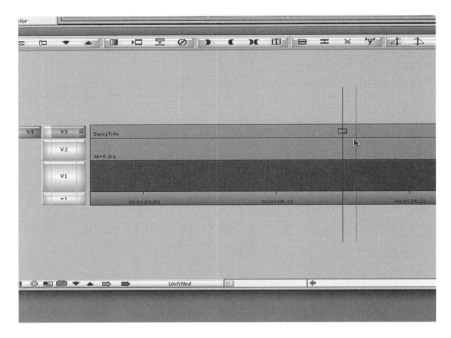

9.43 Editing the Graphic in the Nest with Resulting Nested Pic *(above)*

9.44 The Resulting Picture *(right)*

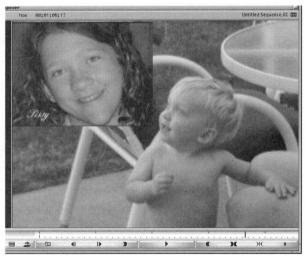

correctly when building it (see Figure 9.43). Once you've created the title, step out of the nest by clicking on the upward pointing arrow, the Step Out button.

The sequence will reappear and your title will be inside the picture-in-picture. Wherever the picture-in-picture effect goes, your title will follow (see Figure 9.44).

Expansion Nesting

Now we'll take a look at expansion nesting and an example of why you would choose this method over step nesting.

We'll start by taking an image that we want to integrate into a historical documentary. The image is faded, the color has a blue cast to it, the people in the shot face the wrong way, and we want to pan across the screen, all the while incorporating a letterbox matte.

As we build the nested effect, we need to pay attention to the audio cue in the narration track, which tells us when to start the pan of the image from one person across the entire group.

In this scenario, expansion nesting is the best solution. There are two reasons: 1. we need to hear an audio cue, which we would not normally hear by stepping in, and 2. we are adding effects to an entire picture, thus there is no need to focus on any specific image within a group of images.

To begin, I like to add a Submaster effect to the top, then expand the Timeline to reveal the added effects inside. The reason I choose the Submaster effect is simple: the Submaster effect has absolutely no characteristics, but it implies that there is something underneath. In essence, it's just a wrapper for nested effects. Some other NLE products call these *containers*.

Once you've placed the Submaster effect on the segment, select one of the segment editing buttons on the bottom of the Timeline. It doesn't matter which one is chosen, because it's only a method of expanding the Timeline to show the nest. With the segment mode selected, double-click on the submastered clip in the sequence. The Timeline expands vertically, showing a video track V1.1. (You can also do this by going into Effects mode first then double-clicking without using segment mode.) We'll drag and drop a mask on top of this segment.

Now double-click on track V1.1. It expands to show track V2.1. In this case, instead of counting vertical tracks, Xpress Pro is counting nested tracks, differentiating between V2, and V2.1. Here we'll add the Flop effect, which reverses the picture horizontally (see Figure 9.45).

Fun, huh? Let's do some more. Double-click on track V2.1 and expand to track V3.1. Here we'll add a color effect. Just drop it on for now. We'll do the adjustments later. Finally, we'll double-click on V3.1 and expand it, revealing V4.1. Here we'll add our Pan and Zoom, so that the picture will be imported from its original file, panned on the audio cue as we discussed earlier. So the processing order goes like this: Pan & Zoom>Color

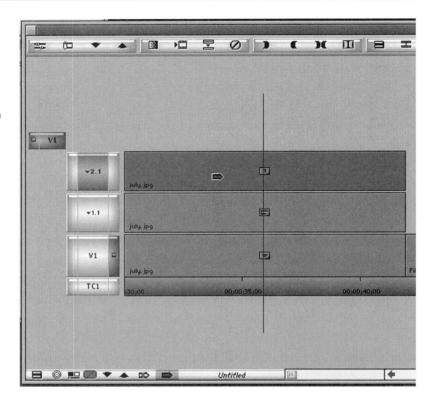

9.45 Expanded Nest on
Timeline—Adding
Effects

Effect>Flop Effect>Mask>Submaster>V1. And the whole process is in front of you, so you can pick each effect and adjust it with the Effect Editor. The audio will play back normally and you can still see the entire nest (see Figure 9.46).

You can also do this process by Alt-dragging/Option-dragging effects on top of each other. For example, drop the Flop on a regular video track, then Alt-drag/Option-drag a color effect, then Alt-drag/Option-drag the Pan and Zoom effect. Once all of the effects are applied, you can go into Effects mode and double-click the Submaster effect to open up all of the individual tracks.

Now that you've made the adjustments, how do you get the nest to disappear back inside of V1 on the Timeline? Again, using a segment-editing mode, double-click on V1. The nest disappears.

In this instance we have created about five layers of effects on one piece of media. Can your system play it back in real time? Probably. Because we are not dealing with five separate streams of video, it is much easier for Xpress Pro to play back, even with five different effects on the single stream.

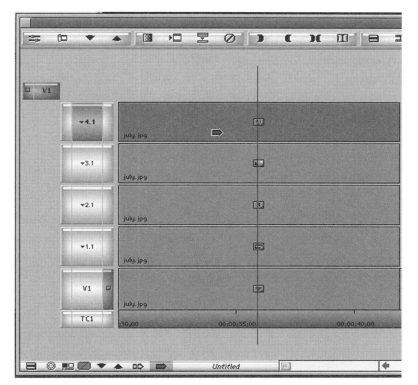

9.46 Effects in the
Expanded Nest

Nesting Order and Autonesting

The order of building nests within nests is very important. For example, if you want to add a color effect and a matte to a picture, the color effect would need to go inside of the matte effect. Otherwise, the matte would show evidence of the color effect as well. Your ability to prevent these issues before they happen will increase through experience and previsualization.

Even when a multiple nest effect has been poorly planned, Xpress Pro has a solution to easily fix this. You can change the order of nested effects inside of the Effect Editor. When an effect is nested inside another effect and Advanced Keyframe mode is selected, the Nesting Priority icon appears for each effect nested inside of the original effect.

In order to use this feature, the base effect on the Timeline must have Advanced Key-framing capability. Without it, you cannot reorder the nest. In the earlier example of expansion nests, we used a Submaster effect, which does not have Advanced Keyframing. To solve this problem, we'll need to add an effect on top of the Submaster.

Autonesting

But how do you place an effect on top of a nest? First, using segment mode, click on the base track of your nest (V1, for example). Go into the Effects Palette. We're going to use a Resize effect, which has Advanced Keyframe capabilities. To autonest the picture-in-picture on top of the Submaster effect, press Alt/Option and double-click the Resize icon in your Effects Palette. The Resize icon should appear on the base track of the Timeline. The reason we chose the Resize effect is because it defaults to 100 percent screen size, so no actual adjustments are necessary.

Effect Priority

Now we'll take a look at the Resize effect in the Effect Editor. At the bottom of the screen is the purple layered icon used to promote the effect to advanced keyframes. Click on this, and the Effect Editor expands. You should also be able to see all of the nested effects inside. To the right of each effect is a blue layering icon. This is the effect priority icon, which allows you to determine the nesting order. You can click and drag the effects vertically to change the order in which the effects are processed by Xpress Pro. Try grabbing the color effect and moving it below the Avid Pan and Zoom. If you do this, the color is added before the image is imported for Pan and Zoom. As a result, the color adjustments won't show. The same is true when placing the Flop or Mask effects at the bottom.

3D WARP

The earliest versions of 3D effects on Avid systems required extra hardware, cumbersome cabling, and mixed results. Now, thanks to OpenGL and advanced video cards, 3D effects are simpler than ever. To a large extent, this development is due to the gaming industry, which had a need for more advanced displays in order to make interactive games in the 3D realm.

The 3D Axis

So far in our discussion of effects, we have discussed how we can manipulate the horizontal and vertical axes, respectively known as X and Y. Now we will focus on the depth axis, known as Z. In order to give objects depth on the screen, the Z-axis can be adjusted so that what normally would be a flat item (such as a video image, which is flat) would need to be manipulated so that pixels would emulate the effects of a third axis, showing depth (see Figure 9.47).

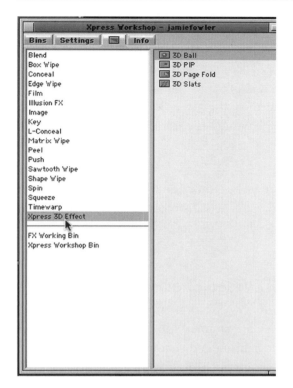

9.47 3D Warp Effects in Effects Palette

We emulate a third axis frequently when using the scale parameter of an effect. For example, if we want an image to "fly" from infinity to full screen, we can adjust a Resize effect so that an image enters at zero size and increases to 100 percent, giving us the impression that it is coming toward us.

But the problem with this type of faux 3D effect is that there is nothing to indicate that there is any true depth of space in the picture. The scaled image is flat, so there is nothing to show that there is a true dimension. As a result, these effects seem rather tired.

In order to allow us to create that third dimension of depth, 3D on Xpress Pro takes form in three different shapes: page fold, balls, and slats.

Page Fold

Page folds have been used in video effects for decades. They give the impression that a page from a book is being turned, complete with the sense of depth in the curled portion of the video. Video editors have commonly used this effect to indicate a change in subject or scenery.

Balls

A 3D ball is not just a circular wipe: it can show portions of a picture with a true Z-axis, forming what appears to be depth in the picture. The image is distorted in a circular fashion to express depth, and it can be spun, to a degree, to implicate a ball shape. The parameters within the Shape parameter can further affect the 3D look of the 3D Ball, changing the amount of distortion that is applied and other parameters.

Slats

Without a Z-axis, the slat shape would appear to be a horizontal wipe. The difference here is that as the slats come onto the screen, the image is distorted so that there appears to be some depth from the "front" of the slat where the image is closer to us, and the "back" of the slat, where it is farther away.

3D Modeling and Shading versus 3D Video Effects

For those of you who have a pretty good idea of how 3D animation works, the concepts of 3D video effects may seem simple. Okay, they are simple. You can add drop shadows and borders to 3D effects, but you cannot offer lighting and shading effects of the object as it travels in space. Remember, Xpress Pro is an editing tool. If you need some fancy 3D effects, you're going to have to export the video to a more appropriate application, then reimport it into your sequence.

Promoting an Effect to 3D

In some cases, an existing effect can be "promoted" to a 3D-type effect. These effects are titles, picture-in-picture, and imported mattes. To promote them to 3D, click on the 3D button in the Effect Editor. You now can adjust these effects choosing one of the 3D shapes.

Promoting a title or a picture-in-picture effect is important. On most high-end video effect editing systems the smooth page turn and 3D transitioning is standard operational procedure. Without 3D promotion, Xpress Pro would have little to match these systems.

Let's do a little experiment. Build a background of video, then create a title and edit it in. What we'll try to do is add a simple effect to bring it on and off the screen. Everyone loves that Page Turn effect, right? OK, if you don't, just pretend you do. So what we have to do is put an effect on our title that will simulate this. If you go to the Effects Palette, you'll find a category called Peel. These Peel effects are strictly 2D, but they are the closest

9.48 A 3D PIP Effect   9.49 A 3D Page Turn Effect on a Title

thing that we have to a Page Turn in the arsenal. (Yes, I know we have 3D effects, but we're pretending here.) So all you have to do is apply this Peel effect on top of the title.

Did you figure out how to do it? The easiest way is to Autonest it. Select the title with one of the segment editing tools and then Alt+double-click/Option+double-click the Peel effect of your choice. What happens?

Before Avid introduced 3D titles, this was a pretty common mistake. What happens is that, because the effect is only two-dimensional, not only the title but also the background peels onto the screen. Ecch. Believe it or not, there was a way to do this. Avid's senior instructor Greg Staten once faxed a copy of the workaround. It was 16 steps and filled an entire page.

Now, when you create a title, you can go into Effects mode, click on the 3D button, select the Page Fold as your 3D shape, and skillfully create a very simple page-turning effect so that the title glides onto the screen in true 3D space, without mucking up your background video.

While picture-in-picture effects don't have the same issues as Titles, the Peel effect just wasn't nice enough for most editors. When you create a PIP, you can click on the 3D button in the Effect Editor and promote it to 3D space. Again, a common reason would be to create a page turn transition using the PIP. But you can also flip boxes onto the screen in 3D, roll a ball of video (in the PIP) onto the screen, create a complex origami-like folding and unfolding of images on the screen—well, you get the idea. The main idea is that people are used to seeing sophisticated effects in 3D on video. Xpress Pro allows you to do this with 3D effects.

EXPERIMENTING WITH EFFECTS

Most video editors have their own arsenal of effects. You can store these templates in a bin of favorites, then transfer that bin to a thumb drive, disk, floppy, or zip drive. Using previously created effects can add a lot of "Wow!" factor to your sessions and impress clients. Or, as one editor told me, "Whoever has the most effect templates wins."

Once you've built up a pretty good effects bin, be sure to copy it and take it with you. Go into the Avid Projects folder, find the project where you created your effect bin and copy it to your favorite portable storage format. USB thumb drives are perfect for this sort of thing, and you can carry them on a keychain, a lanyard, or hook them to your belt or purse. When you see another editor, you can even exchange effect bins! Effect building and sharing is fun. But when someone else has built templates for you (as we have on the DVD-ROM), it makes the process easier and more fun. You can transfer your personal effect bin by dragging it to a project folder on any system and opening it within your project.

If you're really into the effects on Xpress Pro, you haven't seen all of it yet! In the appendix, we will show you some of the AVX Effects developed by third-party software vendors specifically for use on Xpress Pro. These effects packages range from simple pan and zooms to some incredibly brilliant special visual effects. The DVD also has some demos of these plug-ins that you can use for experimentation.

Using quality effects can make all of the difference in the world when creating content that conveys information and presents ideas. Xpress Pro provides the effect engine, but the creative use of these little gems is up to you. When you spend time creating templates and experimenting with the effects in the palette, you are building a library that will please even the toughest clients.

It's hard to edit projects that have a lot of information and little eye candy, and effects can't always save the day. But in many cases, a solid effects arsenal can make all the difference between a sleepy presentation and a glittering performance. And for you, the editor, it can be a challenge to keep your material lively and your job interesting.

Chapter 10

The Title Tool

Avid's Title tool has such a bad reputation. I disagree with this reputation. I like the Title tool. Is it incredibly full-featured? No. Does it have enough features to make it a workable solution for most of your titling needs? Yes. Absolutely. And the really nice thing is that it has just the right mix of features and simplicity. You really can't have your cake and eat it too when it comes to how feature-packed something is and how easy it is to use. It's either very easy but not very powerful, or it's fairly complicated with lots of great features. The Title tool falls somewhere in the middle, but definitely closer to the easy end of the spectrum.

If you want great titling (character generator) options on your Xpress Pro, there are a lot of really good options as AVX plug-ins, especially if you are on a PC. The choices for Macs are much more limited. There are Titling plug-ins from Aston (PC only), Boris (both platforms), Chyron (PC Only), Inscriber (PC only), and Pinnacle (PC Only). Avid also makes their own AVX Titling product called Marquee.

Less attractive (workflow-wise, not image-quality-wise) are external options. You can make great titles in Adobe Photoshop for import into Xpress Pro. Most of the aforementioned AVX Titling programs come with stand-alone versions, so even if you are on a Mac, you could run them on a networked PC and import them. It's even possible to import CG files from the venerable Chyron products.

As I have hinted at already, one of the great things about the Avid Title tool is that it is so easy to use that you don't really need to RTFM (Read the Fine Manual) to be able to use it at all. So why have an entire chapter devoted to it? Because the Title tool is so easy to use, a lot of its bad reputation comes from people who never really read the instructions to know all of its great features. Granted, this will be one of the shortest chapters in the book, but if you have to get by with just the Title tool for doing your CG work, you should read this chapter. And if you're one of those people who has turned his or her back on the Title tool, I may just convert you. There's a whole lot of titling that needs to be done on any project that doesn't require any more power than is available right under this little button. T

The most common way for people to access the Title tool is Clip>New Title or Tools>Title Tool. But the fastest way is to map the Title tool button to your keyboard. (See "Keyboard" on page 42 in Chapter 2 for how to do this.) The Title tool button is in the Command Palette's Effects tab.

Once the Title tool is open, the interface is very simple (see Figure 10.1). It appears that there's just a small toolset box along the bottom.

However, there is also a wealth of additional controls in the menu bar for the application, which gets two new menu pulldowns when the Title tool is open and selected. Many people miss out on all of the options and power available in these pulldowns.

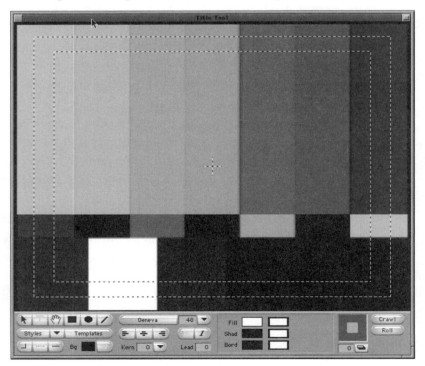

10.1 Title Interface

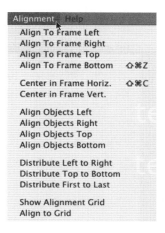

10.2 Two new pulldown menus in the Title Interface

Let's explore the toolset at the bottom of the Title tool first.

Working from left to right there are four groupings of tools. The first group is an assortment of selection tools, styles, and templates. The second group defines the font and its main parameters. The third group defines the colors of the face, shadow, and border of your text and objects. The fourth group defines the shadow parameters and allows you to create rolls and crawls.

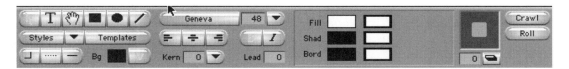

TITLE TOOLS

First Group of Text Tools

In the first group, the arrow key is the Selection tool. It allows you to move objects around the page once they've been created.

The T is the Text tool. This is simply a cursor that lets you type text. You can move the cursor fairly intuitively in most of the ways you would in a standard word-processing application.

I constantly have to switch back and forth between the Selection tool and the Text tool. This can be annoying if you hate the mouse. Luckily there is a very cool tip to minimize the mouse movement. Instead of mousing away from what you're working on to click on the buttons at the bottom, you can Alt-click/Option-click on your text object to toggle between Selection tool and Text tool.

The little hand icon is the Video Placement tool. This is basically a holdover from the days when the Title tool didn't open up big enough on the monitor to display the entire image, so you would use this tool to grab the video image and move it around the screen. I remember having to do this to make sure that full-screen rectangles actually went all the way to the edges. Unless you are using a very low-resolution monitor (that is actually not supported by Xpress Pro), this tool is useless.

The square icon is the Square and Rectangle tool. This allows you to draw rectangles, or—with the Shift key held down—perfect squares. To get a perfect square, you need to hold the Shift key down before you click to begin drawing and continue to hold it until after you've released. The Shift key can also maintain the aspect of rectangles. If you've already drawn a rectangle and you want to make it bigger, but the same exact shape, hold down the Shift key.

You can't create a full-screen gradient using the background color. Instead, use the Square and Rectangle tool. Just draw a rectangle that covers the entire raster and you can create gradients using the Fill Color Blend and Transparency preview.

The circle icon is the Circle tool. This operates the same as the Square and Rectangle tool above, except that it allows you to draw circles and ovals.

The diagonal line icon is the Line tool. This allows you to draw lines and arrows. To draw a perfectly horizontal or vertical line, constrain it using the Shift key.

Below the first row of buttons are two buttons for selecting Styles and Templates. In between them is a small twirl-down triangle for saving styles.

Styles and templates can make your life a lot easier. The difference between a style and a template is that styles simply provide the ability to recall a specific font with specific text parameters (i.e., shadow, color, justification, leading, kerning, opacity, border) or even the parameters without a specific font. A template, on the other hand, defines all of the parameters for a page of text, including positioning and multiple font styles for specific lines or words. This template locks your ability to change anything but the content of the text. This provides for consistency between titles with templates.

10.4   Clicking on the Styles button calls up a menu of saved styles.

Styles are accessed by clicking on the Style button and saved by clicking on the twirl-down triangle to its right. Templates are created and saved by clicking on the Template button.

The bottom row of buttons begins to the left with the Box corner tool. This provides a pulldown menu of various curved corners that can be used to "soften" the corners of boxes.

The dotted line on the button to the right is the Line Attribute tool. This lets you change the thickness of the line that was drawn with the Line tool.

The next button is the Arrowhead tool, which allows you to turn the lines you drew with the Line tool into arrows with arrowheads at either end or at both.

The color picking swatch and pulldown button under Templates allows you to toggle between keying your text over video or using an opaque, colored background. The default for the Title tool is to key text over video. While in the Title tool, you will see a reference frame of video from the point of your Timeline locator in the sequence.

 You can change the reference frame for the background video for your Title by clicking out to the Timeline or the Sequence Monitor, moving to the frame you want and then going back to the Title tool. The Title tool will update to the new frame as soon as your click inside the Title tool.

Second Group of Text Tools

At the top left of this group is the Font Selection button, which opens a pulldown menu of the fonts available to Xpress Pro.

To the right of that is a text entry box for typing the font size.

The pulldown triangle to the right of the text entry box allows you to select the size of the font from a pulldown menu.

Below the Font Selection button are the three text justification buttons: Left Justify, Center and Right justify.

Under the Font Size text entry box are buttons for changing the font style to **bold** or *italic*.

The bottom row of buttons allows you to set the kerning (how far apart the letters are from each other) and the leading (how far apart the lines of text are from each other. The word "leading" comes from the old typesetting days when they would use strips of lead to separate the lines of text. So, the pronunciation of this tool isn't "leeding," but "ledding." While setting the leading between lines is very useful, I find less use for the overall application of kerning. In general, kerning is best done with individual attention to the amount of space between each individual pair of letters. We'll discuss individual kerning elsewhere in this chapter on page 312.

Third Group of Text Tools

All of these boxes help you set the color, color gradients, opacity, and opacity gradients for your text, shadows, borders, and graphic elements (squares, circles, and lines).

The top left box is a color picker for the face of the font. Clicking on this box calls up a small window enabling you to pick from a quick color palette, eyedropper a color from the main display of the Title tool, or call up the full Color Picker.

The middle left box is a color picker for the shadow of the font. It works the same way as the top box.

The bottom left box is a color picker for the border of the font. It works the same way as the top box.

The three white buttons to the right of the color picker boxes are the opacity boxes. From top to bottom, they set the opacity for the face (or fill), shadow, and border of the font.

When boxes appear to the left of the opacity boxes, they allow you to create a gradient of color or opacity. Click on these smaller boxes to set both sides of a gradient using the same tools as the main color pickers. The large box that appears below these smaller boxes allows you to set the direction of the gradient. Simply click on a corner or a side of the large box to change the direction of the gradient.

Fourth Group of Text Tools

The large box with the small lighter-colored box in the center allows you to set the direction of your shadow. Just click on the lighter box and drag in any direction. If you like the direction you've chosen but don't have enough control of the depth of the shadow, you can type in the small text entry box below.

The small shadowed Hyphen button allows you to choose either a drop shadow or an extruded shadow. (Extruded shadows are connected to the font, while a drop shadow appears to be on another plane.)

The Crawl button allows you to create "crawling" text—from right to left. Enabling a Crawl calls up arrow buttons along the bottom of the Title composition area to allow you to pan left and right.

The Roll button allows you to create "rolling" text—like credits. Enabling a roll calls up arrow buttons along the right side of the Title composition area to allow you to move up and down to view all of your text.

MENUS

Object Menu

Bring to Front moves any selected object in the Text tool to the front. In other words, if two objects are in the same geographic space, the "front" object appears on top of or in front of the other object. Bring to Front places this object on the highest or front level.

Send to Back moves any selected object in the Text tool to the furthest back position. If there is a stack of objects in the Text tool, this places the selected object on the lowest or rear level.

Bring Forward moves the selected object forward in the stack of objects one layer at a time. If used enough times, this has the same effect as Bring to Front.

Send Backward moves the selected object backward in the stack of objects one layer at a time. If used enough times, this has the same effect as Send to Back.

Object	Alignment	Help
Bring To Front		⇧⌘L
Send To Back		⇧⌘K
Bring Forward		
Send Backward		
Group		
UnGroup		
Lock		
Unlock		
✓ Safe Title Area/Global Grid		
Preview		⇧⌘P
✓ Safe Colors		
Auto Size Mode		
Add Page		
Bold		⇧⌘B
Italic		⇧⌘I
Font Replacement		⇧⌘F
Make Crawl		
Move To Page		
Copy To Page		
Insert Page		
Remove Page		
Soften Shadow		⇧⌘H

 All four of these menu selections are used to control the appearance of multilayered text objects. They are also useful if you are having trouble "grabbing" or selecting a given object because it is obstructed by other objects. Simply send the obstructing objects behind the one you want to select.

Group allows you to move a group of text objects en masse. This is a useful feature if you have a composition that you like for part of the title, but need to move that group to another location on the screen. For example if you have built a lower-third title with text and maybe an "anchor" graphic and a line separating two lines of text, Group will allow you to select all of these objects and move them together without losing any of the relationships between the objects. Grouping also prevents any of these objects from being changed until they are ungrouped.

Ungroup allows you to release the relative geographic relationships between objects that have been grouped. This is necessary to change any of the grouped elements.

Lock allows you to prevent a selected object or objects from being moved or altered. This may be useful in building certain titles with multiple versions when you want some of the elements to remain in the same state or location from title to title.

Unlock allows you to release Locked objects from their locked state, allowing them to be repositioned or edited freely.

Safe Title Area/Global Grid allows you to see the area of the screen (the interior 80 percent of the full, underscanned raster) that is safe for text information. Because each TV set overscans by a slightly different amount, the safe title area defines the portion of the screen that should definitely "make it home." (My TV set at home has a huge overscan. Almost always, news graphics are just barely visible at the bottom and sides of my TV. The bug in the bottom corner of most TV stations sits exactly at the bottom right corner.) You can turn this grid off if you want, but I would only do this if the grid were interfering in some way with composing your frame. I have never turned off this feature.

Preview is a very useful feature that antialiases your text, allowing you to get a preview of what your text will actually look like when keyed and played over your video. The Title tool commonly displays text in an aliased mode that makes it a little difficult to judge proper kerning when selecting exact letter pair spacing. My most common use for Preview is immediately after attempting to kern text to better judge the final look. If you've never used this before, just type some text and see how the text seems to smooth out significantly and the positioning of the letters slightly changes.

Safe Colors is checked by default to insure that the colors you assign to text objects are legal. This can also be assigned in the Color Corrector's Safe Color mode. The Title tool can let you select from the entire 16 million colors available in the color picker, but most of these colors are out of the range of NTSC or PAL video. Safe Colors is another setting that I have never unchecked, but if you are doing a video that will never see broadcast or tape, in other words, exclusively for distribution as computer files, then I suppose you could disable this setting and get much brighter, more saturated colors.

Auto Size mode automatically deletes and adds pages to a roll as you create and edit rolls and crawls. The only reason to disable this is if you wanted to add some filler pages—using Add or Insert Page—before or after the text.

Add Page allows you to add pages to rolls or crawls. Additional pages are added to the end of the roll or crawl.

Bold is pretty self-explanatory. If you want to make a font bold you can use this menu selection. A similar choice is more easily accessible from the tool bar at the bottom of the Title tool, or by using the keyboard shortcut (Cntl+Shift+B/Cmd+Shift+B).

Italic is also pretty self-explanatory. If you want to make a font italic you can use this menu selection. A similar choice is more easily accessible from the tool bar at the bottom of the Title tool, or by using the keyboard shortcut (Cntl+Shift+I/Cmd+Shift+I).

Font Replacement calls up a dialog when a text object is selected. It is much easier to replace a font using the toolbar at the bottom of the Title tool.

Make Crawl allows you to resize crawling titles instead of dragging the title.

Move to Page allows you to move selected objects to a different page of a crawl or a roll. This is obviously a useful tool when making revisions to credits.

Copy to Page allows you to copy selected objects to a different page of a crawl or roll. If you are trying to format a roll or a crawl, this would be an easy way to create a single page with a particular format and make multiple copies that could then be edited.

Insert Page allows you to insert new pages into a roll or a crawl between existing pages.

Remove Page allows you to remove blank pages only. Once text or other objects have been placed on a page, it cannot be removed using this selection.

Soften Shadow allows you to soften or blur the shadow that you assigned. The minimum softness is 4. (The funny thing is that when Soften Shadow was first introduced on the Avid, even though the minimum softness was 4, the default was 0!) The high end of the range is still similar in this regard because you can type numbers up to 99 in the Soften Shadow dialog, but only numbers up to 40 are accepted. The dialog box for Soften Shadow includes three buttons: OK, Cancel, and Apply. If you know the exact softness you want and don't need to see it before the dialog closes, you can simply type in the number and hit OK without applying it. Hitting the Apply button simply lets you see the softness amount without losing the dialog box. So if you are experimenting to find the right softness, use Apply until you've reached the proper amount, then hit OK.

Alignment Menu

There are a lot of selections in this menu, but we'll address them in groups to keep from being too redundant.

The *Align to Frame* (Left, Right, Top, and Bottom) group allows you to neatly line up all of your selected objects in the Title tool along the Safe Title grid. The trick with these alignments is that the text *boxes* are what is aligned, not the text itself, so if you centered the text inside the text box, then aligned it to the left or right, they would not line up correctly. If you use Align Left, then the text inside those text boxes should also be aligned to the left.

Center in Frame Horizontally and Vertically will center the object within the Safe Title area. For these to look properly centered, the text inside the text objects also needs to be centered.

Align Objects (Left, Right, Top, and Bottom) will align all of the selected objects to the position of the furthest object in that direction. For example, if you Align Objects Left, all selected objects will line up with the object that is the furthest to the left.

Distribute (Left to Right, Top to Bottom, and First to Last) will distribute the objects evenly. The most common use for this is to create a series of lines of text, then use Distribute Top to Bottom to make all of the lines evenly spaced from each other. Once again, these distributions are based on the bounding box of the text, not the text itself. So if you do not get the results you expect, you may need to look at how the text is distributed inside the text box itself. Distribute is the main way that I create title builds and slates. You have much greater control of your text when each line is in a separate text box, then you use the alignment and distribution tools to place them appropriately on the page.

Show Alignment Grid displays a grid of dotted lines that is used when Align to Grid is active. This is handy if you are trying to place text in an orderly fashion on a page.

Align to Grid locks any movement of object in the Title tool to specific intervals on the Alignment Grid. This is obviously a useful tool, but knowledge of this menu selection is usually more of a troubleshooting item when people lose the freehand positioning of text objects. If you are being prevented from placing an object exactly where you want it, chances are that Align to Grid is on, allowing only for placement of the object exactly on the grid.

FACTORS OF CONSISTENCY

Styles

Styles is one of those things that can definitely speed up your editing, especially if you do a lot with text. Do you usually create fonts of about the same size and with approximately the same drop shadow? If so, create a style for it. Even if you use a different font, it'll save you from changing the size and drop attributes.

Two of my main clients had several fonts designed specifically for them. It only makes sense for me to have these fonts and the general attributes that I regularly assign to them saved as styles. At the minimum, it keeps me from having to wade through my font menu. Plus, I rarely use the Avid factory default size of 48. That's huge!

Let's take a look at how to save a style and the attributes that can be assigned to a style. The first thing to do is to create a font style by typing some text, assigning a font, and some attributes to the text. When you've created a look that you like, click on the little triangle to the right of the Style button. This is a pulldown menu that allows you to save the style (which brings up the Title Style Sheet window) or choose a previously saved style.

The Title Style Sheet provides you with a lot of attributes that you can choose to assign or not assign to a given style. In other words, you want to save all of the attributes of this style except for the font, for example. That way, you can type some text in a different font and apply this style without having it alter the font. Another common item to leave unchecked would be the font size, so you could type something in numerous sizes, then apply the style to all of the text, without changing the font sizes you chose for each line or word.

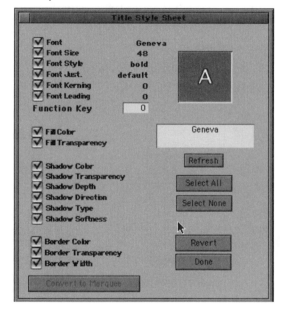

For our first example, pick your favorite font, size, drop shadow type, and color. Save it as a style. Leave everything checked.

One of the great options in the Title Style sheet is the function key designation. With it, you can assign a function key to the style so that each time you're in the Title tool, you can hit that function key to assign the style with a single keystroke. Only Function keys 2–15 can be assigned. This does *not* affect any other items you have assigned to the function keys for editing purposes. It is only active in the Title tool. When you are ready to save the style, it defaults to naming the style the same as the font. Pick something more descriptive. You can even assign it the name of the *purpose* instead of a descriptive name.

For example, name it "Newsroom lower-third style" instead of "Futura with a 3 lower-left semitransparent red drop shadow."

Warning

Styles are User Settings, so if someone else needs to use your Styles, they'll need to be in your user settings or they'll need to copy the Title Styles from your user settings to theirs. (See "Sharing Specific Files between Users" on page 20 in Chapter 2 for directions on copying User Settings from one user to another.)

Styles are not limited to text. You can also create styles for other Title objects, such as lines (sometimes called "rules" in graphic design or typography), squares, or circles. The "font" for these objects comes up as applFont. It's especially important for styles with applFont objects to give them good names instead of the default.

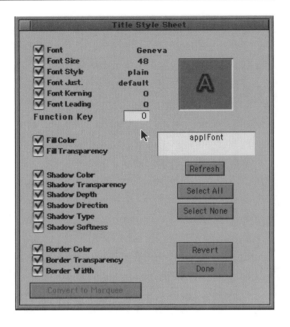

Coming up later in this chapter, you'll learn how to create a soft, semitransparent box that helps light-colored fonts stand out on light-colored backgrounds. This is something I do a lot. Finally I made a style for this soft drop box that I can call up whenever I do this. This is an excellent use of styles to speed your workflow.

Styles can really help with large bodies of imported text. For example, when I onlined a nationally broadcast documentary series, I would have the credit roll delivered as a text file. Then I would simply use styles to quickly provide the specific titles and names with the proper attributes.

Using styles is a no-brainer on regularly recurring projects or shows, but it can also be very helpful to quickly give you a starting look for text for new projects. You can run though a dozen looks for a producer, then customize them from the feedback you receive.

One of the fastest ways to communicate creative concepts with someone is to give them something to react to. Even if none of what you show them is what they want, you'll get much more specific feedback by showing them *something*.

Templates

Templates are related to styles, but they provide a more global, rigid assignment of a look for a title. This is often desired so that all lower-thirds or page builds conform to certain specifications. When you create a template, the page is essentially locked except for being able to edit the text boxes.

Creating templates is fairly similar to creating Styles. You begin by creating a look in the Title tool. When you are finished with the page, click on the Templates button to save the page as a template.

Warning

When creating templates, make sure that your text boxes are as long as possible, because when you call up the template to type into it, you cannot alter the size of the text box. You can only type as much text as the text box will hold. This is actually a good thing. Some networks require that text does not violate the far right corner of the screen, where their network bug sits. So it is good to create a template that has a text box that does not allow text to be typed in this protected area.

Once you've created a template, you can use it by calling up the Title tool, just as you would to create a new title. Before typing anything, click on the Template button and choose Include Template from the pulldown menu. Now, you can change the text in the text boxes.

If the template is positioned inappropriately on the background, you can click on the Template button again and choose Moveable Templates. This allows you to use the selection arrow to reposition the template.

If the template needs to be edited in some way, call it up and select Edit Template to change whatever portion or attributes need to be changed.

Typographic Craftsmanship

Editors are becoming generalists. We need to be experts at so many aspects of postproduction. This is largely part of the greater democratization of the toolset and a result of economic necessities. As with most things, people who are specialists are better at doing things because they focus their attention on nothing but that specialty. Typography is one

Toert   Toert   Toert

10.5   This text appears as it was typed. Note the very large space between the "T" and the "o." Also there is slightly more space between the "e" and the "r" than there is between the "o" and the "e." And finally the "t" is too close to the "r."

10.6   This is much better looking and easier to read than the example in Figure 10.5

10.7   This is the same screenshot as Figure 10.6, only I enabled Preview. On the computer screen, this antialiases the text and slightly changes the kerning sometimes.

of those specialties that we—as editors—are called upon to emulate. Typography is an art unto itself. Some editors are quite good at setting type in the Title tool; others are not. If you are an editor who is faced with doing a lot of design work in the Title tool, I urge you to check out design and typography books to see how the specialists work with type. To improve your editing skills, sometimes you need to branch out and examine other arts, and one of them is typography. How do you choose the proper font? Which fonts should you mix? How can you add interest, added meaning, and focus to words on the page using fonts and their attributes? These are all questions for a much different book than this one, but they are questions you should pursue using books, magazines, and the web.

My main area of concern when it comes to creating good type as a craftsman is simply making sure that each letter pair is kerned properly. It never ceases to astound me as I watch television to see the horrible looking CGs (Titles) that make it to the air. When you type a word in the Title tool, the spacing between the letters is a predetermined distance that is unaffected by the letters that you type before and after it. This means that the letter "o" typed next to a "T" is the same distance from that letter as it would have been if typed next to a "d." Yet, the graphical look of these letters next to each other is very different. Each pair of letters has its own particular design that needs to be massaged for each font. To have good-looking titles that are easy to read, each letter pair needs to be kerned individually (see Figures 10.5–10.7).

To kern a letter pair, place the text cursor between a letter pair and hold down the Alt/Option key while tapping the left or right arrow keys to either bring the letters closer to each other (tightening the kerning) or spread them apart (loosening the kerning). When you have one pair of letters kerned, tap the right arrow key without using a modifier key to move the cursor in between the next letter pair.

10.8   Typed Text
with Video
Background

Warning

You need to check your kerning using the Preview option, which is in the Object menu at the top of the screen. Without Preview turned on, the letters do not quite look like they will when rendered over your final background. (Looking at the Title tool in its regular mode displays aliased type. Preview creates an antialiased display that will more closely resemble your finished Title.)

FREQUENTLY ASKED-FOR FUNCTIONS

Filling Text with Video

Filling text with video is a common request. Luckily it's very easy to do. Type your text in the Title tool using the Video background, not a colored background.

I would avoid shadows or edges. The reason is that when you fill the text with video, it obeys the alpha channel of the title, not just the fill of the text, so if you use a shadow, it will make it look strange. If you don't believe me: experiment for yourself. Who knows? Maybe you'll like the look. Anyway, once your title is created, cut it in to your sequence. Now, use the Step In button to step into the title (see Figure 10.9).

This shows you the title in its two component parts: alpha on the top layer and fill below. The alpha is locked, but you can do anything you want to the fill. Using basic editing techniques, edit either video or a colored or textured background onto the fill layer. (See Figure 10.11 to view the final result.)

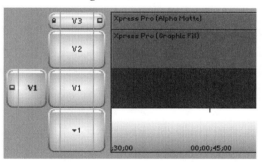

10.9   This title is cut onto V1, but when you step in to the effect, it appears that the title fill is on V2 and the title matte is on V3.

Soft Drop Trick

Oftentimes, even putting a shadow on a font isn't enough to make it legible when it is keyed over a bright or high-contrast background, or sometimes an art director won't want shadows on the font. To help improve legibility, it is common to put a soft-edged, semitransparent rectangle behind the text. The bad news is that you can't make a soft-edged, semitransparent rectangle using the Rectangle tool. The good news is that you can make a soft-edged, semitransparent rectangular shadow.

1. The first thing to do is type your text and position it where you want it.

2. Then draw a rectangle (using the Rectangle tool) that covers your text.

3. Turn the fill transparency of the rectangle to 0. This makes your rectangle disappear.

4. In the Shadow toolset, pull a small drop-shadow of only a pixel or two. Now you should have your rectangle back in black. ("Back in Black" ... that would be a great song title.)

5. Adjust the transparency of the shadow to about 25 or 30, then go to Object>Soften Shadow (or Ctrl+Shift+H/Cmd+Shift+H) and set the softness to about 20 or 30.

OK, you're almost there. Now the text looks shaded, and we don't want that.

6. Go to Object>Send to Back or Send Backwards to place the shadow behind the text. If you need to edit the shadow, you'll need to send the text behind the shadow, so that you can adjust the handles of the rectangle, then send the shadow back behind the text again when you're done.

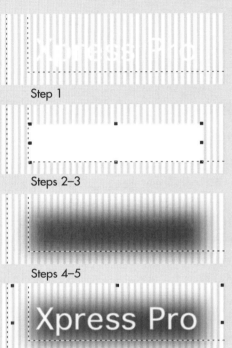

Step 1

Steps 2–3

Steps 4–5

I've even created moving light passes inside text by editing a color into the fill layer, then editing a lighter color in at the end and doing a long thin wipe pattern between the two colors. Another very cool trick that I used when I produced and edited Avid's NAB video several years ago was to create some very subtle, shimmering movement in the text to call attention to it. This really just looked like the titles softly pulsed in brightness. I did this by shooting out the window of my commuter train as I went to work, using a Hi-8 camera (Hey, it was quite a few years ago!) I found some inter-

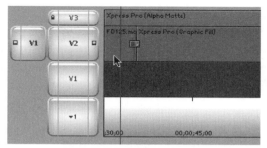

10.10 I cut a clip of ArtBeats' "Food1" stock footage in for the first few seconds of the title, and then used a wipe to transition to the regular fill for the title. You can combine all kinds of effects inside the title if you want or just do straight video.

esting movement and dropped the contrast a lot and blurred the video. I was left with a fairly bright gray video that occasionally had broad sweeps of brightness and darkness. I used that to fill the video using the technique described above. Check the DVD for a complete tutorial on this project, including royalty-free footage that you can edit into your own projects. (See Figure 10.12 to view a similar effect.)

Creating Title Builds

If you edit videos that have title builds, well, I'm really sorry about that. I have to do them too, so I know how you feel. Unfortunately, for lots of editors, creating title pages with massive blocks of type that are supposed to "build" on, one line at a time, is one of the

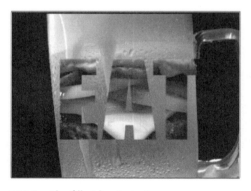

10.11 The fill video is ArtBeats.

10.12 Text filled with video shot from moving train to create random light patterns and energy.

most tedious, unimaginative parts of the job. To make this task a little easier and more manageable, I find that it's easiest to create the builds as separate lines, instead of as a single block of text, using Return to go from one line to the next. If you create a single block of text, it is sometimes difficult to get the pages to build on properly without moving the other lines. Using single lines of text also gives you much greater control over the placement and editing of those lines. Although you can obviously use styles to match the look of your text lines, one of the fastest methods is to duplicate your text blocks with Ctrl+D/ Cmd+D. If you make one duplicate and position it in relation to the first line, the next time you duplicate a line, it will maintain the same relationship. Then you can tweak the space between lines and the justification of the lines using Alignment menu (discussed previously in this chapter).

Usually the best way to create these builds is to make the final page first with the build complete. Then go back and delete the last line, saving a copy of that page. If you do this as a "Save As" instead of a "Save" the Title tool will stay open and you can edit faster. Continue this procedure until you either are at the first line or have deleted all of the "build" lines and are left with a heading or headline.

One of the nice ways to do builds is to have the current line brighter than any of the lines that have already been read. This is very easy to do with this method of building the page from individual text blocks, because it is easier to treat these lines separately than if they were created as a single, large block of text. A nice spin on this technique is to lower the opacity of the completed lines.

When you lower the opacity of text using the Fill opacity, you need to be aware that any shadow that is active on that text remains at full opacity. This can look very odd.

When the Avid creates title media, it is a finite clip with a beginning and an ending. In order to give yourself room for dissolves that start before the edit or to trim the title back, it is common practice to set an IN point on title media that is several seconds in from the start of the clip. The default Mark In for a title is, of course, the first frame of the title. This is like being at the first frame of a video clip.

When dissolving titles in and out, the easiest way to accomplish this is to use the Fade Effect button. I do not recommend this however, because this method causes the title to "bloom" slightly. Unfortunately, the only way to cleanly dissolve in or out a title is to use a regular dissolve.

Altering Titles

To edit a title that has already been cut into a sequence, go into Effects mode and click on the title. This will call up the Effect Editor window. Click on the small button in the far upper left corner of the Effect Editor window, next to the word "Title." This will call up the Title tool with the title you selected inside, ready for editing. Edit and either save the title, or simply close it and save it in the dialog box that comes up when you close the Title tool.

10.13   Effect Editor

Promoting Titles to 3D

One of the most common mistakes is attempting to apply an effect to a title by dropping a 3D effect onto the title. The correct way to make a title 3D is to "promote" the title to 3D. To do this, cut a title into a sequence. Go into Effects mode and select the title. This calls up the Effect Editor. In the bottom right corner of the Effect Editor is a small "wire-frame" cube with the characters "3D" inside the cube (see Figure 10.13). Clicking on this cube promotes the title to a 3D effect and calls up all of the 3D parameters you get when you drop a 3D effect on a regular clip.

If you promote a title to 3D you may want to have other titles use the same move or effect. To do this, go into Effect mode. Select the title that has been promoted to 3D. This calls up the Effect Editor. Now, while holding down Alt/Option, drag the small T button in the upper right corner into a bin. Notice that this places a new effect in the bin titled "3D Title: <name>.01 (Without Src)." If you drag the T without the modifiers, it will save the effect and the accompanying title media. (This is the opposite of saving regular 3D effects to a bin.) Once you have saved the title (Without Src), you can drag and drop this onto any title to apply the same 3D parameters to the new title. And in a special tip within a tip, if you only want to apply certain parameters of the effect—for example, the Scale properties only—to a title that is already 3D, you can drag the effect onto specific parameters in the Effect Editor.

Exporting Titles

One of the overlooked options when deciding how to save a title is the Export option, which is available from the File menu. When you export a title that is created over a video background, the title is saved as a graphic file with an alpha channel. If you create a title that uses a colored background, it is saved without an alpha channel. Using this method would be an excellent way to ensure that a title could not be edited or altered in any way. Once a title has been exported and reimported, it is no longer a title, but a Matte key, as if it had been created in Adobe Photoshop or some other third-party application. My main use of this option is to create full-screen colored backgrounds. If you save these as titles and use them in other effects or as fills for things, they have to be rendered, but if you export them and reimport them (we're talking about titles without alphas, remember) the resulting media file is a regular clip, as if it had been digitized, so it does not have to be rendered.

Importing Text into Title tool

Not only can titles be exported, but text can be imported into titles. Any text that you can copy—even from web sites and emails—can be pasted into Title tool. There are several advantages to this. First off, it's much faster than typing. Second, it absolves the editor of any typos or misspellings. When I online documentaries, cut car spots with disclaimer type, or work on corporate pieces with complex or technical terminology, copy and paste is my friend. It allows a producer to email all of that text information to dozens of people to check and cross-check. By copying and pasting that proofed text, you are hopefully removing one more chance that the project will come back for revisions. (Or at least it helps justify charging for any errors in their text document.)

Rolls

Creating rolls—such as credits—always seems to be a frustrating thing. Importing the text for a roll is one way to make it a little less painful. Once the text is imported into the document, it's useful to use styles to set the look of the text. This helps ensure that one person's name or title doesn't appear any larger or smaller than someone else's. The basic operation and procedures for a roll don't change much from a regular title. Enabling a roll on a title calls up a scroll bar down the right-hand side, so you can scroll through the length of the roll. All other operations are basically the same. Rolling titles are indicated in the bins and in the Timeline with an "RT" in the Title Effect icon.

There are two relatively tricky concepts to understand with rolls. The first is that how fast they roll is related to how long they are. Both of those parameters are controlled in the sequence itself, not in the Title tool. If you cut a rolling title into your sequence and you feel that it is going twice too fast, then you need to reedit it into the Timeline (or trim it) to be twice as long.

If you want a roll to either begin paused or end paused or pause somewhere in-between, those pauses are done by adding keyframes and positioning the titles at those keyframes. So if you want to have a roll begin with a 5-second hold with the first line of the scroll centered in the middle of the frame, cut the rolling title into the Timeline, then go into Effects mode on the title and scroll through the Effect Timeline until the first line is centered in the middle of the frame. (You can also do this with the Vertical Scroll Position parameter in the Effect Editor.) Add a keyframe at that point. Copy the keyframe (Ctrl+C/Cmd+C), select the first keyframe in the roll, and paste the keyframe (Ctrl+V/Cmd+V). Then type "+500" and press Enter on the numeric keypad. This will move you forward 5:00 in the Effect Timeline. Add another keyframe and paste the same keyframe again. That will hold the opening line in the middle of the page for 5 seconds. If you want to have the movement from this position "ease in and ease out," then set the Acceleration parameter to 100. (If that is too much, try another number. I almost always use Acceleration at 100.)

You can also crop the roll either on the sides, or more commonly, top and bottom. This creates a very hard cut-off transition in the key. If you want to soften this transition, don't use Crop. Instead, Alt-drag/Option-drag a Vertical Open Edge wipe onto the Title. It's very hard to see where the edges of the wipe are over a roll, so while I'm setting my level (position) on the wipe, I'll add a border, but bringing up the Width parameter. Once I've got the top and bottom positioned where I want them, I'll reset Width to 0. The softness of the wipe is obviously determined by the Soft parameter.

If you have a very complex effect, and this Vertical Wipe method doesn't work, you can also make a "sandwich" effect. Copy whatever is underneath the rolling title so that it is also above the title. So if it's a simple background video, place that video at the exact same timecodes, below the title (on V1) and above the title (on V3). Then you can apply a vertical wipe to the background video on V3, revealing the rolling title keyed over the same video on V1.

Warning   Titles promoted to 3D cannot be rolled or crawled and titles that have been rolled or crawled cannot be promoted to 3D.

Crawls

Crawls are very similar to rolls. Generally, you want to turn the title into a crawl before you type anything. When you click on the Crawl button, a scroll bar appears at the bottom of the Title tool's main pane, allowing you to scroll horizontally to see all of the text in your crawl. Crawling titles are indicated in the bins and in the Timeline with a "CT" in the Title Effect icon.

Similar to rolls, the speed of a crawl is determined by the length of its clip in the Timeline. The longer the clip, the slower the crawl. If a crawl (or a roll) is trimmed, it does not cut off part of the crawl, but speeds it up, if it is shortened or slows it down if it is lengthened.

Also, like rolls, the direction of a crawl can be controlled by adding keyframes in Effects mode and setting the horizontal scroll position. Pauses can be introduced by copying keyframe data between adjacent keyframes. The movement between these keyframes can be adjusted—either easing in and out of speed or providing linear speeds, using the Acceleration parameter.

CONCLUSION

So, there you have it. Now that you know a little more about the tools available in the Title tool and how to exploit them, you may hate the Title tool a little less. It really is very well designed. Could it have more features? Of course. But for the basic day-to-day slapping together of simple text over video, this tool does what it is supposed to do in a quick, relatively painless manner.

Chapter 11

Importing with Xpress Pro

Xpress Pro offers a variety of options for file imports. With Xpress Pro, you can import shot logs, graphic files, AAF format files, OMF files, and MetaSync files. In this chapter we'll take a look at each type of file and how it can be imported into your sequence.

SHOT LOGS

Shot logs have been around from the earliest days of production. Like most tools, they have evolved to a digital state. A shot log is a carefully prepared database that details the production activity during a shoot. These logs are either generated on a computer or handwritten. Many productions prefer the old-fashioned style, but there are some time-saving advantages to a digital log.

A shot log can be generated with any text-capable tool. Some shot logs are created from popular database applications like FileMaker or spreadsheet applications like Microsoft Excel. There are even some industry-specific applications that can generate shot logs, such as the Executive Producer by Imagine Products.

The workflow of a digital shot log is simple: while on set during the production phase, a script supervisor records specific information about each shot that is recorded or filmed during the shoot. This can include timecode start and end, scene, take, and other shot-specific information. Usually the director's comments are also included, or in some cases whether the director chose to "print" the scene. When the director decides to print a scene, this would mean that he or she wants to see the scene in the dailies. The dailies are the compilation of selected shots from the day's work.

In some cases, the director may choose to print everything, meaning that he or she decided to look at all of the footage shot from that day. But there are certain situations where the director would not want to see everything.

For example, there are a lot of nature films that try to capture a particular moment in time, like a migratory pattern. Lots of footage can be wasted waiting for these moments and the director may choose not to print many shots that were taken in production.

The creation of a shot log and the use of a script supervisor (who normally would record the information) can speed up the postproduction process. It is astonishing to work on complex projects where a script supervisor was not used in order to save money. Usually, this means that the editor, who normally is paid a higher rate, has to do the logging instead. Why would any production do such a thing?

Shot logs can also be created in postproduction, before the editing phase, instead of during actual production. This is usually done with logging software on a low-cost computer and sometimes uses dubs of the original tapes in order to protect them from excessive wear and tear. Care must be taken to ensure that proper tape names are used and that timecode types are not switched if the timecode numbers are entered by hand, which sometimes happens when using VHS timecode window dubs. I've seen plenty of shot logs where four field tapes are dubbed to a single 120-minute VHS cassette and all four field tapes are given the name of the first field tape on the dub. It's much easier to fix this problem before the tapes are actually digitized.

Shot logs are organized so that each entry has a specific space or "field" where information is recorded. Examples of the fields would be Timecode Start, Timecode End, and so on. When the spreadsheet or database is completed, it is exported as a tab-delimited text file. This creates a file with a tab marker between each field. Tab-delimited files are a common way of exchanging textual information between databases.

Shot logs that are created with tab-delimited files and other database programs can be translated with Avid Log Exchange. Avid Log Exchange is included with every copy of Xpress Pro. What Avid Log Exchange can do is transfer a shot log into a format that is readable by Xpress Pro. Once the file is converted through ALE, it can be imported into a bin.

ALE is used primarily for file types that relate to telecine databases. For example, when a film is telecined (transferred from film to video) it almost always goes through some sort of database system that logs the film numbers and their relationship to time-

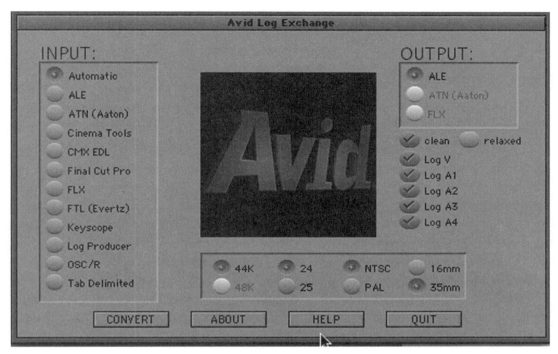

11.1 Avid Log Exchange Interface with Import selected

code numbers on the resulting tape. When you use telecined videotape, it is much easier to import the log from telecine than to go through the tape and log the material manually. Why recreate what's already been done? You can do it with Avid Log Exchange in a matter of moments (see Figure 11.1).

ALE can directly open Aaton (ATN), Evertz, Flex, CMX, Log Producer, OSC/R, and OLE files as well as its own format. ALE is already set up as a drag-and-drop operation, where, if you drop one of those formatted files onto the application icon, it will process the file into an ALE format and save it in the same directory as the originating file.

You can also import FCP, Cinema Tools, and, as mentioned earlier, tab-delimited files into ALE. In order to do this, first run the application, then select File>Import>[Filetype], where the Filetype is either FCP, Cinema Tools, or a tab-delimited File.

First, find Avid Log Exchange. It's located in your Avid Folder. You can put an alias (shortcut) to ALE on your desktop. If the file is one of the abovementioned import types, you will need to open ALE. Otherwise, just drag and drop.

Once the file is converted into an ALE format, you can import it into a bin. In Xpress Pro, create a new bin for the shot log. Next, select File>Import. On the Import menu, select Shot Log as the file format. Navigate to the ALE file that you created from your original shot log and import it. The new clips should appear in the bin.

IMPORTING IMAGES

It is incredibly easy to ignore the not-so-distant past, when integrating graphics into video without a broadcast-specific, expensive character generator was impossible. Most of us who remember those days choose to forget, because there was so little that could be done creatively. But now, anyone with a computer, software, and a bit of talent can create excellent graphics.

Likewise, it used to be difficult to import and export both still and motion graphics. But with Xpress Pro's import interface, the process is very easy. The only true deal breaker associated with importing graphic files is the format of the files themselves.

Xpress Pro supports import of the most common graphic file formats used in video and film. These include Alias (.als), Bitmap (.bmp), Chyron (.chr), Cineon (.cin), Framestore (.fs), IFF (.iff), OMFI (.omf), JPEG (.jpg), Photoshop (.psd), PICT (.pic, .pict), PCX (.pcx), Pixar (.pxr), PNG (.png), QRT (.dbw), Rendition (.6m), SGI (.rgb), Softimage (.pic), Sunraster (.sun), Targa (.tga), TIFF (.tif), Wavefront (.rla), X-Windows (.xwd), and Abekas YUV (.yuv) files. Macintosh systems also can import Photo CD format.

There are some formats that you might encounter that are not on the list. However, there is little doubt that you will be able to find methods of converting an unsupported file type into one that Xpress Pro can read. What you will need for this conversion is the "Swiss Army knife" of graphics—the file conversion application. I use GraphicConverter, a shareware application that is available on the web. Debabelizer is another popular choice.

Once you've converted your files into an Xpress Pro–readable format, you'll need to prep them so that they can fit properly in the frame. Although Xpress Pro has some importing capabilities that ensure that your files come into the system in a clean manner, a little prep work can guarantee a better import

Preparing Still and Motion Graphics for Import

When preparing a file for import, certain criteria must be met in the frame size, pixel aspect, color levels, field ordering, format, and color space of your file. So before we address how to import the graphics, let's make sure that you're up to speed on all of the terminology required to understand how graphics work, and also how they relate to the video signal.

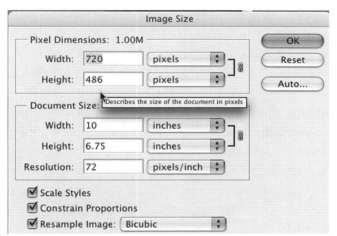

11.2 Checking Image Size in Photoshop

Frame Size

In order for still images to import correctly into Xpress Pro without any improper distortion or other quality issues, the proper frame size must be maintained (see Figure 11.2). The dimensions of the image are expressed in width by height. The measurement unit is in pixels. Xpress Pro accepts DV-sized images, which are 720×480. A normal NTSC image is 720×486, but DV images are smaller in pixel height, removing four lines from the top of the image and two from the bottom. PAL native size is 720×576.

Pixel Aspect

Before we actually import any graphics, we need to cover a couple of key concepts. The first is 601, or ITU-601. ITU-601 is the standard that determines the dimension and pixel sizes of both PAL and NTSC standard definition television images. It also dictates other specifications, including color levels, which we'll discuss later. The 601 standard determines the size and shape of the pixels used in our broadcast images. It may come as a surprise to some, but the pixels for broadcasting are not square. This makes file imports a bit trickier, because most files from common graphics programs like Adobe PhotoShop and even Adobe After Effects contain square pixels.

So, you might ask, why are the pixels different? The pixels created in computer monitors are perfectly square. The pixels encoded in video broadcast signals were and still are…well, not quite square. Once a standard was set, they were referred to as nonsquare. So, you might ask, if the pixels are nonsquare, why not say that they are rectangular? The answer is that they aren't always a perfect rectangular shape. A lot of the shape of the pixel depends on how the image is displayed.

The bottom line is this: if you mapped a regularly sized graphic image pixel-for-pixel into a broadcast format, it would appear to be horizontally stretched out. Now that we've defined the problem, let's take a look at how it is solved. In order to properly import a graphics file generated by computer to video, you can either adjust it using the graphics program or adjust it on import.

In the early days of graphic imports, there weren't very many options. An image would be created at the proper aspect, then horizontally shrunk so that, once imported, the wider horizontal pixels would stretch it back out.

One of the great new features in Photoshop CS, a popular graphics editing application, is the ability to create and view a file using the Pixel Aspect Correction feature. Using this feature, you can create a file that will be the appropriate size for import. When the file is previewed, it can be switched between square pixels or with corrected pixel aspect, which is what it will look like when imported into a video application such as Xpress Pro (see Figures 11.3–11.4).

Now that you've learned the basics of pixel aspects, let's go over the import options regarding pixels and image size using Xpress Pro. Select an open bin and then File>Import. Make sure the File Type is set to Graphic Files.

Now let's go to Options to look at the pixel aspects. Select the Options button. Here are the aspect options with a description of each and how they work.

601, Nonsquare

This option (the default) is chosen for images which have been prepared for import using nonsquare pixels and are the correct size for Xpress Pro. You can use this option when importing any image with nonsquare pixels that maintains a 4:3 aspect ratio. (This is also commonly used when exporting files from Xpress Pro that will be altered in some other program and returned to Xpress Pro.) If images are not big enough to fill the frame (smaller than 720×480, for example) they will have a border of black around them.

Maintain, NonSquare

Maintain refers to maintaining the correct aspect ratio (how wide it is compared to how tall it's supposed to be) of the image. This option prevents a graphic from being squished or distorted when it is imported. Select this option for import when the image contains the correct nonsquare pixels but might vary in size or in aspect ratio. If the image is too

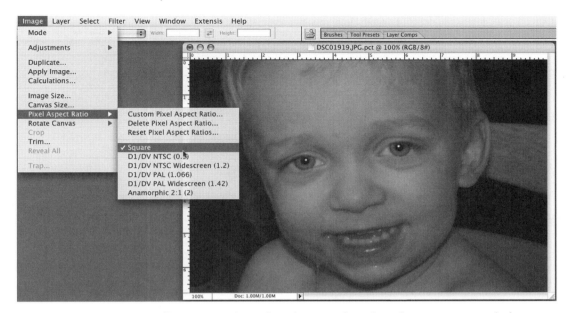

11.3 Pixel Aspect Preview off (square pixels) in Photoshop CS. This is how the image appears before it is properly corrected.

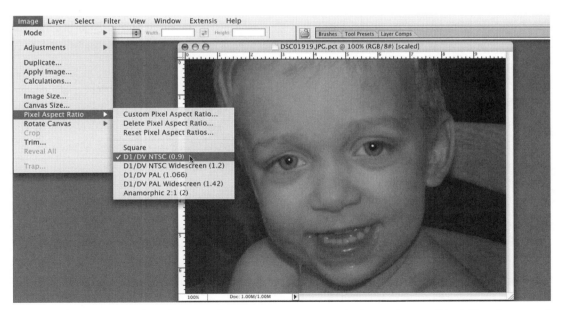

11.4 Pixel Aspect on in Photoshop CS. The image appears normal. This is what it will look like when saved and imported with no correction necessary into Xpress Pro.

big (beyond the 720×480 norm for NTSC DV or the 720×586 norm for PAL DV) the image will be mapped into the proper aspect ratio (shape). If the image is too small, black borders will be inserted. Using this option will not resize the image. This option is primarily used for importing standard NTSC images, where the dimensions are 720×486. Using this option will crop six of the horizontal lines, bringing the image down to the DV standard of 720×480. If the image is too large, then only the middle of the image will be imported, cropping off any portion of the image larger than the standard import size.

Maintain, Square

You can use this import option if you want the original image size maintained. This is used primarily for import of logos, icons, and other items which do not necessarily have to fill the screen. Xpress Pro recognizes that the original contains square pixels and will adjust to fit the proper aspect, but it will not resize the image to attempt to fill the screen.

Maintain and Resize, Square

Xpress Pro uses this option to take an image that was created with square pixels and fill the largest dimension possible, adding black borders on the other dimension in order to maintain the correct aspect ratio. Tall, skinny pictures will import so that they fill the screen from top to bottom and have "pillars" of black on the side. Wide, landscape-aspect pictures fill the screen from side to side with "letterbox" black space top and bottom. This option is used for import of graphic images that were not originally intended for video use, such as stock images. If an alpha channel is used with this type of import, any black borders added by Xpress Pro are made transparent.

Color Levels

When importing a file, you'll need to determine which color levels were used when the file was created and saved. The file needs to be saved in RGB or 601 mode. Most graphic applications don't have 601 color space, but they do contain an RGB option. Either will work fine for import with Xpress Pro.

In Photoshop, the color levels are known as the Color mode. Actually, what is being referred to here is color space. The two color spaces, RGB and 601 (which is also known as YCbCr or YPbPr or, sometimes, YUV color space), have different properties that affect how different colors are represented on your screen. The variance of colors is known as the gamut. Note that 601 color space has a gamut which, if applied to a true three-dimensional space, would be much less dense and far smaller than RGB color space.

For example, you may know that the NTSC setup or black level for video is set to 7.5IRE. The highest or white level is set to 100IRE. So, what about video that is less than

11.5 A: An RGB image imported as RGB.
    B: An RGB image imported as 601—Tonal Range is unnatural.
    C: 601 image imported as 601—Ideal for Video.
    D: 601 image imported as RGB—Elevated Black Levels, Crushed White Levels.

7.5 or more than 100IRE? These levels are generally considered to be illegal or not proper for 601 video.

In RGB color space, equivalent to NTSC 7.5IRE is 16, 16, 16 RGB level and the 100IRE equivalent of white is 235, 235, 235. Very few graphics are created using these restrictions. Most RGB images use 0, 0, 0 for black and 255, 255, 255 for white. As a result, there is more contrast and thus more variance in the allowable colors in that space. But using an RGB picture without adjusting the levels would create an image in 601 space that would not be acceptable. As a result, the brightness of the image has to be attenuated (see Figure 11.5).

In addition to the brightness levels, there are some colors in RGB that cannot be faithfully be reproduced in 601 color space. When we convert the image from RGB to 601 space, the colors in the original RGB image are mapped to the 601 gamut. This gamut mapping can be troublesome and will require some experimentation with graphics to get desirable results. An example of RGB color that is not reproduced well in 601 space is a sunny yellow. Even in grayscale, you can see that the 601 image is not as bright or vibrant as the original RGB image.

11.6 A Sunny Yellow Created in RGB color space, then exported to 601. Even in grayscale, the difference can be seen.

There is one other option that you can choose, RGB Dithered. This option is used for more complex RGB files with color gradations and more complex color effects. The dithering process smooths the image somewhat so that any "stepping" in variations of color will be less noticeable. Dithering smooths the transitions from one color to another.

We tried using the Dither option with mixed results. Where there was little variation, the dithering came through the best. When the image has a big variation in color, you see it less. But if you use a lot of washed backgrounds, particularly in the reds, you will notice a change. Dithering definitely softens the variations. Keep in mind that we're using 8-bit video in a 601 color space as mentioned before. The variations in the color gamut are not as subtle as they would be in RGB or other color space. In addition, because the graphic information is only 8 bit (as opposed to say 10 or 16 bits) the gradations with seem less gradual.

File Field Ordering

When importing video graphic files, Xpress Pro has to determine field ordering from the original source. Field ordering determines how the original file was written, and in turn, how it should be read into Xpress Pro.

You may already know that NTSC and PAL video are made up of two fields. Each field scans every other line in the picture. These two fields "interlace" with each other. For example, if we were to number each line of video, one field displays the odd numbered lines: line, 1, line 3, line 5, etc. Then the other field scans the even numbered lines: line 2, line 4, line 6, etc. Then when the two fields are combined or interlaced, they create what we perceive to be a full-resolution frame.

So which field comes first? The order of the fields—that is, how they are recorded—can differ. The question here is, when a source is recording to videotape or to a file, do the even numbered lines play back first, or do the odd numbered lines? The order of fields is determined by the playback (or in the case of file writing, export) source. The reason that this order is important is that these fields are recorded so that they are "temporally displaced" from each other. In other words, the second field that is recorded, whether it is odd or even, happens later in time than the first field, so if you switch the order, you are actually messing with the space-time continuum, just like a funky episode of *Star Trek*. The more movement in the frame, the worse this problem appears, because you are making the half of the picture that was recorded first look like it happened after the other half.

Here are some examples. With older AVR resolution Avid systems using NTSC or PAL video, the upper or odd field is first. The same is true for Meridien and Xpress Pro Avids using PAL video. However, Xpress Pro writes NTSC video using the lower or even field first. Therefore, if you import a video file that was originally created with Xpress Pro with NTSC video, you should select Even (Lower) Field First.

Before we forget to mention it, any video that is 24p or 25p is created with both fields combined in a progressive frame. If you are importing such files, there is no field ordering.

You can select the Noninterlaced option. Also, images that are created in Photoshop and other still graphic applications will not have field order, so those will also be imported as Noninterlaced.

Now that you have gained the important understanding of field ordering, how can you determine whether a file is odd (upper) or even (lower) field first? Some applications can create files either way. The easiest way would be to contact the creator of the video file and ask how it was created. If the software that created the file is on your system, you can usually find the correct field ordering in the manual or help files.

But if you have neither creator, manual, nor help files at your disposal, the only way to determine the proper field order would be to import the file both ways and compare the results. Once you've imported the file, be sure to label each clip correctly as upper or lower.

Load one of the clips into the monitor and find a place where some motion takes place in the picture. If you are doing a sports video, you're in luck. Using the arrow keys on your computer, step the clip forward frame by frame. The action should all be forward moving. If it regresses occasionally as you step forward, the selected clip uses the wrong field ordering.

If this comparison doesn't work, try this: compare the two clips when playing back at regular speed. One will look a bit more distorted and any horizontal motion might seem jumpy. Additionally, you might see some shapes that are distorted when vertical motion occurs. Again, if you see these things when comparing the two, the distorted clip uses the wrong field order.

Field Order versus Field Dominance

Field ordering is commonly confused with Field Dominance. Although the two sound similar, they are quite different. Field dominance determines which field is used in the frame as the cutting point. All Avid systems are Field 1 dominant.

At first, this term may seem confusing, and it has nothing to do with importing, but let's explain it anyway so you'll know the difference.

If we were to take a continuous stream of raw video, you would not be able to determine frames. In fact, we could say that the "frameness" of the video has not been determined. However, once we record the video, synchronizing it and adding timecode with the picture, it takes on certain characteristics, including two fields for each frame. These two fields, when combined, make up a single frame of video and one frame of assigned timecode. Therefore the first field of video that is recorded for a specific timecode is field 1; the second recorded field is field 2, and then the timecode number advances.

Field dominance is the determination of which field is first temporally in the edit frame and where each cut will occur. Avid systems always cut before the first frame. Therefore it is Field 1 dominant. If it were cut on the second field, it would be Field 2 dominant.

Alpha Channel

The alpha channel of an image determines which parts of the image are seen and which are not when they are keyed. For example, if we were to create a circular logo over a black background and we wanted to just show the logo, we would need to create an alpha channel that defined the black background as transparent and the logo as opaque (see Figure 11.7). Xpress Pro supports alpha channels in most common file formats.

There are a lot of different terms for alpha channels. Video editors have called them mattes, holdouts, cookie cutters, and hi-cons. Graphic artists frequently refer to them as masks or mattes. In any event, they all do the same thing: determine transparency.

If you were to look at an alpha channel, you would see a grayscale image. Normally, the white pixels represent areas of the image which will be seen. Black pixels represent areas which will be masked or matted out. Gray pixels represent varied levels of transparency of the image, with lighter pixels less transparent than darker pixels. Alpha channels are represented in this manner for just about every graphic application that has been created.

However, when evaluating alpha channels, Avid systems read them backward, with black pixels representing opacity and white pixels transparent (see Figure 11.8). Why on earth would they do it this way? Apparently it goes back to film mattes and how they are represented. Matting in film is done exactly opposite of the way Photoshop and other graphic programs create alpha channels. As a result, Avid chose to go with the film industry standard. Keep in mind that in the early days of nonlinear, the personal computer was relatively new. Not all editors were computer operators and not all editors used Photoshop.

11.7 Alpha Channel in Photoshop

11.8 Inverted Alpha Channel—A Common Mistake

Okay, so if you are using graphic files created with a graphics application, remember to choose the invert alpha when importing the file. You can easily tell when the alpha was incorrectly read.

Organizing Your Graphic Files

Xpress Pro's advanced feature set allows you to import files in a relatively easy fashion. Before importing the files, there is one important thing to consider: is there any possibility that you will need these graphics for future use? If there is, you should put them in a permanent folder on your system, preferably inside the Project folder itself. Most graphic files don't take up too much space, and when importing, you'll find that the system has some special features that ease the method of import when you do this. We'll examine those methods later in the chapter. For now, we'll go through a basic importing procedure.

First, create a bin where the imported files will be stored. Select File>Import. The Import Dialog screen appears. For File Type, select Graphic Files (Windows) or Graphic Documents (Mac). Now you can navigate to find those files on your system.

To import multiple files, Ctrl-click on additional files (Windows) or Shift-click on each additional file (Mac).

Once you've selected the files, choose the media drive where you want the imported items to be stored. Xpress Pro is going to take each file and convert it into media that the system can easily read.

Mixing Resolutions

When you import a graphic or animation file, you'll have to determine the resolution of the resulting file that Xpress Pro will create. You can mix resolutions with Xpress Pro, but you cannot mix frame rates. For example, you can put a 15:1s graphic into a DV-25 sequence, but you cannot mix PAL media with NTSC.

Single-Frame Import Duration

When you import graphic files, Xpress Pro creates a media file for each import. With this option, you can select the duration of the media for each import.

Autodetect Sequential Files

Enabling this option allows Xpress Pro to look for a numbered pattern of file names within a folder. This is the method

used to import PICT and other types of animated sequences. Xpress Pro can import all of the files from one of these sequences at once as a single clip, eliminating the need to string them back together frame by frame in Source/Record mode. In other words, each graphic will represent a single frame in the resulting import, which will be a single clip of all of the sequential frames. To import PICT sequences (and other types of image sequences) you only have to select the *first* image of the file sequence. You can also import partial sequences by selecting a file from further into the sequence, for example, you could import PICT.030 and that would start the import 1 second into the image sequence.

Warning Be careful when naming your graphic files. When Autodetect Sequential Files is turned on during an import, if there are two files with sequential numbers, they will be imported as a clip together, with each graphic represented by only a single frame.

SAVING IMPORT SETTINGS

Now that you've gone through the trouble of defining all of the options for importing your files, do yourself a favor and save these settings on your system. If you work with a graphic artist or animation house on a regular basis, it might be a good idea to name the settings after that person or place. That way you won't forget which setting works best. First, go to the Project window and duplicate your Import Settings. (Click on the Import Settings and click Ctrl+D/Cmd+D) A duplicated setting appears in the Settings window. Select this setting and scroll to the right, where you can name it. In this case, we'll name it "My Graphics." You can activate this Import Setting by clicking to the left of it. When the check mark appears next to the setting, it is selected.

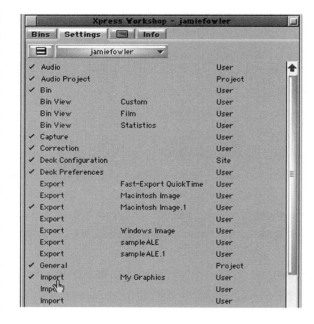

Drag-and-Drop Importing

Once the Import Settings are made, you can drag and drop items from the desktop directly into a bin. Keep in mind that these will be imported using whatever settings were last used. There is only one thing that poses a problem: desktop real estate. If you have a two-monitor system, this procedure can prove fun. Doing this with a one monitor system requires resizing and repositioning. Still it's worth it to try this method out.

IMPORTING AUDIO FROM A CD

When using audio CDs it can frequently be to your benefit to copy the tracks to a project file, much as you did when importing graphics. This way, you have the ability to use the audio without having to track down your CD again. At this point, our lawyers have asked us to remind you to remember to respect all copyrights when doing this.

Importing audio from an audio CD works much like importing graphics, except there are fewer options. To import an audio CD track, select the target bin, then File>Import. When the Import browser comes up, select Files of Type>Audio (Windows) or Show> Audio Documents (Mac). Navigate your way to the audio CD and select the track.

Music CDs use a sampling rate of 44.1kHz. If your Audio Project Settings do not reflect this sampling rate, Xpress Pro will ask you if you want to convert the CD track to the proper rate (see Figure 11.9). Click Yes. The file is imported.

11.9 Sampling Difference Message on CD Import

IMPORTING PHOTOSHOP GRAPHICS

Xpress Pro has some advanced graphic importing capabilities that work well with Adobe Photoshop v6.0 and above. When importing a Photoshop graphic (a .psd file), you can use separate layers and use existing alpha channels. Not all Photoshop settings are supported (blending modes, for example) but with the ability to separate layers comes the opportunity to animate the image in a sequence. It also makes it easier to use Photoshop

Matte Key: thosekids.psd: Layer 5 (With Alpha)	00;00;30
Matte Key: thosekids.psd: Layer 4 (With Alpha)	00;00;30
Matte Key: thosekids.psd: Layer 3 (With Alpha)	00;00;30
Matte Key: thosekids.psd: Layer 2 (With Alpha)	00;00;30
Matte Key: thosekids.psd: Layer 1 (With Alpha)	00;00;30
thosekids.psd: Background	00;00;30

11.10 Multilayered File in Photoshop

SuperBin: ◇ Xpress Workshop Bin

Brief | Text | Frame | Script

Name	Start
thosekids.psd.01	00;00;30
Matte Key: thosekids.psd: Layer 5 (With Alpha)	00;00;30

11.11 Imported Sequence from multilayered Photoshop file

images that were originally created for other uses. This, combined with some of the effects in Xpress Pro's arsenal, can create a lot of "Wow!" factor with your clients.

When you import a multilayered Photoshop file, Xpress Pro will create a separate clip for each layer (see Figure 11.10). It will also create a sequence of all of the layers together, which you can use for animation (see Figure 11.11).

First, go to your Import settings. Under Alpha, select Invert Existing. Doing this will allow Xpress Pro to translate the way PhotoShop creates alpha channels to the way the Avid understands them.

Now you can import the Photoshop file. When importing this file you will be asked whether you want to import it as one flattened layer, a sequence of layers, or a sequence of chosen layers. This third option allows you to ignore layers that you will not use. When you import the file as a sequence of layers, it will produce a matte key clip for each layer and a regular clip for the background. Xpress Pro also creates a sequence with all of the layers in order, just as they were in the original Photoshop file. You can "stair step" the appearance of each layer to animate them on the screen or use other effects to enhance the image (see Figure 11.12).

Warning Photoshop PSD files that are 16 bit will not import properly into Xpress Pro. Before importing any Photoshop files, make sure they are 8 bit. You can do this in Photoshop by opening the file and selecting Image>Mode. If the file is 16 bit, you can change it to 8 bit and save it before import. Otherwise, you will get an error screen and no layers when importing.

IMPORT ISSUES

Batch-Reimporting Graphics

Earlier in this chapter we stressed the importance of keeping graphic images stored on your hard drive. There are several good reasons for this. Should you inadvertently lose the media from your imports, Xpress Pro will remember where the import came from. If it came from your hard drive, it can reimport it more easily than if you imported it from a CD or network location that you would have to find again.

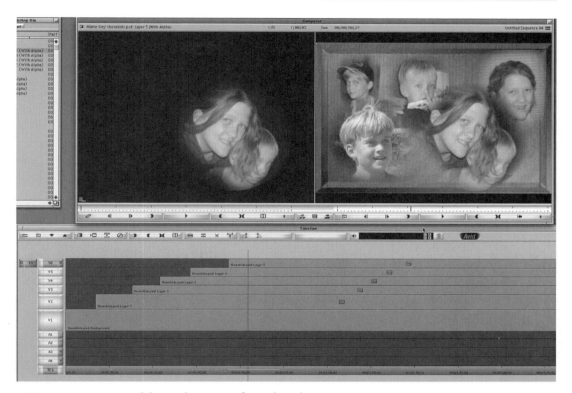

11.12 Animating a multilayered sequence from Photoshop import

Perhaps more importantly, if you are editing an offline version of a program and want to batch-digitize all of the clips and graphics in a higher resolution, Xpress Pro can do this as well.

To batch-import your graphics, first select the sequence that contains the graphics to be imported. Then select Bin>Batch Import. The Batch Import menu appears.

At the top of the screen is a list of graphic files that were imported for the sequence that you selected. You can select or deselect each individual file. Next, choose your resolution and clips to be imported. You'll also need to choose a drive for the import. At the bottom of the menu are two key options. Use Source Compression for OMFI uses the same compression used on an original OMFI file when importing OMF files. This allows you to import at a native resolution and do the import more quickly than normal. For graphic files, leave this deselected. Override Clip Settings with Current Settings, the second option, allows you to import files and change their settings to the current settings that you have selected. For example, if your graphics were previously imported at 15:1s and you have changed the import setting to DV-25 411, it will import at the DV-25 resolution.

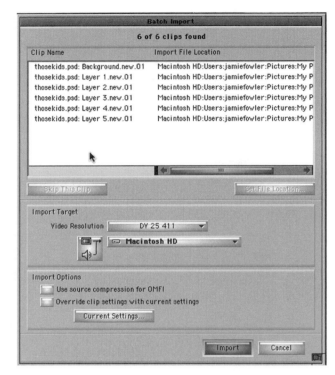

11.13   Batch Import Menu Selection   11.14   Batch Import Menu

Once you've chosen your settings, batch-import the files (see Figure 11.14). They will have their original names but will be created at the new resolution that you have chosen. You can double-check this by changing your bin to Text View and looking at the resolution of the clips.

Importing QuickTime Files

Importing QuickTime files is a fairly simple operation. Be sure to set your Media Creation tool so that it will import files at the resolution that you are using for the rest of your sequence.

Be sure that you have the proper codec for the QuickTime file that you want to import. Without the proper codec installed on your computer, the QuickTime will not import correctly. We'll talk more about codecs in Chapter 14 "Exporting with Xpress Pro" on page 395.

Choose File>Import. The Import screen appears. Select Graphic Files; then navigate to the QuickTime file to be imported. Select the file and press Open. The file will import.

Many of the same rules about field order, color space, aspect, and alpha channels from "Importing Images" on page 324 of this chapter apply to QuickTime files.

Importing OMF and AAF Files

You can import OMF and AAF media into your bins just as easily as a QuickTime or graphic. There is only one major item to remember: be sure to select the format of the file on the Import menu, or it won't show in your file browser.

Select File>Import. When the Import menu appears, select the file format (either OMFI or AAF, depending on the format you wish to import). Navigate to the file and select it. Xpress Pro will import both metadata (information about the media, such as timecode) and the media itself.

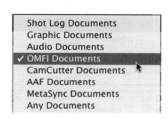

11.15   OMF File Selection
in Import Menu

FUN WITH IMPORTS

Importing files is a pretty straightforward operational procedure, and it's not particularly challenging to your creative side. Our next lesson will take you into a much more subjective world, where your decisions will reflect the quality of work that can be done, using Xpress Pro's powerful Color Correction tools.

Chapter 12

Color Correction

Color Correction is a topic that could take up an entire book of its own. As a matter of fact, our last book did just that. *Color Correction for Digital Video* (CMP Books, 2002) was a platform-, OS-, and product-agnostic book that covered the concepts of color correction for a wide spectrum of users. The theory and concepts discussed in that book had wide appeal from a spectrum of end users that included Avid editors of all stripes, Adobe After Effects artists, Apple Final Cut Pro users, and others.

In this chapter we'll discuss some of the same basic principles, but we will focus our attention firmly on the color correction capabilities of Xpress Pro. We will work within its limitations and show you how best to exploit the great tools that it has.

COLOR CORRECTION TOOLSET

Let's start by taking a look at the Color Correction toolset. Color Correction (CC) in Xpress Pro is a mode, like Trim or Effects. With a default user setting, the way to get into Color Correction mode is Toolset>Color Correction (which can also be activated by pressing Shift+F8). However, there are two other ways to launch into this mode with the touch of a keystroke. As is discussed in "Keyboard" on page 42 of Chapter 2, you can map the Toolset>Color Correction file menu pulldown to any key on your keyboard or your GUI.

Alternately, you could also call up the Command Palette and map the Color Correction mode button that is at the top left of the CC tab. On a Symphony, the Color Correction mode is mapped on the GUI next to the Source/Record, Trim, and Effects modes.

The difference between these two methods is that the version from the Toolset menu also calls up any other settings, keyboards, and screen layouts that you like while you are in Color Correction mode. Try using the Toolset, then the Mode button. You will notice that the windows open in different places and if you customize your Color Correction toolset, then those customized options will not exist when you enter the mode with the button from the Command Palette.

You can't color correct source material. The Color Corrector only works on sequences. So before going into Color Correction mode, load a sequence into the Timeline or Sequence window or quickly create one.

The layout and buttons in this mode are quite intuitive, but there's a lot of cool functionality you can miss if you skip ahead. Even you experienced Symphony editors out there could learn a thing or two about your own machines. Plus, there's a lot of new stuff in Xpress Pro.

THE COLOR CORRECTOR GUI

The GUI is divided into three basic sections (see Figure 12.1). The top is called the Composer window, and there are, in fact, three windows instead of the usual one or two. This allows you to correct your shots in context. You are able to see the shots that precede and follow the shot you're working on, which is important to help each correction seem like part of a cohesive whole. Notice the words above the images in this window—"Previous," "Current," and "Next." These are not just descriptions, though. Just as in Source/Record mode, these words also hide menus. As you move your cursor up to them, the cursor changes to a downward pointing triangle, allowing you to click to see a pulldown menu. The selections allow you to customize the content of each of the three screens. This ability is incredibly powerful, because the key to doing color correction is analyzing and comparing the images.

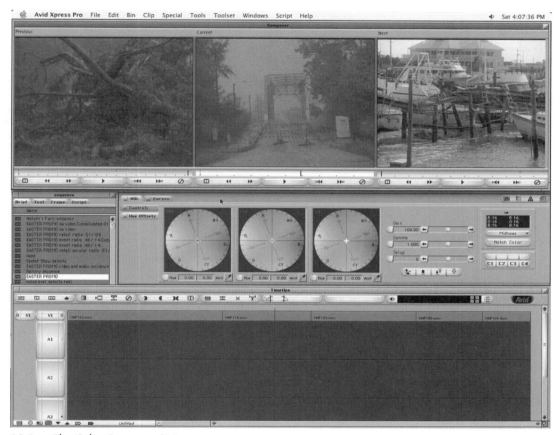

12.1   The Color Corrector GUI

Even though you should be monitoring your corrections on a broadcast-quality video monitor, it is also useful to have the largest images possible on the computer screen. You can drag the Color Corrector Composer window so that it fills the screen from edge to edge. To completely fill my monitor, I had to move the window off-screen a little on the left side to be able to pull the right side open to its full size. This larger size is useful when you are using the eyedropper to identify a specific pixel in the image.

Monitoring in CC Mode

Let's take a look at our monitoring choices. I'll explain what they mean and why you'll need them:

- *Empty:* Allows you to clear the monitor. Why? I don't know. Maybe so you aren't distracted.

- *Entire Sequence:* Allows you access to the entire sequence in the monitor you choose. The best use of this capability is to navigate anywhere in the sequence to compare shots.

- *Reference:* This locks the current frame displayed in the monitor to be used as a reference frame. The two main uses for this are to select an optimal shot to match to, or sometimes as a reference starting point for the current shot, providing you with a side-by-side, full-screen "before and after."

- *Current:* Displays the shot you are correcting. As we've mentioned before, though, you should be correcting the colors while referencing an external video monitor.

- *Previous:* Displays the shot previous to the one you are correcting. This is handy for matching shots in a scene.

- *Next:* Displays the shot after the one you are correcting. This is handy for matching shots in a scene.

External Monitors and Scopes

The optimum way to analyze an image is to view the image on a properly calibrated NTSC or PAL video monitor (not a TV set from your neighborhood electronics store!). You should also have some form of professional external waveform and vectorscope. People are loathe to spend the money, since a good monitor and scopes can easily cost 10 times what you paid for your Xpress Pro, but if you are going to be doing any kind of final online work for broadcast, it really is a must. I like the Sony BVM and PVM series video monitors and the VideoTek VTM-300 series waveform/vectorscope that is displayed using a regular computer monitor. As a matter of fact, if your computer monitor for your Xpress Pro has two inputs, you can put the waveform/vectorscope on the other input and switch back and forth on the same monitor, saving you space and money. I have also worked with scopes that are displayed superimposed on the video monitor (Magni is the brand that I've used in the past), but the resolution of the trace is not quite good enough for the creative uses that are required for good color correction.

We don't have room to explain the proper set-up and calibration for a good video monitor in this book, but it is thoroughly covered in *Color Correction for Digital Video* (CMP Books, 2002) or using any of countless free web resources including www.videotek.com, www.techtronix.com, or www.leader.com.)

- *Second Previous:* Displays the shot before the Previous shot. In other words, two shots back from the current shot. This is another handy reference for maintaining a consistent look throughout a scene.

- *Second Next:* Displays the shot after the Next shot, in other words, two shots forward from the current shot. This is also a handy reference for maintaining a consistent look throughout a scene.

- *Quad Display:* Displays the RGB Histogram, RGB Parade Waveform, Vectorscope, and YC Waveform in a single monitor. These are arguably the four most important displays for analyzing your image while color-correcting. Unfortunately, at the reduced size needed to display all of these, you can't do any detailed work, but this does give you a nice sweeping overview (see Figure 12.2).

- *RGB Histogram:* Displays a graph of the three color channels (see Figure 12.3). The X-axis shows the tonal range: from dark on the left to bright on the right. The Y-axis indicates how many pixels there are at a given brightness value. The histogram can't be used to determine if an image is perfect, but steep spikes on either end indicate either crushed blacks (if the spike is on the left) or blown-out highlights (if the spike is on the right). Also, if the graph is fairly thin on either end or both ends, it indicates a lack of tonal range (low contrast).

- *RGB Parade:* This is a waveform display with each color channel displayed in its own separate "cell." This is an excellent tool for matching shots since you can see the relative levels of each color channel (see Figure 12.4).

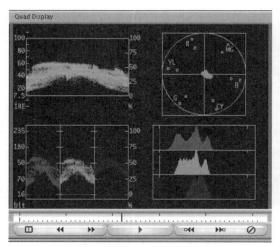

12.2   Quad Display

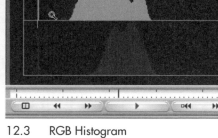

12.3   RGB Histogram

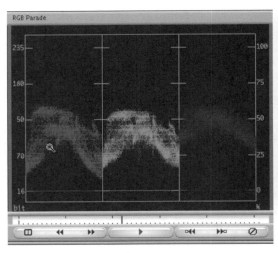

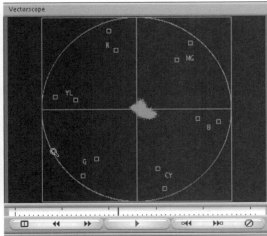

12.4   RGB Parade

12.5   Vectorscope

- *Vectorscope:* Displays chroma and hue information. Hue is indicated by its rotational position around the scope and the chroma value is indicated by its displacement from the center. Any portion of an image with no chroma value (black, grays, and white) appear in the center of the scope and portions of the image with high chroma values appear at the outer edges of the scope. Legal levels cannot extend beyond the area bound by the six small "targets" for the colors of color bars: (clockwise from just left of "noon") red, magenta, blue, cyan, green, and yellow (see Figure 12.5).

- *Y Waveform:* The Y Waveform is a waveform display that only indicates luma values, with the chroma information stripped. This is similar to a standard waveform monitor with a Low Pass filter. If you have safe color limits set, any signal outside of that range is indicated.

- *YC Waveform:* The YC waveform is a waveform display that indicates both luma and chroma. This is similar to a standard waveform in Flat filter mode (see Figure 12.6).

- *YCbCr Histogram:* Unless you are a fairly adept reader of histograms and an expert in conceptualizing in YCbCr space, this won't do you much good. The Y portion of the histogram will display the luma values and the Cb and Cr histograms represent chromatic values of Cb and Cr respectively. This is not an easy way to evaluate either chroma or hue (see Figure 12.7).

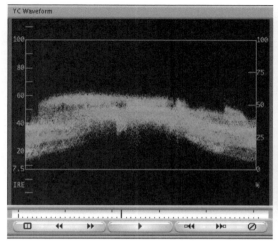

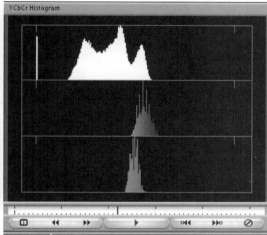

12.6   YC Waveform   12.7   YCbCr Histogram

- *YCbCr Parade:* This is also a very difficult waveform to analyze. The first cell is the same as the Y Waveform, and the next two cells represent the Cb and Cr values. As they expand from their center position halfway up the scale, they indicate increased chroma. A flat centerline position indicates black or white. Cb values above that line are blue hues, while values below it are yellow. In Cr, values above the centerline are red, while values below are cyan.

The active monitor is also displayed in the client monitor or broadcast monitor. This is the preferred place to monitor images during color correction.

Below the images in the monitors in the Composer window are a series of seven soft buttons that can be customized and mapped to the keyboard to minimize mousing. We will deal with their default settings here, though (see Figure 12.9).

- The first button displays a split screen with the original levels indicated on the left and the altered levels on the right. The split screen is easily cropped by dragging any of the four white triangles at the corners of the split screen.

- The next button is the Rewind button. It jumps you to the head frame at the previous transition to where the Locator bar is. This is the same as the Fast Forward button in the regular editing interface.

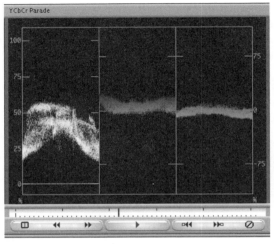

12.8   YCbCr Parade *(left)*

12.9   Customizable Buttons *(below)*

- Next to the Rewind button is the Fast Forward button. It jumps you to the head-frame of the next shot. This is the same as the Rewind button in the regular editing interface.

- In the center of each monitor is the Play button. If you are monitoring Previous, Current, or Next, this Play button will only play that segment. It will not play past either end.

If you want to watch more of the sequence without having to call up the entire sequence in the monitor, map Play Loop to your keyboard or GUI. Using Play Loop instead of Play will cause playback from the locator through the end of the sequence. On some other Avid products, it is also possible to use the Review Edit button to watch the Previous, Current, and—depending how long your Current shot is—Next shots in sequence. Keep an eye out for the Review Edit button in future versions of Xpress Pro. It may trickle down from the higher end products eventually.

- To the right of the Play button are the Previous Uncorrected and Next Uncorrected buttons. These buttons allow you to quickly navigate to shots in the sequence that you have not yet corrected. The locator jumps to the headframes of those shots.

- The final button beneath each window is the Remove Effect button. To start over, or clear all of the parameters of a correction, click on this button. It's the same as the Remove Effect button used to delete Effects created in Effects mode. All of these buttons can be customized to be anything you want, as discussed in "Keyboard" on page 42 of Chapter 2, but I've been working with these buttons in these positions for a lot of years and they seem pretty perfectly chosen.

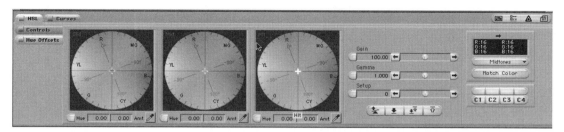

12.10   *Color Correction Tool*

COLOR CORRECTION TOOL

The middle window—under the Composer window and above the Timeline—is the Color Correction tool (see Figure 12.10).

At the top left of the tool are the two Group tabs: HSL and Curves. At the top right are the Color Correction tool buttons. We'll start out with an exploration of the HSL tab.

First, a few words about the behavior of the Group tabs buttons. Clicking in the little box to the *left* of the name of the tab "enables" the tab (which adds all of its parameters into the sum of the correction), while clicking on the tab where the *name* is calls the tab forward so you can view it. You can also switch between tabs using the Page Up and Page Down keys. To restore any tab—and all the parameters inside that tab—to their factory presets, Alt-click/Option-click on the Enable button.

HSL Controls Subtab

The HSL tab has two subtabs: Controls and Hue Offsets. To me, most of the controls in the Controls subtab are worthless for color correction.

Hue should mostly be used if there are some problems with a dubbed tape that was set up wrong and the adjustment should only be made using the color bars from that tape.

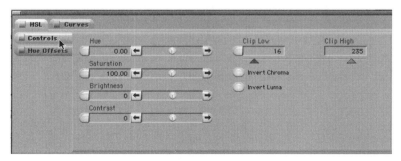

12.11   HSL Tab

Saturation is an important color correction parameter. Obviously, you'll need to use this parameter to increase or decrease the overall strength of the chroma values in your images. This will affect the vividness of the colors.

 As a general rule of thumb, you should apply Saturation last, since it affects all of the tonal ranges in the picture equally, and you will probably be tweaking individual tonal ranges that you will want to bring into balance before adding or subtracting chroma to the overall image.

Brightness is not a good tab for doing color correction. Good color correction is all about control. The more control you have, the better. Brightness is a deceptive parameter that changes all of your tonal ranges at once. The best test pattern to see the effects of tonal corrections is "BWRamp.pct" which is located in your Xpress Pro folder>Supporting Files>Test Patterns. Before you import them, choose the Options button in the Import window and set your Import Options as follows: all of the test patterns are designed to be imported as 601 aspect ratio and 601 levels. The file should also be imported as noninterlaced and ignore alpha. While you're at it, import color bars using the same settings. My favorite bars to use for NTSC are the SMPTE bars, which have many useful features compared to other bars. (For more on importing graphics files with proper levels, see Chapter 11 "Importing with Xpress Pro" on page 321.)

Call up the Y Waveform Monitor in the left monitor and watch it as you raise the Brightness. The entire waveform moves up and down as a unit. This means that the shadows, midtones, and highlights are all affected together. Good color correction tools allow you to control each of these tonal ranges individually. Don't worry, Xpress Pro has just what you need...just not here.

Contrast has the same problem as Brightness: not enough control for serious work. With the Y Waveform displayed in the left monitor, adjust Contrast up or down. You will notice that as you lower the Contrast, the entire waveform compresses towards the center and as you raise it, it spreads equally from the top and bottom. Once again, this indicates a lack of control. It's fine to increase or decrease contrast, but you want control over how much you raise or lower the shadows compared to raising and lowering the highlights. Contrast doesn't give you that ability, but it does exist using other controls that we'll discuss soon. The exception to the rule would be using Contrast more as an effect. For example if you quickly wanted to lower contrast to use the video as a backplate for a Title. If you just want a quick correction without any finesse, then this is your tool.

Clip Low and Clip High are generally best left at their default to keep things legal. Activating clipping is a quick way to bring shots into a legal range for broadcast, but it isn't foolproof and it doesn't provide you with as much control as you can get elsewhere.

The Invert Chroma and Invert Luma buttons allow you to quickly flip the chroma or luma values, respectively. Invert Luma swaps light values for dark values, giving a film-negative effect. Invert Chroma swaps every color for its opposite color on the Vectorscope, called the complementary color. Call up the Vectorscope in the left monitor and watch as you Invert Chroma. The shape of the trace of the Vectorscope flips 180° from where it was. This is easier to see with some images than others. Invert Chroma does the same thing as typing 180 in the Hue parameter. Check it out!

Behavior of the CC Controls

Before we move on, let me explain how the various buttons, sliders, arrows, and numbers behave.

The first box that sits on the left of any parameter is the Enable button. When it is purple (in the default interface color scheme at least), it is active. Clicking on this button toggles between active and inactive. When the button is active, it adds the value of the parameter to the values of all of the other active parameters. Toggling this button is a good way to see whether that parameter is helping or hurting a correction. When you disable a parameter, the numbers still stay right where you left them, but no longer affect the correction. If you want to reset a parameter to the default, Alt-click/Option-click on its Enable button.

You can highlight numbers in the numerical section of the parameter and retype the values. The numbers also display any parameter changes made by using other portions of the parameter controls, like the slider and arrows. Numbers can be entered from the QWERTY keyboard or the number pad. Also, if you click in the numerical area, you can use the Up and Down arrow keys to tweak numbers up and down.

The two arrow keys on either side of the slider allow small incremental changes by clicking on them. You'd probably be better off clicking once in the numerical value area and using the Up and Down arrow keys.

The slider is a fairly intuitive way of dragging the parameter to the values you want. Unmodified, the slider makes fairly gross adjustments. If you want to use the slider for more refined adjustments, hold down the Shift key while sliding.

Match Color Control

The final section of the HSL/Controls subtab is to the far right and is called the Match Color Control. This section allows the use of an Eyedropper to select values of pixels on any of the monitors (or even the Color Picker or anywhere on the GUI with the right settings!). Avid designed this so that you can pick a color using the left box and match it to a color that you've picked in the right box. The thing to realize is that the Match Color buttons work differently in each of the tabs and subtabs, so we will discuss each of these sections in every subtab to explain the differences.

The Match Color Control is a very simple interface. The top two boxes of the interface are two colored boxes with numbers indicating RGB values. Using Match Color in any of the subtabs begins with picking colors for the two boxes. This is done by clicking and dragging from the box with the RGB numbers to the portion of the image on the Current monitor that you want to match. As you drag over various colors in the monitors, you will notice the color of the box changing and the values of the RGB numbers changing.

 For more precise control of the exact spot of your selection, you can Ctrl-click/Cmd-click on the monitor before you select your color. This turns the cursor into a magnifying glass and allows you to magnify any portion of the screen up to 8x. After 8x, it reverts back to normal magnification. You can also do this using Ctrl+L/Cmd+L to magnify and Ctrl+K/Cmd+K to shrink. Note that the blocks that are visible on the screen are not individual pixels. Scrubbing inside of a block will still reveal the values of individual pixels within the block. Also note that the block is just an average color of the individual pixels within it.

Then click in the right box and drag to the color you want the left box to look like. Normally the match color is chosen from one of the other two monitors set to Previous, Next, or Reference. This is an excellent use of Reference. Find a shot where—for example—the skin tones are just right and select an area of skin tone from the reference. There is one more step, but we need to discuss the Match Color Options before we take that last step.

Using the Match Color Eyedroppers

An excellent use of the Match Color eyedroppers is to simply use them as analytical tools. Clicking in an area that should be white should make the individual RGB values almost match. Pure white at 100IRE would be indicated as R:235, G:235, B:235. There's definitely room for a little deviation, but if any one value is lower or higher than the others, it tells you that there is a color cast to the image. The easy casts to understand are if red, green, or blue are higher, then you have a red, green, or blue cast. To figure out and remember the secondary colors, you can use the vectorscope as a mnemonic device.

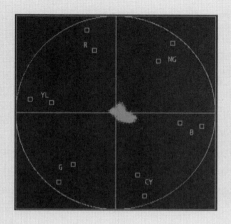

If two of the channels are higher than the other, look at the color that is in between those two colors on the vectorscope. For example, Red and Blue make Magenta, Green and Blue make Cyan, and Red and Green make Yellow. Clicking on an area of gray should also yield closely matching red, green, and blue values, and black should also have matching values for each color channel. This becomes a nearly foolproof method of checking for color casts in each of your luma ranges (shadows, midtones, and highlights).

The trick to this method is that as you drag around an area of the screen that seems to have the same color, the values of the channels shift quite a bit. You need to kind of average the ratios out in your head. You can't rely on the values of a single pixel. (See "Correction Mode Settings" on page 34 in Chapter 2 for how and why to turn on 3×3 averaging for the Eyedropper.)

Another thing that the Eyedropper can be used for is to look for clipping of highlights and crushing of shadows. As you drag around highlights or shadows, if you don't notice any of the slight changes in RGB values that you normally see, it tells you that there is no additional detail that can be pulled out of those areas. In other words, they are clipped or crushed. (Some small fluctuation in RGB values as you drag in the monitor can also come from video noise.)

The Match Color Options pulldown is between the color boxes and the Match Color button. In the default Controls subtab, it will say "H+S+L." Click and hold down the button to reveal the other choices in the pulldown. The options are H+S+L, Hue, Saturation, and Luminance. When you match a color from one shot to another, you must

understand how the two shots are different from one another. Do you really want an exact match? If so, choose H+S+L. On many matches, you only want to match the Hue, Saturation, or Luminance, so choose one of these other options. For example, on a skin tone that is too blue, you may only want to use Hue. For two skin tones that don't match because the lighting changed a little, try matching Luma. For Match Color to work properly, you must also select the proper pixels from each shot very carefully. For example, if there is a nice blue rim light on the subject in both shots, you must carefully choose the portion of the skin tone that isn't affected by the rim light. If the left box is "polluted" by blue and the right box is not, then the Match Color will assume that all of the shot is too blue and would warm up the entire shot too much. If the right box was "polluted" with blue, then it would assume you wanted the entire shot to be much bluer, and it would cool down the entire shot too much. Similarly, if you select an area of the skin that is a little more affected by the intensity of the keylight in one box than the other, the match color will attempt to "fix" the brightness of the image. To see how this works, try to match color on two identical shots. Selecting the wrong portions of the image will radically affect the outcome of the match. So if it's this hard to match two shots that are identical, imagine the problems of matching shots that are different.

Once you have chosen your input and output colors and your Match Type, the only thing left to do is hit the Match Color button and admire your handiwork.

Color Buckets

Below the Match Color Control, in the bottom right corner of the Color Correction tool, are the Color Buckets. These are a great help in color correcting on an Xpress Pro. Avid Symphony allows you to  make corrections to multiple shots that are related to each other in some way, so that an entire tape with a color cast can be corrected in one fell swoop. Xpress Pro lacks that option, but the Color Buckets can function in a similar fashion, allowing you to correct shots with a single click of a button.

Once you have completed a correction for a shot, you can save that correction temporarily in the Color Buckets. To save a correction in the Color Bucket, Alt-click/Option-click on one of the Color Buckets and the correction in the Current Monitor will be saved to that bucket.

To assign the corrections that are saved in the Color Buckets, simply park the Timeline locator on the shot you want to correct and click on the appropriate bucket.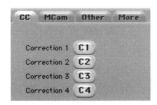

It is possible to assign these buckets to keyboard keys or the GUI. They are available in the CC tab of the Command Palette, indicated as Correction 1, 2, 3 and 4.

Warning The buckets are for temporary storage of corrections only. If your system crashes or you quit out of Xpress Pro, these buckets are cleared.

If you want to save the temporary corrections of the Color Buckets more permanently, they can be saved in a bin. Simply drag the little rainbow-colored box from the bucket to a bin. It is a wise idea to name the correction something descriptive. To put the corrections back in the buckets, simply drag them from the bin.

One of the great ways to judge how well a correction is working is to create several corrections of the same shot and assign them each to a Color Bucket. You can quickly compare the corrections by simply clicking on successive Color Buckets. This is a great way to get a client to buy a correction, especially if one of the corrections is the original shot without any correction. To create an "uncorrected" Color Bucket, simply disable the main HSL and Curves tabs—make sure the little box to the left of the words is not purple—and save that to a bucket.

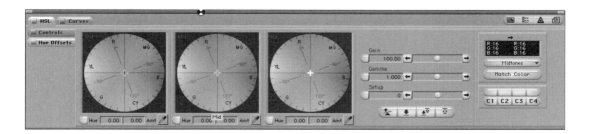

Hue Offsets Subtab

Hue Offsets is the other subtab of the HSL tab. For a lot of your corrections, this will be the most important tab. Let's skip past the cool, colored circles for now and take a look at the sliders first. I want to contrast their behavior with the behavior of the similar-looking, but very different sliders on the Controls subtab. These controls work with the same general operational behaviors as the ones on the Controls tab, so I won't bother to repeat how the Enable button, sliders, arrows, and numerical entry work. If you skipped that part, check out "Behavior of the CC Controls" on page 351.

The top control is the Gain Control. Gain is different from Brightness. While Brightness raised all of the tonal ranges—shadow, midtones, and highlights—the same amount,

Gain is much more selective. Gain will still have some effect on shadow and midtones, but mostly, it affects just the brightest portions of the picture. This kind of control is very useful when doing color correction. If there are pure white portions of your image, they should probably be no brighter than 100IRE on a Y Waveform (or on an external Waveform Monitor in Low Pass filter). Not all video needs to reach 100IRE, but in general, the goal of color correction is to spread the tonal range of the video as much as legally possible.

 While 100IRE is the generally acknowledged peak for a legal level, most broadcasters allow signals that are somewhat higher than that. However, 100IRE is a good target because specular highlights—light shining off glass, chrome, or water, for example—often will peak above 100IRE and the addition of Chroma when monitoring the YC waveform (Flat Pass filter, sometimes referred to as the Composite level (the composite of Luma and Chroma) will also increase the overall video level and needs to monitored carefully. Check with the broadcaster or your dub house on their video specifications.

Let's skip Gamma for now and discuss Setup. Setup controls the darkest portions of the picture. It will have very little effect on highlights and a little more affect on midtones. Setup is actually the first thing you should tweak. This is the base on which all your other corrections are made. Use this control to properly place the setup. Setup is also sometimes called black or pedestal. For NTSC waveform monitors in the United States in Xpress Pro, and for any external scopes fed by the component, composite, or S-Video feeds, the lowest legal limit for setup is 7.5IRE. In Japanese NTSC and in PAL, the legal limit is 0IRE.

Not all pictures should have their darkest tonal range at 7.5IRE—think of a polar bear in a blizzard—but if the picture has something that is really supposed to be black, it should be at 7.5IRE (U.S. NTSC). Don't worry yet that this may make the picture look too dark. We still have a lot of correcting to do.

The middle slider control is Gamma. The Gamma control adjusts the midtones of the image, while leaving the setup and highlights relatively untouched. Gamma is a really important control. Once you have used the Gain and Setup controls to spread the tonal range as much as you can while remaining true to the intent of the image, Gamma can deliver the correct overall perception of overall brightness. Imagine the video signal as a rubber-band. You have nailed the bottom (Setup) down where it needs to be, and you have stretched the top (Gain) up to its legal limit. Now you can use the Gamma control to grab the middle of the rubber-band and move it up or down to give it the look you want.

Shades of Black

Setup, pedestal, black level: how hard can black be to understand? All of you Aussies and Brits and English readers from countries with a sensible TV system (PAL users, in other words) can tune out for a minute. This is a talk for the unfortunate American readers. Here's the thing about setup: analog NTSC black should be at 7.5 IRE on a waveform monitor. You may have read that DV and other digital video formats do not have setup at 7.5IRE. This is correct. But the only place you have to concern yourself about 7.5IRE or 0IRE is on a waveform. If you are monitoring a DigiBeta deck with an SDI feed to a waveform, that scope will show setup at 0IRE. Monitor the same tape with a composite feed to the scope and it will show 7.5IRE. So how do you know which level you should be shooting for on your particular scopes? Well, since we're worried about color corrections that occur inside of the Xpress Pro, load up filler in your Sequence Monitor and look at it on your scopes. That level—whether you have an SDI external waveform or you're just using the internal scopes in the color correction tool—is where black should be. If you look at the internal Y Waveform, that level is at 0 percent on one side of the scope and RGB 16 on the other side.

Look at the YC waveform and the level is at 0 percent on one side and 7.5IRE on the other. This brings up another point: know what the scale of the waveform is when you are looking at it. If you look closely at the waveforms built into Xpress Pro, you may not see the tiny "%" sign and think that 0 means IRE.

   Let's get back to those cool-looking Hue Offset wheels. This is where you can work very intuitively and effectively to eliminate color casts in your images—or to *add* them if that's what you want.

There are three wheels, corresponding to each of the tonal ranges: shadows, midtones, and highlights. Each wheel operates exactly the same, so we don't have to discuss all three wheels separately. The operation of these wheels is incredibly intuitive. The only thing you have to do is drag the small cross in the center of the color wheel *away* from the color you're trying to eliminate. So if your videographer forgot to re–white balance when he went outdoors, and the picture has a blue cast, you drag the center cross away from blue, which means towards yellow. To eliminate a warm, red-

dish cast, drag away from red, towards cyan. Often African-American skin tones have an unappealing greenish cast on video, so you can pull them towards magenta to create a more natural, pleasing skin tone.

> Not all color casts affect all tonal ranges of the picture. Sometimes highlights will turn yellow, while midtones are reddish and shadows are slightly blue. Examine the various tonal ranges of the picture to specifically determine what kind of cast is affecting each tonal range. (Using the Eyedropper is a good way to do this.) Then address that tonal range with the proper correction with the wheel. Symphony has an additional wheel for "master" Hue Offset corrections, but by and large, you don't want to make a master correction anyway, so use all three of the wheels to eliminate the casts that are polluting their specific tonal range.

If you don't want to experiment with which direction and how far to move the crosses, the Eyedroppers under the Hue Offset wheels can do it for you. They operate by clicking on the Eyedropper under the tonal range for which you want to eliminate a color cast, and then clicking on a pixel in the Current Monitor that is in that tonal range. The pixel you choose for this operation is very important. It should be a pixel that is supposed to be neutral, but isn't. If you use the Eyedropper under the Shadow wheel, the pixel you choose should be dark, or better yet, black. Pixels for highlights should be close to white and the hardest pixels to find will be for the midtones, which will require finding a pixel that should be a midvalue gray.

When you do this, you will notice that the automatic corrections are actually displayed on the color wheels. The center crosses on each wheel will move to indicate how the automatic correction compensated in order to remove the color cast from the pixel.

Before we get to the buttons below the Gain, Gamma, and Setup sliders, let's address the differences between the Match Color box in the Controls subtab and the one here in the Hue Offsets subtab.

Match Color in the Hue Offset subtab

The input and output color boxes (with the RGB values in them) work exactly the same. The Match Color button executes your match in this tab, just as it did in the last. The difference is the button/pulldown menu between the Match Color button and the color boxes. In the Hue Offsets tab, your pulldown choices are Highlights, Midtones, and Shadows. The advantage here is that you can match a targeted tonal range. If you just want a color match to take place in a single range, for example, the highlights, this is the match for you. You can even do matches in all three tonal ranges in a single image.

It is possible to choose colors for output or input from the Color Picker. Simply Ctrl+double-click/Cmd+double-click on the color box and the Color Picker will appear. This is a way to perfectly match a specific RGB target. The colors in these color boxes can also be saved to bins for recall later. If you Alt-drag/Option-drag the color box to a bin, the specific RGB color will be saved to use again. The cool thing is that each RGB color has actually been assigned a descriptive name by a bunch of people who got paid to think up several million names for colors. Luckily, you did not have to do this. The color is saved in the bin with this descriptive name and the specific RGB values. You can add to or change this name entirely. If you have a client that likes something—like a logo, or a talent's skin tone—to be a specific color, save it once you've agreed that it is correct and you can refer to it any time in any project. To match to that color, simply drag the color swatch from the bin to the Output Color Box. How cool is that?

Automatic Color Correction

No time to figure out how to do color correction from scratch? Xpress Pro comes to the rescue with four handy buttons sitting directly below the Setup slider in the Hue Offset subtab.

They are (from left to right) the Auto balance, Auto Black, Auto Contrast, and Auto White buttons. There are also three Eyedroppers—one under each color wheel—that automatically remove color casts from each of their respective tonal ranges. Avid recommends starting your corrections by using these tools, making further adjustments from that starting point. Especially if you are up against a deadline or do not feel inclined to learn how to properly color-correct "by hand," this is probably sound advice.

The nice thing about Xpress Pro's Auto Correction is that it actually moves the faders and Hue Offset wheels and Curves just like you would if you did the corrections by hand, so it's fairly easy to tweak them. Looking at what the Auto Corrections do to the parameters is actually an excellent tool for you to learn more about color-correcting, especially when they perform a correction that significantly improves an image.

Like the Match Color tool, the Auto Correction buttons work slightly differently in each subtab, even though they have the same names and the buttons look the same.

Auto Balance in the Hue Offsets subtab adjusts the three Hue Offset wheels, eliminating color casts.

Auto Black in the Hue Offsets subtab adjusts the Setup slider, bringing the shadows down to the lowest legal black level.

Auto Contrast in the Hue Offsets subtab adjusts the Gain and Setup sliders, spreading the tonal range of the image. The highlights are brought to their peak legal level and the shadows are brought to their lowest legal level.

Auto White in the Hue Offsets subtab adjusts the Gain slider, bringing the highlights up to their maximum legal level.

 You should only use Auto Contrast if an image is supposed to have a complete tonal range, including both very bright highlights and very dark shadows. If an image only has bright highlights, but not dark shadows, use the Auto White button. If it contains dark shadows, but is not supposed to have bright highlights, use the Auto Black button. You need to think carefully about your image. Is there anything that is actually fully white? Should any part of the image actually go all the way to black? As you gain experience in color correction, it will become second nature to determine the needs of your images.

In the Hue Offset subtab, using the Auto Correction buttons doesn't even require choosing specific pixels for analysis. You just park on the frame you want to correct in the

Current Monitor and hit the buttons. The only ones you need to use to do the fastest corrections are the Auto Balance and Auto Contrast buttons. Between these two buttons, you eliminate color casts and spread the tonal range of the image. The order in which you use these buttons does matter. In the Hue Offsets subtab you should use Auto Contrast before Auto Balance. (When you use these same controls in the Curves tab, you'll want to do them in the reverse order.)

Warning   These automatic controls only analyze the current frame of the image. If there are any other pixels in other frames in the shot that go darker or brighter, the shot could be "illegal." Avid claims that using these Auto buttons means that images are automatically set within legal limits, but you'll need to be careful anyway. Use these Auto tools as a starting point, but for the best results, you're going to need to use your eyes and finish by hand.

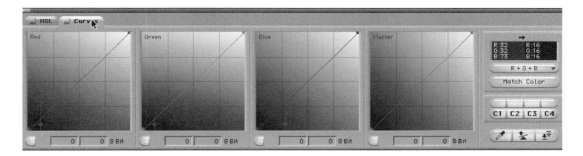

Curves Tab

The final area of the Color Correction tool is the Curves tab. This tab has only two main areas: the four Curves controls and the Match Color area.

Where each of the Hue Offset wheels controlled a specific tonal range, each of the first three Curves controls a specific color channel. The fourth Curve is the Master Curve and it controls overall tonal range—acting somewhat like a graphic depiction of the Gain, Gamma, and Setup controls.

While correcting color problems using the RGB Curves is a slightly less intuitive way for some to correct color casts, it is very powerful because it offers specific control of very precise tonal areas in each color channel. Unlike Xpress DV, which allows you to set only four points on the curve to specify tonal ranges, Xpress Pro—like Symphony—can place as many as 16 points to isolate ranges along each of the curves. But we're getting a little ahead of ourselves. Let's explain how Curves works and why you'd want to do a correction here.

Master Curve

Let's start with the Master Curve, because this will simplify explaining the value and operation of all the curves. To start off with, if you've never used this tool, you may wonder why a tool with a single diagonal line is called the Curves tool. When we're done with a correction, it should make sense.

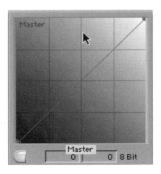

What the diagonal line represents is the correlation between the level of the input pixels—what they look like *now*—and the level of the output pixels—what you *want* them to look like. The input levels are on the horizontal, or X-axis, while the output values are on the vertical, or Y-axis. Since you haven't done any correction to the curve yet, every input value corresponds exactly to every output value, creating a perfect diagonal line. In other words, 0 = 0, 50 = 50, 100 = 100.

If you wanted to bring your black level up a little, you would redraw the curve so that 0 = 10. If you wanted to pull your midtones down a little, you would redraw the curve so that 126 = 110. And if you wanted to bring the whites down, you'd redraw the curve so that 255 = 235. You can perform these "redraws" numerically or by dragging points on the diagonal line itself.

To use the numeric functions kind of kills the intuitiveness of the Curves display but allows for precise numeric control. Put the BWRamp test pattern in your Current Monitor. Click on a point on the diagonal line—which is called a curve

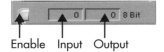

Enable Input Output

Vocabulary Is Key

One of the most important skills for a colorist—or for any creative professional who must collaborate with other creatives—is the ability to communicate effectively. While you're working on tonal range corrections, you may want to communicate specific tonal ranges. In addition to the terms used by the Color Correction tool—shadows, midtones, and highlights—there are other names for specific tonal areas. The values approximately halfway between black and the midtones are called *quarter tones* and the values approximately halfway between the midtones and white are called the *three-quarter tones*. Another term frequently used in describing tonal ranges include *crushed* to describe shadow or black values that are lowered to the point that detail in the shadows is lost. Also, highlights or bright values that are pushed up beyond their ability to hold detail are often described as *clipped* or *blown-out*. An image with a high level of contrast is often described as looking *crunchy*.

whether it is curved or straight—and then type in one of the two numeric panes directly below the curve. The first pane on the left is the input number and the one on the right is the output number. So, if you click on the bottom left corner of the Master curve, the input and output numbers are both 0. To make black brighter, type 0 in the input and 10 in the output. This essentially remaps all of the pixels, but mostly affects the darker tones. It remaps the value of any input pixel that was 0 brightness up to 10. It also remaps the other low value pixels to higher values. To make black darker, type 10 in the input and 0 in the output. This remaps all the input pixels with a value of 10 and below down to 0. Pixels with values above 10 will also be brought down somewhat.

Now let's try a gamma, or midtone, correction using the mouse. Click on the Master Curve right in the middle. You can see that the numeric panes update to give you numeric data on your position on the curve. Drag the center point on the curve up or down. Watch the numeric values in the panes below the curve update. Watch the effect the move has on the BW Ramp image in the Current Monitor. The middle grays get brighter as you move up or back and darker as you move down or forward. Watch the Y Waveform Monitor update after you have let go of the point. If you dragged the center point down, notice the dip in the midtones on the waveform (see Figures 12.12–12.14).

The ability to set multiple points on the curve allows you to very effectively isolate specific tonal ranges. To see this, drag a point in the middle of the curve up and down while watching the current monitor. The deep blacks and brightest highlights are never really affected by even major moves of the midpoint, but the quarter tones and three-quarter tones definitely move. To isolate the movement of the midtones, place a point on the curve about a quarter of the way up from the bottom and another about a quarter of the way down from the top. As you move your midtone, watch how the two new points are "protecting" your quarter tones and three-quarter tones. Two points even closer together will even more completely isolate a tonal range. You need to be very careful about making exaggerated moves between points that are close on the curve. This will create an unnatural look. But maybe that's what you're going for.

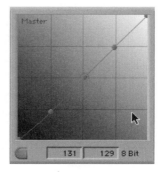

12.15   The Master Curve has points set in quarter tones, midtones, and three-quarter tones.

RGB Curves

The RGB color curves are a little less intuitive but their power lies in the specific control they can achieve over the tonal ranges in each of the RGB channels. Avid added the cool-

12.12 This example represents the uncorrected BW Ramp and its representation in the waveforms. Note the straight Master Curve.

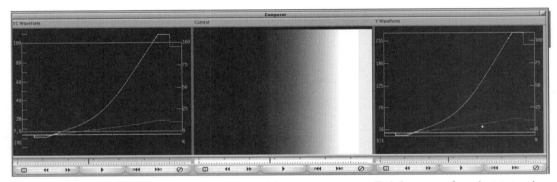

12.13 This example has the gamma, or center, of the Master Curve pulled down significantly. Notice that now, instead of the BW Ramp being gray in the center, it is dark all the way to the center and the waveforms show the midtones are much lower.

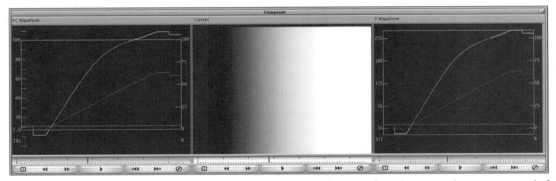

12.14 This sample has the gamma of the Master Curve pulled up significantly. Notice that now, instead of the BW Ramp being gray in the center, the bright gray portion of the image is significantly larger than in Figure 12.12 and the waveforms show the midtones are much higher. Note that in all three figures, the blacks and whites at the extreme ends of the image are still essentially unchanged.

looking color scheme to the Curves to help make them a little more intuitive. You can see by looking at the three-color curve boxes (see Figure 12.16) that lowering the curve in the Red channel will pull a specific tonal range towards cyan. Lowering the curve or moving it forward in the Green channel will pull a specific tonal range towards magenta. Lowering the curve or moving it forward in the Blue channel will pull a specific tonal range towards yellow. Obviously, raising the curve or moving it backwards in any given channel increases the amount of that channel in a specific tonal range.

If you'd like to get a little better understanding of how to adjust these curves, you can get a pretty good lesson by watching what happens when you use the Automatic Color Correction buttons below the Color Buckets in the Curves tab.

Auto Correction in the Curves Tab

The Eyedropper allows you to click on an achromatic (colorless) pixel in the Current Monitor and remove a color cast. To use this button, click on the button, then click again on any pixel in the Current Monitor that appears to have an unwanted color cast. Remember that you can zoom in on the Current Monitor (Ctrl-click/Cmd-click) to more accurately choose the best pixel.

Warning Be careful that the pixel you click on is really white, black, or pure gray, otherwise this will "uncorrect" your image instead of correcting it. You also have to be careful about clicking on multiple points of an image. Every time you use this button, it adds points to the color curves. Sometimes, if you do this too many times in a single image, it can look very unnatural.

Auto Balance adjusts the Red, Green, and Blue Curves to eliminate color casts and Auto Contrast adjusts the Master Curve to spread the tonal range of the image. The highlights are brought to their peak legal level and the shadows are brought to their lowest legal level. Operation of these two buttons is very simple. Just park on a frame in the Current Monitor and click the buttons. They automatically analyze the picture without eye-

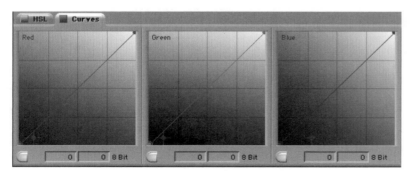

12.16   Three-Color Curve Boxes

Theory of Color Bars

Lowering a specific tonal range in a given channel affects not only the color, but the luminance as well. For this reason, you do not always want to go for the most intuitive fix in Curves. If you want an image to be more yellow, the easiest thing is to pull down the Blue channel, but this also lowers the luminance values of any pixels that have blue in them. The other way to do this correction is to equally raise the same tonal range of each of the other two color channels. To see the difference, attempt some corrections with color bars.

There is some very interesting color theory behind the organization of the individual bars in the color bars test signal. (This is thoroughly covered in our book *Color Correction for Digital Video*.) The basic premise is most easily described by discussing the colors in terms of percentages.

White	Yellow	Cyan	Green	Magenta	Red	Blue	Black
R 100	R 100	R 0	R 0	R 100	R 100	R 0	R 0
G 100	G 100	G 100	G 100	G 0	G 0	G 0	G 0
B 100	B 0	B 100	B 0	B 100	B 0	B 100	B 0

Notice the pattern. In the red channel, the bars with red are paired: two with red, two without, two with, two without. In the green channel, the first four bars have green and the next four don't. In the blue channel, every other bar has blue, while the alternating bars have none.

For an interesting experiment, watch the relative brightness levels of these bars change as you move the midpoint of each color channel up and down. As you raise the Red curve up and down, it really only affects white, yellow, magenta, and red. These are the bars created from some combination of the color channels that includes red. Now move the Green curve. As you raise and lower it, it only affects the first four bars, which are the ones that include green. Adjusting the Blue curve will affect all of the alternating bars, starting with white.

Now compare lowering the Blue curve to raising both the Red and Green curves equally.

droppering. As with the Auto Balance and Auto Contrast buttons in the Hue-Offset subtab, it *does* matter the order in which you click the buttons. In the Curves tab, use Auto Balance before Auto Contrast.

Match Color in the Curves Tab

The Match Color area in Curves works essentially the same as the Match Color areas in the other subtabs. The difference is the choices in Match Type button. The default Match Type is R+G+B. This matches the values of all three color channels. Master matches the overall Master level (tonal range). And the final choice is called Natural-Match. NaturalMatch actually works two different ways: in conjunction with R+G+B or

with Master. Whenever NaturalMatch is "checked," so is one of the other two selections.

NaturalMatch is the best choice when the match is complicated by different lighting conditions in the two shots that you're trying to match. NaturalMatch compensates for the luminance and saturation differences between these difficult to match shots. Natural-Match uses the hue of the output to replace the input hue, leaving the luminance values alone and performing calculations based on luma and hue to derive a natural saturation level.

NaturalMatch gives you a quick way to match even with images with very different lighting.

Color Correction Tool Buttons

The small group of buttons at the top right of the Color Correction tool are called—creatively enough—the Color Correction tool buttons. From left to right the four buttons are Create FX Template, Correction Mode Settings, Safe Colors Setting, and Add Comments.

The Create FX Template button allows you to click and drag a color correction into a bin or onto another segment. This is useful for saving corrections and applying them to multiple segments. Color FX templates can also be applied to just certain parameters of another segment. To do this, instead of dragging the template onto a segment or into the Current Monitor, drag the template onto a specific parameter or tab. This same procedure also works for regular visual effects in Effects mode.

 You can also save color correction templates with the Save Correction button which is located at Tools>Command Palette>CC Tab. Map this button to your keyboard or your UI. Clicking on this will automatically save the current correction to a bin.

Correction Mode Setting allows access to Color Correction Settings that can also be accessed from the Settings list in the Project window. These Settings are discussed in detail in "Correction Mode Settings" on page 34 in Chapter 2.

Safe Colors Setting allows access to Color Correction Settings that warn you of shots in your sequence that are illegal or out of standard video specifications. These Safe Color specifications are customizable according to the demands of any broadcast outlets or duplicators with whom you work. Details of how to set these customizable settings are in "Safe Colors" on page 49 in Chapter 2

When the Safe Colors Setting is changed from the default (Ignore) to Warn, it alters displays in several areas to warn you of levels outside of the specs that you set. The primary area where you will notice these warnings is in the top left corner of the Current monitor. The Warning display is made up of five columns of three dashes. The first, yellow column indicates the composite value of luma and chroma. The second, white column indicates just the luma value. The next three (red, green, and blue) columns indicate the color gamut for each color channel. A safe level is indicated by the colored dash located in the center of the column. If the colored dash is at the top, the level is above the legal limit and if the colored dash is at the bottom, it is below the legal limit. If there are no dashes at all, then that specific frame of the segment on which you're parked is completely legal.

Safe Color warnings are also indicated in the Y Waveform and the YC Waveform as changes in the color of the trace. For example, the Y Waveform's default green trace turns white where the signal exceeds proper specification.

The Add Comments button allows you to make comments on a certain correction for any number of reasons. Primarily this would be useful if your edit was going to be finalized or onlined in a Symphony. While you are in Color Correction mode, you can view these notes. Any segment with a comment is indicated by the Add Comments button being highlighted in yellow.

NOW...FORGET THE BUTTONS

We've covered all of the tools to make your corrections, the questions now are, "Why?" and "Which ones to use when?" Answering those questions was the main gist of our *Color Correction for Digital Video* book. That book hardly covered any of the specific operational items that we just covered in this chapter, but was about how to analyze your images for color problems and which tools to use to correct them.

We can't possibly cover all that in the same kind of depth here, so here's a quick overview of general concepts:

- Use the waveforms and histograms to analyze your image. Are the highlights bright enough? Are the shadows dark enough? Your objective in most instances is to spread your tonal range over the entire legal spectrum.

- Using your Vectorscope and Eyedropper tool, look for unwanted color casts. The Eyedropper is very useful in finding these casts. Is anything in the picture supposed to be completely white or completely black? Use your Hue Offset wheels or automatic tools to eliminate these casts. But be careful. Some casts are a good thing. This is one of the shortcomings of the automatic tools. They often eliminate desirable color casts like the buttery yellow of a bowl of popcorn or the warm, romantic glow of a sunset.

 You can use the same Ctrl/Cmd modifier that allowed you to magnify the screen to more accurately choose the right pixel on the screen to zoom into in the Vectorscope, waveform, or any of the monitoring tools. So if you want to get a closer look at any point on any of the tools, just zoom in. Also, if you have the Zoom In and Zoom Out tools mapped to your keyboard, you can use those, too. Here's a tip within a tip: I mapped my Zoom In and Out buttons (which have a little plus (+) and minus (-) sign in a magnifying glass) to my + and − buttons as a mnemonic device to remember where they are.

- General tonal corrections should be made with the Gain, Gamma, and Setup controls, not the Brightness and Contrast controls. Most experienced colorists start by setting the black level, then the highlights, and finally gamma. After the tonal ranges are set, move to color-balancing the image in the same order. Once the first pass has been made, another set of tweaks may need to be performed because the various levels and controls interact with each other.

- When adjusting parameters, think of focusing a camera. You never stop focusing the first time you get something into focus. You usually overshoot the focus a bit, just to make sure you can't get it even further in focus, then settle back to the correct level. A similar style is needed with the Color Correction controls. When setting the levels for shadows and highlights, watch the waveform. Raise or lower the levels until the shape of the trace begins to flatten out. That "flattening" is a sign of "clipping" or "crushing." Both of those mean you're losing detail.

- Severely under- or overexposed images are often salvageable using the precision tonal control of the Master Curves. Isolate and correct specific narrow tonal ranges with points on the curve.

- Look to the shadows—not the dark tonal values, but the shadows cast by lights—as a strong visual clue as to the correct contrast and general luminance of a shot. Outdoors, if the shadows are long, that means dawn or dusk. The contrast shouldn't be too strong and the levels should possibly be a bit more subdued. At noon, shadows will be short. This indicates high contrast and brighter values. Take clues from the practicals on the set. Should the video be bright or not?

- Use color correction to help tell your story and influence the emotions of your audience. Visual clues created with color can put the audience in the middle of the story—in the right place to accept the story—before a word is spoken or an edit has been made. Color and music work very similarly to provide subliminal clues to the audience about the current emotional beat of the storyline and the emotional state of the characters in the story.

- Learn to pick your battles. Usually projects have deadlines and the amount of time you can spend on a correction is limited. So choose where your color correction efforts are best spent. Give the automatic tools a chance to quickly whip shots into shape. It they don't work, spend more time getting them to form a cohesive whole with the rest of the shots in the show.

- Watch lots of TV, especially commercials, to see how color is used to tell the story. I mention commercials because they generally have the longest amount of time per shot spent on color correcting. Look at skin tones especially, because everyone knows what a skin tone should look like. Why or how did they deviate from a normal skin tone? What other colors, like sky and grass and water, can you tell were altered? What was the purpose of going for that look? Try to copy the looks of some of these spots and shows using your own footage as practice.

ADDITIONAL COLOR CORRECTION WISDOM

Color corrections in the Color Correction mode cannot be keyframed. If you want to be do a keyframed color effect, use Color Effect in the Effect Palette, which is accessible from Tools>Effect Palette>Image>Color Effect.

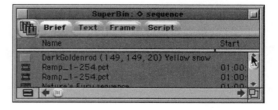

You can Alt-drag/Option-drag colors from the Color Matching boxes to a bin and save them as custom colors. You can then click that custom color and drag it from the bin into the Match Color control at any time, or, if you have the Eyedropper Picks from Anywhere in Application option selected (in the Corrections Settings in the Settings list of the Project folder), you can select a custom color by clicking on its swatch in the bin using the Eyedropper. This is a handy feature, because if your client buys off on a skin tone or the color of a logo, you can save that color in a bin. You can then load that color back into the Match Color control whenever you need to make a match based on that color.

Applying the Same Correction to Multiple Segments

While Symphony has numerous ways to apply the same correction to multiple segments based on establishing certain relationships between the segments, the easiest way to apply the same setting to multiple segments in Xpress Pro is actually done using the bin and the Timeline in either Effects mode or Source/Record mode. This is the same method used to apply the same visual effect to multiple segments.

1. Create a color correction.

2. Save it to a bin by dragging it into a bin from a color bucket or from the Create Effects Template button at the top right of the Color Correction tool.

3. In Source/Record mode go into Segment mode by clicking on either the red or yellow segment arrow at the bottom of the Timeline (or using your keyboard if you have mapped it to the keyboard).

4. Shift-click on all of the segments for which you wish to apply the effect. You can also choose segments by lassoing them from left to right in segment mode. For a clip to be selected by lassoing, the Lasso must encompass the entire clip. Partially lassoed segments will not be selected.

5. In the bin, double-click on the color correction template you wish to apply.

Saved templates are also available in the Effects Palette by clicking on the name of your sequence, which should be at the bottom left. Then the saved color corrections will appear in the right column of the Effects Palette or the Effects tab of the Project window (see Figure 12.17).

12.17 *Saved Color Corrections (on right)*

COLOR CORRECTION TUTORIAL

One of the tools that engineers use to set up multiple camera shoots is the chip chart.

The purpose of this chart is to ensure that all of the cameras have the same levels of black and white, that the responses across the midtones are the same, and that there are no color casts through any of the tonal ranges.

This can be done by wiping between cameras and adjusting them until the eight gray chips, plus the black-and-white chips, are even with each other on a waveform monitor. Also, since there should be no saturation level in an image made up entirely of shades of black and white, the Vectorscope image of all the cameras should be perfectly in the middle.

The image in Figure 12.18 is on the DVD (called Accu-Chart Grey Scale) and you can import it (601 color and aspect) and watch the waveform and vectorscope as you change the color cast or tonal values of certain tonal ranges. There is also an image on the DVD called "Bad grayscale" which we will use for the tutorial. The goal will be to match the badly white-balanced, poorly exposed image with the good image (see Figure 12.19).

You can cheat and use the Auto Correction tools, but they won't quite get you all the way

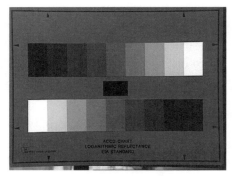

12.18 This is an EIA, logarithmic grayscale chart from Accu-Chart. Used by permission of Vertex Video Systems and Nalpak Sales.

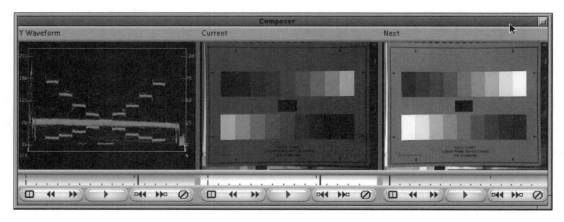

12.19 The bad image should be in the Current Monitor and the good image should be in the Next Monitor. If you don't have an external scope, you can place your scopes in the other monitor.

there. If you use the Auto Correction tools in the Hue Offset tab, you can see that all of the ranges need to lean more toward blue/cyan. That should be obvious by seeing how reddish-yellow the image is. Undo the Auto Correction and let's try to do this from scratch, just like Mom used to do.

The first correction that any colorist usually makes first is to spread the tonal range, so let's make sure that black is 7.5IRE and white is 100IRE and gray is pretty close to the middle. I'd do this in the Hue Offset tab, using the Gain, Gamma, and Setup controls while watching the Y Waveform.

The black levels look pretty good. I did play with them a little to see if I could go up or down with them a bit. The blackest part of the picture is the little chip in the center of the chart. That shows up as a thin green line, horizontally centered, right near the 16-bit/ 0% line on the Y waveform. If you bring it down much more, it starts to turn white, which is your indication that the signal is illegal. On scopes that don't change color, you look for it to cross the "black line" (0 or 7.5, depending) and that the thickness of the line doesn't start to flatten out.

 If the shape of the waveform trace (the green fuzzy lines) flattens out at either the top or the bottom as you make a correction, you are clipping the levels and losing detail. Make sure the blobby shapes in the waveform don't start to squish into different shapes; otherwise you are clipping or crushing the signal.

Once I determined that the shadows were black enough, I brought the Gain up to about 145. You may notice that some of the signal is illegal, but this is actually not part of the chart. You need to be conscious of all the portions of the picture, but for this exercise, we're just worried about getting the chart to match. You may also notice that the lighting on the chart isn't quite even. The white chip at the

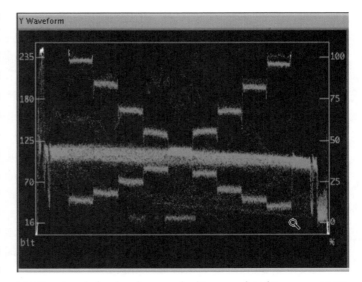

12.20   Levels for the chart are looking good. Whites are at 100 percent white, blacks are at 0 percent black, and gamma is about where it should be.

bottom left is slightly brighter than the white chip at the top left. Get the brightest chip to the peak, legal level.

Warning

> If you use the Safe Color warnings in Xpress Pro, and you have black lines on the sides of your image, these lines are illegal blacks, and your system will warn you that something is illegal, but if you try to correct the entire image so that these warnings go away, your black levels will be incredibly elevated. The Safe Color Warning software takes every single pixel of the image into account.

Gamma is tough to set. Because this is a logarithmic chart, the correct gray level isn't simply 50IRE. It's more like 45IRE or even 40IRE. The signal difference between chips five and nine should be about half of that between steps one and five. There's not a lot to worry about for a specific level of gamma, because gamma is generally set "to taste" anyway. If you are trying to match cameras, once the white and black is set, pick the camera with your favorite gamma level and match the other camera to it. Our good image is a little brighter in the gamma than the bad one, even after the blacks and whites have been set. Try to get the gray of the background of the chart to be the same level. One good way to do this is by color-picking the gray level of the backgrounds and looking at the numbers. On the good chart I get R111, G105, B88, which indicates that even the good chart is slightly warm. I happened to shoot these charts while I was setting up for an interview, so being a touch warm is a good thing. The bad chart shows R117, G85, B50. The reds are about the same level, but the bad image is going to have a lot of blue pulled out of it eventually, so let's look to the green channel, noting that the gamma of the bad image is about 20 percent lower than the good image. You can also see this with the Waveform Monitor. I pulled the gamma up on the bad image to about 1.153. To compare the images, I clicked back and forth between the bad and the good in the Timeline while I watched the thick line that goes all the way across the middle of the waveform until they were both at the same level.

With the levels matching, we can work on the color differences. The first thing we have to do is call up a signal analysis tool that makes sense for the job. We need the Vectorscope, which measures the amount of color and its orientation, or hue, on what is essentially a color wheel.

What controls do we have for color? Saturation is one, Hue is another, the Hue Offset wheels are a third, and the Curves are another. Since this image is supposed to be all gray anyway, you could cheat and pull about 50 percent of the saturation out and you'd be left with a pretty good match, but as soon as you saw any color on that image, your cheat wouldn't work any more.

Looking at the Vectorscope, try to use Hue to solve the color problem. The big blob of color that starts out pointing towards the yellow target on the vectorscope will just rotate from one vector to another. What you want it to do is go into the center, where gray, black, and white are supposed to be. Hue is not the way to go.

Let's try the Hue Offset wheels. This is the way a colorist would approach the task. Start with the Shadow wheel first. Pull the center cross point in exactly the opposite direction that the blob is. That would be almost straight toward blue. Try to get the blob right in the middle. You won't be able to do it with just the Shadow wheel, because parts of the yellowish blob will need to be controlled by the other two wheels. If you want to, you can cheat again and click on the Auto Balance button. Look at the numbers in the text panes under each wheel. That's pretty much the right target to hit, although for me, it makes the image slightly blue. You can do better than the Auto Balance. Just remember that the scopes aren't the only thing. What you really need to use is your eyes. Remember that each wheel alters only one specific tonal range, so as you move the shadows towards blue, just look at the black and dark gray portions of the picture and see if they are getting too blue. Glance over at the Vectorscope occasionally to confirm your suspicions. Maybe occasionally check the color of black using the Match Color boxes to look at the numbers. R, G, and B should be pretty much equal on black, gray, and white.

You'll also notice that as you move the colors around, you'll need to adjust the initial levels a bit, altering the black levels, gammas, and highlights. It's like a little dance.

Okay, once you've got it pretty well dialed in, reset the Hue Offset corrections and give it a try using the Curves. This is much less intuitive with this particular image. Remember that the image is very yellowish, with a lean toward red as well and that all of the tonal ranges are affected, though the shadows are closer than the midtones and highlights. Using that information, look at the Curves. You need to move away from red and yellow. To pull away from red, you can obviously just lower the entire curve toward the cyan area. And the bottom of the Blue curve is yellow, so you can move that curve up

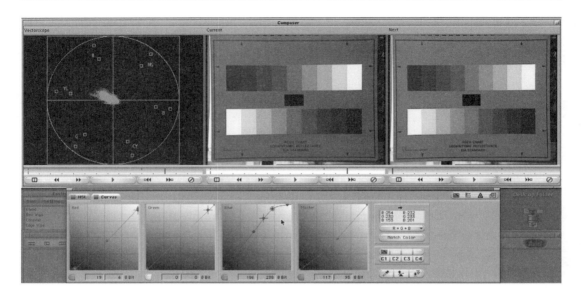

away from the yellow area. Making these corrections makes big jumps in the luminance levels though and you need to compensate using the Master Curve.

Keep at it for a while. Reset the curves every once in a while to start over. (Alt-click/ Option-click on the Enable buttons for each curve.)

Try using the Auto Correction features in this tab and see what effect it has on the curves.

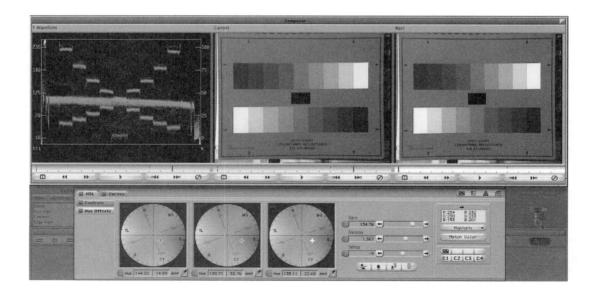

You can use the understanding of the effect each of these tools has and how we analyzed the effect they had on the image to correct many of the real-world examples you will encounter as you explore the powerful color correction tools in Xpress Pro.

MORE ON THE DVD

Check out the color correction tutorial on the DVD for more discussions of common fixes that you will face, along with some creative uses for color correction.

Chapter 13

Output

Xpress Pro allows you to output your sequences and footage in a number of ways. One of the most common is the digital cut, where the media is played back from the system and output to a recording medium such as videotape. Some other NLEs call this "printing to tape." Digital cuts can also be made to any source that can capture an audio or video signal in real time. This could include specially enabled CD recorders, DVD recorders, on-air servers, and DAT recorders (for audio only).

PREPARING FOR A DIGITAL CUT

Before you make a digital cut of your sequence, take a little extra time to prepare the sequence for output. This preparation could mean the difference between a solid output of the sequence and an unqualified disaster. Here is a list of things you should do:

1. Put Bars and Tone Media at the head of your sequence.

2. Add a Slate to identify the sequence.

3. Render effects.

4. Convert Audio sample rates.

5. Calibrate signals between Xpress Pro and your deck.

6. Configure your input deck in the deck configurations setting.

7. Output using the Digital Cut tool.

Adding Bars and Tone

While adding bars and tone may seem a bit extravagant for a digital cut of a viewing copy, it ensures that the playback fidelity of your sequence is accurate. Even if you decide not to include bars and tone in your digital cut to videotape, it's a good idea to put them on your sequence for calibrating Xpress Pro with your deck. Doing this will assure you of a good quality output, and it keeps you from looking like a hack.

Format

The formatting of a tape can vary by program, including the length and duration of bars and tone. That said, here is a common way of formatting videotape program material:

1. One minute (60 seconds) of bars & tone
2. Ten seconds of black (filler)
3. Ten seconds of slate (created using the Title tool)
4. Ten seconds of black (again, using filler)
5. Begin program

So if you were to begin the sequence at timecode 01:00:00:00 (a common standard), here's how your bars and tone would begin in the sequence:

Table 13.1   Format for Bars & Tone with Sequence (Common)

Start timecode	End timecode	Source
00:58:30:00	00:59:30:00	bars and tone
00:59:30:00	00:59:40:00	black (filler)
00:59:40:00	00:59:50:00	slate (from Title tool)
00:59:50:00	01:00:00:00	black (filler) or countdown
01:00:00:00	end of show	your sequence

13.1   Bars and Tone in Timeline

Changing the Timecode Start of Your Sequence

Because the default timecode for a sequence in the Avid is 1:00:00:00, the first order of business is to change the timecode start of your program. This can be done before or after adding the bars, tone, filler, and slate. To change the timecode start number on your sequence:

1. Click on the Sequence Monitor.

2. Press Ctrl/Cmd+I.
    On Windows, you can also right-click on the monitor for a pulldown menu called Get Info.

3. The sequence information appears (see Figure 13.2).

4. The beginning timecode and the name of the sequence appear. If the timecode is dropframe (with a semicolon [;] between the numbers, enter **58;30;00**. If it is non-dropframe (with a colon [:] between the numbers, enter **58:30:00**.

5. The system knows that these entries will mean a zero timecode. Thus they will appear as 00:58:30:00 or 00;58;30;00.

    Now you're ready to add bars and tone. But first, we have to create them.

13.2   Sequence Information Menu

Adding Tone

To add tone:

1. Select your Audio tool (Ctrl/Cmd+1).

2. Click on the Peak Hold (PH) button.

3. Select Create Tone Media.

4. The Tone Media menu appears.

13.3   Tone Media Information Menu

Setting Tone Media Levels

The Tone Media Levels are preset at −14dB. Some digital systems are set for −20dB. When in doubt, go with the default. On most systems, −14dB digital equals 0VU analog.

Tone Media Frequency

The Tone Media Frequency is preset at 1000Hz. This is the standard for most recorded video media. However, some audio post houses prefer using a variety of tones at different frequencies. If your digital cut is going to an audio house for sweetening or for mixing, it's a good idea to check with them first before adding tone to your digital cut. You can also add a series of tones to properly identify individual audio tracks.

Be sure to check out the Bars & Tone reference sequences on the enclosed DVD.

Tone Media Length in Seconds

This controls the amount of tone media created. Sixty seconds is the default and the standard.

Number of Tracks

The number of tone tracks to create should be determined.

- If the output uses discrete tracks going to separate channels, tone media should be created for each track. This includes stereo pairs.

- If the output uses a mono output, tone should only be put on one channel.
  This is done to avoid adding volume to the tone. Two tone tracks mixed together would be additive, creating a louder tone signal than desired. If the tone is placed on a single channel only, it will be mixed into a mono signal that registers correctly on the audio input of the record machine.

After these items are selected in the Create Tone Media menu, you will need to select a bin for the tone clip and a drive where the tone will be rendered.

Adding Bars

SMPTE Bars, the most commonly used test pattern, is imported to Xpress Pro as a PICT file. You can find the SMPTE Bars in the Avid>Avid Xpress Pro>Supporting Files>Test Patterns folder (see Figure 13.4). There are several other test patterns available in this folder.

Before importing the bars, you should change your import settings so that the right amount of media will be imported. To do this:

1. Go to the Project window and select the Settings tab.

2. Select Import settings.

3. Under the Single Frame Import heading, change the number of seconds to 60.
   This will add 60 seconds of bars media when the SMPTE bars are imported.

   To import SMPTE bars:

1. Select a target bin for your bars clip.

2. Go to the File menu and select Import.

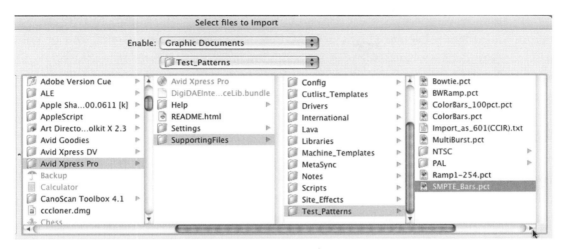

13.4   Locating SMPTE Bars in Test Patterns Folder

3. Make sure the file type is Graphic.

4. Navigate to the Test Patterns folder and select SMPTE Bars.

5. Import this file. The new bars clip is added to the bin.

Now you can edit your bars and tone into your sequence. Be sure to select all tracks and Splice.

Adding a Slate

Adding a slate will help you identify the sequence, the creation date, the total running time, and other information (see Figure 13.5). The slate can be created in the title tool and doesn't have to be too fancy. In fact, some of the most incredible commercials and video trailers for motion pictures use plain old black background slates with white Helvetica type. But you can decide for yourself. Be sure to allow 10 seconds of black after the slate.

13.5   A Typical Slate

In some cases, you may want to add a countdown from 10 seconds to two seconds before the program begins. This is usually done for broadcast only. Again, you or your producer can decide what is adequate. A countdown can be generated using the title tool. Some effects footage libraries have fancy countdowns. Of course, no one will see this except the client, yourself, and whoever uses the tape.

Render Effects

Xpress Pro's Expert Render can determine exactly how many of your effects will need to be rendered in your sequence before you do your digital cut. Expert Render tends to work on the safe side, so that your sequence should play back without failure. If you really want to play it safe, and you have the time, you can render everything.

Rendering with Software Only

If you're using the software only, select Special>Enable Digital Video Out. You'll notice that your Digital Video Toggle may have switched colors. The reason is that for output, you have to turn off real-time effects. What does this mean? Well, you're going to be rendering all the effects in your Timeline. This may take awhile. We highly recommend a thorough study of the AVX Appendix on page 421 while rendering. Who knows? You might learn something new.

Before we go any further with your digital cut procedure, let's talk about offline resolution. If you used 15:1s, you will not easily be able to get a digital cut out of Xpress Pro. When you select Special>Enable Digital Video Out, Xpress Pro beeps at you and informs you that only DV-25 sequences can be used when non-real time mode is selected. What does this mean? Basically, Xpress Pro does not want to output single-field, poor-resolution video.

There's a workaround for this, but it will take a little time. And keep in mind that your sequence is still going to look like 15:1s video.

You can transcode your sequence to DV-25:

1. Select the 15:1s sequence in your bin. Then select Bin> Consolidate/Transcode.

2. When the Consolidate Transcode menu appears, select Transcoder and make sure that DV-25 is selected.

3. You'll also need to select a target drive. In this case, you'll be creating a new sequence.

4. Transcode the sequence. A new sequence with the suffix ".transcode" will appear in your bin, along with all of the clips.

5. Once the transcoded sequence is made, load it into the source monitor and again select Special>Enable Digital Video Out.

This time the toggle button should turn blue without any errors.

6.   Mark an IN point at the beginning and an OUT point at the end of your sequence. Select Clip>Render In/Out.

You could also select Clip>Expert Render In/Out, but let's face it, with software only, you're going to render all of the effects. Fortunately, you're using a very fast computer so this won't take much time at all…right?

Note   You can also use this procedure with 28:1 if you are working with 24p or 25p projects.

Rendering with Mojo

If you're using the optional Mojo, you can rely on Expert Render to let the system determine which effects will need to be rendered in order to play back your sequence. Here's how to set it up: Mark an IN at the beginning of the sequence and an OUT at the end and highlight all of your tracks, both video and audio. Select Clip>Expert Render. The Expert Render menu appears. Select the Prepare Effects For Digital Cut option at the bottom of the menu and click OK. The system will render the necessary effects and you're ready to proceed.

13.6   Using Expert Render for Mojo output

Converting Audio Sample Rates

Before performing a digital cut, you have to convert all audio sample rates to the same spec. To do this:

1.   Select your sequence in its bin.

2.   Select Bin>Change Sample Rate.

You could optionally right-click (or Control-click on a Mac) on the sequence and choose Change Sample Rate.

3.   Choose the correct sample rate and the quality of audio that you wish to create.

For a final layoff, this should always be High.

4.   You can also choose to delete the original audio. If you do not choose this, duplicate clips will be generated with the new sample rate.

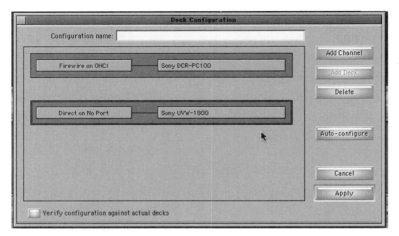

13.7   Deck Configuration
Settings

5. Xpress Pro creates new media for clips in the sequence that do not have the correct sample rate. Your conversion is complete.

Calibrating for Output

Before outputting, you'll want to measure the output of the audio tone using the Audio Tool against input meters on your record deck. If the deck has adjustable levels for record input, optimize your levels appropriately. Usually this means simply zeroing the level of tone, but you should also test the levels going to the deck using the loudest portion of your sequence to make sure no clipping occurs and to ensure that the tone is truly representative of your program levels.

Configure the Record Deck

Before performing a digital cut, make sure that your deck is connected and properly configured.

There are two different control interfaces that can be used in deck configurations which were discussed earlier, RS-422 (Also referred to as "Direct") and OHCI (IEEE 1394, or "FireWire") With either of these protocols, the communication is two-way, and your Xpress Pro can poll the deck or camera to determine its model and make.

Sometimes, however, Xpress Pro does not properly identify the deck or camera. Keep in mind that there are now many decks and cameras on the market, and although the protocols are common, the methods of implementation are not. So the best thing to do is to go to your deck configuration settings and do it yourself.

First, go to the Project window and click on the Settings tab. Locate the Deck Configuration settings and double-click.

It may take a moment or two for the deck templates to load. The deck templates contain information about how to control the most commonly used decks. If your deck is not among the templates, you can still use a generic template and configure it for your deck.

 If you know which decks you'll be using regularly and want faster configuration, go to Hard Drive>Programs (Mac: Applications>Avid Xpress Pro>Supporting Files) and open the *Machine Templates* folder. Inside this folder are all of the templates for machines available in Xpress Pro. You can remove some of the templates that you are sure you will not be using. It's a good idea to *move* them, not delete. You never know what kind of editing job may walk into your life. Once the folder has been reduced to just your commonly used decks, the load time for configuration decreases dramatically.

If this is your first time using Deck Configuration, you will need to click on the Add Channel button. The Channel Options appear. You can choose between Direct (RS-422) and OHCI (IEEE 1394 or "FireWire").

On Windows machines, usually an RS-422 to RS-232C adapter (such as Addenda's Rosetta Stone) is used for controlling the deck. The deck is therefore connected to one of the two RS-232C serial ports built into your system. On Windows systems, you must choose between the Com 1 and Com 2 RS-232C ports.

RS-422 control can also be established on Macintosh systems. It requires either a serial to USB adapter such those made by Keyspan or a third-party card, such as Gee Three's Stealth card. The Keyspan adapter and the Stealth card (and many others like them) will allow direct connection between the RS-422 connector on the deck and the card on your Mac. In Deck Configuration, this is shown as the "Direct" choice.

If you are using a hardware codec or Mojo and want RS-422 control, you should choose either the Com 1//Com 2 selection (Windows) or the direct selection (Mac).

Once you've added your channel, it's time to add a deck. Click on the Add Deck button, and the Deck Selection window appears. In order to properly select a deck, you must choose the manufacturer first. For example, if your deck is a Sony DSR-11, choose Sony. The list of Sony configured decks will appear. Scroll down the list and select DSR-11.

If your deck is not listed under the manufacturer's name, you might be able to find the template on Avid's website. Avid frequently adds or creates new templates because new decks and cameras come out frequently.

Another option would be to select a Generic deck. A generic deck follows standard protocols for controls of OHCI and RS-422 controllers. It is not particularly sensitive to the full capabilities of a specific deck, but it can fulfill the needs of just about any deck.

If your deck has neither RS-422 or OHCI capability, you'll need to control the deck manually. In cases such as these, there is no need to configure a deck, because the deck cannot be controlled by Xpress Pro. When you access the Digital Cut tool, select Local for deck control. In the deck control section, you'll notice that No Deck appears where time-code would normally be.

Deleting Deck Configurations

If you need to delete a previous deck configuration, do the following:

1. Go to your Project window and click on the Settings tab.

2. Select Deck Configurations.

3. Click on the deck and shift click on the channel. Or you can lasso them both in the Deck Configuration tool.

4. Press Delete.

The deck configuration disappears.

THREE METHODS OF DIGITAL CUT

There are three ways to perform a digital cut (see Figure 13.8). The first is an insert edit. Insert editing assumes that you have a deck or camera that can perform insert edits, that you use a blacked-and-coded videotape (a tape that has a black signal recorded from beginning to end using continuous timecode, usually by setting the deck to Regen), and that recording will be frame accurate. Remote machine control is maintained by Xpress Pro. Insert-type recording assumes that the control track, a signal that is synchronous and assures smooth recording, is already recorded onto the tape.

The second method of recording is called assemble edit. Assemble editing requires a machine that can be remote controlled by Xpress Pro. The difference between assemble and insert is that with assemble editing, the tape only needs to be blacked and coded up to the starting timecode. From the point of the digital cut, assemble editing creates new time-code, video, and a control track. In the case of assemble editing, the control track continues recording where it left off previously. As a result, an assemble edit looks smooth, but actually contains a new sync recording. For purposes of deck cueing, we highly recommend that you black and code the tape beyond this point by at least an additional five sec-

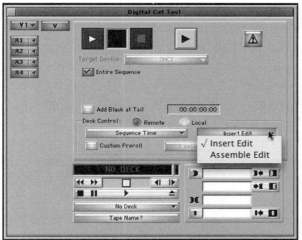
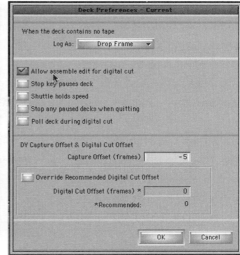

13.8   Three Different Recording Modes: Insert,
         Assemble and "Crash"

13.9   Assemble Edit Enabled in Deck
         Preferences

onds. When the deck goes into Record mode, the timecode is generated through the deck and is continuous.

In order to use Assemble mode, it must be enabled in your Deck Preferences first. When you open your Deck Preferences (from the settings in your Project window), select Allow Assemble Edit for Digital Cut.

Which decks and cameras support these two modes? The best way to find out is to look at the Avid web site, www.avid.com. There are so many decks and cameras out on the market that it would be impossible to list all of the supported decks in this book. On the Xpress Pro page, there is a link to a list of supported decks and cameras. Some decks are partially supported—that is, they may be able to do insert edits but not assemble edits—and others are fully supported.

Warning

One thing that is important to consider: FireWire (IEEE 1394) protocol is not always frame accurate. There is a lot of dependency on the deck, the transcoder (if necessary), the FireWire card, and finally the software. As a result, if you are controlling your deck by FireWire, assemble, and sometimes even insert digital cuts will not be available, because in order to make frame-accurate edits, Xpress Pro needs a recorder that can make frame-accurate edits! If you use RS-422 control of your deck, you may have frame-accurate remote control of your deck, but again, the deck must be able to make insert or assemble edits.

Many decks are configured only for hard or "crash" recording, which is the third method of making a digital cut. Crash recording is simple: Hit the Record button on your deck and play back the digital cut. If you choose this method—by far the easiest of the three—you will want plenty of black at the head and tail of your sequence. Otherwise, the untidy crash record will be seen, which is never good at presentations. In the case of crash recording, you can set your deck to Local control on the Digital Cut tool and start recording as you press the Play button for the digital cut.

Crash recording is a way to do a digital cut to a deck that is not controlled by Xpress Pro. There can be many reasons for doing a digital cut with this method. The most common is that not all decks are controllable by Xpress Pro. For example, VHS decks normally have neither FireWire or RS-422 serial controls.

We have finally gone over the options and are ready to actually take a look at the Digital Cut tool.

THE DIGITAL CUT TOOL

The Digital Cut tool will look different, depending on whether you have a software only system or a system with optional Mojo.

Software Only (Without Optional Mojo Interface)

Let's take a quick tour of the Digital Cut Tool (see Figure 13.10) and spend some time on the key elements.

13.10 Digital Cut Tool

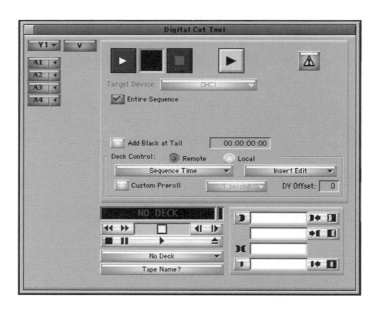

At top left you'll notice a track selector, much like the one on your Timeline. If your deck is configured to a FireWire device, there is a single column, representing the enabled tracks in your sequence. You'll also see a single column if you are using a locally controlled deck. If your deck is a non-FireWire device with RS-422 control, there is a second column of tracks where you can select the channels to record on the deck.

The big buttons to the right of the Track Selector panels control the digital cut. When you click on the red button, the digital cut will begin. Much like the Capture tool, you'll get a blinking light (to the right of this button) when the digital cut is in progress.

To the right of the blinking light is a blue Stop button. When recording or previewing a digital cut, you can click on this button to stop the process. (You can also press the Escape key on your keyboard.)

The yellow button is used to preview your digital cut. If you are inserting the sequence onto a tape that already has materials on it, it is highly recommended that you preview the digital cut. It is better, in fact, if you try the digital cut on a blank tape first. There is nothing like that all-is-lost postapocalyptic feeling that you get when you've ruined a master tape. If it has never happened to you before, trust us, it's not pretty. When you do this preview, you want to monitor the output of the deck, not the output of the Avid. Monitoring the deck will show you what the preroll and postroll will look like. And take one more moment to make sure you are not in Assemble edit.

Below the buttons is a Target Device pulldown menu. If you are using a remote controlled deck with FireWire, this would normally be OHCI. This menu lists all of the target device types that are currently connected. If it is grayed out, Xpress Pro doesn't see your deck. If you're doing a crash edit in local mode, it normally would be grayed out.

Below that are two checkboxes. Select the top one if you are indeed outputting your entire sequence. If not, leave it deselected and be sure to mark your INs and OUTs on the sequence. The second checkbox is for adding black at the tail of your digital cut. If you're doing an assemble edit or controlling the deck locally, this is especially important. Because an assemble edit ends by stopping the deck in a crash-record mode, you'll want to add plenty of black at the tail to keep the sequence looking smooth for a while after the sequence has played. Usually 30 seconds is good. Some tape duplication facilities require two minutes of black after program end. Look at it this way: if your sequence is going to be played back in a conference room and some manager type is doing a presentation around it, there very well could be a minute or more before he or she stops the tape.

You might also consider adding some black at the tail if you are doing an insert edit. Even though the tape already has black on it, oftentimes the level of black doesn't match the output of your Xpress Pro. As a result. the end of the sequence, where one normally fades to black, could look like a glitch, where Xpress Pro stops recording and the black from the tape continues playing. Mismatched levels are common in broadcasting and they don't look particularly good. However, if you are inserting footage into the *middle* of a sequence, then make sure you do *not* have Add Black At Tail selected.

If you have chosen an insert or assemble edit, Xpress Pro has a pulldown menu that determines where the digital cut will take place. The menu gives you three options:

- *Sequence Time,* where the tape timecode matches the sequence timecode exactly
- *Record Deck Time,* where the digital cut will begin at the exact timecode where the deck is parked before you begin the digital cut
- *Mark In Time,* which can be determined by marking an IN point using the timecode registers near the bottom of the Digital Cut tool.

One thing to remember if you are doing NTSC video: be sure that the tape timecode and your sequence timecode use the same frame code mode—that is, they both need to be either dropframe or non-dropframe timecode.

Again, if you are remotely controlling the deck, there should be a menu to the right of the previous menu. This will select whether you are insert or assemble editing. If there is no menu here, you have selected Local mode. If the menu does not have the Assemble option in it, you will need to adjust your deck preferences accordingly to enable it.

Below the pulldown menus is the preroll time, which might need to be adjusted to properly make an edit on your deck (again, only if remotely controlled) and a DV Offset. The DV Offset is used when doing a digital cut using FireWire. Sometimes, when doing a digital cut to DV-25, the audio and video do not arrive at the same time. Adjusting the DV Offset will fix this problem. For your deck, there is a predetermined offset built into the template. If you use a transcoder, the chances of a delay are even greater. Many of the more common transcoder templates are listed in the deck configuration menus. When one is chosen the default offset is automatically selected.

Although it looks like a direct entry box, the DV Offset is controlled through your deck preference settings. If you do a digital cut, but the audio and video don't seem to be in sync, you'll need to open your deck preferences and override the recommended DV offset with a number of your choosing. The bad news about overriding the recommended offset is that you will have to determine the correct number of frames through trial and error. The good news is that it should remain consistent, so long as you use the exact same equipment. So once the settings are made, save them. An easy way to determine the offset is to lay a sequence off to tape that consists of a few seconds of filler, flowed by a beep synchronized to a single frame of white or bars or video, followed by more filler.

If you receive the error "No coincidence point found," it probably means that your deck or your tape or both are "write protected" or "record inhibited." Pop or slide the record inhibit button on the tape or flip the record inhibit switch on the deck and try again.

The rest of the Digital Cut tool should be familiar to you. We covered all of it in the Capture chapter. Be sure that the right deck and tape name are selected. If you are controlling the digital cut locally and doing a crash record, none of this is necessary. No marks need to be in the Marks Register unless you are recording your digital cut at a specific Mark In timecode. One slight difference is that there is no Mark Out button. That's because the length of your sequence or marks on the sequence determines the OUT point, plus any black filler you've added.

Digital Cut with Mojo

Mojo accelerator allows a few more options when you create a digital cut. It can work as a transcoder to Composite, Component, or S-Video analog decks. It can output real time effects. It can output uncompressed video.

The greatest advantage of Mojo is the lack of rendering required when completing a digital cut. Although all of the preparations should be completed as with a digital cut without Mojo, you do have the capability of playing back uncompressed video and some real time effects.

Once connected to your deck by FireWire from Mojo, Xpress Pro can control the deck. The only significant difference that you will see on the Digital Cut tool when used with Mojo is that you can enable Effects Safe mode. Effects Safe mode will determine which effects need to be rendered before performing a digital cut. Enabling Effects Safe will prevent video underruns or other playback issues. With Effects Safe mode selected, click on the Record button for the digital cut to begin. After rendering, the system will perform the digital cut.

Chapter 14

Exporting with Xpress Pro

Xpress Pro has a dazzling array of export options. You can export media, data, information about your sequences, projects, still graphics, QuickTime files, and more. There are very few limitations, and even those can be exceeded by adding more software, video and audio codecs, and digital media applications to your system.

For example, you can:

- Export individual frames

- Export AVI, QuickTime, RealMedia, DV Streams, or Windows Media

- Export audio files for mixing on a Digital Audio Workstation (DAW)

- Export files to convert them from one file type to another

- Export sequences for use on other systems

- Export MPEG streams for use with DVD authoring

- Export files for a transfer between Avid systems

- Send sequences to other applications for use

- Save files to Avid Links, such as Audiovision, D\S Compositions, or ProTools formats.

EXPORT SETTINGS TEMPLATES

Before we run off into the diverse world of exporting, let's take a look at some export settings. In Chapter 2 "Settings" we discussed different ways of creating and saving Settings templates. With Xpress Pro, you already have three export templates that were created for you (see Figure 14.1). They are:

- *Fast Export as QuickTime Movie:* This setting will create a fast export of a Quick-Time movie using the Avid DV codec. It will create a movie that is "Same As Source," meaning that the exported QuickTime will be the same size as the captured source footage and use the Avid DV codec. If you have the optional Mojo, you can export an uncompressed sequence to QuickTime.

- *Macintosh Image:* Using this default setting will export a single PICT file. Which PICT will export? That's determined by your Mark In point in the sequence. It's seems like an odd moniker for a setting because, of course, Adobe Photoshop for Windows reads PICT files just fine, right? Wrong. The resulting export would not open in Photoshop 6 for Windows because, according to the error message, Photoshop for Windows reads rasterized PICT files only. However, some other Windows applications can open it.

- *Windows Image:* This setting will export a single BMP file. Like its Macintosh counterpart, a Mark In point determines which single frame is exported and the name doesn't necessarily imply that bitmaps cannot be opened by Macs.

To simplify my settings I changed the Windows Image Export Setting to BMP and the Macintosh Image Export to PS MAC (see Figure 14.2).

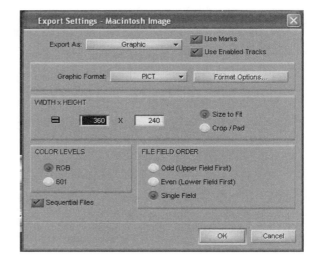

14.1   Export Settings Templates *(above)*

14.2   Changing Export Settings *(right)*

You might want to try your hand at creating some new settings as well. Duplicate your PS Mac settings (Ctrl+D/Cmd+D) and open them up by double-clicking on them. Select JPEG as the file type and make sure that Sequential Files is deselected. Use Marks should be selected. Once you've set it up, rename the setting to JPEG. Now you have a few export options in your arsenal. We've created several export settings templates on the DVD-ROM. These settings can be imported with your other settings and used for easy drag-and-drop exporting without even having to create new templates.

Before we thoroughly discuss exporting frames and audio files, let's get right to the most elaborate kind of export: your sequence. While exporting single frames is a relatively easy process, exporting a sequence can be a bit more tasking. There are many formats and options. Let's start by taking a look at QuickTime.

You should have QuickTime already installed on your system. QuickTime is a media playback system developed by Apple Computer. The QuickTime Player has become quite a versatile tool for digital artists. If you haven't used it yet, you might be surprised at how much it can do. It is somewhat more advantageous to have QuickTime Pro. QuickTime Pro adds some versatility to how QuickTime reads, imports, and exports files through the player. It's also an inexpensive option.

WHAT'S A CODEC?

When I first learned the basics of Adobe's Photoshop application, I was told that the key to manipulating single images was through plug-ins. The more plug-ins you had, the more things you could do. And as a result, I probably have purchased at one time or another just about every commercially available plug-in for Photoshop.

For QuickTime, the key element is the codec. The more codecs you have, the more versatile QuickTime becomes. Have you ever downloaded a video and wondered how on earth they got such a beautiful picture on such a small file? Usually it's the codec. The same is true when the results are less than satisfactory. Codecs make the difference between a very good QuickTime file and a very bad one.

What is a codec? A codec is a compressor-decompressor, and every QuickTime file uses a codec to determine exactly how it is compressed. There are many different compression methods. Some are free and can be found on the Internet. Others, which use proprietary algorithms and can create the best files in the smallest formats, can be expensive.

Which codec is best? It usually depends on how you'll use the file. For example, if you were exporting a sequence that was to be played back on the desktops of employees in a small company with very old computers, it might be wise to determine what software codecs they have available and how fast their computers can read files. If you intend to output to a CD-ROM, the speed of the CD-ROM that will be reading your files is very important.

On the other hand, if you're creating a file that is an intermediary, that is, not intended for playback but just for transferring from one application to another, uncompressed quality might better suit you.

When selecting a codec, you're given several options on how the codec will write the file, including the quality level that you want the file to be. Remember to test, test, test! Try outputting a segment of your sequence and reading it on a target computer—a system that is exactly like the one that will be used to view the file. It's better to discover playback issues sooner than later.

Using and Copying Codecs

The most common QuickTime export error is the lack of similar codecs on the target computer. In other words, while your Xpress Pro may have a dozen or so different codecs, not all computers do. Without the proper codec, the computer will not be able to play back your file at all. Usually, the user receives a message that the computer cannot read the file because software has not been installed.

So long as you have permission to transfer the codec that you want, it can be done, but be sure to check for licensing before doing this. The Avid codec is distributed for free from Avid's web site at www.avid.com. Any system that regularly uses QuickTime files from your Xpress Pro should have the Avid codecs installed.

14.3   Codecs in the System 32 Folder in Windows

If you're running Xpress Pro on Windows XP, your codecs are located in the folder [drive name]:Windows/System32/ (see Figure 14.3). Normally these files are hidden in the folder, but you can get Windows XP to reveal them. If you're running Xpress Pro on Macintosh (OS X), the codecs are located in the folder Macintosh HD/ Library/QuickTime. The Avid QuickTime codecs are for Meridien Uncompressed, Meridien Compressed, the Avid DV Codec, and another QT codec for ABVB and Nuvista Avid media. All of these codecs cover the gamut for exporting to every Avid system ever made.

The type of codecs available for your computer will vary, depending on whether you're running a PC or Mac. For example, you can export an Audio Video Interleave (AVI) file with a Windows computer, but not normally with a Mac.

EXPORTING A SEQUENCE

Let's start by exporting a sequence. From here, we'll go through all of the options and dialogs. At first, this may seem a bit cumbersome—there are a lot of questions that the system needs to have answered before exporting—but once you've created settings and are satisfied with the results, exporting sequences can be a drag-and-drop operation.

There are a few things to check before we begin.

- *All Media Online:* Make sure that all of your media is online. No, you can't export what isn't there (but wouldn't it be nice?). A fast way to check for this on your sequence is to load it into the Record Monitor, click on the Timeline Fast menu and select Clip Color>Offline. Any offline clips will show in the Timeline. You'll need to find these and import, capture, or relink them before exporting the sequence. Also, check out the tip and accompanying figure on page 115 in Chapter 4 "Media Management" about using Set Bin Display to do thorough searches for offline media.

- *Audio Sample Rate:* If any clips contain different sample rates other than the one you've chosen as the default rate for your sequence, you need to convert these before exporting. You can view the sample rates of each clip in your bin, then select Bin>Change Sample Rate to convert any mismatches.

- *Audio and Video Levels:* What you see is what you get (WYSIWYG). All audio levels, pans, video levels, effects, and anything else you did to the sequence are going to be exported. Make sure that these levels are all to your satisfaction. Despite any false hopes you might have, exporting will not improve your work. Trust me on this one, I've tried.

- *Render Everything:* If you render it now, it won't have to be rendered during export. If you don't, you could be in for a long export. Bottom line is that while Xpress Pro can play back in real time, there is no real-time support for other file formats. As a result, the system will have to think through every unrendered effect during export and render it.

- *Drive Space:* Here's something that is absolutely necessary to know: a partial QuickTime file is not a QuickTime file. It is worthless, void, zilch, nada, naught. In order for your file to work, it has to be completely exported. Until that moment comes, you have a worthless file on your system. You're going to want plenty of drive space to make sure that the export comes all the way through. If the system runs out of space, it'll tell you. If it does it after exporting 93 percent of your sequence, you're going to need a little time alone. Better safe than sorry. If your sequence is very long, you might consider breaking it up into segments before exporting.

QUICKTIME MOVIES

There are two different types of QuickTime files. They are:

- *QuickTime Reference Movie:* Exporting sequences as QuickTime Reference creates a file that references the media already on your system. The OMF files that Xpress Pro uses are basically played back within a QuickTime wrapper, making the reference file very small. This type of export goes very fast and is quite convenient for playback. The instruction set is so small that there is very little concern for drive space. However, it is absolutely dependent on the media that you already have on your system. If you move it to another computer without the media, it is worthless. If you delete the original media from your system, a QuickTime Reference file that points to that media will not play back, because the referenced files aren't there.

- The most common reason for using QuickTime Reference movies is to use the existing media files for other applications on your system. Whereas it once was considered taboo to put other applications on Avid turnkey stations, it is now quite commonplace. So, for example, if you need to export a reference file to be imported into Adobe After Effects or Apple Shake for compositing, you can easily do this with QuickTime Reference format. The media is already on your system, and there are no compatibility issues. It saves time for the export and drive space for media, and you can go right to the next application. This is also an excellent option for files that you intend to compress or reformat further using a program like ProEncode or Cleaner.

- As a matter of fact, Xpress Pro has a menu function called Send To that will allow you to export and send a file to another application. We'll discuss this function later in the chapter on page 403.

- *QuickTime Movie:* The second method of QuickTime export is as an independent QuickTime movie with media created by a codec. Creating this type of file will depend on the codec and settings that you choose. It is much larger than the reference file, but it is also a free-standing file, meaning that you can copy it to another system and it will play back fine, so long as the other system has the same codec. It is not dependent on existing media from Xpress Pro.

Exporting a QuickTime Reference Movie

Okay, you've checked all of the items mentioned and observed all of the caveats. Let's start with a simple export: a QuickTime Reference movie.

First, select all of the tracks that you want to export in the Track Selector panel. If you want to export the entire sequence, clear all of your IN and OUT marks. If you're only exporting a portion of the sequence, determine the exported section using a Mark in and a Mark Out. Be sure to enable all of the tracks that will be exported.

Now, select File>Export. A box with Export As appears (see Figure 14.4). For the moment, we'll assume that you haven't created any custom settings. Click on the Options button. The Export Settings window appears. At the top, there is an Export As setting. Click on it to reveal all of the different file types available. Choose QuickTime Reference. Once chosen, you're given some new options (see Figure 14.5). For now, let's select every-

14.4   Export as Box

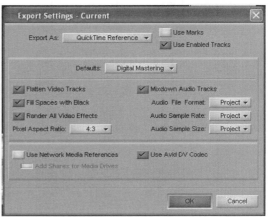

14.5   Export Settings Window

thing, with the exception of Network Referencing. Be sure to select Use Enabled Tracks so the right media references will export. You'll flatten the video tracks, insert black in the blank spaces, render all effects, and go with your project settings for audio sampling, file format, and sample size. You'll also use the Avid codec.

And just why would Avid have its own codec? Two main reasons: getting the file in and out of your system using the codec is generally faster, and using the Avid codec ensures that the quality of the file remains the same as the original. There are so many different compression schemes out there that a book could be written about it. As a matter of fact, Ben Waggoner offers a rather lengthy study of compression in *Compression for Great Digital Video: Power Tips, Techniques, and Common Sense* available from CMP books.

You may have also noticed that there is a Digital Mastering setting. The options in this pulldown menu are shortcuts to choosing the Export options already in the menu. There are two choices with this menu, Digital Mastering and Fast Draft.

Digital Mastering flattens the video tracks, fills blank spaces in the sequence with black, mixes down the audio tracks, and renders all effects. The other option is Fast Draft. Fast Draft will get the sequence out quicker. It fills blank spaces with black and flattens the video tracks. The only problem with Fast Draft is that if the effects are not rendered, they will not show up in the resulting QuickTime. If you're just doing something for general reference, it could suffice, but normally, you're going to want to choose Digital Mastering.

When you're creating a QuickTime Reference, one of these selections, Fill Spaces with Black, is very important. If this isn't done, the resulting reference file may have difficulty playing back any blank spaces in your sequence. Always select this option.

Saving the Export Settings

Notice at the bottom left of the Export Settings Options menu there is a Save As... button. This is not for saving the export, but rather a method to save your Export Settings. Go ahead and click on it and save these settings as Xpress Pro Workshop. You'll notice that this is now in your Settings menu as one of your Export options.

Drag-and-Drop Exporting

Okay, it's been pretty tedious so far, so let's have a bit of fun. Let's export our QuickTime reference file, but instead of saving it through the Export menu, we'll drag and drop it with the settings that we just created (see Figure 14.6).

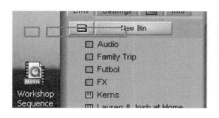

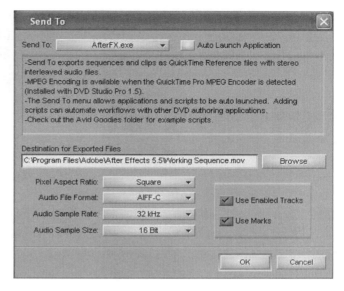

14.6   Drag-and-Drop Exporting
        (above)

14.7   Send To Menu *(right)*

First, activate the Export Settings that we just created in the Settings tab of your Project window. There should be a check mark next to those settings. Now, select the sequence in its bin and drag it off to the desktop. I realize that this may require you to move a window or two out of the way, especially on a PC, but it's worth it. Instantly your sequence turns into a QuickTime reference movie. Cool, huh?

Another Way of Exporting: Send To

As we mentioned, the big advantage to QuickTime Reference files is that you don't go through the time to create new media files nor do you have to worry about having enough drive space to create them. With Xpress Pro, you can export a QuickTime Reference (or for that matter, any type of export) then send it to another digital application as long as it is on the same machine. This method of export goes directly from the Xpress Pro bin to the target application. The function is called Send To. Here's how you do it.

First, make sure that your Export Settings are correct. You want to export as a Quick-Time Reference file, flatten tracks, and fill spaces with black. Once you've created the Setting, make it active and select your sequence in its bin, then select File>Send To (see Figure 14.7).

The Send To menu appears. You first will have to show Xpress Pro where the other application exists. Click on the Browse button and find the application that you want to use. You'll probably want to enable the tracks on the Timeline and make marks before you do this. Once you've found the application, Xpress Pro will export it to wherever you choose. The only real advantage of using Send To is that you can launch the next application automatically from Xpress Pro. In some cases, the application will automatically load the sent export file as well. When you work back and forth between applications, this is a nice convenience, but be sure to have plenty of physical RAM on your system if you're going to have both apps open at the same time.

Exporting QuickTime Movies

Now that you know how to make reference files, it's time to do a true export. Let's move some media with a QuickTime movie export. A QuickTime movie export basically puts a QuickTime wrapper on media files created with your codecs. Here, options are abundant and the results vary greatly.

To start, prepare your sequence just as mentioned previously in "Exporting a Sequence" on page 399. Now take a look at the sequence in your Timeline. If you want to export only a portion of the sequence, be sure to mark an IN point and an OUT point. You'll select the Use Marks option in the Export options. If you want to export specific tracks from the sequence, make only those tracks active. You'll want to choose the Use Enabled Tracks option in the Export options.

With the sequence selected (either by clicking on the Timeline or the Record Monitor) select File>Export. You can name the soon-to-be-exported QuickTime here, then click on the Options button (see Figure 14.8).

Warning
Choose before you export. If you forget to select the Record Monitor or Timeline, whatever was last selected on the interface will be exported. The Export menu is conditional. In other words, its content varies, depending on whether a bin, sequence, clip, or other media is selected. Whenever you're unsure, it's easier to just stop the export, click on the proper item, and begin exporting again.

The Export Options button leads to a variety of different formats, which in turn leads to even more specific formats. First, click on the Export As pulldown menu (see Figure 14.9). There is a list of different types of media exports available on your system, everything from OMF and AAF (which we'll describe later) to the QuickTime formats. Are there any tilde keys in front of the formats in your menu? For example, on my Xpress Pro system, I have a ~MPEG 4 option. The tilde indicates that this export option has not been qualified with Xpress Pro and is not supported by Avid. Nonetheless, the option exists and you can try it out as an export if you wish.

Let's select QuickTime Movie (be careful not to select QuickTime Reference or QuickTime Media Link) and take a look at more options. Be sure to select your Use Marks and/or Use Enabled Tracks options if needed. Just below that is the Save As Source

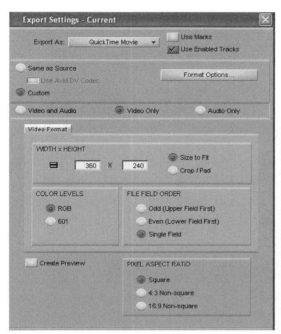

14.8   Export QuickTime Movie Selected *(left)*

14.9   Export QuickTime Options *(below)*

option. When you save the QuickTime Movie the same as its source, you're essentially putting a QuickTime wrapper on Avid media. There are two options here: to save it as source or to customize the QuickTime. If you customize it, the Use Avid Codec button deflates, and you're given yet another Options button: this one entitled Format Options.

Format Options

When you customize your QuickTime Export, you have a myriad of options. These options primarily are concerned with which QuickTime codecs will be used. There are both audio and video codecs. Click on the Format Options, and you will see another window, where the current options are displayed. Here the audio and video are separated and there are settings that can be made. You also have Filter and Size options for video and some streaming options if you intend to use your QuickTime on the Internet. The streaming options can be deselected if Internet use is not intended.

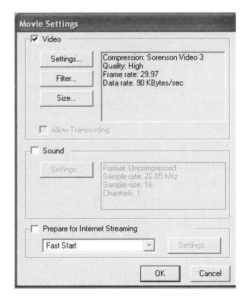

14.10   Video Settings Pulldown *(left)*

14.11   Audio Format Options *(below)*

Video Settings

When you click on the Video Settings button, a Compression Settings pulldown menu appears. In this menu, you can choose the QuickTime codec that best suits your needs. The number of settings available depends upon the type of computer, the enabled media capabilities and the amount of software that you own. My Xpress Pro system is pretty bare-boned in this department, yet I have a choice of 27 different codecs. Once your codec is selected, you can select a Quality Setting below the pulldown menu.

Where do we go from here? Well, with some codecs, you have even more options! Are you counting how deep the Options menus go? So far, we're up to number four. Try this: select the Avid ABVB NuBus codec, then adjust the quality. Surprise! A hidden Option screen!

There are so many codecs on the market that it would be impossible to discuss the details of each one here. Again, Ben Waggoner's book, *Compression for Great Digital Video: Power Tips, Techniques, and Common Sense,* discusses the majority of codecs on the market and comprehensively covers their strengths and weaknesses. For integrating QuickTimes with other Avid applications, it is always best to use the Avid codec. For web, CD-ROM, and FTP, our favorite codec is Sorenson Professional. It's pricey, but the results are beautiful and the file sizes are manageable—and it's quite rare when both features are attributed to a single codec.

Other Exports   **407**

Audio Codecs

You can choose from a variety of audio codecs for QuickTime. Usually uncompressed is the way to go, unless you have a need to compress the audio in a different format for a special purpose. Be sure the sampling rate and sample size are the same as your audio project sample in order to avoid downsampling issues.

Prepare for Internet Streaming

Last on our list of Format Options are the choices that can be made when creating a QuickTime for video streaming. There are three:

1. *Fast Start:* Fast Start allows your QuickTime to begin streaming on the Internet before it is completely downloaded. For those of us who remember the first Internet QuickTime downloads, this is especially important. For everyone else, you may wonder why this option isn't always mandatory.

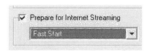

2. *Fast Start with Compressed Header:* This method of preparation is actually a bit better for Internet streaming. It works exactly the same as Fast Start, but with one major advantage. The header portion of the QuickTime is compressed so that it can be read more quickly by the Internet client. The QuickTime will not stream until the header is completely read. A smaller header allows for a faster start on the stream.

3. *Hinted Streaming:* This type of preparation is for use on video servers. The file does not begin streaming until it receives a Hint track for each track of video and audio. The hint track allows the server to divide the file into packets for more efficient Internet delivery. When selecting this option, you either need to know how your video server works or contact someone who does. The encoding, packet size, and method of delivery will need to be chosen in further options menus.

Once you've selected the audio and video codecs, filters, frame sizes, and Internet options, save the QuickTime movie. It might take a while to export, depending on the codec and the length of your sequence. While you're waiting for the export to finish, you can keep reading!

OTHER EXPORTS

Other Movie Formats

You can also export your movie in other formats, such as DV Stream or MPEG formats, when available. These formats are readable on a QuickTime player, but are not specifically created for QuickTime.

DV Streams come in two flavors: standard DV-25 (NTSC or PAL) and DVC Pro (also in NTSC and PAL). When you choose to export to DVC Pro, the audio automatically locks to 48kHz, the DVC Pro standard.

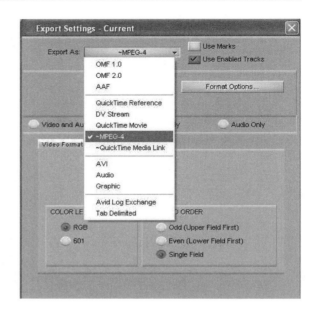

Graphics

Xpress Pro has the ability to output single frames and multiple frames in sequence. These frames can be used for a wide variety of reasons. For example, some might use them as references for publications or possibly for manipulating through graphic imaging applications.

Keep in mind that the image quality of single-frame exports are severely handicapped by the resolution of NTSC and PAL. If you've never worked with print before, here's a brief explanation: A standard definition frame export from Xpress Pro is 720 pixels wide and 540 pixels tall. The most basic printed image usually contains a minimum of 300 dpi. Many printers prefer 600 dpi. So if you do the math correctly, your exported image would best be suited for print at a size of anywhere from 1.2 to 2.5 inches wide.

All of this is based on theory that you would even use a video image for print. A more common use for exported graphics is for use in a graphics-editing application. In some cases, you might need to export a sequence of frames for animation, compositing, rotoscoping, or some other dynamic media imaging. Either way, Xpress Pro can handle these types of exports with ease.

Single-Frame Graphics

Xpress Pro can export a lot of different file formats. The first order of business is to determine which format you'll need to export. To see the variety of options, find the frame that you want to export. It can be from a clip, subclip, sequence, or an effect. You can export from either the Source or Record Monitor. When Xpress Pro exports a graphic, it chooses whichever monitor is selected, so be sure to enable the correct one. Any frame works. Once you've found the frame, place a mark IN on it. The mark lets Xpress Pro know

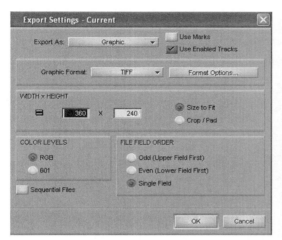

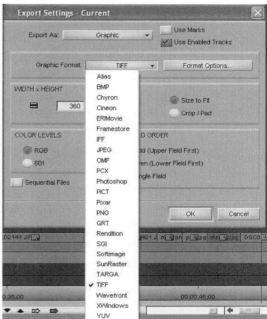

14.12   Graphic Export Menu *(above)*

14.13   Potential File Formats for Export *(right)*

which frame is to be exported. From there, select File>Export. If you have other things to do before exporting, be sure to click on the frame before accessing this menu, because the Export menu is conditional. In other words, if you were to click on a bin, the system would assume that you were trying to export a bin or perhaps a sequence (depending on exactly what was clicked in the bin) but it wouldn't know that you are trying to export a frame.

When the Export menu comes up, select the Options pulldown menu. From here, select Graphic, and the Graphic Export menu appears. To the right of the menu is the Use Enabled Tracks and Use Marks selectors. Again, Xpress Pro determines the graphic by your marks if Use Marks is selected. If you don't make a mark or don't select this option, Xpress Pro will export the graphic from wherever you parked your position indicator on the highlighted monitor. In order for the graphic to export with the Use Enabled Tracks option, you will need to enable the video track. Otherwise, nothing will be exported, although you will not get any error messages.

There are a number of file formats to choose from. In recent years, Avid has added to the Export options and can now export a graphic for just about any use or manipulation. The file formats range from simple web use to files that can be used on high-end workstations.

Multiple-Frame Graphics

Exporting a multiple graphic sequence works much like exporting a single graphic with one exception: you can create multiple individual files, one for each frame. If you work with animators or do much rotoscoping (i.e., painting frame by frame) then this is probably a common use for you. Individual frame exports can, for some applications, be easier to deal with than a QuickTime movie or other streaming media. The frames would need to be contiguous in the sequence in order to be exported in this automated fashion. If they are not contiguous, you can edit a sequence together and make them that way.

To export multiple frames in a sequence, select Sequential Files on your Export Graphic Options menu. If you are only exporting a portion of your sequence or of a clip, be sure to make a mark IN and OUT at the intended start and finish; otherwise the entire piece will export. When you save a sequence of files, you'll also probably want to put them in a separate folder. A desktop dump can become extremely messy.

 Although it may seem tempting to export these files over a network directly to a server or directly to a CD-ROM or other removable storage medium, this is not necessarily the best solution if the write-speed to that storage medium or server can't keep up with how fast the Xpress Pro can export. Instead, export to the fastest drive you can send to, which is usually your internal drive or one of your media drives. Once the export is completed, you can then transfer the saved files to the removable medium or server.

As you export sequential frames, Xpress Pro will take whatever name you assigned in the Save dialog and add a number, beginning at 001. So, for example, if you exported sequential files with the name "Untitled Sequence" (you DID name your sequence, didn't you?), Xpress Pro will name the first exported file Untitled Sequence 001, then Untitled Sequence 002, and so on until it finishes unloading each single frame in the marked sequence. From there, they can be moved for whatever purpose you intend. It's good to remember that some file formats produce larger files than others, so make sure you have plenty of drive space for the export. Unlike QuickTime and streaming media formats, in the event of a power outage, whatever individual files were exported will be usable. Just pick up the export with a new mark from wherever you left off. Or better yet, purchase an uninterruptible power supply. In the long run, you'll be thankful anyway.

AUDIO FILES

Later in the chapter, I'll discuss how to export complete information for using audio with digital audio workstations. These file types are specifically intended for working with entire sequences of audio using different interchange formats.

But first let's discuss the options when exporting single clips or sections of audio without the complexities of needing to define your sequence, individual audio edits, and transitions. You can create single audio files with Xpress Pro that can be used with a variety of applications, from the high-end audio workstations to a simple audio application.

Xpress Pro also has the ability to export individual or entire sequences of audio files. Select the sequence or the clip of the audio that you want to export. As with graphics and QuickTimes, you'll want to make marks and enable tracks according to your needs.

You can select a clip, sequence, subclip, or any other form of audio media. You can also select the audio by selecting it directly from a bin, but be mindful of the no-brainers—if you select Use Marks in your export dialog and the clip in the bin has no marks, there will be no audio exported.

There are two choices of audio format when exporting. WAV files originated with Windows PCs and now are compatible with QuickTime. They are not normally considered professional standard. The other format, AIFF-C is pretty much the industry standard. Almost all audio workstations and applications that use audio will accept an AIFF-C format.

You also have a sampling choice. If you intend to create a file for an audio CD, you'll want to use 44.1kHz sampling. If you're doing an export of DV material not intended for audio CD using 4 channels of sound, 32kHz is the normal sampling rate. And if you have audio sources sampled at the higher (and thus superior) rate of 48kHz, you can use those for the file. Again, the end purpose will normally define which setting to choose. You can also default to the sample chosen for your project.

The audio file can be exported as either mono or stereo. Any stereo exports will include any panning set in your edited sequence or source clip. Be careful not to inadvertently cause volume to double by panning one track center and the other to one side. When using stereo, WYHIWYG (what you hear is what you get). Fortunately, most audio exports go fairly quick. So if you mess it up, you can go back and reexport the file.

Finally, you must select a sampling size. Audio editing has developed to the point where sampling size is incredibly accurate. As a result, the old industry standard of 16-bit audio has been superseded by 24-bit, which is superior, but to most nonaudiophiles, not that detectable. You can choose the larger sampling, but before you do, make sure that wherever the file goes, the equipment can support it. Some audio facilities still use 16 bit and have no intention of changing that standard anytime soon. Better to drop a dime on the audio facility than to export the wrong sampling size. Audio post facilities also frequently have the ability to downsample. For most consumer audio uses and programs you are probably safest at 16 bit.

OMFI AND AAF

Exporting OMFI Files

Open Media Framework Interchange, also known as OMFI, is a file format that can be transferred to other platforms and other applications. It was developed primarily by Avid and is supported by a group of OMFI partners, developers, and software companies that cooperate with the standard in order to allow import and export of files and information using OMF formats.

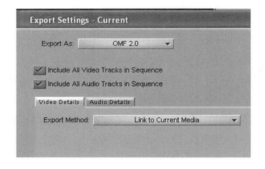

The intention is to allow one digital media application to allow import and export of files and compositions to another. By allowing the applications to "speak" to one another through importing and exporting, we, the users, don't have to deal with extreme measures, third-party software and any undocumented solutions to move media from, say, an editing application to an animation application. Over the years, OMF Interchange files have become accepted by most applications, and as a result, they are a very good way to move media, but only where both applications accept the format.

There are two different types of OMF file. Compositions are fairly small files that define how an exported sequence or sequences are constructed. These files primarily consist of what is referred to as metadata. Much like your sequence bins in Xpress Pro, these are data files *about* media and the way it is assembled—and don't consist of the media itself—so they do not take up a lot of space. The second type of OMF file is the media itself. You can export audio media, video media, or both. Audio is a much smaller file size.

Acceptance in the marketplace of OMF has been mixed, but one area that immediately embraced OMF was audio. Almost every audio workstation made has some form of OMF capability. As a result, exporting audio files and compositions through OMF is quite common.

OMF comes in two flavors: version 1.0 is supported by older audio workstations and works quite well in most situations; version 2.0 was developed a little later and incorporated some changes. The result is that more applications can use OMFI. Once again, before deciding on whether to use 1.0 or 2.0, the best bet is to call the facility that will be using the file and talk directly with the engineer who will be using the files. Once you've created a successful test, name the Export Setting for the name of the facility it's going to.

Exporting AAF Files

Another form of export is AAF, Advanced Authoring Format. AAF is very similar in concept to OMFI and it does basically the exact same thing. That is, you can export sequence information (compositions) in AAF or you can export compositions with embedded audio and video media.

Why the two different standards? Whenever you get commercial software developers to allow some form of access to proprietary software, compression, and functionality, it gets tricky. Some applications are OMF-compliant, others are AAF-compliant. Your Xpress Pro is both. So long as there is some method of moving media from one application to another, it's good, right?

Whether your target application is OMF- or AAF-compliant, the methods of export are exactly the same.

Exporting OMFI and AAF Compositions and Media

Now that you've gone through the trouble of determining which form of OMF or AAF you will be exporting, let's do the export. Just like any other export, it begins with selecting the item to be exported (i.e., a sequence or a clip) then File>Export.

Click on the Options button and the Export Options window appears. Select your format in the Save As pulldown menu. You can choose between OMFI 1.0, OMFI 2.0 and AAF. The types of options for each format are exactly the same, so you're just determining which type of interchange file will be created.

The next decision is what you want to export to the interchange format and how it will be exported. You can:

- *Export an OMFI or AAF file with links to the Current Media:* Choosing this method will create a composition file that has links to the media that is already on your system. If you choose this method and send this file to another system, the application that uses it will have to be able to recapture the media in order to bring it online. Compositions are very small files, so this method is great for sending through ethernet or small media drives.

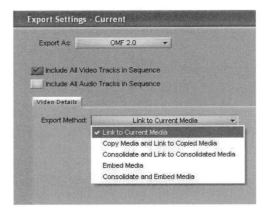

- *Copy Media and Link to Copied Media: This* is the method to choose if you want to make copies of the media on another drive and create a composition with links to that media in its new location.

- *Consolidate Media and Link to Consolidated Media:* If you're in a situation where the sequence is long and needs to be consolidated so that you do not have huge amounts of media files from the original clips, you can consolidate it first. ("Consolidating" on page 126 in Chapter 4 "Media Management" contains much more information on consolidation and transcoding.) Doing this will make the resulting media files fewer and smaller. This option, like the previous Copy Media option, creates links between the composition and the resulting media files. Normally it is used for moving onto a separate drive when the project needs to go to another system.

- *Embed Media:* Using the Embed function will create one single file with both the composition and the media files enclosed. So long as you have a drive big enough to support it, embedding media is a good way to keep track of your media. But make sure that the target application can support it. This makes a nice clean package to deliver, but it definitely puts all your eggs in one basket. It's a big file that will take a while to create, and if it isn't perfect, it's useless.

- *Consolidate and Embed Media:* This last Export option will consolidate the media first, so that you do not have a lot of extra media embedded in the file, then it will embed it into a single file.

Once you've chosen a method of export for audio and video files, save and export.

Some Caveats for OMFI and AAF Exports

An important note to Macintosh users: when exporting SDII files, OMFI and AAF cannot embed this file type. To fix the problem, export with links to the files, so long as the target application and system can read SDII. Without linking the files, they will not import correctly through these interchange formats. Also, SDII files are not compatible with PCs, so this is a less-than-ideal sharing medium.

Note   Project settings and interchanges: If you have a project with a rate of 23.976 fps but the audio was captured at 29.97 fps, the interchange formats will not accept this.

Using AvidLinks for OMFI and AAF Export

In order to make the OMFI and AAF export process simpler, Xpress Pro has a shortcut method of getting the information out. This shortcut is called AvidLinks. AvidLinks uses specific templates to allow you to do quick exports to other Avid applications. Using the AvidLinks function will save you the time of developing templates and manually exporting. You might compare this function to something like a wizard for developing OMFI and AAF files without the trouble of configuring them.

In Xpress Pro, there are three different AvidLinks for export. You can choose between AudioVision, Digidesign ProTools, and Avid|DS. Each AvidLink uses a different template. AudioVision exports an OMFI 1.0 file with embedded AIFF-C audio media. The ProTools AvidLink exports as an OMFI 2.0 file with options for either embedded or external AIFF-C files. The Avid|DS export uses AAF composition only files with links to the media.

To use the AvidLinks function, choose the media objects that you want to export in your bin. Select File>AvidLinks (see Figure 14.14). The AvidLinks choices will appear in a submenu (see Figure 14.15). Select the application. A Save menu appears. Select the destination and change the filename if necessary. The file is exported.

PROJECTS BETWEEN SYSTEMS

One of the biggest advantages of using Xpress Pro is compatibility. The projects and bins created on your system are compatible with other Avid systems. This can make a huge difference when the need for moving from one system to another occurs. You can also transfer Site Settings, User Settings, and Project Settings right along with your project in a very easy manner.

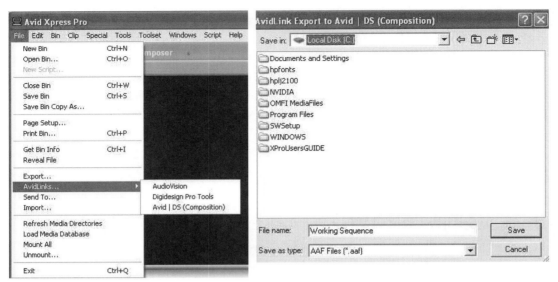

14.14   AvidLinks Menu Selection   14.15   AvidLinks Options Menu

Combine this with the fact that your system dongle can move to another computer and it is both Mac- and PC-compatible—it makes for a lot of versatility.

Exporting the necessary project and user files is fairly straightforward and can be done in just a few minutes. In Chapter 4 "Media Management" we discussed how to move project media. In this instance, we're just moving files and settings, not the media itself. The result is a smaller set of files that could fit on a floppy, a CD-ROM, USB thumb drive, or other portable storage.

My personal preference for storage is a thumb drive, one of those little USB thingies that look sort of like dongles but contain storage. Mine holds 256MB, enough for any project, Settings files, and a lot more space left for anything else I want to add. The obvious advantage is that you can put these little drives in your pocket or on a keychain. Most of these work with both Macs and PCs, so you can even store some files that work cross-platform, like Microsoft Word or Excel spreadsheets.

The business of exporting projects between systems was covered previously in Chapter 4. If you're following this book from cover to cover, that was quite a ways back! So, to refresh your memory, we'll discuss it again, adding a few extra tips to see if you paid attention. To transfer a project, first locate your Avid Projects folder and open it. Find the project that you want to move and drag it to your target drive. It's that simple (see Figure 14.16).

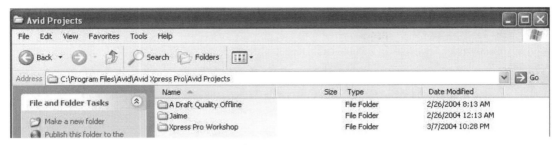

14.16 *Project Folders on an Xpress Pro Windows System*

There are a few caveats for moving projects. Both your source and target systems have to have compatible releases of Avid applications, otherwise the bins might be incompatible. In other words, you will not succeed if you intend to move a project from say, your Xpress Pro to an Avid Media Composer NuBus system, circa 1994. Before moving your project, be sure that the target system can read your project bins.

Here's another important consideration: the fonts need to be installed on both systems in order for the titles to look the same. Without this, you're probably going to have to do some adjusting of the titles before continuing the project on the target system.

Finally, make sure the bins and fonts work on the new system before blowing away your media on the source system. There is nothing worse than moving a project, then discovering that it will have to go back to its original system, knowing full well that you deleted all of your media. Time is precious. Choose your steps wisely!

Since project files are generally small files, it may be a good idea to email them or FTP them to the new system and do a quick test to see that the files arrived in good order and are compatible. You could even Re-create Title Media before any of the other media had arrived to check that the fonts and Title tool information worked as expected.

PROJECTS AND BINS TO AVID|DS

You might already know that Avid has a high-end compositing and HD system known as Avid|DS. This system was originally developed by a company known as SoftImage, which was acquired by Avid. The architecture and functionality of the Avid|DS is unique. As a result, if you want to export a project or bins to Avid|DS, you'll need to do more than drag and drop. To transfer between the two, you have to export using Avid File Exchange format.

Avid File Exchange is relatively new. It is compatible with Avid|DS systems v6.0 and above. It allows Avid|DS users to conform projects in high-end systems that were originally edited in Xpress Pro.

To export in Avid File Exchange, select the Project window or the bin to be exported, then choose File>Export. The Export menu opens. Under the Save As Type, select Avid File Exchange. The project or bin will export.

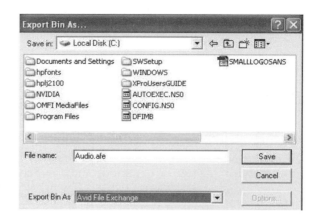

Avid File Exchange is a one-way format. You can export in AFE, but Xpress Pro does not allow import of AFE files.

BINS TO DATABASE APPLICATIONS

If you like to use database applications and are developing a digital archive of information about your footage, you can export your bins to tab-delimited files for import into most database systems. The tab-delimited file is the most common text file format used by database applications, and exporting a bin using this format is very simple.

There are a couple of things to remember when exporting as tab-delimited. The first is, WYSIWYG (what you see is what you get). In other words, whatever information is shown in the current display of the bin is exactly what will show up in the tab-delimited file. Be sure to set the proper bin headings so that all of the information that you need is contained in the bin before exporting the tab-delimited file.

Interestingly, a file exported as tab-delimited will not include bin headers. You can, however, export the file as Avid Log Exchange format, which will include the headers. Either file can be read on most database and spreadsheet applications.

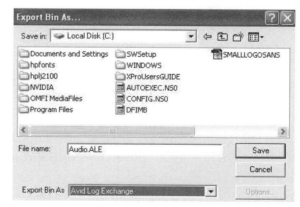

MAKE, MANAGE, AND MOVE

Avid Technology has claimed that their projects "Make, Manage, and Move" media. With so many export options, it's no wonder. You can customize and create many export templates for every different potential use. Choosing and creating the correct Export options can be as unique as your User Settings.

To simplify things a bit, we've included some common Export Settings for all formats on the DVD-ROM. Using these Settings makes drag-and-drop exporting a cinch. Be sure to load these Settings into your machine and try them out.

Here's how to do it: find the Settings file named Export on the DVD. Copy it to the Avid Users folder on your computer. With Xpress Pro running and the Settings selected in the Project window, select File>Open Setting File. Navigate your way to the Export file that was copied into the Avid User folder and open it. The file opens in a separate window. You can select each Setting from the Export Settings file window and drag it to the active Settings area of your Project window. Once you've loaded the settings, try them out and customize to your own specifications.

Appendix

AVX Effects from A to Z

AVX stands for Avid Visual Extensions; it allows third-party plug-ins that are written specifically for Avid effects architecture to link with Xpress Pro and Avid's other editing products to provide increased effects capability.

There are two main ways that these plug-ins link with the host application. One is to adopt the Avid interface, so that when you are setting parameters and interfacing with the plug-in, the effect seems to be completely a part of the rest of the Avid interface. The other method is for the plug-in to provide an interface that is completely outside of the Avid interface. These types of plug-ins usually take more time to master because they function almost as if they were a new program, but they are also generally much more feature-rich. As you examine the screenshots from the various plug-in manufacturers it is quite obvious which ones adopt the Avid interface and which provide their own. Don't let these interfaces influence your opinion of whether they will be powerful enough for you or too difficult to master. There are powerful plug-ins that use the Avid interface and "foreign" interfaces that are easy to master.

Additionally, there are two different AVX versions, 1 and 1.5. (Avid is currently developing AVX version 2.) One of the most interesting qualities of AVX 1.5 is that the plug-in manufacturers can use the Sequence (or Effect) Monitor to display plug-in interface information. The first plug-in I ever saw that used the Sequence Monitor was

SpeedRamp, by 3-Prong. It displays a ramp of motion effect speed changes in the Monitor. For many of the plug-ins that use a custom interface, such as the Ultimatte plug-in or SpiceMaster, you access the custom interface by using the Options button, which is generally located at the top left corner of the Effect Editor.

Warning Having numerous AVX effects installed in your AVX folder can cause launching Xpress Pro to be quite slow. Don't load new AVX effects at crucial times. Allow plenty of time for troubleshooting, and be patient the first time you launch after loading new AVX effects. If you watch the bottom of the Avid splash screen during launch, you can see when the system is checking for, and linking, all of the AVX effects. Try to only load one new plug-in at a time. This will help you troubleshoot which effect is the cause of any problems. Also, if you have a lot of AVX effects and know you'll be doing sessions that won't require them, you can temporarily move them to their own "Disabled AVX Effects" folder. This will allow the system to launch quicker.

There's not really much to say about AVX effects without discussing the specifics of the individual third-party effects. AVX effects, when installed, appear in your Effects Palette along with all of the other effects. Applying them is the same as applying any other effect.

Installing AVX effects is a pretty simple affair. Generally they are self-guided installations that automatically put everything in the right place. Some plug-ins ask you to identify the proper folder where you want the plug-in to be placed. In those instances, navigate to your Avid Xpress Pro folder/Supporting Files/AVX Plugins.

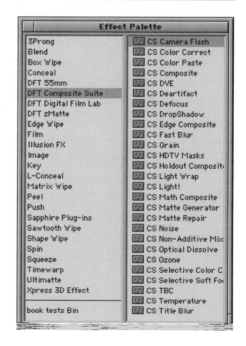

The more RAM in your computer, the better off you are for rendering AVX effects. RAM helps increase the chunks of visual data that have to be passed back and forth between the plug-in and the CPU. Processor speed also helps. But don't be too afraid of AVX. Many effects render quite quickly.

Most plug-ins allow you to download the latest versions from their web site. We have included many AVX plug-ins on the DVD, but we also encourage you to check out the web sites of the AVX vendors for the most up-to-date versions of their plug-ins, especially if you are reading this after 2004. Most plug-in vendors are also very good at offering support, tips, training, and "goodies" on their web sites.

For a list of all the current AVX partners, the web site www.avid.com/partners/avx/displaypartners.html should have an up-to-date listing. The list used to create this appendix was downloaded in early November 2003. Since then, new partners may have been added and others may no longer be providing solutions for Avid. Also, some of the vendors who only provide solutions for Macs or PCs may have added the other platform.

Let's explore some of the solutions from the individual vendors.

3-PRONG

www.3Prong.com

3-Prong has numerous plug-ins for Avid. You already have some of 3-Prong's technology inside your Xpress Pro without ever downloading their software: they developed the waveform/vectorscope displays in the Color Corrector. All 3-Prong effects use the Avid effects interface.

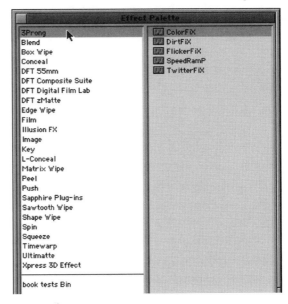

ColorFiX (Mac and PC)

ColorFiX is a color correction plug-in that provides you with dozens of additional color correction controls for your Xpress Pro. Before the widespread dispersal of color correction capabilities to the lower-end Avid products, ColorFiX was an indispensable tool for doing fine color correction on any non-Symphony Avid. ColorFiX still offers capabilities that are beyond those of the built-in Color Corrector in Xpress Pro.

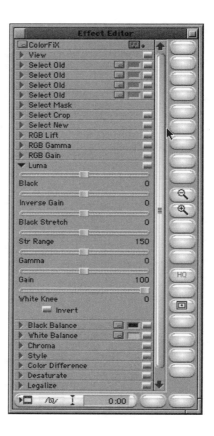

Primary in these abilities is Secondary Color Correction, allowing you to select a color range and change it to a new range without affecting other colors in the image that are outside of that range. To accomplish this, you select the range with the Select Old parameters, which include an Eyedropper for selecting the color you want to replace. You can even select multiple colors by using the other Select Old parameters. Then you can adjust these ranges using the Select Mask parameter, which includes the ability to expand or contract the luminance or chrominance range, tolerance, blur the matte that is created by the selection, and blend the resulting color change back in to the original. The new replacement color is chosen with the Select New parameter.

 Use each of the Select New parameters to choose the extremes of the range of colors you want to select, for example, the most or least saturated portions of a specific color or extremes in luminance or hue. Then use Join and the Select Mask options to combine them. There is also an Exclude option to deselect a specific portion of the entire range.

Additional noteworthy parameters include View, which allows you to switch between the Input, Output, and Mask. The Mask is especially useful when doing secondary corrections, to see how much of the image is being affected by the selections. Make sure that you disable View (the box to the right should be gray, not purple) before rendering. If you leave it enabled, you will render either the input or the mask—which could actually be useful! Mute Legal turns all the legal portions of the picture black and white, leaving illegal colors at full chroma. There's also a "featherable" cropping tool to further isolate corrections.

The tools for fine-tuning tonal ranges are very well refined, though they are all based on simple sliders, which is fairly unintuitive.

Black Balance and White balance controls allow for automatic balancing of color casts. Note that if you click on the Options button, it calls up the Color Picker which has a magnifying glass in the top left corner. This icon allows you much more accurate control in eyedropping your colors.

Styles provide you with control over two of my least favorite effects: solarize and posterize. But, hey, if you've got a need for them, they're here.

Color difference gives you slider controls for the Cr and Cb, which are the color difference channels. This is not a very intuitive method of altering colors, and I'd suggest that if you've got the power of Xpress Pro, you use that instead of playing with these particular parameters.

Desaturate allows you to control attenuation of chroma values in just the whites and blacks, leaving the midranges alone. This is an effective method of losing color casts in the areas where they are most obvious, many times without interfering with the other tonal ranges.

Legalize offers several important color ranges that can be limited selectively.

For more information on how to use ColorFiX go to the folder Xpress Pro>Supporting Files>AVX Folder>3Prong>3PAVXUGContents.html. This calls up the help for all of the 3-Prong effects.

DirtFiX (Mac and PC)

DirtFiX allows you to remove film scratches and dirt as well as tape dropouts and hits.

The basic operation is extremely simple. You create a box around the problem spot, adding keyframes to each field of video that is affected. DirtFiX then uses clean portions of other frames or fields to repair the problem.

Although this is very similar to the Scratch Removal feature on some Avid products (Symphony, Adrenaline, and late-model Media Composers), there are some differences. One of the nice differences is that with DirtFiX, only fields with keyframes are affected, so fields without problems do not become "contaminated" with problems from adjoining fields. If DirtFiX doesn't appear to be working, the most common error is that no keyframe has been set.

Scratch Removal can be applied in several ways, but one of the easiest ways allows the Scratch Removal button to automatically add edits when it is applied. This saves render time and additional keystrokes in adding the Add Edits around the effect. DirtFiX cannot operate like this, so it is necessary to add edits around the problem footage manually.

It is possible to add DirtFiX to a shot as a transition effect instead of the typical segment effect concept, so you could add a single edit at your defect and apply DirtFiX to the Add Edit itself. If you try this method, the effect should be centered on the transition.

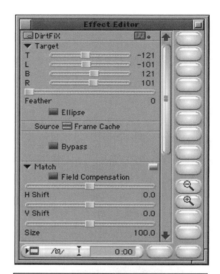

Also, while Scratch Removal can remove multiple hits or pieces of dust using a single effect, DirtFiX requires a separate layer and effect for each "hit."

As of this writing, DirtFiX will not work with real-time Effects Preview on, so you need to click on the little green Real-Time Effects button in the upper right corner of the Timeline. If that button is blue, then DirtFiX will work fine. Once the effects are rendered, the real-time effects can be reset to "on."

FlickerFiX (Mac and PC)

FlickerFiX removes flicker or other changes in brightness, contrast, and color levels. I have used this to even out exposure shifts when cameramen shoot using auto-iris controls. It can also solve some problems with fluorescent lights or film transfers. However, FlickerFiX cannot remove some types of flickers, like instances when the foreground and background are flickering in different ways.

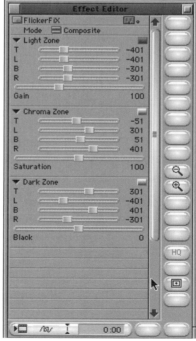

FlickerFiX measures the average luminance levels within a user-defined zone. Operationally, this is pretty simple. When you click on the Other Option button, FlickerFiX takes a snapshot of the values; then, while it renders each flickering field, the differences in the levels are analyzed and adjustments are made automatically to match the reference.

The main tip with FlickerFiX is that you definitely don't want to use every parameter with which you are presented. For most of your problems, use the Composite mode with the Light Zone only enabled. This is the default.

Just drop a FlickerFiX on a segment, go into Effects mode and drag the Light Zone box from the upper left corner to a light section of the image that doesn't have much movement or detail. If there's a lot of movement in the shot, you may need to add keyframes to hand-track the area selected. Pick a field with the level you'd like to use as a reference, then just press the Other Options button to set the reference value. Click OK and render.

Placing these zones is critical to successfully removing flicker. Choosing an area where contrasting detail doesn't move in or out of the zone is important, since this detail can be accidentally perceived by the software as flickering levels. The selected zones must remain unobscured during the entire course of the effect.

The Light Zone measures and fixes gain flicker. (Gain flicker is seen in a waveform monitor as movement in the top, highlight portion of the waveform.) Make sure that the bright area you choose is not clipping, since this will minimize the changes in luminance levels between dark and light.

The Chroma Zone measures and fixes flicker in Saturation. This should be used if chrominance levels are flickering, which is fairly rare. Try to place this in a saturated area with several different colors.

The Dark Zone measures offset flicker. (Offset flicker can be seen in a waveform monitor as movement in the bottom, shadow area of the waveform.) Place this over a dark and unsaturated area of the image. Once again, try to avoid any areas where the blacks are crushed.

Sometimes, problems that you can't solve with FlickerFiX can be solved with TwitterFiX, which uses field blending to average out any differences. TwitterFiX is separate from FlickerFiX but is not sold separately. Its operation is so simple and obvious, I'll just include it here. All TwitterFiX does is blend the two fields of a frame together. This can eliminate the flickering of fine detail, like fine lines in computer-generated graphics from imported third-party programs like Adobe Photoshop, Adobe After Effects, or Alias Maya; or in footage shot of line art or printed material, like newspapers. The only parameter in this effect is the amount of blending. The most effective amount of blending is the default of 50 percent, so you generally shouldn't adjust the parameters once it's applied.

SpeedRamP (Mac and PC)

With SpeedRamP, you can smoothly change motion speed or fix motion problems, such as 3:2 pulldown artifacts.

As many as nine different keyframes can be set to vary speed changes within a clip. In addition to the ability to "ramp" speed changes, its many other options allow increased image quality over the basic Avid motion effects. Since Avid has added Timewarp effects,

Image courtesy of Artbeats.

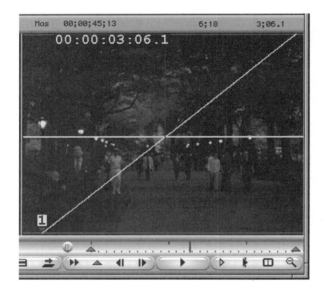

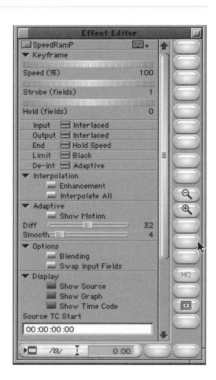

there is *slightly* less need for SpeedRamp, but the Timewarp effects are incredibly limited in what they can do compared to SpeedRamP.

Warning

In order to operate SpeedRamP, you must turn off Real-Time Effects in the upper left corner of the Timeline. It is the fairly big green button next to the word "Avid" in the Timeline. Once the effect is set and rendered, you can toggle Real-Time Effects back on.

Generally speaking the more control and power that a piece of software gives you, the longer the learning curve. That's essentially true with SpeedRamp. It is a very powerful plug-in for dealing with motion and field issues of many types. Learning how to control this power will take a little time, but luckily, the Help files and tutorial that are provided with SpeedRamP are excellent. Use them to familiarize yourself with what the product is capable of before you plunk down your hard-earned cash. My guess is that if you have the patience to learn this software, you'll decide you can't live without it.

One of the main tricks with SpeedRamP is that it operates differently than Avid motion effects, which are created as sources and cut into the sequence at their proper speed. SpeedRamp can work on the clip in the Timeline, but if you are slowing down an effect, then you will not see all of the footage that is in the Timeline clip. For example, if you drop a 50 percent SpeedRamP on a 5-second clip, the clip cannot get any longer in the Timeline, so you will still have a 5-second clip, but you will only see the first 2 seconds and 15 frames of the clip in its slo-mo'd state. So in anticipation of using SpeedRamP, you want to make your clip length be the final length, but understand that once the clip is slowed down, not all of it will be seen.

The other trick is with speeded up shots. SpeedRamP does not have access to any of the footage that is not in the Timeline, so if you want to create a 5-second clip at 200 percent speed, you need to cut a 10-second clip into your Timeline. However, since the clip is running through frames twice as fast, the Timeline segment will actually cut to black halfway through the clip once it is rendered. You cannot trim away the remaining black. To cut to your next shot before the black, you must add the next shot on the video track above the speeded up segment.

One of the coolest things SpeedRamp can do—that you don't really pick up from its name—is to simulate the look of film by simulating the look of 3:2 pulldown. The way film—shot at 24 frames per second—is interpolated into NTSC video—running at 29.97 frames per second—means that one film frame is recorded on two video fields, then the next film frame is recorded on three video fields. This causes a slight strobing that people associate with footage shot on film. Even though this causes undesirable motion artifacts, people associate these artifacts with film, which is perceived to have greater value. Thorough directions for achieving this film-look are in the Help documents with the plug-in.

Alternately, if you actually shot film and want to do slo-mo in the Avid, SpeedRamP is the way to go, since it can account for the 3:2 pulldown of the film and create much smoother slo-mo than the basic Avid motion effect that treats every frame the same.

A useful, though possibly intimidating component of SpeedRamP is the graphical interface that shows up in the Effects Monitor. This graph represents source time against program time. If the yellow line in the graph is moving from lower left to upper right, then time is moving forward, if it is running from lower right to upper left, then time is running backwards. (In Avid motion effects terminology, this would be a negative speed effect.) A straight horizontal line indicates a freeze or pause and the steeper the line, the faster the speed. The graph is not a user interface. It is purely informational.

WaveScope (Mac[1] and PC)

The WaveScope plug-in allows you to have access to a luminance waveform, a composite waveform, an RGB Parade waveform, a YCbCr waveform, a vectorscope, an RGB Histogram, and a YCbCr Histogram.

The easiest way to use this plug-in is to apply it to its own video layer, which should be the topmost track. With Render on the Fly enabled, the scopes will appear in your monitor, just like any other unrendered effect. If you want to see them moving, you'll need to render the effect for the duration that you want to examine. (The trial mode only monitors the bottom half of the image, until you pay for the plug-in.)

Each of the scopes has color coding to help detect illegal levels. There are numerous parameters that can be set to control the "look" of the display and the customizable signal limits that will trigger warning colors.

Obviously, there are scopes in Xpress Pro, but if you're looking for scopes that are available in editing mode, this will fill the bill. I'm a big advocate of scopes in general, but if you are creating a product for broadcast, I have to recommend putting the money that you might spend on WaveScope into a real-time, high-resolution, "outboard" scope such as those made by Leader, Tektronix, and VideoTek. But WaveScope is better than not monitoring your signal at all.

ASTON   www.astondes.com

Pico plug-in (PC only)

Pico is Aston's plug-in for doing titling. This is one of several CG options if you're looking for something better than the Title tool. (See the rest of the AVX plug-ins for other titling options.) I would recommend the Aston AVX product if there are other Aston products in your facility. Pico is essentially the same as Aston's offline CG generator, Ego. It allows you to interface with their other hardware-based products. Another consideration in buying CG products is whether it is available as a stand-alone product, so that CG work can be done on another machine, then imported. This is the case with Pico, which allows you to create titles with their Ego product offline. Ego is free for downloading, so you could even have a client, producer, or other postproduction partner create titles for you, or approve and edit titles that you've completed.

Also, if you are considering switching the platform or OS of your editing workstation, you will want to make sure that the product is available on that platform or OS—though these availabilities change over time as manufacturers add or drop their support for cer-

---

1. As of the writing of this book, this plug-in could be installed on a Mac but did not work. The problem is expected to be fixed.

tain platforms. Pico, as with all of the other title generators, uses a custom interface instead of the Avid Effects interface.

Another consideration for purchasing software plug-ins is what features it has and how much the software "thinks" like you do. Some people find certain programs very intuitive, while others do not. Since most of these programs can be downloaded for free, try them out to find which one is right for you. Some may have more features, and a steeper learning curve. Some may provide just what you need and not much more. Find what's right for you, but also consider how universally the software is used if you intend to use freelancers or will hire other editors to work with the software.

BORIS   www.borisfx.com

Boris is one of the pillars of the AVX partnership. It has a variety of products that are found in many Avids around the world. Boris's support for Adobe After Effects and other NLEs also adds to its appeal, adding to the number of people that are familiar with the standard interface. Boris products also have the useful ability to be run as stand-alone products, apart from Xpress Pro, so that effects work can be designed on a separate machine, freeing up the Xpress Pro for editing and other functions.

Boris Continuum (Mac and PC)

Continuum is one of the AVX plug-ins that uses the Avid interface, making the learning curve a little easier. There are more than 90 filters that are part of Continuum, including Film Grain, Light Zoom, Cartooner, Vector Displacement, Particles, and natural filters such as Fire, Rain, Snow, Sparks and Stars. Continuum allows you to animate all these effects over time, including the ability to animate 3D lights and cameras and the ability to map video to 3D shapes.

Although there isn't enough room in this appendix to go through all 90+ filters, the basic categories of effects are:

- *Color and Blur:* About 20 filters allow for altering the colors of a clip, plus blur
- *Distortion and Perspective:* About 20 filters for 3D shape and particle effects
- *Effects filters:* About 20 filters for a variety of effects, such as Film Damage
- *Generators filters:* About 20 filters for generating marble, brick, clouds, comets, fire, snow, sparks, etc.
- *Key and Matte filters:* About 10 filters for choking mattes, affecting alpha channels, etc.

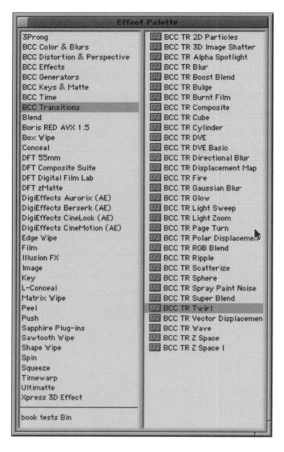

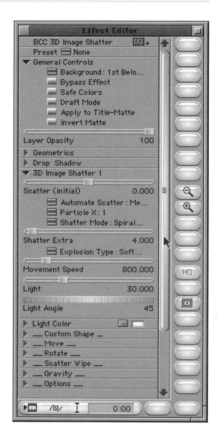

There are also a variety of Time filters which allow for smooth ramping of video speeds and real motion blur. These temporal motion effects are more advanced than the ones allowed in the regular Xpress Pro interface.

The Avid-style interface is simplified, but there's still a lot to learn once you install Continuum, as proven by the 500+ page manual that comes with the plug-in. However, to simplify operations and get you up and running as fast as possible there are a wide range of drag-and-drop preset effects. These effects can be customized or left as is. And you can create your own preset effects.

One of the advantages of Continuum is that the filters, when applied to Avid Titles, only affect the title itself and not the background video. One common editors' complaint is when effects manipulate both the Title and the background.

Some of my favorite things in the package include the Displacement Map filter, which uses luminance from one source to displace (distort) the pixels of another source. There are even a group of special displacement map images provided with Continuum that you can use as transitions. Particle effects using Grid spacing is a great transitional device, especially when used with custom shapes. The Cartooner filter uses edge detection to draw outlines, turning a video source into a cool, animated outline. You've got to be very subtle when adjusting parameters in this effect. I was always a big fan of DigiEffects' Aged Film effect, and Boris Continuum has a similar effect called Film Damage that provides a real look to footage by adding scratches, dirt, hair, grain, and water spots. It also allows you to add flicker and shake to make the footage appear like it's being projected. Shake imitates projector transport problems and gate weave. Light Zoom is a popular look, especially on Titles. And Continuum has a Jitter filter that allows you to randomly jitter a number of parameters—such as geometrics—over time.

A new version is due around the time of the publication of this book that will include the only real-time AVX plug-ins from a third-party developer.

Boris FX (Mac and PC)

For many people who are not satisfied with the 3D DVE effects of even the high-level Avid products, Boris FX has long been the de facto Avid effects engine. Boris FX is billed as "an integrated effects application." Its capabilities go well beyond 3D DVE moves, including compositing, particle effects, filters, importing files with resolution independence, and acting as a bridge to many Adobe After Effects plug-ins. It also offers real-time previews of many effects by using the effects power of the OpenGL card in your system.

As with the other AVX effects, having these capabilities inside your Xpress Pro allows you to complete effects without the need to export and re-import your video to and from a third-party effects package. However, all that power means that the learning curve is substantially higher than most AVX plug-ins because you're essentially driving a whole new application that is simply piggy-backed onto the host. And unlike Continuum, the user interface for Boris FX and Red are definitely not the Avid interface. It is much more After Effects–like, with its own Timeline and menu structure.

While inside of the FX plug-in, the effects are independent of the video resolution constraints of Xpress Pro, except for the video used from the Xpress Pro's Timeline. But QuickTime files and other media imported directly into the FX Timeline are not constrained by resolution. In addition FX offers Vector Paint tools for masking and compositing, Vector spline editing for rotoscoping and masks, and Spline Primitives, such as heart, wedge, and grid shapes, which can be used for many purposes. You can even import Adobe Illustrator or EPS files as splines.

If all of that sounds like too much to grasp on top of all the other software applications you have to master, then do what I do and use the Boris Library Browser to access hundreds of preset effects. Even if you have the time to dive into the myriad effects and parameters that FX provides, the preset effects are a fast way to get an effect started. I don't know of anybody who's not under some kind of deadline and having a jumping-off point for effects can help you spend less time on effects and more time on the rest of the project. These prebuilt effects are in the Keyframe Library, which on a Windows computer is automatically installed to the Users Install Directory\Boris FX, Inc.\Keyframe Libraries\FX Keyframe Library. On a Mac it goes to Library\Application Support\BorisFX\FX Keyframe library.

Operation of Boris FX takes place in its four main windows and its own set of menus. The main windows (clockwise from upper left) are the Controls window, which provides access to the parameter sliders and other controls; the Composite window, which allows you to see your effect and do some hands-on manipulation; the Timeline window, which allows you to add keyframes and manipulate effects on an unlimited number of video tracks; and the Project window, which is kind of a cross between Avid's Project window and a bin.

The tutorials in the documentation are a good place to start for an understanding of the basics. If you don't like tutorials, then open a new project from the File menu and navigate to the Keyframe Library described previously. Ctrl+0/Cmd+0 will play the effect as a RAM preview. There are hundreds of effects. Find the ones you like and deconstruct them to see how they work. Once you get good enough to create your own from scratch, you can save them to the Library Browser for easy recall.

Boris Graffiti (Mac and PC)

Boris Graffiti (see next page) creates broadcast-quality vector titles and graphics. Graffiti's titles can be still, animated, 2D, or 3D. Features include animatable vector paint for creating write-on effects, animated kerning, and custom vector backdrops. Graffiti can animate text on a path and has spline tools that can create paths and even alter the shapes of individual letters. Additionally, you can apply any of over 20 filters to titles to create unique title effects. Graffiti is OpenGL accelerated and ships with hundreds of preset effects so you can get started quickly. One of the cool features—similar to Avid's own Marquee Text tool—is Convert to Container, which places each letter on a separate track so they can be individually animated. Obviously, Graffiti uses a custom interface instead of Avid's effect interface.

Like the other Boris products, Graffiti has a number of preset effects for both static and animated titles that can be called up and modified.

Boris Red (Mac and PC)

Boris Red is the sum of the other three Boris products. Red combines the filters from Continuum, the effects from FX, and the titling from Graffiti in a single product. But because they are integrated, the whole is more than the sum of its parts. Red 3GL also includes a chart editor to create animated 2D and 3D motion charts, including line, bar, and pie styles. Red also allows you to import Adobe Illustrator/Photoshop layers for easier and quicker integration from those commonly used products. Red can even extrude 2D Illustrator files into 3D objects.

Because Red is basically a combination of the three other Boris products mentioned previously, I won't run down all of those same individual features again, but there are some things that are unique to the Red combo including motion tracking and stabilization (much better than that available in even the high-end Avids), corner pin, and a stand-alone effects "engine" that can run separately from the host. Also, some of the features updated or added in the latest version (as of the printing of this book), Red 3GL: an expanded 3D Effects Environment, direct placement and editing of Titles on a video image, and Optical Flow Technology, which is Boris's term for super smooth slo-mo.

Basically anytime you can't get an effect done with the built-in Avid effects, Red is the place to go. I have to admit that I do not use Red to its fullest extent. Red's documentation actually exceeds the documentation for Xpress Pro in pure volume, weighing in at nearly 1,300 pages. So, I tend to go in and modify the prebuilt effects so I can get back to

Boris Graffiti

editing, but even using such a limited amount of its capability, the program is indispensable.

In addition to the thorough documentation, Red 3GL has over 200,000 customers worldwide working with over 20 NLEs including Adobe, Apple, Avid, Canopus, DPS, Discreet, in:sync, Incite, Matrox, Media 100, Sony, and Ulead. Boris also has free (can you believe it?) phone tech support, and the 200,000 users mentioned above have developed a great online community at Boris's web site—a lot of combined wisdom to tap into.

CHYRON   www.chyron.com

Lyric Plug-in (PC only)

For the veteran editors, this titling product certainly would have a nostalgic appeal, if nothing else. Chyron is so ubiquitous as to have its brand-name stand for the entire product category, like Kleenex or Xerox. Despite the fact that I haven't created a CG on a Chyron product for at least 10 years, I still find myself telling producers, "I'll Chyron the

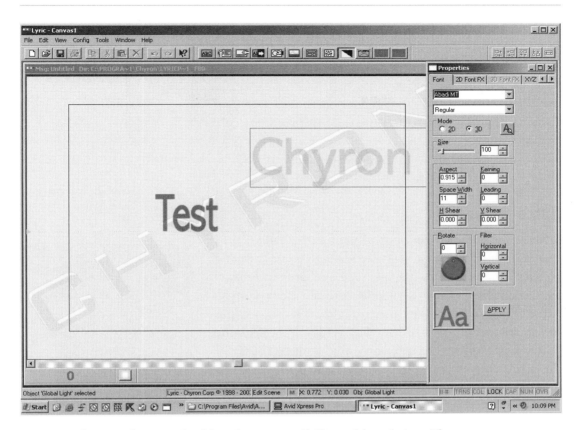

names in later." If you're looking for compatibility with existing Chyron or even some Quantel products in a facility, or you have the need to use CG work that has already been created on other Chyron products—like the Infinit! or Duet, then this is definitely the AVX plug-in for you. As with all of the other AVX plug-ins for CG, Lyric calls up a custom UI. This UI offers a ton of great formatting and import options for bringing in text, fonts, and graphics and allowing you to create style sheets and templates. All of this appears in a custom Chyron interface instead of the Avid effects interface.

Lyric allows for rolls, crawls, full-page titles, and lower-thirds. It can create keyframable animations and "FlipBook" animations. It can animate text on a curve and supports doing rolls and crawls in multiple simultaneous windows.

CLEAREFFECT

www.cleareffect.com

CLEAReffect manufacturers these plug-ins, which are bundled together with hardware by partner Ocean Systems. The following plug-ins are all part of the dTective system, which is a forensic video tool for analyzing crime scene video and surveillance camera footage.

Though the software can be purchased separately, Ocean Systems packages Avid hardware together with CLEAReffect software and training for a total package developed for police departments, legal firms, and private and government agencies. These plug-ins could be used in regular postproduction, but their intended purpose is specifically for forensic video analysis. All of these tools use the Avid effects interface, but some also have stand-alone versions that have their own interface.

dPlex (PC only)

dPlex is the generally the start of the forensic video analysis workflow. Most surveillance footage records multiple camera angles onto a single tape in a process known as multiplexing. dPlex allows the forensic video investigator to de-multiplex the camera angles, creating a single full-frame image (if that is what is desired). Without dPlex, much of this footage can only be played back by the proprietary video systems that created them. Many options are provided for selecting the camera and displaying other cameras as well. Once a single stream of video has been isolated from the multiplexed tape or datastream, the other dTective AVX effects can be applied to bring out lost detail or isolate important details.

DVELOPER (PC ONLY)

dVeloper uses frame averaging, gamma correction, and specialized filtration to remove noise, grain, and even obstructions from snow and rain to provide lost detail that is not available from a single frame of the footage. Multiple frames are captured and averaged together, eliminating noise and enhancing the usable detail in the image. This plug-in does not work on handheld or panning footage or with moving objects within a still frame. It

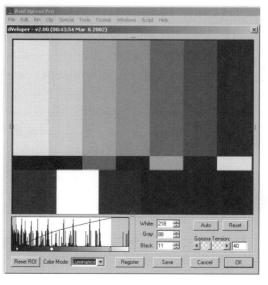

would be possible to use motion tracking and stabilization from another AVX plug-in like Boris Red to stabilize the image first, however.

MAGNIFi (PC only)

MAGNIFi allows the forensic specialist to zoom in to any user-defined area of video. This is not unlike a simple picture-in-picture effect or resize using Avid's built-in effects, except that the output area can be clarified using any of twelve mathematical filters. Also, where a typical PIP effect requires two video tracks, MAGNIFi can create a PIP with a zoomed-in version of a selected area keyed over the full frame footage using a single video track.

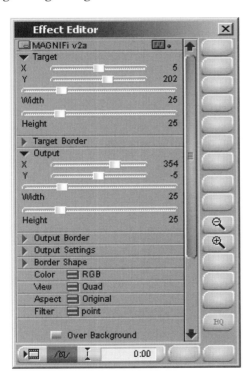

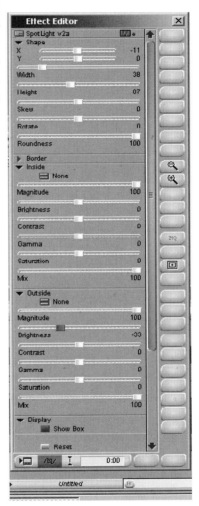

SpotLight (PC only)

SpotLight allows the forensic analyst to highlight an area of video that is of interest or to obscure an area to hide sensitive information. This tool is not really for analysis so much as it is for preparing a video to be viewed in court. If a person needs to be isolated in a crowd, the video specialist can use SpotLight to draw a shape around the person and darken or obscure the rest of the frame, helping to focus attention to the desired area of the frame. All of the tracking of the highlighted area must be done manually using key-frames.

DigiEffects   www.digieffects.com

DigiEffects had some of my favorite AVX plug-ins but it seems they have dropped AVX support for almost all of their products. Now their products are designed for Adobe PhotoShop and After Effects compatibility and DigiEffects promotes the use of Profound Effects' Elastic Gasket and Boris's RED and FX as bridges that allow their AE plug-ins to be used with Avid. Since these are no longer true AVX plug-ins, I won't go into them in detail, but the packages include Aurorix, Delerium, and Berserk as well as CineLook and CineMotion.

Digital Film Tools   www.digitalfilmtools.com
Composite Suite (Mac and PC)

Composite Suite includes 28 visual effects plug-ins that were, until a few years ago, only available in-house at Digital FilmWorks, a Los Angeles–based film effects facility. The Composite Suite plug-ins are aimed at those who need serious, specialized control over their composites. If you're happy dropping a Matte key in a Timeline or using the Luma key in the Avid Effects Palette, you probably don't need these plug-ins, but if you know what a premultiplied alpha is or whether a key needs to be choked, then you have got to have these plug-ins.

Just a list of the compositing plug-ins in the package should tell you if this is the package for you: Composite, Drop Shadow, Edge Composite, Holdout Composite, Light Wrap, Math Composite, Non Additive Mix, and Optical Dissolve, plus tools specifically designed for combining imagery such as fire, smoke, and explosions. There are also plug-ins for DVE, Matte Generator and Repair, Film and HDTV Masks, Film Grain and Noise, Fast Blur and Defocus, Selective Soft Focus, Deartifacting, Color Correction, and Light! for creating lighting effects that appear to have been the work of the D.P., but were actually added in post. As you can see, there's plenty for the serious compositor to drool over, but there are some really cool plug-ins for ordinary editors to quickly use on an everyday basis, too. Fast Blur (which you can download for free) is very nice, as is the cool-looking Camera Flash plug-in and the Selective Soft Focus, which allows you to do soft focus effects based on a matte that you can create in any number of ways. I like to use Selective Defocus using luminance as a matte. I also occasionally use the basic Composite effect instead of Avid's built-in Matte key for more control of the way the key looks on difficult effects.

For the more complex compositing work I usually depend on specialists who know more about the tools and craft than me, but if you love to composite realistic effects and you'd prefer to do it yourself, this suite of plug-ins is probably what you need. One thing I can say for this package is that this product has such great documentation that a lot of what I know about compositing came from the manuals that shipped with the product. Another thing that helps make these plug-ins quick and accessible is that they use the standard Avid Effects interface.

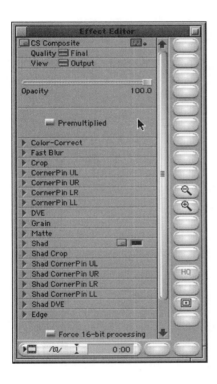

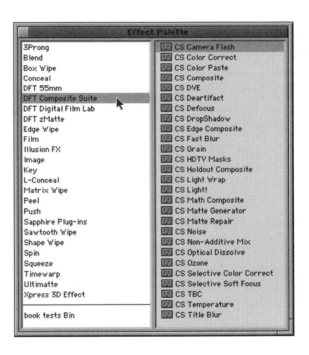

55MM (Mac and PC)

55mm simulates the look of popular glass camera filters, specialized lenses, and film and photographic processes. The set of plug-ins includes Black Mist, (my personal favorite) Black & White, Bleach Bypass, Center Spot, Color Correct, Color Grad, Combined Grad, Cool Mist, Defocus, Diffusion, Dual Tint, Fast Blur, Faux Film, Fluorescent, Fog, Glow, Grain, Infra-Red, Light!, Low Contrast, Matte Generator, Mist, ND Grad, Night Vision, Overexpose, Ozone, Polarizer, Selective Color Correct, Selective Grad, Selective Soft Focus, Skin Smoother, Star, Streaks, Temperature, Tint, Warm Mist, and Warm/Cool.

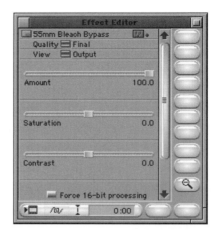

These are very nice, quick, drag-and-drop solutions to make your images look… well, sexier. All of the plug-ins have plenty of parameters that can be adjusted to get just the look you want, but they are also have very well set default parameters that allow them to be used very quickly without a lot of thought other than "Yeah, that looks very cool."

This is one of those plug-ins that you download, drop it on stuff and you'll know pretty much instantly whether you've just got to have it, or if you can do without.

Digital Film Lab (Mac and PC)

Digital Film Lab simulates a variety of film looks. The effect parameters that are available in the Effect Editor are Color Correct, Bleach Bypass, Low Contrast, Flashing, Overexpose, Diffusion, Blur, Grads, Grain, and Post Color Correct. You can also load one of over 150 preset looks, instead of tweaking your own.

The presets are not done like most other plug-ins, but they definitely save time. Basically, the guys at DigitalFilmTools tweaked the levels for you and saved them off to bins that they install into your AVX folder. So to use the presets, you go to File/ Open Bin and navigate to your AVX folder>DFT DigitalFilmLab folder>Effects Folder. Inside the effects folder are a series of bins with names like Black and White, Diffusion, and Looks.

Looks definitely had the coolest presets, including Bleach Bypass Cool, Color reversal, Day for Night, Nightvision, Punchy, and Warm Desaturated (which reminded me of watching "Starsky and Hutch" for some reason). I'd suggest opening all of the bins and making a master bin for these looks, then weeding through them and making another bin of just your favorites.

Color Correct manipulates the Black and White, Hue, Saturation, Brightness, Contrast and Gamma, Red, Green, Blue, and Tint values of the image. Bleach Bypass effectively superimposes a black and white image on a color image, increasing contrast and reducing saturation. Flashing is an optical process to lower contrast by flashing the image with light. Overexpose simulates the look of overexposed film. Diffusion reduces contrast and creates a glow around highlights or shadows. With Blur, the entire image or portions of the image can be blurred. Grad simulates Color Grad or ND (Neutral Density) Grad filters. Grads are especially good for improving the look of the sky. Grain simulates film. And Post Color Correct lets you add do more color work after all of the other operations have been processed.

zMatte (Mac and PC)

zMatte is a greenscreen and bluescreen keyer. I am a big fan of the Ultimatte AdvantEdge AVX plug-in, but if the steep price tag of the Ultimatte product is out of your league, then this could fill the bill for about one-fifth the price. zMatte is very quick at delivering a nice-looking initial key, but I had a trouble finessing some difficult-to-key items like smoke. zMatte uses the Avid Effects interface, which I think is a little limiting, but there are still some pretty good tools for manipulating the image after the initial key is set up. For pure quality, there are some better green- and bluescreen keyers out there, but there's nothing at this price point that matches it and it definitely blows away the Avid RGB keyer.

GenArts   web.genarts.com

Sapphire Plug-ins (Mac and PC)

The Sapphire plug-ins is a big collection (193 at last count) of very high-end effects. Obviously with a number like that, we can't discuss them all, but they all provide really unique looks to your projects as well as give your Avid increased, specialized compositing capabilities. The compositing stuff took a while for me to understand, but GenArts provides some excellent tutorials that walk you through them step by step. Basically their "RGBA" plug-ins solve the age-old Avid problem (Can you have an "age-old problem" on a product that was invented in the late '80s?) that effects added to higher tracks also sometimes affect lower tracks.

One of the cool features of Sapphire plug-ins is that they allow you to render at reduced resolutions so you can test the parameter settings of your effects faster. They also support dual-processor rendering to speed things up. Both of these are very good things, because some of the effects in this package really need some rendering horsepower, especially if you take certain parameters to extremes.

The groupings of effects include Light Effects like a Lens Flare that automatically tracks to a light source, Lightning, Glints and Glares, and Glows—including my personal favorite, Glow-Darks. There are also Blurs, Edge Effects including EdgeRays, Embosses, Lensing Effects, Stylize, Warps and Shakes, Wipe transitions (most of which are lame), Dissolve transitions (some interesting twists on the basic dissolve), Grain (including a nice Film effect for making video look like film), Fractal Clouds, Fog and Depth Effects, Kaleidoscope effects, Procedural textures, and a series of plug-ins under the names Color & Math Ops

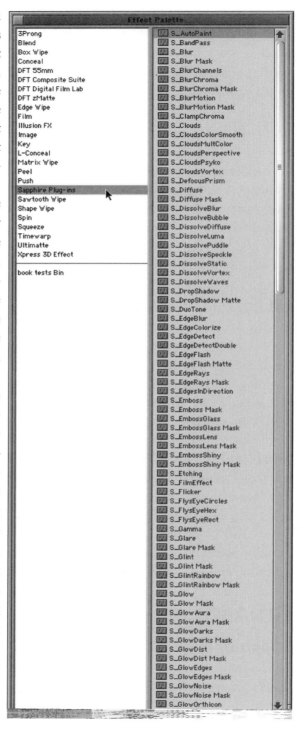

and Matte Operations, which provide you with sophisticated color and compositing tools.

Browsing through the looks that you can create with these plug-ins will probably make you drool, but some of the hidden depth to these effects is that many of them use multiple images to create very unique effects. For example, there are several plug-ins that allow you to make light rays shoot out from the edges of your images or from a matte key or title, but Sapphire has a twist on this effect that lets you use another image—still or moving—to create a matte for the rays of light, giving them much more life and energy by making them more organic looking. There is also an effect that allows you to control the amount that an image is blurred by using a grayscale image to determine the amount of blur applied—the brighter parts of the grayscale image are, the blurrier the corresponding parts of the primary image are.

If you are an effects wizard, or wish you were, this is definitely a set of plug-ins to check out. They can definitely add some "Wow!" power to a project. Some of these plug-ins, despite using the Avid Effects interface, do have a bit of a learning curve, but the HTML-based help is very well done and the initial default settings give good starting points for all of the effects.

INSCRIBER   www.inscriber.com

Inscriber TitleMotion AVX (PC only)

TitleMotion is a titling plug-in. I first used TitleMotion in a post facility that had a linear DigiBeta suite that included the full, hardware-based Inscriber CG. We started using the TitleMotion plug-ins for the four Avid suites so that we could move projects from room to room, including the DigiBeta suite. We easily swapped graphics from room to room and were able to have assistant editors prepare titles for sessions in other suites that were not being used. When picking one of the AVX plug-ins for your Avid Xpress Pro, one of the most important features is whether it is compatible with the other titling products in your facility or in the facilities of your clients and the other people you may share files with. In the past, that's the reason I've used TitleMotion in a few facilities and it may be the reason you'll pick the Chyron, Inscriber, Pinnacle, or Boris product over one of the others.

TitleMotion allows you to create animated title effects very easily and it has a full library of static titles and animation templates to instantly create intricate looks and complex animations, including logos and other graphic elements, without a lot of work. I spent some time when I first got TitleMotion looking through the animations and text styles, making note of the ones that I liked. Knowing what is in the prebuilt styles and animations saves a lot of time during a session.

Colors and texture maps can be applied to the foreground, edges, and shadows of text. Text can also be beveled for a sculpted 3-D appearance, and any word or line can be rotated or set on a customizable spline path. Most editors I know will appreciate the integrated spell-checker. TitleMotion can also import text, which is a workflow that I strongly recommend for titling: get the producer or client to provide all the correct spellings, job titles, and legal wordings as text files that you can import to reduce errors.

One very cool feature of TitleMotion is Logo Compose, which has a drawing toolbar for creating spline-based objects and geometrics with full control over extrusion, colors, blends, shadows, and textures. You can also import backgrounds from file formats such as TGA, BMP, PSD, and JPEG files. Logos can also be imported as text objects, so they can be sized, shadowed, and manipulated just like text.

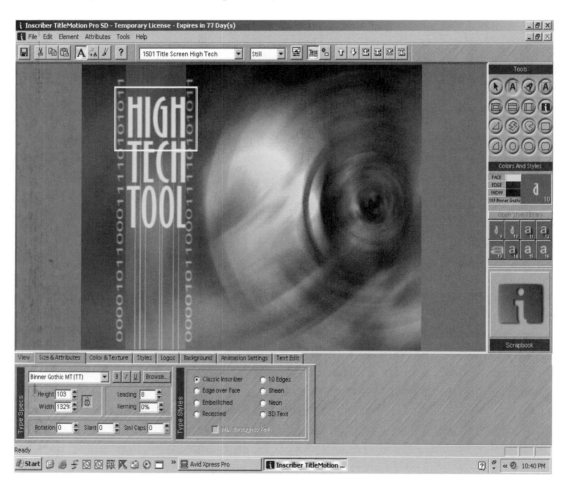

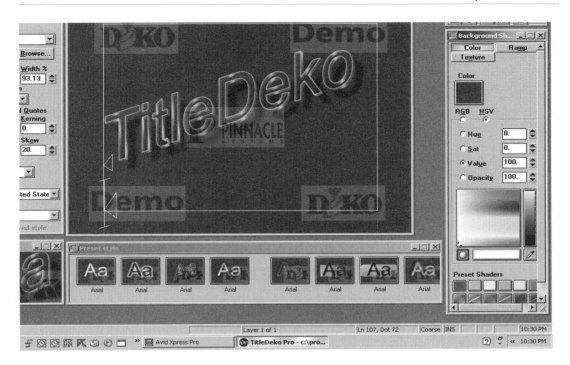

PINNACLE SYSTEMS

www.pinnaclesys.com

TitleDeko Pro (PC only)

TitleDeko Pro is another titling AVX plug-in. This product is fairly similar to the Inscriber product and at least one nationally broadcast TV show has both of these products installed side-by-side in their NLE suites.

The feature set is very similar to TitleMotion; it has the ability to import logos, photos, and other graphics; a spell-checker; fine typesetting controls; and a wide variety of text effects for different looks. For me, the deciding factor between any of the CGs has to be determined by whether you have used any of the products before, and whether you need to interchange files with other facilities or suites that already have one of these products. There are pretty ardent fans of both of these products. If you are looking for a top-drawer titling package, download the demos and see which interface and feature set appeals to you the most. As with all of the titling plug-ins, TitleDeko has a wide assortment of preset styles that are excellent places to start when trying to develop a style for text treatment.

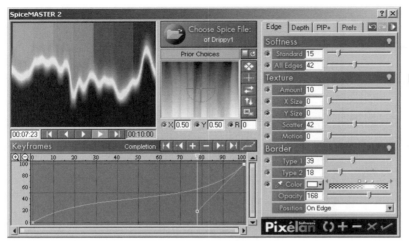

Pixélan

PIXÉLAN

SpiceMaster (PC Only)

www.pixelan.com

Spice effects are customizable, organic wipes. I am not one to use wipes, generally, but these are without a doubt, the coolest, most customizable wipes you'll ever see. Each wipe is the product of a unique grayscale image. The custom wipe interface transforms that simple image by allowing you to reposition it, change the direction, radically alter the softness of the wipe, and even allow multiple thicknesses and colors and textures of edging. There is a very easy to use library of effects that play back in motion as you preview them; you can easily try dozens of wipes with different speeds and parameters in seconds. You can also organize your favorites in their own library.

One of the cool features of the user interface is the wipe graph, which allows you to control the speed and direction of the wipe with a Bezier curve. Lots of these effects look really good with a little "ease-in/ease-out" to them.

Although these are primarily transition devices, they can definitely be used as segment effects to reveal or mask between two sources. You can even "freeze" the wipe and use it as an organic matte or frame for another effect. For example, create an organic matte to wipe between the clean backplate and a blurred version. Or use a super-soft, organic wipe that is almost invisible to bring on an effected version of a shot.

These wipes are similar to the Avid Plasma wipes, but the Spice shapes are much cooler, and without the Spice interface, the Avid Plasma wipes just aren't nearly as good.

PROFOUND EFFECTS

Elastic Gasket (Mac and PC)

www.profoundeffects.com

So maybe you're looking through these AVX plug-ins, wishing you could find one that does what your favorite Adobe After Effects plug-in can do. Well, this is the plug-in for you then. Elastic Gasket acts as a bridge between the AVX architecture and After Effects plug-ins. When you install Elastic Gasket into your AVX folder, what do you see? Nothing. It does absolutely nothing. You can't even see it in your Effects Palette. Ah, but add a few choice After Effects plug-ins to the AVX folder and you'll see what Elastic Gasket does. All of the After Effects plug-ins in your AVX folder can now be seen and used in your Effect Palette.

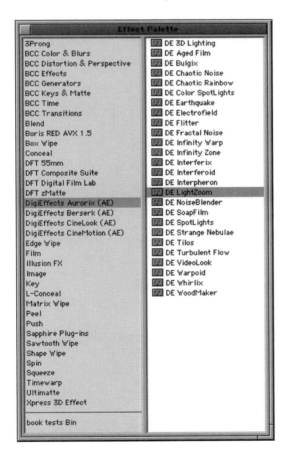

The only disappointing thing is that you can't use the effects that are bundled with After Effects with Elastic Gasket. Check the Profound Effects web site for a list of currently compatible plug-ins. There are some that do not work through Elastic Gasket. Also, there is this warning from the Profound Effects web site: "If you are using a Carbonized host application on the Mac OS X operating system, (which Xpress Pro is) you must use Carbonized or Mac OS X-compatible versions of the After Effects plug-ins. Your Classic (non-Carbonized) plug-ins will not work with Elastic Gasket on the Mac OS operating system. Check with each vendor for their plug-ins' Mac OS X-compatibility."

Move (Mac and PC)

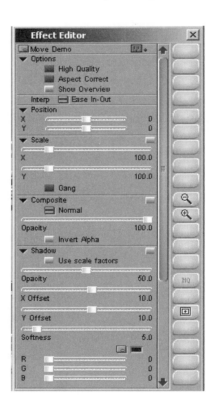

Move lets you pan and zoom over high-resolution (up to 6400×6400 pixels) stills, similar to a motion control camera or animated camera stand. Move is designed to minimize the demands such image manipulation would usually have on RAM. Usually, an 8000×8000 pixel color image takes 256 MB just to load the entire image into memory. But Move only loads what it needs so RAM requirements never exceed what is normally needed for a video resolution still. Move is easy to use, adopting the Avid Effects interface.

Profound Effects has done a good job creating smooth movement with sub-pixel sampling that is definitely necessary to get good-looking movement on images. They allow for various types of typical camera-stand moves including ease-ins and ease-outs.

The very cool thing with Move is that you can use Adobe Photoshop layers with alpha for layered transparency with a drop-shadow.

RE:VISION EFFECTS, INC.   www.revisionfx.com

ReelSmart Motion Blur (Mac and PC)

This plug-in is pretty much self-explanatory. It creates realistic motion blur. I've experimented with this plug-in and in addition to just getting a very "true" looking motion blue, you can really take it to extremes and get incredibly cool looking, stylized motion that is very surreal and dreamy.

The way that ReelSmart Motion Blur is able to create such a realistic motion blur is that it carefully tracks the motion of every pixel. This is very similar to motion tracking and image-stabilization. As a matter of fact, you can use the tracked data from one scene and apply it to another scene for truly wild effects. Motion Blur can also help with strobing motion effects using its frame-blending mode. You can even use this plug-in to *remove* motion blur from shots, making them clearer.

ReelSmart Twixtor (Mac and PC)

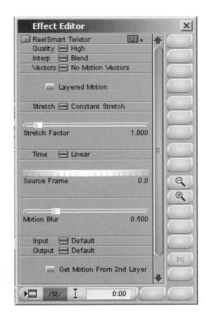

With Twixtor you can dramatically speed up or slow down shots in sequences without ending up with jerky, strobe-like motion. Twixtor does this by synthesizing unique new frames, warping, and interpolating frames of the original sequence. This is accomplished using the same motion tracking algorithms employed in the Motion Blur plug-in.

STAGETOOLS   www.stagetools.com

MovingPicture (Mac and PC)

MovingPicture lets you use the entire resolution of a still image (up to 8000×8000 pixels) to pan and zoom, creating moves that are typical of a motion control rig or animation stand. An option allows you to rotate the image or to move the camera in 3D space to skew the image, which provides variety in creating shots from stills.

MovingPicture is really easy to use. I know that most editors never bother reading the manual, and MovingPicture is definitely one of those pieces of software that is so intuitive that you can just dive in. Basically, all you have to do is reposition and resize a box to indicate the portions of the image you want to show at various keyframe points. Although this plug-in uses its own user interface, there's really no learning curve for it. Though, as usual, after reading the manual I did learn to unleash some additional capabilities of the software.

A small window in the UI allows you to preview your move in real time. It's a really teeny little window, but you get the idea of what you've done. All motion is field-rendered

and calculated at the sub-pixel, so there's no stuttering or jittering. One very cool thing is that MovingPicture supports alpha channels.

If you want to be able to access your moves from your Timeline, you can use the plug-in version or you can install the stand-alone version of the program, which generates QTs or AVIs, on another computer. This frees up your editing computer to edit.

The stand-alone version—called Producer—even comes in a free non-rendering version that a director or assistant editor could use to work out the moves, then import those moves into either a rendering version of Producer, or a plug-in version.

Another plus of MovingPicture is its ability to create Macromedia Flash SWF movies of moves created in Producer.

MovingParts (Mac and PC)

MovingParts animates images and effects. You can use it for animating 2D logos or creating animatics using alpha-channeled images. If you feel constrained by the number of video tracks you have to work with or by your ability to keyframe, MovingParts can animate up to 32 images over motion video.

MovingCharts (PC only)

MovingCharts allows you to create animated charts.

ULTIMATTE   www.ultimatte.com

Ultimatte AdvantEdge (Mac and PC)

I've been using Ultimatte plug-ins for a number of years. And before that, I used the hardware-based systems. The new AdvantEdge system is the best and easiest to use yet. (For those familiar with AdvantEdge in the Symphony Ultimatte, this is totally different.)

When you first add Ultimatte to a greenscreen or bluescreen key, it asks how many layers the effect is. Usually you just want to use 2. There is the bottom track, which is the background, and the top track, which is the greenscreen and will eventually become the foreground element, once it is keyed. You can also add mattes and screen correction effects to the basic two tracks.

The old AVX version of Ultimatte used the Avid Effects interface. There were about a million parameters to set. The AdvantEdge plug-in uses a custom effects interface that is launched by clicking on the Options button, the way all of the other plug-ins with custom

interfaces work. Disturbingly, the Xpress Pro interface vanishes for a few seconds before being replaced by the Ultimatte interface. You must have a dongle to operate this plug-in to get rid of the watermark. The interface is very friendly and easy to use, though you can't really get started without reading the manual. Take the time to explore all of the functions and read the excellent .pdf files on the web site about creating good greenscreens.

One of the cool things that Ultimatte did was create a special way to improve the keying of DV-sourced greenscreen material. Most editors agree that you just can't get a good key off of a DV source because the 4:1:1 color space and lower resolution don't give you enough to work with. Although that was the standard wisdom, it needs to be rethought with this plug-in. I've been able to pull some very believable keys shooting greenscreen on DV with this plug-in.

Also, if you are an old Ultimatte expert, all of the old parameters are still there to adjust if you want to get your hands dirty; they just keep those controls hidden from view unless you call them up.

ZBIG   www.slick-fx.com/slickfx/zbig

Zbig (PC Only)
Zbig Easy (PC Only)

Both of these plug-ins are for chroma keying. The full version has many more parameters for fine-tuning greenscreen and bluescreen effects. This is especially useful in cases where the footage that needs to be keyed hasn't been shot perfectly. The Easy version has a reduced, easy-to-use interface that is also cheaper.

Though my allegiance lies with the Ultimatte keyer, it is also much more expensive than Zbig, which also provides a very good key, and if you look at the opening splash screen credits of the Ultimatte plug-in, whose name do you see? Zbig's: Zbigniew Rybczynski. So this is definitely not a "no-name" knock-off.

Though there are places on the web that claim to be able to provide this plug-in, Zbig's home page claims that all of their technology was licensed to Ultimatte and that sales of this software have been discontinued. We included it in the book because it is still linked to Avid's AVX Partner web site.

Index

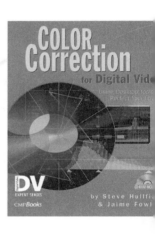
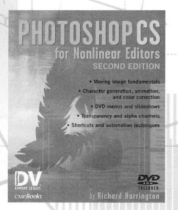

Creating Motion Graphics with After Effects, Volume 1: The Essentials

3rd Edition, Version 6.5

Trish Meyer & Chris Meyer

Master the core concepts and tools you need to tackle virtually every job, including keyframe animation, masking, mattes, and plug-in effects. New chapters demystify Parenting, 3D Space, and features of the latest software version.

$59.95, 4-color, Softcover with DVD, 448 pp, ISBN 1-57820-249-3

After Effects On the Spot

Richard Harrington, Rachel Max, & Marcus Geduld

Packed with more than 400 expert techniques, this book clearly illustrates all the essential methods that pros use to get the job done with After Effects. Experienced editors and novices alike discover an invaluable reference filled with ways to improve efficiency and creativity.

$27.95, Softcover, 288 pp, ISBN 1-57820-239-6

Lighting for Digital Video and Television
2nd Edition

John Jackman

A complete course in video and television lighting. Detailed illustrations and real-world examples demonstrate proper equipment use, safety issues, troubleshooting, and staging techniques. This new edition features a 8 page 4-color insert and new chapters on interview setups, and low-budget lighting set-ups.

$39.95, Softcover, 256 pp, ISBN 1-57820-251-5

What's on the DVD?

The DVD contains video tutorials, sample footage, and demo plug-ins for Xpress Pro users. Also included are importable settings and royalty-free stock footage from the authors and from Art-beats. Some of the demo plug-ins are Mac only, some PC only. Mac OSX is required for Mac users. QuickTime is required to play back the tutorials.

A note from Boris to accompany the trial version of the software:
Here is your serial number: BCCTNB-300AEMP-29501. Once you've decided you're ready to purchase, visit the following link for instructions: http://www.borisfx.com/esd/instructions.php.

Additional tutorials and related files can be downloaded by following the links on the page for this book at www.cmpbooks.com

Updates

Want to sign up for e-mail updates for *Avid Xpress Pro Editing Workshop*? Visit www.cmp-books.com/maillist and select from the desired categories. You'll automatically be added to our preferred customer list for new product announcements, special offers, and related news. Your e-mail address will not be shared without your permission, so sign up today!